The Economics of
INEQUALITY,
DISCRIMINATION,
POVERTY,
AND MOBILITY

The Economics of
INEQUALITY,
DISCRIMINATION,
POVERTY,
AND MOBILITY

Robert S. Rycroft

M.E.Sharpe
Armonk, New York
London, England

Library of Congress Cataloging-in-Publication Data

Rycroft, Robert S.
  The economics of inequality, discrimination, poverty, and mobility /
Robert S. Rycroft.
     p. cm.
  Includes bibliographical references and index.
  ISBN 978-0-7656-2326-3 (cloth : alk. paper) — ISBN 978-0-7656-2327-0 (pbk. : alk. paper)
  1. Income distribution—United States. 2. Poverty—United States. 3.
Equality—United States. 4. Discrimination—United States. 5. Social
mobility—United States. 6. Economics—United States. I. Title.
  HC110.I5R895 2008
  339.2'20973—dc22   2008045834

Printed in the United States of America

The paper used in this publication meets the minimum requirements of
American National Standard for Information Sciences
Permanence of Paper for Printed Library Materials,
ANSI Z 39.48-1984.

∞

| CW (c) | 10 | 9 | 8 | 7 | 6 | 5 | 4 | 3 | 2 | 1 |
| CW (p) | 10 | 9 | 8 | 7 | 6 | 5 | 4 | 3 | 2 | 1 |

For my family

Contents

Preface

A metaphor with widespread applicability in the field of economics is "slicing the pie." Economists are wont to speak of the economic goals of efficiency and equity. What is meant by efficiency and equity? The terms can be defined in a fairly obscure manner by using words or mathematical equations, but it is simpler to imagine a pie. The efficiency goal is associated with the size of the pie. An efficient economy produces a large and rapidly growing pie (the pie, of course, represents the goods and services that give us our standard of living). The equity goal is associated with how big a slice each of us receives. An equitable economy provides everyone with their "just desserts." As a society, we aim to both grow the pie rapidly and slice it equitably. What makes this interesting is the feedback loop from how we slice the pie to how fast it grows. Many economists believe efforts to slice the pie more equitably slow the growth of the pie. Others believe judicious reslicing may, in fact, speed the growth of the pie. This book discusses important aspects of "slicing the pie"; why the pie is sliced the way it is, what the connection is between how the pie is sliced and how rapidly the pie grows, what happens if people get a slice that is "too small," how the slice received changes over the course of a career, and how our slice influences what our children can expect to receive. In other words, this book is about the economics of inequality, discrimination, poverty, and mobility.

The contents of this book are useful for anyone who wants to bring themselves up to speed on these issues, but its primary intended use is as a textbook for students enrolled in undergraduate economics classes that deal with any combination of these issues. The book originated out of frustration. For literally decades, I have taught an undergraduate economics course at the University of Mary Washington (UMW) called Poverty, Affluence, and Equality. The course is about "slicing the pie" in the context of the United States (it is not an economic development course). The source of my frustration was the lack of an adequate textbook. In my judgment, most existing textbooks were not comprehensive enough, nor did they cover the material at the level of rigor I thought appropriate for undergraduates in an economics course. I was faced with two choices. I could either fume or do something about it. Initially I fumed, but not much came of that. I then decided to do something about it, and this book is the result.

The book has a very deliberate structure. It begins with the inequality problem—

how the pie is sliced. We first look at the functional distribution of income in a pure market economy. This allows the basic tools of demand and supply to be introduced (it would be helpful if students had taken principles of economics before taking this course, but not essential). Then we move in the direction of an explanation of the personal distribution of income by considering the impact of individual differences in tastes, tolerance for risk and time preference, the direct and feedback effects of government policies that explicitly or implicitly redistribute income, and the influence of discrimination. Next we look at the problem of "a slice too small." How do we measure poverty, how many people are poor in the United States, what are the fundamental causes of poverty, and what policies do we employ to combat it? Finally, we look at how the size of a slice changes over a career and across generations. What factors influence intra- and intergenerational mobility and wealth accumulation, distribution, and inheritance?

What distinguishes this book are the following:

- Detailed (but not highly mathematical) development of the economic theory underlying the analysis: To fully understand the issues in the fields of inequality, discrimination, poverty, and mobility, students need to have a good grasp of economic theory. In particular, to understand the very contentious debates over the appropriate policies in these areas, students need to be aware of the trade-offs involved, which requires an adequate grounding in economic theory. This book takes pains to develop the theories of labor demand, labor supply, investment in schooling and on-the-job training, incentive-based compensation schemes, intergenerational mobility, efficiency wages, reciprocity in the labor market, tax incidence and the incentive effects of taxes, among others and also addresses the efficiency aspects of policy proposals.

  I felt the available relevant textbooks shied away from this methodology, probably because the student audience for this type of course was thought to be so multidisciplinary (along with economics majors, courses like this would be sought by sociology, psychology, anthropology, political science, international affairs, English, history, and business majors, among others) that an emphasis on "real" economics might scare them away. In my experience, this is not the case. My students are typically a wide-ranging, multidisciplinary crowd, but they have managed to handle the economics I have presented to them (even if they haven't necessarily loved it), so I believe economists do not need to be timid about using their specific disciplinary tools.
- Greater emphasis on mobility: In recent years, economists have made great strides toward understanding and appreciating the significance of intragenerational and intergenerational mobility. Only a fraction of this work has made it into textbooks. This book provides expanded coverage of mobility issues that can be understood by typical undergraduates.
- Greater emphasis on wealth accumulation, distribution, and inheritance: Leaving these topics out of a discussion on what is ultimately the well-being of people seems like a major omission. I devote one full chapter and parts of a few other chapters to a discussion of these issues.

- Greater emphasis on discrimination law: Discrimination law and the court decisions that interpret it are an important part of the analysis of discrimination. Most undergraduate textbooks, in my judgment, do a fairly superficial job of dealing with these topics. This book provides expanded coverage on these issues. Most notably, there are discussions of several relevant Supreme Court decisions presented in a detailed, informative, and colorful manner. This material will help support classroom discussion of these issues.
- Full and fair treatment of the controversies in the fields: The economics of inequality, discrimination, poverty, and mobility are chock-full of controversy. Examples of contentious issues include the minimum wage, the appropriate way to measure poverty, how much mobility exists, comparable worth, whether the Supreme Court has interpreted the antidiscrimination statutes correctly, the efficiency and equity of affirmative action, and the optimal degree of redistribution, to name a few. These controversies are given full and fair treatment and are presented so that instructors can use the textbook material as a means to motivate a variety of classroom discussions and debates.

Courses in inequality, discrimination, poverty, and mobility are among the most idiosyncratic offered by economists. Every instructor has his or her own take on what should be covered. This book is not just an overview of my Poverty, Affluence, and Equality course. Rather, it is my course-and-a-half, or my course plus another. I have included far more material than I could possibly cover in a single semester. With classes devoted to debates on important topics, student presentations of papers, classroom discussions of assigned readings, and instruction in how to do research, write, and speak in the discipline, not to mention tests and homework, there is simply not enough time to cover all this material. In the class's current incarnation, I cover none of the chapter material in its entirety and I completely skip some topics presented here, such as Chapters 4, 8, and 17. I doubt if anyone could cover all this material in a semester, even if they were to do nothing but lecture (which I do not encourage). Conceivably, this book could be used for two semester-long courses, if this is at all possible.

Another aspect of the idiosyncratic nature of the course is that even if professors could agree on the topics, they are unlikely to agree on how to evaluate conflicting empirical evidence (does raising the minimum wage reduce employment opportunities or not?), and the normative aspects of policies (how much redistribution is required in a just society). As implied earlier, I believe that this book could be used by professors coming from many different points along the ideological spectrum (except for the extremes at both ends). I think I have aired controversies fairly by discussing conflicting points of view as their adherents would want them to be discussed. See if you agree.

I am intolerant of any analysis that ignores such bulwarks of economics as the laws of scarcity, demand and (theory of) supply, and comparative advantage. There is no such thing as a free lunch, and even policies that would appear to have the widest base of support deserve to have their costs identified. I believe prices are determined by demand and supply, not whim, and what happens in one market has bearing, frequently unintended, on many other markets. I believe, in most instances, that voluntary exchange is mutually beneficial, whether within a country or across national borders. Government attempts to restrict voluntary exchange may be beneficial, but must be justified.

I would like to acknowledge several people and institutions that have helped me complete this project. Thanks are owed to UMW for giving me a semester sabbatical that allowed me to write most of the first draft of this book, and my many students in Poverty, Affluence, and Equality over the years who have told me in many ways what the level of rigor and topical coverage of this book should be. I have received helpful comments from Dr. Mary Ellen Benedict of Bowling Green State University and Rachel Greszler, a friend, former student, and professional economist. Stephanie Rzepka (editor *extraordinaire*) and Sarah Restaino, both students at UMW, provided invaluable editorial feedback. Catherine Stewart and Stephen B. Davis, both students at UMW, also helped in the preparation of this book. I also owe a debt of gratitude to Dr. Kristin Marsh of the UMW Sociology Department whose suggestion that we each sit in on the other's course (Social Stratification in her case, and Poverty, Affluence, and Equality in mine) for a semester helped me return to a manuscript that had lain dormant for too long. I also want to thank the staff at M.E. Sharpe, particularly Lynn Taylor, economics editor, Angela Piliouras, production editor, and Molly Morrison, copyeditor.

I also thank the following individuals and organizations for allowing me to incorporate their essays, tables, figures, and data in the book: the American Economic Association, National Bureau of Economic Research, Luxembourg Income Study, Derek Simpkins, Federal Reserve Bank of Atlanta, Federal Reserve Bank of Boston, Arthur B. Kennickell and the Federal Reserve Board, Ernie Ackermann, Donald Boudreaux, the Federal Reserve Bank of Minneapolis, the *Industrial and Labor Relations Review* and Cornell University, Princeton University Press, Elizabeth Elzer, Urban Institute, Ann Harper Fender, Jean Fletcher, Peter Gottschalk, and Sheldon Danziger.

Robert S. Rycroft
Fredericksburg, Virginia
July 2009

The Economics of
INEQUALITY,
DISCRIMINATION,
POVERTY,
AND MOBILITY

1 The Pie and How We Slice It

INTRODUCTION

The income "pie" in the United States exceeded $13.8 trillion in 2008.[1] If sliced equally among the over 300 million residents (U.S. Bureau of the Census [USBC] 2007c), each man, woman, and child would have received nearly $46,000. A four-person household would have had an income of nearly $184,000; a pretty decent standard of living.

But the pie is not sliced equally. Some people barely make enough to survive. Others earn more in a year than most of us will earn over our entire career or several careers. Annually for the last several years, *Parade* magazine has published a special report called "What People Earn." The report includes commentary on the current state of the economy and how it affects income and job opportunities. But the most memorable feature of the report is the accompanying photo gallery of a randomly selected group of Americans that lists each individual's name, age, occupation, hometown, and income. The 2008 report included many middle-income people, such as Renita Rhodes, a thirty-one-year-old software engineer from St. Louis, Missouri, who earned $72,000; Paula Daigle, a thirty-five-year-old Spanish teacher from Fairhaven, Massachusetts, who earned $38,400; Bruce Hossler, a fifty-three-year-old truck driver from Madison, South Dakota, who earned $45,000; and Tracy Todd, a thirty-four-year-old 911 supervisor from Decatur, Illinois, who earned $54,500. The list included several low-income people, such as Keith Moore, a nineteen-year-old theme-park worker from Del City, Oklahoma, who earned $11,400; Jose Lara, a sixty-two-year-old cargo sorter from Fresno, California, who earned $16,300; and Sue Gage, a fifty-two-year-old janitor from Shelby Township, Michigan, who earned $10,700. And it included several "superstars" with astronomical incomes, such as Miley Cyrus, a fifteen-year-old singer/actress from Los Angeles, California, who earned $18,200,000; John Paulson, a fifty-two-year-old hedge fund manager from New York, New York, who earned $3.5 million; and Oprah Winfrey, a fifty-four-year-old TV personality from Chicago, Illinois, who earned $260,000,000 (Brenner 2008).

This book is about how we slice the pie. The issues involved are important for two big reasons. The first is the perception of economic justice. While most people do not believe in equal slices for all, their sense of economic justice is offended if some people receive slices that are "too small" (Okun 1975, 94–5). And some people are upset if others receive slices that are "too big." The second reason is the connection between the relative size of the slices and the size of the pie itself. Many economists would argue that there is typically a trade-off between the size of the pie and the equality of the slices (Okun 1975). If we slice the pie more equally, we could end up with a smaller pie; or others would argue that contrary to the previous assertion, the pie could be sliced more equally and made larger by judicious slicing (Haveman 1988).

The "slicing the pie problem" will be dealt with as four separate pieces, but this approach is only for expositional convenience. Each piece is tightly interlocked with the others, and the connections will be made clear. The first piece, the *inequality* piece, explains how the marketplace and government policy interact to determine the relative size of the slices consumed by different people: How are the owners of the factors of production rewarded in the marketplace? How and to what extent does government policy redistribute income and what impact does it have on incentives? The second piece, the *discrimination* piece, investigates whether the size of a slice depends on race, ethnicity, gender, or any of a host of factors that do not represent individual "merit," and the impact of government policies to combat the problem. The third piece is the *poverty* piece. Poverty means a slice "too small." How do we define too small, how many people receive slices too small, and are the people or the economy to blame? The fourth piece is the *mobility* piece. Can people with small slices today reasonably hope to get larger slices later in life? Is there hope for their offspring? Is mobility in the long term an antidote to inequality in the short term, or does short term inequality prevent long-term mobility?

None of these issues is the exclusive domain of the discipline of economics. A comprehensive understanding requires a multidisciplinary approach that combines insights from economics with sociology, psychology, political science, history, law, and philosophy. But the truth is that this book emphasizes economic analysis.

The issues involved are extraordinarily controversial. In fact, competent scholars are quite capable of holding diametrically opposed views on all the big issues. Regarding inequality, "Among advanced Organization for Economic Cooperation and Development (OECD) countries, the United States has an exceptionally high degree of income inequality, standing in what Denny Braun calls 'a class by itself' at the top of the inequality pyramid" (Page and Simmons 2000, 29) can be juxtaposed with, "Far from experiencing a dramatic U-turn in recent years, inequality in 1995 was roughly the same as in 1972 and substantially lower than the level attained in 1947" (Slesnick 2001, 131). Regarding racial discrimination, "Race and ethnicity play a central role in understanding the structure of inequality in the United States" (Lundberg and Startz, 2000, 269) can be juxtaposed with, "At the heart of these retreaded 1960s arguments is the notion that statistical disparities between groups are strange and sinister, and can only be explained by discrimination based on 'stereotypes.' What I discovered in the course of my 16 years of research, . . . is that statistical disparities among groups is the rule—not the exception—in countries around the world" (Sowell 1998b). Regarding gender discrimination, we have, "The same forces that tend to constrain the earnings of minorities and lower-income classes also operate to limit the employment and income opportunities of women (Schiller 2004, 204) juxtaposed with, "We conclude that complaints about systematic economic discrimination against women simply do not square with the evidence" (Furchtgott-Roth and Stolba 1999, xi). Regarding poverty, "In no other developed country is the poverty rate as high as in the United States" (Mangum, Mangum, and Sum 2003, 10) can be juxtaposed with, "We have indeed eliminated poverty in the United States. By historical standards, no one—not a single person in our civilization—lives in poverty" (Boudreaux 2005). With respect to mobility, we have, "It is also true that income inequality as conventionally measured has been increasing since the late 1960s and that this has not been accompanied by any *increase* in mobility rates. Thus, growing annual income inequality implies growing lifetime income inequality as well" (McMurrer and Sawhill 1998, 6) juxtaposed with, "Annual snapshots of the income distribution might deserve attention if we lived in a caste society, with rigid class lines determining who gets what share of the national income—but we don't live in a caste society. . . . To argue that upward mobility is being lost, we would have to show that the poorest remain stuck where they are, with little hope of making themselves better off. Nothing could be further from the truth" (Cox and Alm 1999, 72).

Are you ready for some controversy?

WHAT'S IN THE PIE?

The preceding section talked about an "income pie." The pie that we should be concerned with consists of something known as utility. The term *utility* is used by economists to refer to the feeling of satisfaction that an individual gets from consuming goods and services. People are assumed to attempt to maximize their utility—to try to act in such a way as to make them as well-off as possible. A successful society, then, creates the most utility possible and allocates it equitably among persons, or, to continue the metaphor, bakes the largest pie it is capable of baking and slices it in the most equitable manner.

Utility comes from the bundle of goods and services consumed, recognizing that this bundle consists of more than just obvious items such as food, clothing, and shelter. Utility is also a reflection of how healthy we are, how secure we feel, what civil rights we have, how much leisure we enjoy, how respected and loved we are, the quantity and quality of our friends, how much fulfillment we get from life, how much fun we have, and many other qualities of life. There is no way to directly measure the amount of utility received from a bundle of goods and services. People cannot express the number of *utils* (a util is one unit of utility) they receive, and it is not possible to attach electrodes to a person's head and measure them. In principle we could measure utility indirectly by asking people how much they would pay for each of the items in the bundle and then adding all items, but there would be little reason to be confident in the answers (for example, how much would you pay for the amount of fun you have?).

In short, a measure of people's utility does not exist, and so it is impossible to say precisely how the utility pie is cut. Does this mean that the book should stop at this point? Maybe it should, but economists are loath to simply surrender when faced with data shortcomings. Instead, they make do with what they have, which means using approximations.

What is the best approximation of utility? In the preceding section and throughout much of the rest of this book, people's income is used to represent their level of well-being. This makes a certain amount of sense. Income is a major determinant of how many tangible goods and services one can buy, and may very well be positively correlated with health, security, and most of the other intangible factors that influence utility.[2] Also, income data are widely available in large time-series as well as cross-section data sets. But rich people are not always happy, so there are obviously gaps. Income data is supplemented with whatever else is relevant and available, including but not limited to data on wages, earnings, wealth, consumption, occupational status, unemployment, and surveys of who has health insurance, whether people feel safe in their homes, ownership of consumer durables, and many other bits and pieces of data. The measurable pie has many components.

THE PLAN FOR THIS BOOK

Conceptually, the book is divided into five sections: Inequality, Discrimination, Poverty, Mobility, and Final Thoughts. Part I, Inequality, consists of seven chapters. Chapters 2, 3 and 4 introduce an admittedly "unrealistic" pure market economy and build a model to explain the *functional distribution of income*, or the distribution of income among factors of production. In Chapters 5, 6, and 7 complications having to do with individual tastes (regarding desired work hours, the assumption of risk, and time preference), institutions, and government policy are introduced to permit an explanation of the *personal distribution of income*, or the distribution of income among persons or groups of persons, such as households and families. Chapter 8 asks the question, "What should the distribution of income be?" and reviews a variety of philosophical approaches to the issue of economic justice.

Part II, Discrimination, has three chapters. Chapter 9 reviews data on economic differences between demographic groups, explains the economic definition of discrimination, and develops competing models of discrimination. Chapter 10 explains how economists measure the extent of discrimination, and discusses why identifying discrimination is a tricky business. Chapter 11 looks at employment antidiscrimination laws, controversial landmark Supreme Court decisions in the field, and the contentious issues of affirmative action and the policy of comparable worth.

Part III, Poverty, consists of two chapters. Chapter 12 discusses the "official" measure of poverty in the United States, the extent of poverty in the United States, competing explanations for why people are poor, and competing definitions of poverty. With respect to the latter issue, the appropriate definition of poverty is no mere academic squabble. By one reasonable definition, poverty is higher now in the United States than it was three decades ago! By another reasonable definition, poverty has been eliminated! Chapter 13 defines welfare and reviews the current welfare system in the United States.

There are three chapters in Part IV, on mobility. Chapter 14 explains how consideration of the extent of economic mobility can shine a different light on the issues of inequality and poverty, develops some economic models explaining intragenerational earnings mobility, and discusses the controversy over the best way to measure mobility. Chapter 15 looks at intergenerational earnings mobility. Among the topics covered are controversies regarding the measurement of intergenerational mobility, why it pays to be born rich, why "rags to riches" stories still take place, and several current policy issues. No discussion of mobility would be complete without giving consideration to the accumulation and transfer of wealth. This is explored in Chapter 16. Among the topics discussed are wealth inequality in the United States, wealth accumulation over the life cycle, the accumulation of huge fortunes, why people leave bequests, the impact of bequests on inequality and incentives, and the so-called death tax.

Part V, Final Thoughts, contains Chapter 17, which offers policy strategies to deal with the "slicing the pie problem" from various locations along the ideological spectrum.

Defining Terms: Wealth, Income, Consumption, and Money

The terms *wealth*, *income*, *consumption*, and money are used in any discussion of inequality, discrimination, poverty, and mobility. People frequently exhibit some confusion about what these terms really mean. If you are confident in your understanding of these terms, you may skip this section, but I would counsel against overconfidence.

Wealth

Your wealth is the sum of the assets you own that can be used to provide you with utility. Your house is an asset. It gives you shelter, contentment, and status. So is that Picasso hanging on the wall, because you get pleasure from looking at it. Your car is an asset because it is a convenient source of transportation. Stocks and bonds are assets because the former gives you ownership rights in a corporation, a right to collect dividends, and the potential for capital gains, and the latter gives you interest income and potential capital gains. If you own a factory, the facility is an asset because it can be used to produce a product that can be sold for a profit. Your education and job skills are also assets because they can be used to procure a job and earn income. Notice that the utility you receive from wealth can come in many forms. Money is only one of them.

In theory, at least, a monetary value can be placed on your assets. The value of an asset is what the asset would fetch in the marketplace. The monetary values of homes, cars, paintings, stocks, bonds, and factories are easily grasped since these goods are bought and sold all the time. The monetary value of your education and skills may not be as obvious, particularly since you cannot sell yourself and buy anyone else. Without providing formulas here, suffice it to say that the asset value of your education and skills is related to the earning power they create. Workers with more education and skills typically are able to earn more, which makes the asset value of their education and skills greater.

However, your wealth is not simply your assets. Rather, it is your assets minus your liabilities, sometimes referred to as net worth. Liabilities are your debts. They must be subtracted from assets because you have to pay your debts. In a sense, some portion of your assets must be dedicated to paying off your debts, and cannot be used to provide utility for you. Frequently, liabilities are incurred to purchase assets. For example, many families take out a mortgage to buy a home. If your only asset is a house worth $400,000 but you still owe $100,000 on your mortgage, your net worth is $300,000 (= $400,000 − $100,000).

Wealth is an example of what economists call a stock variable. The variable can only meaningfully be measured at a particular point in time. For example, the value of your car can be determined at 5 P.M. on July 17. At 6 P.M. the value may have changed due to a variety of factors. It does not make any sense to talk about what your car was worth last year because what it was worth may have changed from hour to hour.

INCOME

The term *income* refers to the utility received from using your assets. The interest, dividends, capital gains, profits, wages and salaries, and, for assets that do not yield a monetary return, the enjoyment received from using assets (such as the comforts associated with living in your house and gazing at your Picasso) are all forms of income.

Income is a flow variable. This means the amount of income can only meaning-fully be measured over a specified period of time. Income can be measured annually, monthly, weekly, or hourly. It is impossible to measure it at a specific point in time. What I earn this very second cannot be computed, but if I work an hour I might receive $25. If I work 40 hours at $25 per hour, then my income will be $1,000 for the work week.

Clearly wealth and income are related concepts. What connects them is the *rate of return*. The rate of return measures the income received from wealth relative to the value of the wealth that generated the income. If $100 of wealth yields $5 of income each year, then the rate of return is approximately 5 percent ($5/$100). The actual formula used to compute a rate of return is much more complicated, however, this simplification will suffice for now.

CONSUMPTION

You have two options with the utility you receive from wealth. You can enjoy it right away or you can use it to acquire additional wealth. The former action is called consumption. If you buy a meal and eat it, or purchase an item of clothing and wear it, or you take a trip and go sightseeing, you are consuming because you are getting enjoyment from that item or activity right up front.

The latter action is called investment or saving. The two terms *investment* and *saving* really mean the same thing because they are actually identical activities. Investment means to acquire wealth. Saving means to abstain from consumption—to sacrifice current enjoyment. But if you abstain from consumption, how do you use the funds? To acquire wealth. So investment and saving are essentially the same thing. How do you acquire wealth? You can either buy an asset or reduce your liabilities. Either way raises your net worth dollar-for-dollar. As we will see later, some economists think consumption is a better measure of long-term well-being than either income or wealth.

Table 1.1

Share of Aggregate Income Received by Each Fifth and Top 5 Percent of Households, All Races, 2006

Households	Share of Income (%)	Income Limit	Mean Income
Lowest fifth	3.4		$11,352
Second fifth	8.6	$20,032	$28,777
Third fifth	14.5	$37,771	$49,223
Fourth fifth	22.9	$60,000	$76,329
Highest fifth	50.5	$97,030	$168,170
Top 5 percent	22.3	$174,000	$297,405

Source: United States Bureau of the Census, accessed on February 1, 2008 at http://www.census.gov/hhes/www/income/histinc/h02ar.html.

MONEY

In everyday language, the word *money* is frequently used in place of wealth or income. "She is worth a lot of money" or "he made a lot of money last year." Strictly speaking, this use of the word money is not very precise and is, in fact, misleading. Precisely used, the term *money* refers to a special type of asset. It is the asset (one of only a few) that can be used as a medium of exchange in the economy. For further elaboration see any money and banking textbook.[3] Consequently, the word *money* will be used carefully and infrequently in this book.

THE "OFFICIAL" DATA AND REPRESENTING INEQUALITY

THE LEVEL AND DISTRIBUTION OF HOUSEHOLD INCOME

In 2006, median household income in the United States was $48,201. Household income was measured using a statistic the U.S. Census Bureau calls *money income*. Money income is the cash income received by individuals fifteen years of age and older with the exception of realized capital gains, lump-sum payments from insurance companies, workers' compensation, or pension plans. Then this income is aggregated for every member of the household.

This measure of income was not distributed equally, however. One commonly used method to represent its distribution is shown in Table 1.1.

Construction of the Table

The most widely used and readily accessible source of information about incomes in the United States comes from the Bureau of the Census (USBC 2007d). Income data is gathered as part of the annual Current Population Survey (CPS). The CPS surveys approximately 66,000 households, usually by phone,[4] during March of each year,[5] to obtain income, employment, and family structure data. The survey-taker will talk only to an adult, but no effort is made to verify that what the adult says is accurate.

Figure 1.1 **Real Median Household Income, 1967–2006, in 2006 Dollars**

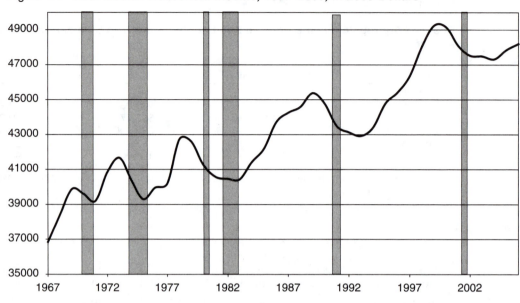

Source: United States Bureau of the Census; NBER designated contractions in shaded areas

Among the types of income included are earnings, unemployment compensation, workers' compensation, Social Security benefits, Supplemental Security income, public assistance, veterans' payments, survivor benefits, disability benefits, pension or retirement income, interest, dividends, rents, royalties, educational assistance, alimony, child support, financial assistance from outside of the household, and other income. The unifying theme is that all these forms of income come in money form. The CPS is only one of several sources of income data in the United States.[6]

Table 1.1 was constructed in the following way. First, all the households in the United States were lined up from highest to lowest income. Second, on the basis of income the households were divided into five groups with the same number of households in each. The 20 percent of households with the highest incomes were listed as the "highest fifth" group. The 20 percent with the next highest incomes were in the "fourth fifth" group, and so on, so that the poorest 20 percent of the households were in the "lowest fifth" group. Third, the total income of each fifth and each fifth's income as a percentage of total household income were computed.

The "Income Limit" column shows the incomes that constitute the boundary between the groups. For a household to be in the lowest fifth, its income had to be below $20,032. For a household to be in the highest fifth, its income had to exceed $97,030. (Which group does your household fit in? If you are like most people, you think you are lower in the distribution than you really are.) The mean income column gives mean income within each fifth. The poorest fifth had an average income of $11,352. The richest fifth had an average income of $297,405. The proportion of income received by the top 5 percent and the income required for admittance to that exalted group is also reported.

Figure 1.1 shows CPS real median household income in the United States for the

Figure 1.2 **The Log-Normal Distribution**

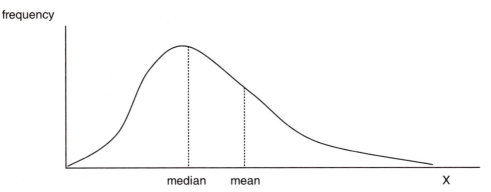

Figure 1.3 **The Normal Distribution**

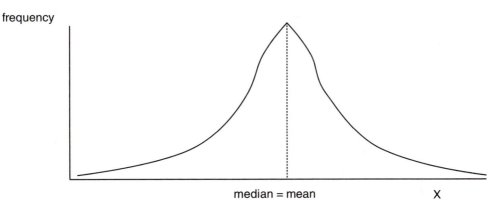

period 1967 to 2006. The periods during which the economy was in contraction as determined by the National Bureau of Economic Research are shown in gray (National Bureau of Economic Research 2008). Note that while the long-term trend for income was positive, there were several periods of declining income that coincided with cyclical downturns in the economy.

Mean household income in 2006 was $66,570. This was higher than the median income of $48,201. That the mean household income exceeds the household median is not unusual. In fact it has been that way ever since we began keeping track. The reason lies in the distribution of household income. The distribution consistently looks like Figure 1.2. Most people are bunched around the median, but there is a long, thin tail that extends to the right, and the high incomes in this tail cause the mean of the distribution to exceed the median.

A distribution with this characteristic is called *lognormal distribution*. The lognormal distribution gets its name from the fact that if you were to measure X in terms of its natural logarithm, the resulting distribution would be the familiar bell-shaped and symmetric normal distribution in which the median equals the mean (Figure 1.3).

The Lorenz Curve

Working with tables is not always convenient, particularly when there are many numbers on the table. A graphic device that is commonly used to represent the inequality of distributions is the Lorenz curve.[7] Figure 1.4 shows the Lorenz curve for the 2006 household distribution of income. The degree of inequality is represented by how "bowed-out" the curve is relative to the 45° line connecting the bottom left-hand and upper right-hand corner of the box. The more bowed-out the curve, the more unequal the distribution.

The Lorenz curve can range between perfect equality and perfect inequality. With perfect equality every household has the exact same income. Graphically that would be represented by a Lorenz curve that followed the 45° line. Perfect inequality would be a situation where one household had all the income and every other household had nothing. Graphically that would be a Lorenz curve that followed the bottom horizontal axis and the right-hand side vertical axis.

Constructing a simple Lorenz curve is not difficult. The first step is to compute the cumulative share of income. Table 1.2 replicates the listing of the share of household income received by each quintile in 2006 as shown in Table 1.1. The right-hand column in Table 1.2 shows the cumulative share of income. The cumulative share percentage for a quintile measures the percentage of income earned by that quintile plus all lower quintiles. In 2006 the cumulative share value for the lowest quintile is 3.4 percent, exactly the percentage of total income earned by the quintile. The cumulative distribution value for the fourth quintile is 12.0 percent, which is equal to the 3.4 percent earned by the lowest quintile plus the 8.6 percent earned by the fourth quintile. The

Figure 1.4 **The Lorenz Curve, 2006**

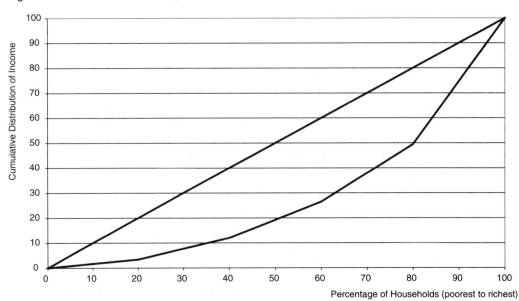

Source: United States Bureau of the Census

Table 1.2

Share of Aggregate Income and Cumulative Share of Income Received by Each Fifth of Households, All Races: 2006

Households	Share of Income (%)	Cumulative Share of Income (%)
Lowest fifth	3.4	3.4
Second fifth	8.6	12.0
Third fifth	14.5	26.5
Fourth fifth	22.9	49.4
Highest fifth	50.6	100.0

Source: United States Bureau of the Census, accessed on February 1, 2008 at http://www.census.gov/hhes/www/income/histinc/h02ar.html.

26.5 percent cumulative share for the third quintile is the 3.4 percent of the lowest quintile plus the 8.6 percent of the second quintile plus the 14.5 percent of the third quintile. The remaining cells are filled in similarly.

Next, plot the cumulative share for each quintile. Finally, connect successive points with straight lines. The result is Figure 1.4.

A Lorenz curve based on five quintiles is an approximation of the true Lorenz curve. As the number of income categories increases, the curve becomes more precise and more "curved."

In the case of perfect equality, each quintile would earn 20 percent of the income. The cumulative distribution values by quintile would be 20, 40, 60, 80, and 100 percent. Graphing these would result in a 45° line. The case of perfect inequality is difficult to construct if you only have quintiles to work with. Here the lowest, fourth, third, and second quintiles would earn 0 percent and the highest quintile would earn 100 percent. The cumulative distribution values would be graphed along the bottom horizontal axis up until 80 percent of the families. Then a diagonal line would shoot up to the upper right-hand corner. As the number of income categories increases, the perfect inequality curve would approach the appearance ascribed to it earlier.

The Gini Coefficient

A mathematical way to represent the degree of inequality is the Gini coefficient.[8] The Gini coefficient is derived from the Lorenz curve. In Figure 1.5, two areas, A and B, are specified. The Gini coefficient for that distribution of income is area A/[area(A + B)]. The Lorenz curve runs from 0 to 1. If 0, the distribution is perfectly equal. That makes sense graphically because the only way for the Gini to be 0 is if area A is 0. Area A would be 0 only if the Lorenz curve was a 45° line. Perfect inequality is a Gini of 1. To get a Gini of 1, area A must equal area (A + B). That would only occur if the Lorenz curve followed the bottom horizontal and right-side vertical. The official Gini coefficient in 2006 was 0.470.

The Gini coefficient is relatively easy to approximate by just remembering a few geometrical formulas. Notice that area (A + B) is simply a triangle. The area of a

Figure 1.5 **Relationship between the Lorenz Curve and Gini Coefficient**

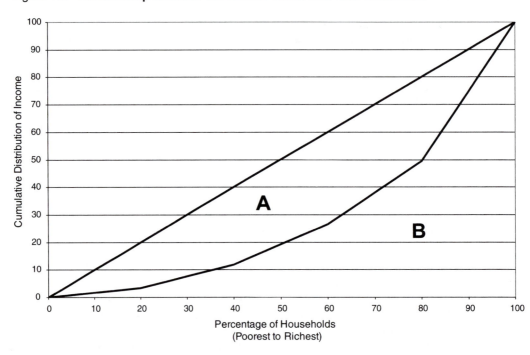

triangle is ½ b × h, where b is the base of the triangle and h is the height. Area A might be difficult to compute directly, but it can be obtained indirectly. Notice that area B consists of five sub-areas. To see that more easily, see Figure 1.6. Call the five sub-areas H, I, J, K, and L. Area H is a triangle. Areas I, J, K, and L are rhombuses. The area of a rhombus is ½ b × (h$_1$ + h$_2$), where h$_1$ is the height of the left-side of the rhombus and h$_2$ is the height of the right side.

Applying these formulas to the data in Table 1.2 gives a Gini coefficient of 0.4348, a tolerable approximation.[9]

The 90/10 Percentile Ratio

Increasingly popular with the USBC, the 90/10 percentile ratio method is another way to represent income inequality. It compares the income of the household at the 90th percentile of the income distribution to the income of the household at the 10th percentile. The 90th percentile disposable income is the income that exceeds 90 percent of all incomes (90 percent of all households earn an income less than that amount). The 10th percentile disposable income is the income that exceeds 10 percent of all incomes. The 90/10 percentile ratio is simply the income at the 90th percentile divided by the income at the 10th percentile. In the United States in 2006, that ratio was 11.08 (USBC 2007d, 38). That means the income at the 90th percentile was 11.08 times higher than the income at the 10th percentile ($133,000 versus $12,000). The USBC also reports 95/20, 95/50, 80/50, and 20/50 percentile ratios.

Figure 1.6 **Computing the Gini Coefficient**

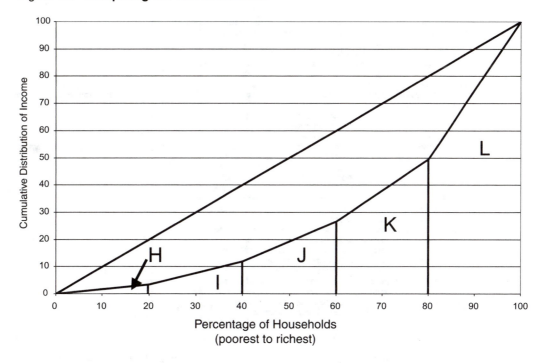

Percentage of Households
(poorest to richest)

Comparative Inequality

How does income inequality in the United States compare to that of other countries? Figure 1.7 shows the 90/10 percentile ratio for a sample of countries. There are only two countries in which income inequality is higher than in the United States—Russia and Mexico.

CRITICISMS OF THE MEASUREMENT OF INEQUALITY

For a long time critics have pointed out that the "official" CPS measure of income makes some major omissions. There are four omissions that are particularly significant.

- The CPS omits a substantial source of money income, namely, capital gains.
- The CPS does not make any allowance for the taxes people pay.
- The CPS omits all kinds of in-kind income. In-kind income is income in the form of goods or services, rather than money. An example would be food stamps. Many poor people are eligible to receive food stamps. Food stamps are coupons that have a monetary value attached and can be used to pay for food items in stores.[10] Receiving food stamps is similar to receiving income,[11] but what the recipient actually gets is stamps, not money, so their value is not included in the recipient's income. Medicaid is another example of in-kind income. Medicaid is a health insurance program for the poor. Since the poor

Figure 1.7   **International 90/10 Percentile Ratios**

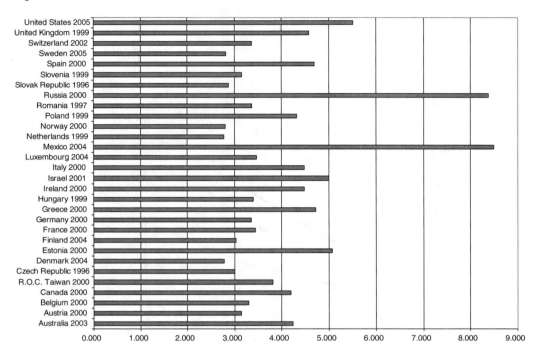

Source: Luxembourg Income Study (LIS) Key Figures, accessed at http://www.lisproject.org/keyfigures. htm on 16 June 2008

receive a service, namely, health care, and not money, the value of this program is not considered part of their income. Of course, the nonpoor also receive various forms of in-kind income. Homeowners, for example, receive the benefits associated with living in their own houses and these benefits are not included in their income.

• The CPS omits the benefits from various public goods, such as national defense and public schooling. Since they do provide utility to their recipients, they are properly considered income.

These omissions are not the result of lack of awareness on the part of the USBC; there is no organization that understands better how to measure income.[12] Data availability and conceptual problems associated with measuring particular types of income are the cause of the omissions. While data are available for measuring realized capital gains, data on unrealized gains are not.[13] People keep track of realized gains for tax purposes. No one has any reason to keep track of unrealized gains. Instead of measuring just part of capital gains (the smaller part), the USBC opts to exclude all the gains. With respect to in-kind income, there is no generally accepted method of measuring the value of the various goods and services that make up in-kind income. Is $100 in food stamps equivalent to $100 in income? If you would have voluntarily spent the $100 in income on food, then it is. But if that

$100 would have been allocated differently, say $80 on food and $20 on something else, then that means the last $20 of food obtained with food stamps was not worth as much to you as if the money was spent for that something else. Similar problems haunt the valuation of public goods. What is a year of public schooling or a cleaner environment worth to a family?

Despite these problems, for many years now the bureau has experimented with other measures of income that attempt to account for some of the omissions discussed earlier. Currently, the USBC produces estimates of three measures of income in addition to money income (USBC 2008, 2). They are:

- Market Income. This measure includes all money income but adds realized capital gains and the imputed return to a homeowner from living in his or her own house (also known as imputed rental income) and subtracts work expenses (excluding child care) and all government cash transfers.[14] Of course, imputed rental income and work expenses can at best be estimated, and the estimates hold only for large classes of people, not particular individuals. Market income, by excluding government benefits that come in the form of cash transfers, is an attempt to measure what people's income would be if their only source of income was what they could earn through working and renting out the other productive resources they own. Subtracting work expenses causes market income to more accurately be a measure of the net return to working. Whether market income measures what it purports to measure is problematic, however. It excludes government benefits, but does not adjust for how people's behavior would change if they were not eligible for government benefits. For example, if people did not receive Social Security benefits, fewer would be retired.
- Post–Social Insurance Income. This measure uses market income but adds non-means-tested government transfers. Non-means-tested government transfers are government benefits for which eligibility does not depend on income. The category includes such programs as Social Security and unemployment compensation. Eligibility for these programs is extended to people who have worked and contributed to the system by paying taxes.[15] It does not include public assistance, a program that people become eligible for essentially by not working. Individuals on public assistance do not have to pay taxes into the program.[16] To many, social insurance benefits have an entirely different standing than welfare. They are in a sense "earned," while welfare benefits are charity.
- Disposable Income. This category includes all money income and makes some of the same adjustments to it that market income does, by adding realized capital gains and imputed rental income and subtracting work expenses. It does not subtract government cash transfers, but rather adds the value of noncash (in-kind) transfers. Finally, it subtracts a variety of taxes, including federal payroll and income taxes, state income taxes, and property taxes on owner-occupied houses. In short, disposable income is an attempt to measure what people actually have to spend. It comprehensively includes what they earn in the marketplace and benefits received from government (with the exception of the shared value of public goods), and subtracts work expenses and most taxes.

Figure 1.8   **Median Income of Households by Income Definition: 2006**

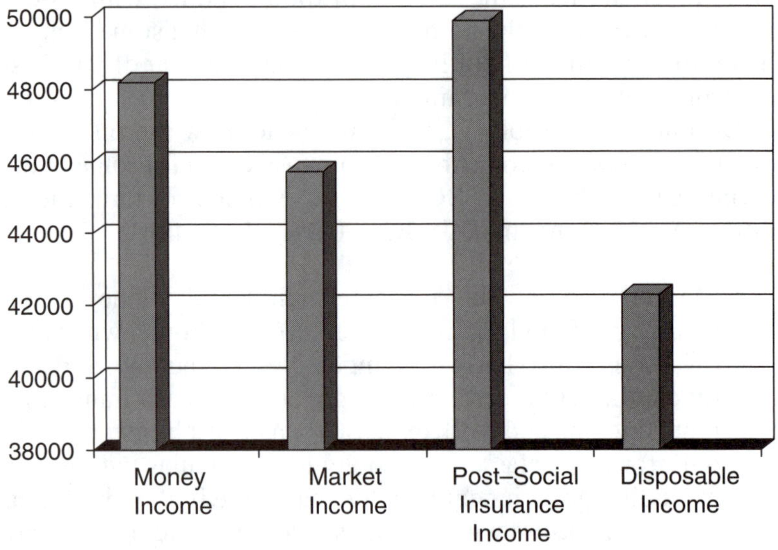

Source: United States Bureau of the Census 2008. Table INC RD-AEI 3.

Figure 1.8 shows median household income in 2006 for each of these measures. While market income includes some categories of income not in money income, the exclusion of government benefits and work expenses drives its value down significantly. Adding back non-means-tested government benefits places post–social insurance income much above money income. Taking into account taxes causes disposable income to be much less than the other three categories.

Not surprisingly, using different definitions of income makes a difference in the calculation of the distribution of household income. See Table 1.3 (2005 data is used in the construction of the table because the 2006 distribution is not yet available). The share of the lowest quintile increases by over 29 percent while the share of the highest quintile is reduced by a little more than 6 percent between money income (the official measure) and disposable income. The Gini coefficient falls slightly above 7 percent. The more interesting comparison is between market income and disposable income. Here the share of the lowest quintile is increased 194.6 percent, the share of the highest quintile is decreased 12.2 percent and the Gini coefficient falls 15.2 percent. Subject to the caveat mentioned earlier regarding the interpretation of market income, these results show that government policy has the effect of redistributing income in the United States.

CONCLUSION

The goal of this chapter was to introduce and describe the facets of the "slicing the pie problem." Quotations from professional economists illustrated just how widespread the range of opinions can be on any one of the four key issues—inequality,

Table 1.3

Share of Aggregate Household Income by Quintile and the Gini Index, 2005

Quintile	Money Income	Market Income	Post–Social Insurance Income	Disposable Income
Lowest	3.42	1.50	3.24	4.42
Second	8.79	7.26	6.59	9.86
Third	14.42	14.00	14.33	15.33
Fourth	23.03	23.41	22.80	23.11
Highest	50.34	53.83	51.03	47.28
Gini index	0.450	0.493	0.447	0.418

Source: United States Bureau of the Census 2007a. *The Effect of Taxes and Transfers on Income and Poverty in the United States: 2005* (P60-232), Table 3, accessed May 2009 at www.census.gov/prod/2007pubs/p60-232.pdf.

discrimination, poverty, and mobility. These controversies will be explored in subsequent chapters. The terms *wealth, income, consumption,* and *money* were also defined. An initial assessment using "official" data on the degree of income inequality in the United States was undertaken. Various ways inequality could be presented—tabular display, Lorenz curve, Gini coefficient, and 90/10 percentile ratio—were shown. Alleged shortcomings of the "official" CPS measure of income were discussed and while measurement controversies can be deadly, that charge hardly holds in this case. The picture of inequality that emerges is sensitive to decisions made regarding measurement issues. We will encounter similar measurement controversies in later chapters. Next, we will employ the tools of economic analysis (and anything else that comes in handy) in an attempt to explain how the pie is sliced.

QUESTIONS FOR REVIEW AND PRACTICE

1. Is a person's money income a good approximation for their total utility? Explain.
2. Gwendolyn owns a house, a car, and a portfolio of stocks with market values of $450,000, $25,000, and $100,000, respectively. She also has $2,000 in a checking account. She still owes $150,000 on her home mortgage and $5,000 on a car loan. What are Gwendolyn's assets, liabilities, and net worth? How much money does she have? Gwendolyn works as an art appraiser, earning $75,000 a year. Assume her consumption is $70,000 and the remaining $5,000 is invested in stocks. What are Gwendolyn's assets, liabilities, and net worth? Assume that, instead of buying stocks, Gwendolyn uses the $5,000 to pay off her car loan. What are Gwendolyn's assets, liabilities, and net worth?
3. A society consists of fifteen single individuals. Their incomes are as follows:

$100,000	$75,000	$25,000	$35,000	$150,000
$80,000	$15,000	$45,000	$85,000	$90,000
$110,000	$135,000	$95,000	$70,000	$60,000

Use the data to construct a table showing the percentage of total income received by each quintile. Then compute the cumulative distribution and use it to construct a Lorenz curve and Gini coefficient using the method described in this chapter.

4. Go to the U.S. Bureau of the Census Web page (www.census.gov) and follow the Income link. Find the data to allow you to construct a table like Table 1.1 for the current year or any year your instructor assigns. Draw the Lorenz curve and compute the Gini coefficient using the method described in this chapter.

NOTES

1. The pie being referred to is the nation's Gross Domestic Product (GDP). GDP measures the production of goods and services.

2. Robert H. Frank and Ben S. Bernanke include a table in their *Principles of Economics* textbook, which shows that, compared to the least developed and all developed countries, the industrialized countries have better outcomes with respect to life expectancy, infant mortality, the under-five years mortality rate, births attended by skilled health personnel, prevalence of HIV/AIDS, undernourished people, school enrollment, and adult literacy (Frank and Bernanke 2007, 511). In the United States, poor people are more likely to report housing problems such as leaky roofs; pests; broken windows; exposed electrical wiring; plumbing problems; holes in walls and floors; and neighborhood problems such as safety concerns, streets in need of repair, trash or litter in the streets, smoke or odors, and abandoned buildings (Rogers and Ryan 2007).

3. A leading textbook in the field is Frederic S. Mishkin, *The Economics of Money, Banking and Financial Markets,* 7th ed. New York: Addison-Wesley, 2004.

4. Households without phones are excluded this way. Today, there are very few households lost because of the lack of a phone. This method also excludes people without households, which is probably a bigger problem.

5. Of course, every ten years it surveys all households as part of the constitutionally mandated census.

6. The census bureau produces two other widely used sources of data: the *Survey of Income and Program Participation* (USBC 2007a), and the *Longitudinal Employer-Household Dynamics* (U.S. Department of Labor, Bureau of Labor Statistics [BLS] 2007b). The Internal Revenue Service's *Statistics of Income* provides a fairly comprehensive measure of income on a national basis (Internal Revenue Service 2007). The BLS is a good source of wage and earnings data (U.S. Department of Labor, BLS 2008). There are also many cross-sectional and longitudinal data sets that have been generated as part of various research projects. Compared to the *Statistics of Income* and BLS national data, these data sets are much more detailed, but have much smaller sample sizes. Two of the more important data sets are the *Panel Study of Income Dynamics* (PSID) and the *National Longitudinal Surveys* (University of Michigan 2007; United States Department of Labor, BLS 2007b).

7. The Lorenz curve is named for M.O. Lorenz who introduced the technique in 1905 (Lorenz 1905).

8. The Gini coefficient was developed by Corrado Gini in 1912 (Gini 1912).

9. See "The Lorenz Curve and the Gini Coefficient" for a computer tutorial on constructing the Lorenz curve and computing the Gini coefficient (Rycroft undated).

10. There are extensive rules regarding what items food stamps may be used to buy and where they can be bought.

11. An interesting exercise done in most microeconomics courses is to show that $X of food stamps is not exactly equivalent to $X in income. See Robert Frank (2008, 73–76).

12. Admittedly, the Internal Revenue Service (IRS) is also pretty good at it, but the IRS is no better than USBC.

13. Gains are realized when the asset in question is actually sold. If you buy a stock at $100 and sell it for $115, you have realized a $15 capital gain and you have 15 additional dollars in your pocket. If you do not sell the stock, you still have a capital gain of $15. You are $15 wealthier, but instead of having cash in your pocket, you have stock in your portfolio that is worth more. This is an unrealized gain.

14. Government cash transfers refer to all government benefits that are made available to people in cash form. They include Social Security; supplemental security income; public assistance; unemployment compensation; workers' compensation; veterans' payments; and survivor, pension, and disability benefits from certain sources. Many of these benefits will be described in more detail in Chapter 7.

15. Programs with these characteristics are typically called social insurance.

16. These programs are frequently called welfare. See the extended discussion in Chapter 12.

PART I

INEQUALITY

2 | Labor's Slice of the Pie

INTRODUCTION

Money does not grow on trees. (I bet you've heard that before.) Ultimately a society's sustenance is obtained by it putting its factors of production (land, labor, capital, and entrepreneurship is one commonly used comprehensive listing) to work to produce goods and services. Compensation (rent, wages, interest, and profit) is paid for the work performed. This compensation, of course, does not just go to inanimate factors. Rather it goes to real people because, in a capitalistic society, most of these factors of production are privately owned by persons, families, or households.[1] The amount of money that goes to (the owners of) land, labor, capital, and entrepreneurship is what constitutes the functional distribution of income.

This is the logical starting point for understanding how the pie is sliced in the United States. The logical starting point is a long way away from the ending point. For one thing, in a modern economy people are not *either* landlords, workers, capitalists, or entrepreneurs. Most individuals are landlords, workers, capitalists, *and* entrepreneurs. They own their own labor power, to be sure, but they also own a portfolio of entre-preneurial ability and financial and real assets. Most "workers" have entrepreneurial spirit in some areas, such as savings accounts, mutual funds, and 401(k) plans, and some own land, buildings, machinery, and tools. People rent out their labor plus all the items in their portfolio in order to earn their daily bread. Consequently, the functional distribution is not a very useful end-product. The distribution of income resulting from supplying factors depends on the pattern of individual ownership of labor, entre-neurial ability, and financial and real assets, and the relative return on each.

Secondly, the income received from supplying factors of production can be redis-tributed by voluntary and involuntary transfers. The word *transfer* refers to money volunteered by or taken from some people and given to other people, often in an attempt to help the disadvantaged or to modify the market's distribution of income. Unlike rent, wages, interest, and profits, which are compensation given to reward the rendering of current productive services, transfers are provided to recipients who are incapable of rendering current services.[2] Private charity is a clear example of a vol-untary transfer. Most transfers would not exist without a government with the power and resources to raise the necessary funds (by taxation and borrowing) and organize the distribution of benefits. Prominent examples of government transfers are Social

Security benefits, welfare payments, unemployment compensation, and alimony (the payment of alimony is a consequence of a legal system that allows for alimony and enforces court orders to pay), and the taxes and borrowing to pay for them. The "voluntary" nature of these transfers is open to dispute. Certainly, "We, the people" have given our consent to the existence of a government with these powers. Of course, those who get outvoted are understandably unhappy. An example of an involuntary form of transfer is theft. In virtually all societies, the net impact of all these transfers, taxes, and borrowing is to redistribute income from rich to poor, although that is not true of all transfer programs.

Thirdly, a complicating factor is the feedback effect from transfers and taxes to the income earned by supplying factor of production. Presumably, transfers and taxes have incentive effects. The taxes on some people and the transfers to others might reduce both of their incentives to provide productive efforts. Consequently, while the income people receive is equal to income earned minus taxes paid plus transfers received, taxes paid and transfers received will influence the amount of income earned. An attempt to re-slice the pie by transfers and taxes may result in the pie shrinking in size.

To avoid having to deal with this complicating factor at the start, initially our analysis will be placed in the context of a *pure market economy*. A pure market economy is a competitive, capitalist economy of households and firms without a significant government sector. About the only thing government does is specify weights and measures and enforce contracts. It does not touch redistribution. In addition, we will assume no one is a bigot and institutions are not rigged against certain groups of people. We will learn how the pie is cut among factors of production in such an economy. Once we understand income distribution in this very simple economy, we will then be able to introduce a government sector that taxes, borrows, supplies public goods, and redistributes income. Explaining the rationales for why government does what it does, and investigating the feedback loop from government policy to market outcomes will expand the story. Following that, we will add discrimination to get a fuller picture of why the pie is cut the way it is.

To start us off, this chapter will build a model to analyze the workings of the labor market. The important outputs are the wage and employment level of labor, which together give us labor's slice of the pie.

A MODEL OF THE LABOR MARKET

Widespread public opinion seems to be that wages are set arbitrarily at the whim of an employer. If the employer is sensitive to the well-being of his employees, he might generously pay a "living wage." If the only sensitivity the employer has is to the bottom line, he drives wages down to rock bottom. As an example of this way of looking at things, consider the following argument by a writer decrying Wal-Mart's low wages: "Make no mistake: Wal-Mart could afford to pay its workers more. Wal-Mart's $240 billion in sales last year make it bigger, economically speaking, than Indonesia, the world's fourth most populous nation. Look at the *Forbes* list of the world's top ten billionaires and you'll see that four of them are members of Wal-Mart's Walton family. And just half of the $7 billion in profit the company made last year would have been enough to give every employee a raise of at least $1.50 per hour" (Cox 2008). Apparently the only trade-off involved is with profits and whether the employer will dine on hamburger or Kobe beef.

The alternative view that is promoted by economists is that wages and employment levels are determined in the labor market by the forces of demand and supply. Likewise, other factor prices and employment levels are determined in their respective markets. Looking at it this way reveals a host of trade-offs, or complications, that the "whim" approach to wages overlooks. Granted, wage policy does influence how well the employer dines, but it also influences the flow of capital and entrepreneurial talent to the firm, the level of employment for the labor in question, and the level of employment of all the other factors the firm uses. Employers simultaneously pay the lowest wage possible and the highest wage feasible. To better understand this point, we need to study the markets in which factors of production are bought and sold, starting with the labor market.

MODELING THE LABOR MARKET

Consider the labor market for labor of type X. Let X be any type of labor you are familiar with, for example, firefighters, registered nurses, accountants, graphic designers, administrative assistants, or construction laborers. Assume that many industries use labor of type X, many people have X skills, and all people with X skills are equally talented and have the same "work ethic."

The Demand for Labor

The market for labor of type X can be depicted graphically. In Figure 2.1, the horizontal axis measures the quantity of X. The vertical axis measures the compensation of X, which includes wage or salary plus fringe benefits. For simplicity, we will call it the *wage*. D is the demand curve for X.

One interpretation of D is it shows the quantity demanded at different wages. For example, if the wage of X was $100,000 per year, all employers would want to hire a total of 50,000 X workers. Find $100,000 on the vertical axis and trace a straight line to D at point *A*. Then trace a straight line down to the horizontal axis where it hits 50,000. If the wage of X was $75,000, the quantity demanded would be 75,000, and so on.

The negative slope of the demand curve is representative of the law of demand: the lower the wage the greater the quantity of labor demanded. Essentially there are two reasons for the law of demand. One reason is as the wage falls, X becomes relatively cheaper than the other factors of production that could be substituted for it. This is known as the substitution effect. For example, consider the production technology employed at a car wash. There are many ways cars can be washed. One way is to hire a bunch of workers and give them buckets and sponges. Another way is to employ a completely automated system where the customer deposits the money, fits the car tire into a slot, and sits in the car while it gets pulled through the car wash. If wages are low, the former method might be used. If wages increase, the workers might all

Figure 2.1 **The Demand Curve for X**

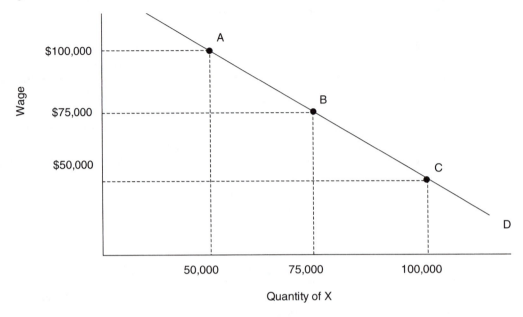

be fired and be replaced by the automated system. Substitution does not only take place between labor and capital. It can also take place between different types of labor. For example, if the wage of registered nurses rises, licensed practical nurses might be hired in their stead to take blood pressure and other vital signs. The second reason is as the wage of labor falls, the firm's costs of production fall allowing it to lower its price and expand production. If the firm produces more, it will need to hire more labor. This is known as the *output effect*.

A second interpretation of the demand curve is that it shows the maximum wage that employers would be willing to pay to hire any quantity of X. (It depends on how you look at it—horizontally or vertically.) Employers would not be willing to pay more than $100,000 each to hire 50,000 X (of course, they would love to be able to pay less). The most they would pay to hire 75,000 X would be $75,000. The additional 25,000 X workers are less productive than the first 50,000 X workers.

Shifts in the Demand Curve

The demand curve does not just stay in one place. It can shift due to changing conditions in the labor market. In Figure 2.2, the original demand curve is D. An increase in demand can be represented by demand curve D'. The demand curve D can be said to have shifted. The actual shift can variously be described as an outward/rightward/upward shift (take your pick). The meaning of an increase in demand is clear. Take the wage $100,000. If the demand curve is D, the quantity demanded of X is 40,000. If the demand curve is D', the quantity demanded is 60,000. At wage $75,000, the quantity demanded is 75,000 with demand curve D and 95,000 with demand curve D'.

Figure 2.2 **Shifts in the Demand Curve**

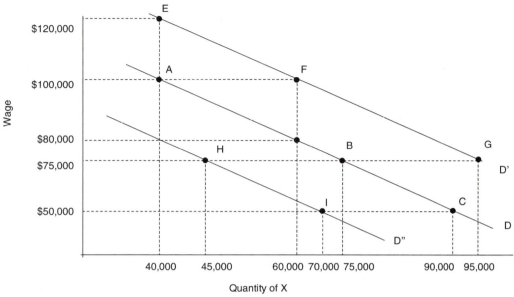

The alternative description focuses on employers' willingness to pay. At any quantity of X, demand curve D' represents a greater willingness to pay. At quantity 40,000, employers are willing to pay $100,000 if the demand curve is D, but $120,000 if the demand curve is D'. At quantity 60,000, willingness to pay is $80,000 with demand curve D and $100,000 with demand curve D'.

What would cause the demand for X to increase? One factor is an increased demand for the goods and services that X helps produce. A second factor is whether the productivity of X increases. One way for X's productivity to increase is simply for X to work harder, but X can be more productive even if X does not sweat more. Consider the following example. Assume a worker is tasked with plowing a field. This could be done a variety of ways. One way is to give the worker a sharp stick and let him have at it. Another way is to give him a tractor and a plow. Obviously, the worker will plow more land more quickly the second way, making the worker more productive. Why is this worker more productive? Is the worker working harder? Doubtful. Sitting on a tractor, likely in an air-conditioned cab these days, is not working harder than trying to turn over earth with a stick. The worker is more productive because he has a better tool to work with. In addition to better tools, labor productivity can also increase if labor acquires better training, is better managed, or is healthier.

An inward/leftward/downward shift in the demand curve (for example, from D to D") is called a decrease in demand. Causes are a fall in the demand for the goods and services produced by the labor or if labor becomes less productive. A reduced demand for labor means that employers will want to hire fewer workers at every wage or else are less inclined to pay for the services of workers.

The Elasticity of Demand for Labor

The law of demand holds for X like any other good or service. If the wage rate rises, less X will be demanded. But by how much will the quantity demanded of X fall? Will it fall by a large amount or just a little bit? The elasticity of demand is a measure of how much the quantity of X demanded changes as a result of a change in the wage. The formula for elasticity of demand is $E_d = | \% \Delta Q_d / \% \Delta w |$, where E_d is elasticity of demand, Q_d is quantity demanded, and the symbol Δ means "change in." Please note the absolute value symbol. If absolute value was not used, then elasticity of demand would always be a negative number because if w rises, Q_d falls and vice versa. If a wage increase of 1 percent causes the quantity demanded of labor to fall 2 percent, then $E_d = |-2\%/1\%| = 2$.

If $E_d > 1$, we say demand is elastic. Elastic means changes in quantity demanded are highly responsive to changes in w (the percentage change in Q_d exceeds the percentage change in w). If $E_d = \infty$, then demand is said to be perfectly elastic. If $0 < E_d < 1$, then demand is inelastic. This means quantity demanded is not very responsive to changes in w (the percentage change in Q_d is less than the percentage change in w). If $E_d = 0$, demand is perfectly inelastic. If $E_d = 1$, we say demand is unit elastic. Of course, E_d cannot be less than 0 (because we are using absolute value).

There is a relationship between elasticity of demand and the earnings of X. Assume the earnings of X = w*L. What would happen to the earnings of X if the wage rate rose? What makes this a complicated problem is that if w rises, then L falls so the impact on the earnings of X will depend on their relative movement. If w rises by a greater percentage than L falls in percentage terms, then the earnings of X will rise. If w rises by a lesser percentage then L falls in percentage terms, the earnings of X will fall.

Here is where elasticity of demand comes in. Elasticity tells us the relative percentage movement of the two variables. If $E_d = 2$ and w rises by 1 percent, L would fall by 2 percent and the product of w*L would have to fall. If demand is elastic, then an increase in the wage rate will lower the earnings of X. But if w falls by 1 percent, L will increase by 2 percent and the earnings of X will rise. If demand is elastic, a decline in the wage rate will increase the earnings of X.

If demand is inelastic, then the opposite occurs. Assume $E_d = 0.5$. A 1 percent increase in the wage will lower L by 0.5 percent and raise the earnings of X. A 1 percent decrease in the wage will increase L by 0.5 percent and lower the earnings of X.

If demand is unit elastic, every percentage change in w will be matched by the exact same percentage change in L. That means that regardless of the change in w, there will be no change in the earnings of X.

Figure 2.3 shows two demand curves, D and d, which intersect at point A. Clearly d is steeper than D, and while it is natural to say that d is less elastic than D, that would be wrong or at least misleading for the following reasons.

Let $\%\Delta Q_d$ be represented by $\Delta Q_d/Q_d$ and let $\%\Delta w = \Delta w/w$: $E_d = | \Delta Q_d / Q_d / \Delta w / w |$. Rearranging gives us $E_d = | \Delta Q_d / \Delta w / Q_d / w |$. The numerator of that expression is the reciprocal of the slope of a demand curve. The denominator is simply an arbitrary point on the demand curve. Demand curve d is a straight line, which means the slope is the same at every point. But Q_d/w will differ from point to point. In

Figure 2.3 **Elasticity and the Slope of the Demand Curve**

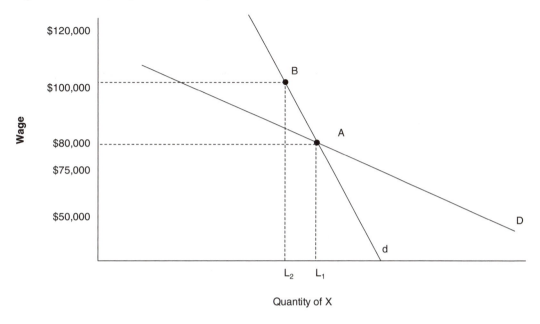

Figure 2.3 Q_d/w differs between points A and B, which implies that the elasticity of demand will differ between points A and B. In other words, along a demand curve, elasticity of demand will be different at every single point,[3] with elasticity rising as we move up a demand curve.

Thus when it comes to comparing demand curves, the only meaningful way to compare elasticities is by looking at the demand curves where they intersect, because that is where Q_d/w is the same for both curves. Differences in their slopes will cause measured elasticity of demand to differ. At point A demand curve d is less elastic than demand curve D. But demand curve d might be more elastic at point B than D is at A.

The Market Supply Curve of Labor

The supply curve of labor shows how many workers are willing to work at different levels of compensation. Continuing with the example of X, Figure 2.4 shows a hypothetical supply curve (S). The horizontal axis measures the quantity of X, and the vertical axis measures the wage of labor.

One interpretation of S is it shows the quantity supplied at different levels of compensation. At a wage of $50,000, no X would offer their services. This wage is called the reservation wage. At $75,000 a year, the quantity supplied would be 75,000. Find $75,000 on the vertical axis and trace a straight line to S at point A. Then trace a straight line down to the horizontal axis where it hits quantity of X = 75,000. If the wage of X was $100,000, the quantity supplied would be 115,000, and so on.

The positive slope of the labor supply curve shown is supported empirically (Rosen and Gayer 2008, 419), but is not the only logical outcome. Labor supply curves could

Figure 2.4 **The Supply Curve of X**

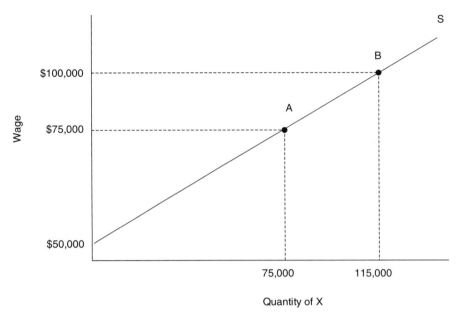

have a negative slope or be what is called backward-bending (a backward-bending supply curve has a positive slope at low wages, but a negative slope at high wages). Why the labor supply curve might take on these different shapes is discussed in Chapter 3, but, given the empirical evidence, that issue need not detain us here.

A second interpretation of the supply curve is that it shows the minimum wage that employers would have to offer in order to hire any quantity of X. At a wage below $50,000, employers would be unable to hire anyone. Why? All X would have a better alternative opportunity. To keep it simple, assume the only alternative to work is to leave the labor force and consume leisure. The utility of the leisure is such that $50,000 is not enough to persuade anyone to give it up. Of course, people have different tastes for leisure. Some people may not enjoy leisure very much and be willing to work for a little over $50,000. Others may place a higher value on leisure, which necessitates a higher wage to induce them to give it all up in exchange for a job. Here employers would have to offer $75,000 to be able to hire 75,000 X and $110,000 to hire 115,000 X. In a more realistic model, there would be more alternatives to work. In addition to leisure, people might opt for housekeeping, child care, and going to school. In these cases the wage would have to be high enough to make it worthwhile for people to hire a cleaning service or a nanny and go to work. Or the value of additional schooling might be judged to exceed the wage.

Shifts in the Supply Curve

Like the demand curve, the supply curve of labor does not stay fixed in one place. It can shift due to a variety of influences. In Figure 2.5 let S be the initial supply curve.

Figure 2.5 **Shifts in the Supply Curve**

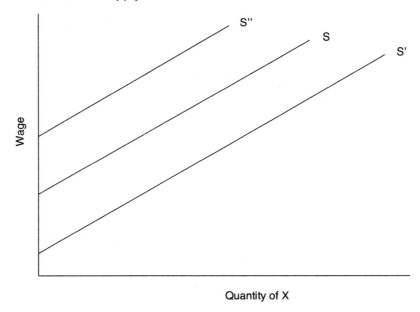

If the curve moves to the position inhabited by S' then we say the curve has shifted outward/rightward/downward and call the shift an increase in supply. An increase in supply results from any factor that increases the number of people willing to work and that increases the willingness of individuals to work. Examples of the former factors include natural increases in population, increased immigration, or an increased labor force participation rate. Examples of the latter factors include changes in tastes (toward work and leisure) and nonwage aspects of jobs. An example of a nonwage aspect might be pleasant working conditions. If employers suddenly made pleasant working conditions available to all employees, the willingness of people to work at all wages would be increased.

If supply curve S moves to S" we would say it shifted inward/leftward/upward and call that a decrease in supply. Factors that decrease the number of people willing to work and that decrease the willingness of individuals to work cause a decrease in supply.

The Elasticity of Supply of Labor

There is an elasticity of supply the same as there is an elasticity of demand. Elasticity of supply measures the responsiveness of labor supply to changes in the wage rate. The formula is $E_s = \% \Delta Q_s / \% \Delta w$, where E_s is elasticity of supply and Q_s is quantity supplied of labor. Note there is no absolute value sign. This is because increases in wages could be associated with either an increase or a decrease in Q_s.

The terminology of elasticity of supply is the same as for elasticity of demand.

If $E_s > 1$, we say supply is elastic. Elastic means changes in quantity supplied are highly responsive to changes in w (the percentage change in Q_s exceeds the percentage change in w). If $E_s = \infty$, then supply is said to be perfectly elastic. If $0 < E_s < 1$, then supply is inelastic. Inelastic means changes in quantity supplied are not very responsive to changes in w (the percentage change in Q_s is less than the percentage change in w). If $E_s = 0$, supply is perfectly inelastic. If $E_s = 1$, we say supply is unit elastic. E_s can be negative, but there is no special terminology that goes with negative values of E_s.

The rest of the analysis that applies to elasticity of demand applies to elasticity of supply as well.

Equilibrium

Figure 2.6 shows the market demand and supply curves for X. The eye is naturally drawn to a particular place on the graph, namely, the intersection of the demand and supply curves. If we draw a vertical line directly downward from the intersection to the horizontal axis we get quantity of X 75,000, which is called the equilibrium quantity. If we draw a horizontal line directly leftward from the intersection to the vertical axis, we get the wage $75,000, which is called the equilibrium wage.

What is meant by the equilibrium quantity and wage? An equilibrium anything is a stable anything. A market in equilibrium is a market that tends to stay put. There are no forces causing price and quantity to change from their equilibrium values. Paradoxically, the meaning of equilibrium is probably best understood by considering a market that is not in equilibrium.

Let the going wage be $100,000. At that wage, the number of X who would desire employment is 115,000, found by tracing a horizontal line from $100,000 on the vertical axis to the supply curve and dropping straight down to the horizontal axis. The quantity demanded of X 50,000 is found in a similar manner. Thus the number of people who want employment exceeds the number of jobs made available. What eventually will happen is that the wage rate will fall. The motivating force for the decrease cannot be precisely pinpointed. Maybe employers will sense that they can hire capable X for less and begin offering a lower wage. Or maybe unemployed X will start getting desperate and offer to work for less. Either way, the wage rate will fall. Consequently, $100,000 cannot be an equilibrium because market forces associated with the surplus of X act to push the wage down. As the wage rate falls, the number of workers desiring work will decrease as some will decide that alternative uses of their time are preferable to employment. Graphically there will be a movement down the supply curve. As the wage falls, employers will increase the number of X they want to hire. Using relatively more X and relatively less of the other factor of production makes more economic sense. Graphically, there is a movement down the demand curve. In short, the surplus shrinks.

If the wage rate is $50,000, there will be a shortage in the market. At $50,000 employers will want to hire 140,000 X, but no X want jobs. The shortage will force up the wage. Again, the motivating source cannot be pinpointed. Desperate employers may begin offering higher wages to snatch X away from other markets or X may

Figure 2.6 **Equilibrium in the Market for X**

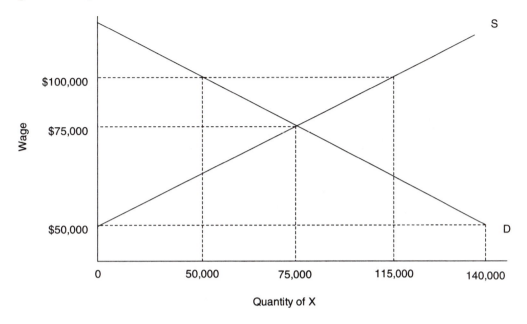

simply demand higher wages. Either way, the wage rises and the shortage will shrink away as the higher wage forces a movement up the demand and supply curves. Again, not an equilibrium situation.

Wage $75,000 is equilibrium for the following reason. At that wage the quantity demanded of X is 75,000 and the quantity of X supplied is 75,000. Everyone who wants a job can get one. Employers can hire all they want. There is no reason for the wage to change and, consequently, it does not. The market is in equilibrium because the wage and quantity of X are stable.

Using the Model

The model is used to make predictions about what will happen in the labor market when certain events take place. The way this is done is as follows:

1. The market is initially assumed to be in equilibrium.
2. Then an event is assumed to take place, something that will affect the willing-ness of employers to hire labor or the willingness of workers to seek employ-ment. Graphically this event will shift either the demand or supply curve. (Events that shift both curves at the same time are possible, but uncommon.) The most challenging part of the exercise is figuring out what the event means in terms of a shift of a curve.
3. The curve is then shifted, and the impact on equilibrium wage and quantity is determined. (Until this type of analysis is second nature to you, it never hurts to actually draw a little graph.)

Figure 2.7 **An Increased Demand for Accountants**

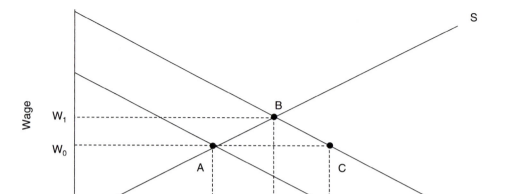

Quantity of Accountants

An Increase in the Demand for Labor. Referring to Figure 2.7, let the initial demand and supply curves for X be D_0 and S, respectively. For the sake of realism, let X be accountants. The market is in equilibrium with wage equal to w_0 and quantity equal to L_0. Next assume an Enron-type scandal erupts prompting Congress to pass legislation enforcing stricter accounting standards on firms and necessitating the hiring of more accountants. This event will shift the demand curve to D_1. The rationale for the outward shift is either that firms want to hire more accountants at every wage or that firms are willing to pay more for any quantity of accountants.

The result of this is easily seen on the graph. The equilibrium quantity of accountants increases to L_1 and the equilibrium wage increases to w_1. The dynamics of the process could be explained as follows: The increased demand for accountants leads to a shortage at wage w_0 (L_2–L_0). In response to the shortage, firms begin offering higher wages. In response to the higher wage, more people with accounting skills enter the labor force in search of accounting jobs.

At this point a frustrating issue of terminology must be dealt with. The shift of the demand curve from D_0 to D_1 is called an increase in demand. Any time the demand curve shifts its position, demand is said to have changed. This makes sense because the word *demand* does not mean a specific amount, like quantity of labor 75,000. Rather, it means the entire schedule, all the wage-quantity combinations. If demand increases, the entire schedule will change, and the quantity demanded at every wage will increase thereby shifting the curve outward.

As the wage rate rises, this leads more people to seek work. The quantity supplied of labor increases from L_0 to L_1. Graphically this is represented by a movement from point A to B along supply curve S. More labor is supplied, but this is called an in-

Figure 2.8 **An Increased Supply of Accountants**

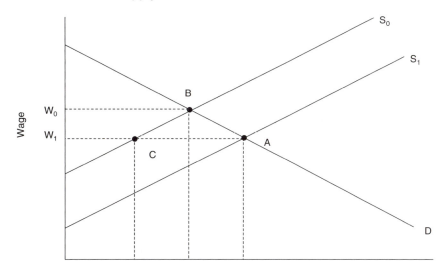

Quantity of Accountants

crease in quantity supplied. Since the supply curve does not shift, there has not been an increase in supply. Got that?

An Increase in the Supply of Labor. Continuing with the accountant market, let the market for labor initially be in equilibrium with demand curve D, supply curve S_0, equilibrium wage w_0, and equilibrium quantity L_0 (Figure 2.8). Let the event be the passage by Congress of a law that would permit easier immigration of people with accounting skills into the United States. This event will shift the supply curve from S_0 to S_1. At any wage, the quantity of accountants offering their skills will be greater. Alternatively, accountants will be willing to work for a lower wage because there is more competition for jobs.

The effect of this will be to push down the equilibrium wage to w_1 and increase the equilibrium quantity to L_1. One way to describe the sequence of events is as follows: At the initial wage w_0, the outward shift in the supply curve creates a surplus of accountants. This will cause the wage to drop. As the wage drops, employers will hire more labor because of both the substitution and output effects.

Graphically, the outward shift in the supply curve is called an increase in supply. The movement along the fixed demand curve from A to B is called an increase in quantity demanded.

The "Temporary" Nature of Unemployment. Assume the labor market for accountants is in equilibrium at wage w_0 and quantity L_0, as in Figure 2.9. An important feature of equilibrium is that the market clears. The quantity demanded of labor equals the quantity supplied. This means all the accounting jobs employers want to offer at

Figure 2.9 **The Temporary Nature of Unemployment**

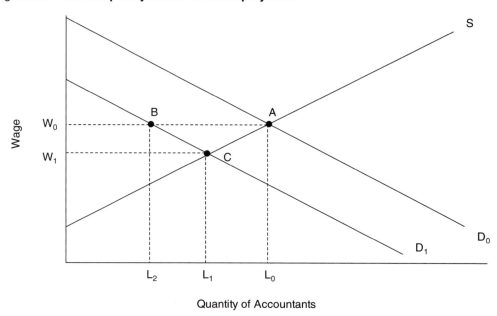

wage w_0 will be filled and every accountant who wants to work at wage w_0 will be employed. The situation can reasonably be described as one of full employment for accountants. Of course, not every accountant in the economy has a job. There are accountants who would not work unless the wage exceeded w_0. However, these people are not unemployed. They are simply out of the labor force.

Now assume the economy hits a rough patch and falls into a recession. Firms are forced to make layoffs. In Figure 2.9, there has been a decrease in demand represented by an inward shift of the demand curve to D_1. If the wage rate is slow to adjust to the new reality, a surplus of accountants results. At wage w_0 the quantity demanded of accountants is L_2 while the quantity supplied is L_0. Since L_0–L_2 accountants would like jobs at wage w_0, but are unable to obtain them, it makes sense to describe them as being unemployed.

If conditions do not change, the unemployment will not last forever. Eventually accountants who want jobs, but are unsuccessful, will catch on to the new reality and moderate their wage demands. Employers will help this process along by lowering their offers. As the wage falls toward w_1, some accountants will leave the labor force as represented by a movement down supply curve S from A to C. As the wage falls, employers will increase the number of accountants they want to hire as represented by a movement along demand curve D_1 from B to C. The result will be a new full-employment equilibrium at wage w_1 and quantity L_1. Fewer accountants will be working, but those no longer working do not want to work at the new wage. The fact that they left the market means they had better opportunities elsewhere. The unemployment in this case was only temporary. There is nothing the theory can do to put an exact measure of time on "temporary." And, undoubtedly, to the people directly affected and many watching it happen, such "temporary" unemployment seems like forever.

DEMAND AND SUPPLY ANALYSIS OF LONG-TERM WAGE GROWTH AND CROSS-NATIONAL WAGE DIFFERENTIALS

Wages are higher in the United States than in Bangladesh, and they are higher in the United States today than they were in the United States 200 years ago. Why? The answer, like the answer to most problems in economics, is demand and supply.

With respect to the United States/Bangladesh differential, the labor demand and supply curves intersect at a higher wage in the United States than in Bangladesh. Figure 2.10 shows this. To provide a full explanation of this, we need to explain why the demand and supply curves hold the positions they do.

The demand curve for labor in the United States is generally "higher" than the demand curve for labor in Bangladesh. Recalling our earlier discussion, the height of the demand curve reflects the productivity of labor. U.S. labor is more productive than Bangladeshi labor. Some reasons for this are:

1. Labor in the United States has more capital to work with than labor in Bangladesh.
2. Labor in the United States works with more technologically sophisticated capital equipment.
3. Labor in the United States is more educated and has better work skills.
4. Labor in the United States is better managed.
5. Labor in the United States is healthier.

The relative importance of these factors is obviously significant, but will not be addressed.

Of course, greater productivity is only part of the story. The other part has to do with supply. The supply of labor is relatively less in the United States than in Bangladesh. This is the result of a variety of factors, including a slower rate of population growth, a lower labor force participation rate, a shorter workweek, and more vacation time.

Keep in mind is that both demand and supply play a role in this explanation. One is no more important than the other. The fact that labor in the United States is more productive than labor in Bangladesh does not "guarantee" higher wages in the United States. Higher wages require relatively scarce labor.

The explanation for higher wages in the United States today than 200 years ago follows a similar line. Over time, residents of the United States have saved and this has allowed the accumulation of capital. Research and development has led to technological breakthroughs that have been incorporated into the capital. Workers have received more schooling and training and are actually healthier. These factors have all contributed to shifting the demand curve for labor outward. All would have been for naught if the supply of labor had grown rapidly, but, in fact, labor supply growth actually slowed down. The end result was growing wages in the United States.

Figure 2.10 **Cross-National Wage Differentials**

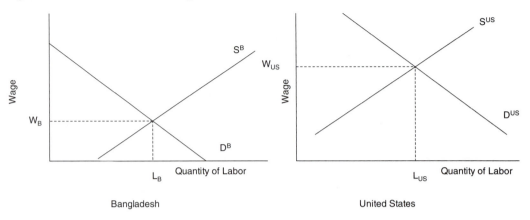

Bangladesh   United States

CONCLUSION

There is no model more basic to economists then demand and supply. In this chapter the model was used to analyze the labor market. The theory might appear to be frighteningly technical, and it is. But do not lose sight of the intuition behind the curves. What ultimately determines the wage a worker earns? The answer is always demand AND supply. Do some workers earn high wages because their jobs are particularly "important" for society (a demand factor)? Not necessarily. Do some workers earn high wages because they are particularly productive (a demand factor)? Not necessarily. Jobs may be very important and workers may be very productive, yet wages may be low simply because there are many people who are capable of doing that job (a supply factor). Take the case of teachers. Teachers do a very important job. Literally the future of society is in their hands. Yet teachers are not particularly well paid because many people possess the skills to do an adequate job. The relatively high demand for teachers is offset by a high supply. Electrical engineers (the folks who design and build computers, among other things) are highly compensated. Yes, they do an important job, but is it any more important than teaching our children? The difference is that electrical engineering is a hard course of study at which only a few succeed. Electrical engineers in a relative sense are scarce. The high demand for them is associated with a relatively low supply, which leads to a high level of compensation. Superstar actors are extremely well compensated. Not taking anything away from the entertainment they provide, it is difficult to argue that their services are vital to society in the same way that teaching and electrical engineering is. Nonetheless, they are highly compensated because the talents needed to be a superstar—acting skill, good looks, and charisma—are highly scarce.

Which factor is more important, demand or supply? To paraphrase Alfred Marshall, one of the greatest economists of all time, which blade of the scissors is more important in cutting the paper? They are both important and neither one is more important than the other. So it is in the case of demand and supply of labor.

For other purposes, the models discussed in this chapter are inadequate. They were developed using intuition, but intuition is a decidedly nonrigorous approach to economic modeling. Economists like to ground their models in theories of individual behavior. Chapter 3 shows how the demand and supply curves can be built up from models of utility-maximizing households and profit-maximizing firms.

QUESTIONS FOR PRACTICE AND REVIEW

1. Surpluses of labor cause wages to fall and shortages of labor cause wages to rise. Tell a plausible story to explain both phenomena. Why are wages stable at equilibrium?
2. Draw a graph to illustrate the effect of each of the following events on wages and quantity in the market for registered nurses (RNs).
   a. An increase in the demand for RNs
   b. An increase in the supply of RNs
   c. A decrease in the demand for RNs
   d. A decrease in the supply of RNs
3. Draw a graph to illustrate the effect of each of the following events on wages and quantity in the market for registered nurses (RNs).
   a. Changes in immigration law make it easier for foreign nurses to come here and work as RNs.
   b. A serious disease epidemic spreads among people who work in hospitals.
   c. A law is passed mandating that hospitals must have more RNs available at all times.
   d. A law allows doctors to use licensed practical nurses to do some of the jobs RNs used to do.
4. Figure 2.11 (page 42) shows the demand curve for carpenters. Compute the elasticity of demand for carpenters at points A and B.
5. Let the labor market in the United States consist of two types of labor, skilled and unskilled workers. Skilled and unskilled workers complement each other. The assistance of unskilled workers allows skilled workers to be more productive in the skilled jobs. Being able to work with unskilled workers makes skilled workers more productive. Assume there is a wave of illegal immigration into the United States consisting of unskilled workers who could be substituted for U.S. unskilled workers. What will happen to wages for both unskilled and skilled workers? Draw graphs showing how you reached your conclusions.

NOTES

1. To be precise, people can own land and capital and their own labor and entrepreneurial ability. They cannot own the labor or entrepreneurial ability of another person. That would be a system of

Figure 2.11 **The Demand for Carpenters**

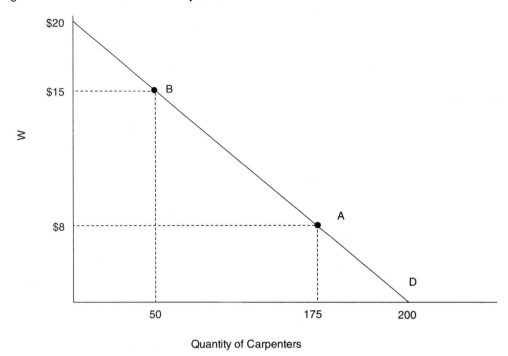

Quantity of Carpenters

slavery, which is the antithesis of capitalism. Also, even in a capitalistic society some factors of production are owned by government, for example, bridges, roads, and national parks.

2. We need to be careful not to be too judgmental here. Social Security recipients may not be working now, but they worked at one time and paid Social Security taxes. Similarly, beneficiaries of unemployment compensation were workers who lost their jobs through no fault of their own. As Chapter 13 will show, most welfare recipients today must either work or actively receive training. A recipient of alimony may have sacrificed his or her own career for the sake of the family. Thieves do work, but not in a way we want to encourage.

3. There are some exceptions. A horizontal demand curve will be perfectly elastic at every point on it. A vertical demand curve will have an elasticity of 0 at every point. Demand curves that are rectangular hyperbolas will have the same elasticity at every point.

3 | The Foundations of Labor's Slice

INTRODUCTION

The usefulness of the theory of demand and supply in explaining a wide variety of phenomena related to labor markets should be clear. However, the demand and supply curves in the previous chapter essentially "fell down from out of the sky." The slopes of the curves and how they shifted were essentially determined using intuition. This chapter seeks to build a firmer foundation for these curves with which a number of labor market and income distribution issues can be better understood.

To build this foundation, we will make use of two venerable models from the mainstream of economic theory. The Marginal Productivity Theory of Distribution will be used to derive the firm's demand curve for labor. The market demand curve will then be shown to be the summation of the firms' demand curves. The theory of rational choice will be used to derive the individual's supply curve of labor. The market supply curve will likewise be the summation of these individual curves. Putting market demand and supply curves together is what allows us to do the analysis of Chapter 2. With suitable extensions of the theories in subsequent chapters, everything else will follow.

LABOR DEMAND

DERIVING THE FIRM'S DEMAND CURVE FOR LABOR

What determines a firm's demand for labor? To answer this question, first simplify by making the following assumptions:

- Every firm sells its output in a perfectly competitive product market.
- Every firm produces output using a single type of labor (L) and a single type of capital (K), and no other factor of production.
- Every firm is a profit maximizer.
- Both labor and capital are homogeneous. This means every unit of labor is identical to every other unit of labor in terms of skills and motivation. Every unit of capital is identical to every other unit of capital.
- Labor and capital are both hired in perfectly competitive factor markets.

Table 3.1

The Production Function in Table Format

		CAPITAL			
		1	2	3	4
	1	1,000	1,500	1,900	2,200
	2	2,100	2,600	3,000	3,300
	3	3,100	3,600	4,000	4,300
LABOR	4	4,000	4,500	4,900	5,200
	5	4,800	5,300	5,700	6,000
	6	5,500	6,000	6,400	6,700
	7	6,100	6,600	7,000	7,300

- The wage is the only cost of labor.
- The length of the workweek and other working conditions are fixed.

The relationship between a firm's use of factors of production and its output is called the *production function*. A production function can be represented by an equation, chart, or graph. For example, the equation $Q = 1312.9*K^{.25}L^{.75}$, where Q is quantity of output, is a production function because by entering values for K and L on the right-hand side, we can compute Q. A tabular representation of this equation is shown in Table 3.1.

Now add one more assumption. The quantity of labor used can be changed almost instantaneously. If the firm decides it wants to use more labor, it can hire additional workers today and have them start tomorrow morning. If the firm decides it wants to use less labor, it can lay off workers right this very instant. But it takes some time for the firm to change the quantity of capital it uses. Additional capital equipment is not something you can just pick up off the shelf in a store. Rather, the firm needs to place an order and wait for the equipment to be manufactured, shipped, and set up and this cannot take place overnight. Let us say, for the sake of argument, that it takes a month. (The length of time will differ from industry to industry, and even firm to firm, based on the technology in use.) Therefore, any time period less than a month constitutes what is known as the *short run*. The definition of the short run is the period of time during which one of the factors of production is fixed in supply. That factor is called, fittingly enough, the fixed factor. Here capital is fixed in supply for a month. The factor that can be varied in supply, here labor, is the variable factor. Longer than a month is considered the long run. In the long run, all factors of production are variable. Over a period longer than a month, the firm can change the quantity of both labor and capital that it uses by any amount.

In the short run let the firm's quantity of capital be 1. Therefore the Q values in the column headed by capital of 1 are what the firm can produce in the short run.

Table 3.2 is derived from Table 3.1. It shows the marginal product of labor for each quantity of capital. The marginal product of labor is defined as the increase in total output from hiring one more unit of labor. Assuming we are in the short run with the quantity of capital equal to 1, the following relationship between the amount of

Table 3.2

The Marginal Product of Labor

			CAPITAL		
		1	2	3	4
	1	1,000	1,500	1,900	2,200
	2	1,100	1,100	1,100	1,100
	3	1,000	1,000	1,000	1,000
LABOR	4	900	900	900	900
	5	800	800	800	800
	6	700	700	700	700
	7	600	600	600	600

labor and the marginal product of labor holds. If 0 units of labor are employed, the firm produces nothing. If the firm hires one worker, then output is 1,000 (from Table 3.1). Hiring that worker caused output to increase by 1,000 units (from Table 3.2). If a second worker is hired, output rises to 2,100 units (from Table 3.1), an increase of 1,100 units (from Table 3.2). The marginal product of the second worker is 1,100, and so on.

Be careful here. The marginal product of the second worker is 1,100. That means hiring that worker caused output to rise by that amount. It does not necessarily mean that the second worker produced that amount. Since output is produced by two workers working with one machine, it is impossible to say who produced how much.

Note what happens to the marginal product of labor as more labor is hired. Initially it rises from 1,000 to 1,100. That is because of the benefits associated with specialization and division of labor. Two workers can produce more than twice what one worker produces because the workers are able to divide the tasks and become especially adept at their specialized tasks. However, after the second worker, the marginal product of labor falls. This is a result of the law of diminishing returns. As you add more of the variable factor to the fixed factor, the increases in output eventually begin to diminish. This is because of congestion and coordination problems. Adding more factory workers results in congestion. There are more and more workers milling around the machines, maybe bumping into each other. It is also more difficult for management to coordinate a larger workforce. The increase in the marginal product of labor from one to two workers is not problematic. All the law of diminishing returns says is that eventually the increases in marginal product will get smaller and smaller. Eventually the problems associated with congestion and coordination will overwhelm the benefits of specialization and division of labor. A graph of the marginal product of labor is shown in Figure 3.1.

Assume the firm's output sells for $1.50 a unit. Since the firm is a perfect competitor in the product market it will be able to sell all it wants at that price. Multiplying that price by the marginal product of labor gives what is variously called the value of the marginal product (VMP), marginal revenue product (MRP), or marginal value product (MVP) (see the third column of Table 3.3). The VMP (my favorite) measures the economic value of what the worker produces.[1] Hiring the first worker causes

Figure 3.1 **Graphical Representation of the Marginal Product of Labor**

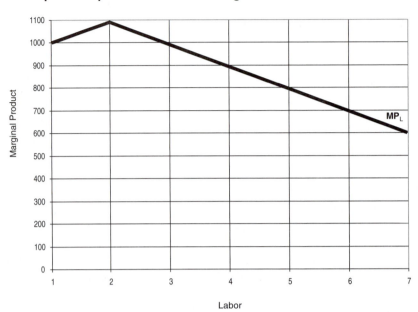

output to rise by 1,000 units. Since those units can be sold for $1.50 each, the firm's revenue will rise by $1,500 (= $1.50 * 1,000) as a result of hiring this worker. Hiring the second worker causes the firm's revenue to rise by $1,650, and so on. Notice that after the second worker the VMP falls as more labor is hired. Since every unit can be sold for the exact same price, the decline in VMP is completely the result of diminishing returns.

A graph of VMP is shown in Figure 3.2.

Now we are ready to determine how many workers the firm will hire to maximize profits or minimize losses. Assume the wage rate is $1,200. From our assumption that the firm hires labor in a perfectly competitive labor market, it follows that the firm can hire all the labor it wants at that price.

To do this, we will employ *marginal analysis*, the analysis of small changes. Referring to Table 3.3, start at the point of 0 labor. Is it worthwhile for the firm to hire the first worker? The first worker contributes to the firm by producing output that can be sold. The VMP tells us how much the firm benefits. In this case, the benefit is $1,500. Of course, this worker must be paid; in this case, $1,200. Would you hire a worker who contributed $1,500 to your revenue while costing you $1,200? Of course you would.

Once the first worker is hired would you hire a second worker? Again look to VMP and wage. The second worker contributes $1,650 to revenue but costs $1,200. Another no-brainer. Hire that worker.

What about the third worker? Again this worker contributes more than he or she costs. Hire that worker. Do likewise with the fourth worker. What about the fifth worker? Here the worker's contribution equals what the worker costs. The firm does

Table 3.3

Table of TP, MP, VMP and W

		TP	MP	VMP	W
	1	1,000	1,000	$1,500	$1,200
	2	2,100	1,100	$1,650	$1,200
	3	3,100	1,000	$1,500	$1,200
Labor	4	4,000	900	$1,350	$1,200
	5	4,800	800	$1,200	$1,200
	6	5,500	700	$1,050	$1,200
	7	6,100	600	$900	$1,200

Figure 3.2 **Graphical Representation of the Value of the Marginal Product of Labor**

not benefit by hiring the fifth worker, but does not lose anything either. In short, the firm is indifferent about hiring that worker.

Would a sixth worker be hired? No. The sixth worker costs $1,200 but only contributes $1,050 toward the firm's revenue.

What general rule is in use here? Clearly hire labor as long as VMP > W. Do not hire labor if VMP < W. Stop hiring labor when VMP = W[2].

In Figure 3.3, the wage line is drawn in. The firm will hire labor until the VMP schedule intersects the wage line, which takes place at five workers. What the graph makes clear is that the real choice is not between four or five workers. Rather it is between 4.99999 and 5 workers—a trivial distinction.

Figure 3.3   **Graphical Determination of the Firm's Level of Employment**

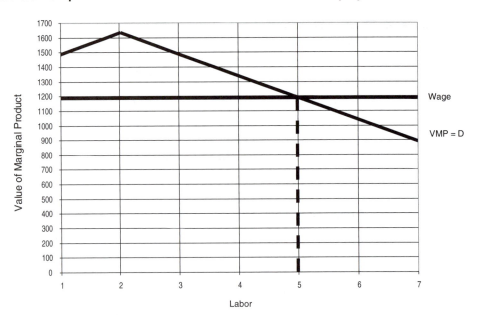

Now consider this thought experiment: By assumption every worker is identical to every other worker. Select one of the six workers at random and send that worker home. How much does the firm's revenue fall? $1,200. In fact, that is true for any of the six. The absence of any one of them costs the firm $1,200. In an important sense, you could say any of those workers is worth $1,200 to the firm. And what are they paid? $1,200. Each worker is paid a wage exactly equal to what the worker is worth to the firm. Does that make the outcome "fair"?

Here we need to be clear on a few things. Saying a worker is worth $1,200 *to the firm* is not the same thing as saying the worker is simply worth $1,200. What human beings are actually worth is a metaphysical question that this model does not presume to answer. Some might object to saying that each worker is worth $1,200. Was it not the case the VMP of the first worker was $1,500? Here it is good to recognize that workers are probably not hired one after another. They are hired as a group. If hired six at a time, it is impossible to say who the first worker is. More importantly, the high VMP of the first worker is simply a consequence of the fact that diminishing returns have not yet set in. The last workers hired are not less productive. They are just unlucky enough to be caught up in the congestion and coordination problems. Labor is homogeneous by assumption so each worker is worth the same as every other worker.

Back to the question of the fairness of the outcome. The answer, of course, is that there is no objective way to say what is fair. But that does not make it against the law for you to have an opinion. So what do you think?

Now consider other wages. What if the wage was $1,350? How many workers would the firm hire? Using the VMP = W rule, the firm would hire four workers. Graphically trace a horizontal line from $1,350 on the vertical axis of Figure 3.3 to the VMP schedule. If the wage was $1,050 the firm would hire six workers using the same rule. At any wage, the number of workers hired can be found from the VMP schedule. What does that make VMP? A demand curve. By definition a demand curve shows the quantity demanded of something at alternative prices. That is exactly what the VMP schedule does for labor. The VMP schedule is the firm's demand curve for labor.[3]

SHIFTING THE LABOR DEMAND CURVE

The firm's demand curve for labor is not fixed in place for all time. The demand curve D in Figure 3.4 is simply the demand curve from Figure 3.3 minus the upward sloping segment as explained in endnote 3. Demand curve D' represents an outward/rightward/upward shift.[4] Regardless of the word used to describe the shift, we call it an *increase in demand*. Demand curve D" is an inward/leftward/downward shift representing a decrease in demand.

Shifts are caused by any factor that can change VMP. Since VMP = P*MP, any factor that changes P or MP can shift the curve. If the price of the firm's product rises, for example, perhaps as a result of a rise in demand for the product, the VMP of the factors hired by the firm will increase and shift the curve rightward. A fall in price would shift the curve inward.

MP changes as a result of actions that change the productivity of the factors. In the case of labor, several events could cause a rise in the marginal product of labor. The acquisition of more capital (or any other factor in a more complicated model) would make labor more productive. Technological changes could also make labor more productive. Managerial changes that induced more effort from the workforce could also raise MP.

Figure 3.4 **Shifting the Firm's Demand Curve for Labor**

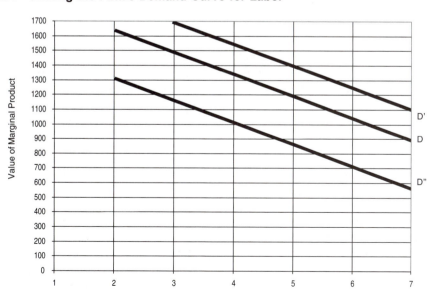

ELASTICITY OF DEMAND

An elasticity of demand can be computed for the firm's demand curve as it is for the market demand curve (see pages 30–31 for a review).

In Chapter 2 we discussed the relationship between elasticity of demand and the earnings of labor. In this chapter, we will change the focus and look at it from the employer's point of view. The employer is concerned with his or her wage bill (how much the employer pays out in wages). The wage bill is also given by the expression $w \times L$. What would happen to the wage bill if the wage rate rose? Employers are paying more for each worker, but likely will reduce the level of employment. The impact on the wage bill depends on the relative movement of w and L. If w rises by a greater percentage than L falls in percentage terms, then the wage bill will rise. If w rises by a lesser percentage than L falls, the wage bill will fall.

Elasticity works the same here as in Chapter 2. Elasticity tells us the relative percentage movement of the two variables. Assume E_d was equal to 2. If w rises by 1%, L would fall by 2% and the product of $w \times L$ would have to fall. If demand is elastic, then an increase in the wage rate will lower the wage bill. But if w falls by 1%, L will increase by 2% and the wage bill will rise. If demand is elastic, a decline in the wage rate will increase the wage bill.

If demand is inelastic, then the opposite occurs. Assume $E_d = 0.5$. A 1% increase in the wage will lower L by 0.5% and raise the wage bill. A decrease in the wage of 1% will increase L by 0.5% and lower the wage bill.

If demand is unit elastic, every percentage change in w will be matched by the exact same percentage change in L. So, regardless of the change in w, there will be no change in the wage bill.

THE MARKET DEMAND CURVE

The market demand curve for a factor of production is obtained by adding together the firm demand curves for that factor. However, the addition process is not a simple one. (Those not interested in the gory technical details can skip the next paragraph.)

In Figure 3.5, ΣVMP_1 is the horizontal sum of all the firm's demand curves for labor when the price of the good in the market is P_1. At W_1 the quantity demanded of labor is L_1. Now let's say the wage rate falls to W_2 and, as a consequence, each firm hires more labor. Doing so will cause each firm to increase production, which will lower the price of the good in the marketplace to P_2. At P_2 the VMP schedules for each firm will shift inward and ΣVMP_2 will lie below ΣVMP_1. The result is that the total quantity of labor hired will be L_2, not L_3, and the market demand curve is the curve D, which cuts both ΣVMP curves.

MONOPOLY IN THE PRODUCT MARKET

One of the previous assumptions is that the firm is a perfect competitor in the product market. What if we drop that assumption? What if the firm is a monopolist (single seller), or oligopolist (one of a few sellers), or monopolistic competitor (one of many

Figure 3.5 **Market Demand Curve for Labor**

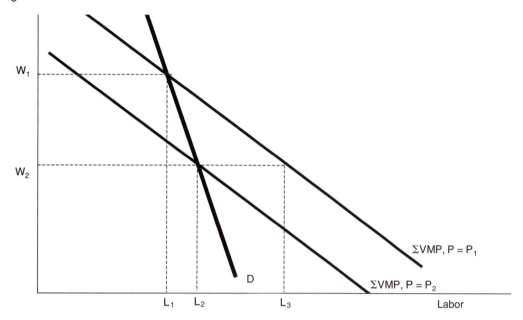

sellers of a slightly differentiated product), or, more generally, an imperfect competitor in the product market?

Retain all the other assumptions from the previous perfect competition case, but with a different production function (equation unspecified) (Table 3.4). The first two columns in Table 3.4 show the short run production function for the firm. As employment increases, output initially rises at an increasing rate (due to specialization and division of labor) but eventually, diminishing returns set in (due to congestion and coordination problems). The column labeled P shows the price the firm has to charge to be able to sell that quantity of output. The imperfect competitor status of the firm can be seen by the fact that the firm must lower the price it charges in order to sell additional output. The next column shows the firm's total revenue (TR), computed by multiplying price by the quantity produced. Short run costs of production can be broken down into variable costs (VC) and fixed costs (FC). Labor at a wage of $300 per unit is the only variable factor and the sole source of variable costs. The capital input is the source of the fixed costs. Only variable costs are shown. The reason is that "bygones are bygones." In other words, in the short run the fixed costs are irrelevant. The next column shows TR − VC. If the firm is a profit maximizer, the choice of how many workers to hire is clear—6. This holds whether fixed costs were $100, $1,000, $10,000, $1,000,000, or anything else.

The next column of Table 3.4 shows the marginal product (MP) of labor. Note that MP initially rises, and then falls. The next column is labeled MRP for marginal revenue product and shows the increase in the firm's total revenue from hiring one more worker. While this reads the same as VMP in the perfectly competitive case, we also said VMP was equal to P $\times$ MP$_L$, and that is what is in the column labeled

Table 3.4

Demand for Labor-Monopoly in the Product Market

Labor	Q	P ($)	TR ($)	VC ($)	TR–VC ($)	MP	MRP ($)	VMP ($)	W($)
1	1,000	1.00	1,000	300	700	1,000	1,000	1,000	300
2	2,100	0.95	1,995	600	1,395	1,100	995	1,045	300
3	3,300	0.90	2,970	900	2,070	1,200	975	1,080	300
4	4,400	0.85	3,740	1,200	2,540	1,100	770	935	300
5	5,400	0.80	4,320	1,500	2,820	1,000	580	800	300
6	6,300	0.75	4,725	1,800	2,925	900	405	675	300
7	7,100	0.70	4,970	2,100	2,870	800	245	560	300
8	7,800	0.65	5,070	2,400	2,670	700	100	455	300
9	8,400	0.60	5,040	2,700	2,340	600	–30	360	300
10	8,900	0.55	4,895	3,000	1,895	500	–145	275	300
11	9,300	0.50	4,650	3,300	1,350	400	–245	200	300
12	9,600	0.45	4,320	3,600	720	300	–330	135	300
13	9,800	0.40	3,920	3,900	20	200	–400	80	300
14	9,900	0.35	3,465	4,200	–735	100	–455	35	300
15	9,900	0.30	2,970	4,500	–1530	0	–495	0	300
16	9,800	0.25	2,450	4,800	–2350	–100	–520	–25	300

VMP. The VMP is the economic value of what the marginal worker produces, which is equal to price times marginal product, but in the imperfectly competitive case the value of what the worker produces is not equal to the increase in the firm's revenue. This is because in order to sell more the firm has to lower the price it charges, and this holds not just for the new units, but also the old.

Figure 3.6 shows MRP and VMP graphed. Which one is relevant for employment decisions? The firm does not much care about the value of what the worker produces, but cares deeply about its profits. Therefore, the MRP schedule is the relevant one from the standpoint of hiring. The firm will hire labor as long as MRP > W and will stop hiring where MRP = W.

An interesting result here is that at the equilibrium point—using the table it is 6 workers, on the graph it is 6 and a fraction—the VMP of the worker exceeds MRP. Therefore workers get paid a wage that is less than the value of what they produce. This difference is sometimes called *monopolistic exploitation*.

The discussion of elasticity and the market demand curve is no different when there is monopoly in the product market.

LABOR SUPPLY

LABOR SUPPLY AS A CHOICE

To earn a living in our simple economy, people must supply the factors they own. People owning labor (their own labor; owning anyone else's labor has been ruled out) will supply their services in the labor market. Economic theory can be used to explain how much labor people will supply to the labor market.

Figure 3.6 **The MRP and VMP Schedules**

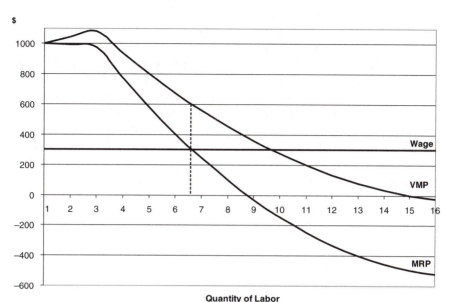

The mainstream theory of labor supply is based on the theory of rational choice. You are likely to be familiar with the basics of the theory of rational choice already. This theory is simply conventional microeconomic analysis. It assumes that individuals seek to maximize utility and make decisions by balancing costs and benefits of alternative choices. The theory most often used to explain consumer demand for goods and services can be easily extended to labor supply once we have an appropriate definition of goods and services.

Assume the existence of a rational consumer in the marketplace. Do not be put off by the use of the term *rational*. This is a term that economists understand very differently than the average guy on the street. To many average guys, a rational individual is greedy, cold, calculating, and utterly despicable. To economists a rational individual *can* be all of these things, but does not have to be. Essentially, a rational individual is someone who does not knowingly behave in a manner contrary to his or her self-interest. Does that make the person greedy? Not necessarily. It ultimately depends on how people define their self-interest. If making other people happy is your goal, then there is nothing irrational about giving away your worldly goods. Nearly everyone is generous to some degree and a few become notable philanthropists. But rational philanthropists do not waste their funds. If you care about others and care about how others perceive you, you are neither cold nor irrational. In a sense rational people must calculate, but they do not have to calculate down to the last penny. Many of us feel that being that precise is just not worth it, which is perfectly rational. Given all that, what is there not to like about rational individuals?

Before going further, it might be worthwhile to consider the following discussion, which uses the theory of rational choice to explain labor supply as if you had a choice about how many hours you work. Many of you probably doubt you have much of a choice. You show up at work when the boss says to show up and leave when the boss says you can leave and that is all there is to it. Admittedly, over short periods of time you probably do not have complete flexibility in your hours of work (at least if you, like most people, are not self-employed), but over longer periods of time there is a substantial amount of flexibility. Consider the sorts of labor supply choices that people make all the time. Some volunteer for overtime; others refuse it. Some work part time; others work full time. You can quit your job and take some time off. You can moonlight (work a second job). You can choose between jobs where the work is intermittent or steady. For example, many construction workers cannot work on days when the weather is bad, and many teachers have summers off. Associates striving for partnerships at law firms may put in a backbreaking number of billable hours each year. If you have worked too many hours over your lifetime, you can retire. Or you can work until you drop. And, in many jobs, you have discretion over how much effort you put in each day.

THE BUDGET CONSTRAINT

In the context of the labor supply problem, assume the individual can consume two goods, where the goods are defined in such a way that we can solve our problem. One good is income, which can be used to buy all other goods and services. The other good is leisure time. In this simple model there are only two uses for your time: work and leisure. If we know how much leisure you choose to consume, we also know how many hours of labor you choose to supply. One other assumption is that when you work, you can earn a wage of $10 per hour, but have no other source of income.

Now we are ready to graph the budget constraint (Figure 3.7). The horizontal axis of the graph measures the number of hours of leisure consumed. The horizontal axis, however, cannot go on forever. There is an absolute upper limit to the number of hours of leisure you can enjoy over any time period. Using a 30-day month as our standard, the horizontal axis must cut off at 720 hours (= 24 hours per day * 30 days). At any point on the horizontal axis you can read the number of hours of leisure and the number of hours of work, where hours of work is measured in the leftward direction from the right-hand end of the axis. The vertical axis measures income earned. There is not an absolute upper limit on how far this axis can run.

The next step is to draw in the consumer's budget constraint. The budget constraint shows all the combinations of leisure and income that the consumer could consume. What if the consumer chose leisure 24 hours a day for the entire month? The consumer would end up with 720 hours of leisure, but no income. Plot that as point A. What if the consumer worked 24 hours a day for 30 days? The consumer would end up with 0 hours of leisure and $7,200 in income (= 720 hours worked × $10/hour). Plot that as point B. Between these two extremes the individual consumes amounts of both leisure and income. At point C, the person consumes 360 hours of leisure, which allows 360 hours for work that can be used to earn $3,600. Connecting all the possible points gives the budget constraint BA. The constraint shows the limitations that the person faces. Point D is impossible. There is no way 360 hours of leisure could be

Figure 3.7 **The Budget Constraint**

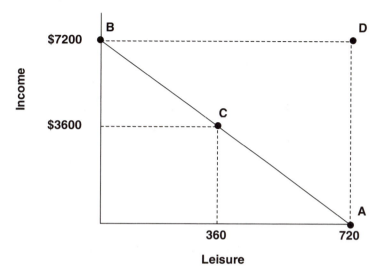

consumed and $7,200 in income earned. The 360 hours of work allowed would not be adequate for earning $7,200 at the $10/hour wage.

Choose any two points on the budget constraint, say A and C. Point A is denoted as (720, $0), where the first number in parentheses is the value on the horizontal axis and the second number is the vertical axis value. Point C is (360, $3,600). The slope of the line segment connecting A and C is $\Delta Y/\Delta X$. Doing the computation yields slope = (0 − $3,600)/(360 − 0) = −$3,600/360 = −$10. The value of the slope is simply the negative of the wage rate. Intuitively, the wage rate tells us how many dollars of income the consumer would have to give up to get an additional hour of leisure. To get an additional hour of leisure, the person would have to work one less hour. If you work one less hour you give up the wage you could have earned, namely, $10.

INDIFFERENCE CURVES

Now look at Figure 3.8. The budget constraint is no longer visible, but ten points representing combinations of leisure hours and income are. Don't be concerned whether these combinations are feasible or not. Each of these points would provide the consumer with a certain level of utility. As you already know, utility is not directly measurable, but that does not prevent us from talking about it as if we could measure utility. For example, point F might represent a combination of leisure and income that gave 50 utils of utility. Point H might give 175 utils, and so on. If you compare any two points (say points F and C), you can say the following: either the utility at F is greater than at C, the utility at C is greater than at F, or the utility is exactly the same.

Now find all the points in the quadrant (visible or not) that yield the exact same level of utility. Assume E, F, and G provide the same number of utils. If you connect

Figure 3.8 **Indifference Curves**

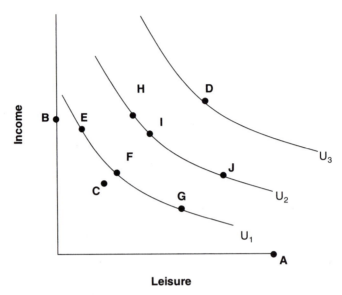

these points along with every other invisible point that provides the same utility, you get what is known as an *indifference curve* (denoted U_1). An indifference curve shows all combinations of the two goods that yield the same level of utility. People would be indifferent as to which point they were at on the curve, and hence the name.

The indifference curve has a negative slope. If you take the absolute value (in other words, ignore the negative sign) of the slope, you get an important concept known as the marginal rate of substitution (MRS_{IL}) of income for leisure. The MRS measures how many dollars of income you would be willing to give up to get an additional hour of leisure. The absolute value of the slope at point E > the absolute value of the slope at point F > the absolute value of the slope at point G. This means the MRS at E > MRS at F > MRS at G. Comparing E and F, the consumer is willing to give up more dollars to get an additional hour of leisure at E than at F. Does this make any economic sense? At point E the consumer is working many hours and has relatively little leisure. The less leisure you have the more valuable an additional hour is likely to be. This greater value is represented by the number of dollars you are willing to give up to get it. By the time you get to G you are consuming many hours of leisure. Another hour might not be worth all that much and the consumer is unwilling to give up many dollars to get it.

There is not just one indifference curve on the quadrant. The quadrant consists of many, many points (an infinite number, to be exact). Each one lies on some indifference curve. For example, H, I, and J lie on an indifference curve (U_2) that lies above the indifference curve containing E, F, and G. D lies on another indifference curve (U_3) that is even higher. A, B, and C also lie on indifference curves, but they are not drawn in.

Comparing indifference curves, we can say the following. As we move from lower

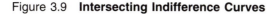
Figure 3.9 **Intersecting Indifference Curves**

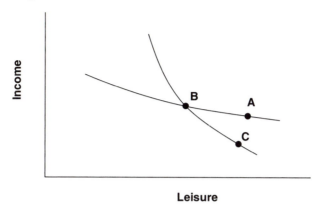

to higher indifference curves (from U_1 to U_2 to U_3) our level of utility increases. That can be seen by comparing points F and I. Point I has to be considered better than point F. At point I the consumer has more leisure and more income than at F. If I is preferable to F, then every point on U_2 has to be preferred over every point on U_1.

By the way, one important characteristic of indifference curves is that they cannot intersect. Figure 3.9 shows two intersecting indifference curves, but that would lead to a weird (inconsistent) outcome. Since points A and B are on the same indifference curve, they should yield the same level of utility. Since points B and C are on the same indifference curve, they should yield the same level of utility. Since A = B and B = C, A should be equal to C. But since A is on a higher indifference curve than C, A cannot be equal to C. This weird outcome will not occur if indifference curves do not intersect.

EQUILIBRIUM

In Figure 3.10 we have made visible again the budget constraint along with the indifference curves U_1, U_2, and U_3. What point in the quadrant will the consumer choose? How many hours of leisure (and, consequently, how many hours of work) and how much income will the consumer select? By assumption, the consumer is rational and wants to achieve the highest level of utility possible. Geometrically that means the consumer wants to choose the point on the budget constraint that is on the highest indifference curve.

Inspecting the graph, the answer is obvious. Of all the points on the budget constraint, the one on the highest indifference curve is I on U_2. At point I the indifference curve is just tangent to the budget constraint. At a point of tangency, the slopes of the two curves are equal to each other. This implies MRS = W.

Consider point E. This point is obviously on a lower indifference curve, but we can analyze it a little more completely. At E the MRS > W. What does that mean? The MRS tells us how many dollars you are willing to give up for an additional hour of leisure. W tells us how many dollars you have to give up for an additional hour

Figure 3.10 **Equilibrium**

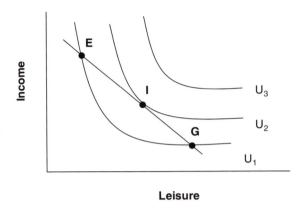

of leisure. If the amount you are willing to give up exceeds the amount you have to give up, then leisure is a bargain. The additional leisure costs you $10, but since you would have been willing to pay more, your utility must increase. Therefore E could not be a point of utility maximization because you can raise your utility by moving to the right.

The analysis at point G is similar but more confusing. We need to introduce the marginal rate of substitution of leisure for income (MRS_{LI}), which measures how much leisure you are willing to give up to get another dollar of income, or, what you are willing to work for. The MRS_{LI} is simply $1/MRS_{IL}$. At G what you are willing to work for is less than what you can work for. It would make sense to work additional hours because you make more than you require to do that work.

At point I, $MRS_{IL} = W$. Since the income you are willing to give up is exactly equal to the income you have to give up, you cannot benefit by consuming more leisure. At point I, $MRS_{LI} = 1/W$. Since the money you earn by working an additional hour is just equal to what you would require to work an additional hour, you cannot benefit by working more. If you cannot make yourself better off by working more or working less, you must be maximizing your utility right there.

CHANGES IN INCOME

What if the consumer acquired a nonlabor source of income? For example, she opened an interest-earning savings account or bought an interest-earning bond or won the lottery. For the sake of argument, assume this new source of income paid $1,000 per month.

The new income would change the budget constraint. On the graph, it would shift it out parallel to the original budget constraint. (See Figure 3.11, which displays the original budget constraint BA.) Without the new source of income, if the consumer works 0 hours, she will earn $0. With the new source, even if she works 0 hours, she will still have an income of $1,000 a month. That gives point K. If the consumer works 720 hours, she earns $7,200 from labor but the $1,000 is added to that for a

Figure 3.11 **An Increase in Income**

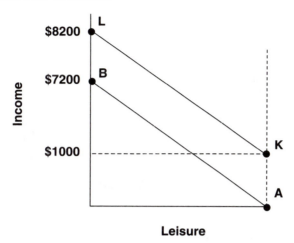

total income of $8,200, which is point L. Connecting points K and L gives the new budget constraint. Since the wage rate has not changed, the slope of the new constraint is the same as the old, meaning the two lines are parallel.

With this new budget constraint, the consumer is able to reach combinations of leisure and income heretofore unavailable. The rational consumer will find the point on the new constraint that touches the highest possible indifference curve. As Figure 3.12 shows, the new equilibrium is one in which she is working fewer hours than before. This is the most likely outcome. It seems reasonable that leisure is a normal good.[5] If the additional income leads to greater consumption of leisure, it must mean fewer work hours.

Changes in Wages

Now remove the nonlabor income and consider what impact a change in the wage rate has on hours of labor supplied. At the wage of $10 per hour, the budget constraint is BA. Now let the wage rate rise to $11 per hour. The budget constraint will change as follows (Figure 3.13): If the consumer works 0 hours, the budget constraint will still intersect the horizontal axis at 720 hours of leisure and $0 income. But if the consumer works 720 hours the budget constraint will intersect the vertical axis at point M. The 720 hours will yield $7,920 (= 720 × $11). Essentially the budget constraint rotates around point A.

With the new budget constraint the consumer can select a new combination of leisure and income. The new combination will place the consumer on a higher indifference curve. In this case, as shown in Figure 3.13, the new equilibrium is one where the consumer chooses to work more hours.

The individual's labor supply curve can be derived directly from the budget constraint/indifference curve graph. There is a wage rate and number of hours of labor supplied at each equilibrium point. These can be transferred to a graph like the one

Figure 3.12 **Equilibrium with Higher Income**

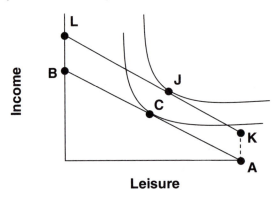

Figure 3.13 **Changes in Wages**

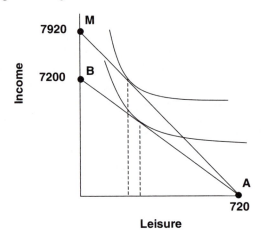

in Figure 3.14 to yield a familiar-looking labor supply curve. Since the consumer chooses to work more hours when the wage rate rises, the labor supply curve has a positive slope.

Individual labor supply curves need not always have a positive slope as the following discussion explains.

INCOME AND SUBSTITUTION EFFECTS

The impact of a wage increase on hours of labor supplied is theoretically ambiguous. That essentially means "it depends." What does it depend on? It depends on the relative strength of the income and substitution effects. First these effects will be explained intuitively, a relatively simple matter. Next they will be explained graphically, which is a relatively complicated matter.

Any wage increase impacts individuals in two ways. It increases the potential

Figure 3.14 **Individual Labor Supply Schedule**

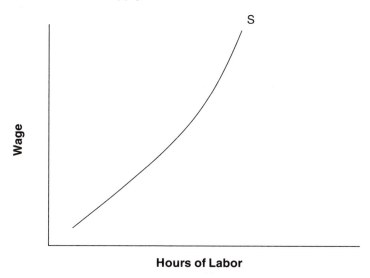

income of the individual. The income you earn from working x hours is greater at the higher wage than the lower wage (obviously). As we saw above, if income rises, the consumer is likely to respond by working fewer hours when everything else held constant. That is the income effect. But everything else is not held constant; the wage rate is equal to the price of leisure. Every hour of leisure consumed costs the amount that could have been earned by working: the higher the wage, the greater the cost of leisure. As the law of demand teaches us, when something costs more, people will consume less of it. This is the substitution effect.

The higher wage rate causes a substitution effect that leads the consumer to want to work more and an income effect that leads the consumer to want to work less. Whether the consumer works more or less depends on the relative strength of the two effects.

Figure 3.15 shows three individual labor supply curves. The curve in graph A has a positive slope indicating that hours of labor supplied increase as the wage rate rises. This will occur if the substitution effect is stronger than the income effect. The negatively sloped supply curve in graph B shows a case in which the income effect is stronger than the substitution effect. Graph C shows the interesting "backward-bending" supply curve. Here, the substitution effect predominates at lower wages, but the income effect is stronger at higher wage rates.

The graphical analysis of the income and substitution effects is challenging. Referring to Figure 3.16, let the initial budget constraint be line BT and the initial equilibrium be point C on indifference curve U_1 with L_1 hours of leisure and $L_1 - T$ hours of work. Now assume the wage rate rises so the budget constraint rotates to MT and the new equilibrium is point N on indifference curve U_2 with L_3 hours of leisure and $L_3 - T$ hours of work. The total effect of the wage increase on hours of work is to increase them by $L_3 - L_1$. To see the income and substitution effects, do the following:

Figure 3.15 **The Income and Substitution Effects**

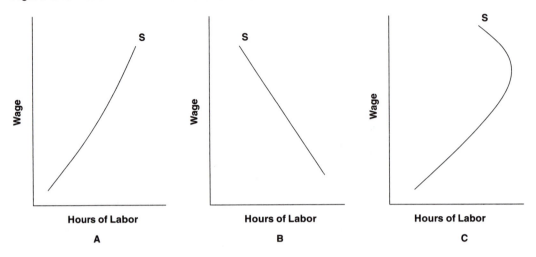

A   B   C

Figure 3.16 **Decomposing the Income and Substitution Effects**

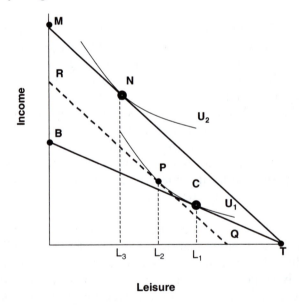

Leisure

1. Take budget constraint MT and shift it parallel to itself until it is just tangent to the original indifference curve U_1. That is the dashed line RQ.
2. Call the point of tangency P. At that point, hours of leisure is L_2 and hours of work is $L_2 - T$.
3. The change in hours of work from $L_1 - T$ at point C to $L_2 - T$ at point P is the substitution effect. The reason is this: the movement from point C to P is just the effect of the higher wage. Income has been held constant since you are still on the same indifference curve.

Figure 3.17 **Graphical Decomposition of Income and Substitution Effects: Income Effect Dominates**

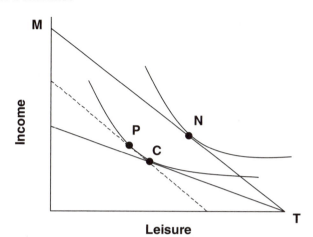

4. The change from point P with $L_2 - T$ hours of work to point N with $L_3 - T$ hours of work is the income effect. Since the budget constraint shifts outward, there has been an increase in income. Since the budget constraint's slope has not changed, the wage rate has been held constant.

   Review these steps slowly until you understand. Do not be concerned if it takes you several tries.

   Now consider the following case. In Figure 3.17 the total effect of the wage increase was to reduce work hours. To decompose it into the substitution and income effects, shift the budget constraint MT inward and parallel to itself until it is just tangent to the old indifference curve. The movement along the indifference curve from C to P is the substitution effect and leads to more work hours. The movement from P to N, from the old to the new indifference curve, is the income effect. Here the income effect is so large it completely offsets the substitution effect. The end result is fewer hours of work.[6]

ELASTICITY OF SUPPLY

The responsiveness of an individual's supply of labor to a change in the wage rate is measured by elasticity of supply. The formula to calculate this is identical to the formula for market elasticity of supply from Chapter 2. The categorizations of elasticity of supply in that discussion also apply here.

MARKET SUPPLY CURVE

To go from the individual labor supply curves to the market supply curve is a fairly straightforward process. Add the individual supply curves horizontally. Assume Car-

Figure 3.18 **From Individual to Market Supply Curve**

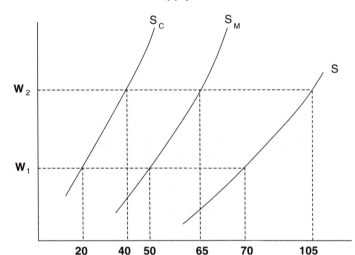

rie and Miranda are the only participants in the labor market. In Figure 3.18, S_C is Carrie's supply curve and S_M is Miranda's. At w_1 Carrie wants to work 20 hours per week and Miranda wants to work 50 hours. For the market, at the wage w_1, the total amount of labor supplied would be $20 + 50 = 70$ hours. Doing the same at each wage rate yields the market supply curve S.

How do we interpret the market supply curve? In Figure 3.19, the curve shows the lowest wage required to persuade someone to work. At a wage of $15.30, one worker will want work. What about everyone else? That wage is not high enough for them. They have alternative uses for their time that they value at more than $15.30, unlike worker 1. This wage is sometimes called the *reservation wage*. Reservation wage reflects the value of all alternative uses of time, jobs, or leisure activities. At a wage of $15.31, two workers will offer to work. One of those workers is the guy already willing to work at $15.30. The second is someone who just became willing after the wage hit the $15.31 level. At a wage of $15.32, three workers want work: the two workers who were willing to work at lower wages plus someone new, and so on.

RENT

Refer again to Figure 3.19. Assume the equilibrium wage is $15.32. At that wage, three workers will want work. Note that all the workers except worker 3 will end up working for a wage higher than their required rate. Worker 1 would have worked for $15.30 and worker 2 would have worked for $15.31. The difference between the wage they work for and their reservation wage is called *rent*. Rent is the return to a factor of production in excess of its reservation price. In this example, worker 1 will receive $0.02 in rent. Worker 2 will receive $0.01 in rent. Worker 3 does not receive any rent because she is working for exactly her reservation

Figure 3.19 **Interpreting the Supply Curve**

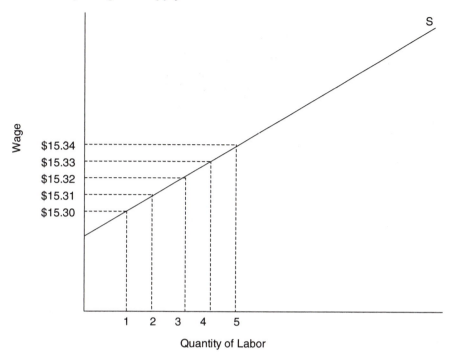

wage. Total rent in the market is $0.01 + $0.02 = $0.03. Graphically the rent is equal to the triangular area above the supply curve but below the wage line out to the level of employment.

SHIFTS IN THE CURVE

Like the demand curve, the supply curve of labor does not stay fixed in one place. It can shift in reaction to a variety of influences. In Figure 3.20 let supply curve S be the initial supply curve. If the curve moves to the position inhabited by S' then we say the curve has shifted outward/rightward/downward and call the shift an increase in supply. An increase in supply results from any factors that increase the number of people willing to work and that increases the willingness of individuals to work. Examples of the former factors include natural increases in population, increased immigration, and an increased labor force participation rate. Examples of the latter factors include changes in tastes (toward work and leisure) and nonwage aspects of jobs. An example of a nonwage aspect might be the availability of fringe benefits. If employers suddenly made health insurance available to all employees, that would increase the willingness of people to work at all wages.

If supply curve S moves to S", we would say it shifted inward/leftward/upward and call that a decrease in supply. Factors that decrease the number of people willing to work and the willingness of individuals to work will cause a decrease in supply.

Figure 3.20 **Shifting the Supply Curve**

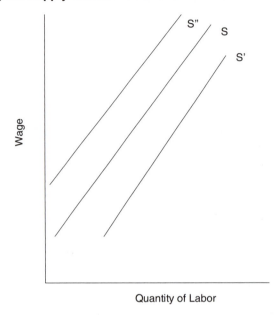

How do people react to changes in wages? Given the ambiguity of the theory, the answer becomes an empirical matter. While economists have studied the issue for a long time, no clear consensus has emerged. For males aged 20 to 60 years, the evidence points toward a nearly vertical supply curve. Rosen and Gayer believe that a reasonable estimate of the elasticity of supply is about 0.05 (Rosen and Gayer 2008, 419). If a normal work year is 2000 hours, this estimate implies that a 1% change in the wage rate would cause a 1 hour change in the number of hours worked.

The estimates for married women differ significantly from study to study. Rosen and Gayer report approvingly of Blau and Kahn's "reasonable" estimate of supply elasticity of 0.4 for this group (Rosen and Gayer 2008, 419; Blau and Kahn 2007). This means a 1% wage decrease will cause married women to reduce work by 8 hours, the equivalent of one day off.

The importance of good estimates of relevant labor supply elasticities cannot be exaggerated. These estimates apply directly to a number of important policy issues, most notably the effect of taxes on labor supply. Tax increases of nearly any type have been anathema to conservative politicians for several decades largely because of the supposed negative impact on work effort. The evidence has not been kind to the most extreme versions of this view.

An interesting sidelight is to note that politicians and economists are frequently "not on the same page" when it comes to policy matters even if they share the same ideological label. Harvey Rosen was a member of the Council of Economic Advisers and chaired it for over three months under President George W. Bush. He could easily be called a "conservative" economist. Nonetheless, his views of the effect of taxes on labor supply reflected in his public finance textbook lie at some variance to those of his boss George W. Bush, a "conservative" politician and advocate of tax cuts. This is not a trait unique to conservatives. "Liberal" economists sometimes differ from liberal politicians, even those they work for. In Chapter 4 we will discuss at some length the issue of the minimum wage. While the evidence on the issue remains mixed, the clear preponderance supports the notion that minimum wage increases can be harmful to vulnerable groups in the labor market. This has not stopped liberal politicians from being strong advocates of minimum wage increases, however. Liberal economists have been reluctant to be cheerleaders in this regard.

Estimated elasticities for younger people, older people, and single women are higher than in the case of married women.

FAMILY LABOR SUPPLY ISSUES

Although developed in the context of a single individual choosing between work and leisure, the basic theory of labor supply is also applicable when we allow additional uses of time (work at a job, work at home, obtaining schooling and training, and leisure, for example) and people to form into families.

Assume Pat and Kim[7] meet, fall in love, and decide to form a family. Pat and Kim have three uses for their time: market work (working a job), housework, and leisure. Figure 3.21 shows Pat's and Kim's labor supply curves (S_p and S_k respectively) to the market. Ignore S_k' for the time being. Note that Pat's reservation wage is much higher than Kim's ($25 v $15). This could reflect Pat's high evaluation of leisure, but more likely is the result of Pat's superior productivity in housework.

If Pat is a superior homemaker and the wage rate is less than $25 per hour it might make sense for Pat to stay home while Kim enters the market and earns money. Of course at a high enough wage, it would make sense for both Pat and Kim to enter the market and hire Rent-A-Maid to take care of the house.

Figure 3.21 **Family Labor Supply**

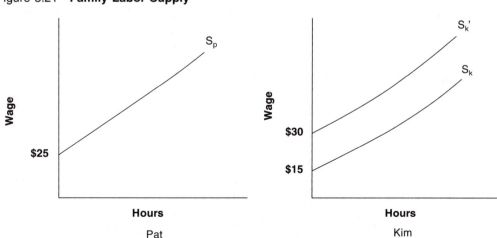

What if you doubt that couples make labor supply decisions on a purely rational basis? For example, what if Pat was male and Kim female and the prevailing social norm was that females stay home even if they are less productive in housework? This does not invalidate the use of this model. Essentially the prevailing social norm could be monetized so that Kim's labor supply curve would shift to S_k'. In that case, Kim's reservation wage would reflect not only her productivity in housework but also the distaste from the standpoint of the family of allowing her to work in the market. Even in this case, Kim might work if the wage were high enough. To absolutely prohibit Kim from working, set her reservation wage at ∞.

Conclusion

The market demand and supply curves of labor from Chapter 2 did not just fall down out of the sky. Rather, they were derived from well-established theories of how firms and individuals act in the marketplace. The approach of this chapter reflected the characteristic individualistic focus of economics. Individuals are the actors in the economy and economic events emerge from the behavior of many individuals, each of whom attempts to maximize their well-being in an environment characterized by scarcity.

The firm's demand curve for labor was shown to be a consequence of the technological constraint imposed by the law of diminishing returns and the firm's goal of maximizing profit. Adding the firms' demand curves (a complicated process) yields the market demand curve. An important intuitive notion is that the wage both reflects and rewards the worker's productivity. The public perception identified in Chapter 2 that wages reflect little more than employer whim and that the only trade-off of consequence was how the pie was sliced has been refuted. An important lesson is that wages out of line with what the market would generate not only impact how the pie is sliced but how large the pie ultimately will be. Government tinkers with market-determined wages only at its peril, as will be discussed in greater detail in Chapter 5.

A model of an individual maximizing utility from the consumption of goods and leisure yielded the individual supply curve of labor. Adding individual supply curves (an easier process) yielded the market supply curve. The aspect of the analysis most at odds with public perception was the role of individual choice in labor supply decisions.

Questions for Review and Practice

1. A lawn-mowing firm produces output using capital and labor. In the short run the quantity of capital is fixed. The production function is shown below. Using Table 3.5:
   a. Fill in the Marginal Product (MP) column.
   b. Assume the firm charges $50 for mowing a lawn. Fill in the Value of the Marginal Product (VMP) column
   c. If wages are $150 per day, how many lawn mowers will the firm hire?
   d. What is the firm's total revenue and wage bill equal to?

Table 3.5

Production of Mowed Lawns

Number of Workers	Number of Lawns Mowed per Day	MP	VMP
0	0	—	—
1	5		
2	11		
3	16		
4	20		
5	23		
6	25		
7	26		

Table 3.6

Short-run Production Functions and Demand Curve

Labor	Q	P
1	100	$2.00
2	190	$1.90
3	270	$1.80
4	340	$1.70
5	400	$1.60
6	450	$1.50

2. Are workers paid what they are worth? Examine the problem from all angles.
3. Table 3.6 shows the short-run production function and demand curve for a firm. If labor's wage was $92, how many workers would the firm hire? Is this labor being paid the value of its marginal product?
4. Peter earns $10.00 per hour and receives no nonlabor income. Draw Peter's budget constraint for a week, assuming Peter must sleep 8 hours a day. Now assume Peter inherits a trust fund that pays him $100 per week, but he continues working at the same job. Draw Peter's new budget constraint.
5. This week Sally has 112 hours to devote to either work or leisure. Draw Sally's budget constraint if her wage is $25.00 per hour. Legislation mandates that any work hours over 40 for the week must be paid at time-and-a-half. Draw Sally's new budget constraint.
6. Seth has a nonworking spouse and three children. Seth earns $10 per hour in take-home pay and works 40 hours per week. The $400 per week Seth takes home means Seth's family lives below the poverty line. In an attempt to save Medicare, the government enacts a 10% tax on all workers. This reduces Seth's take-home pay to $9 per hour. To protect poor families, the government gives Seth per $40-per-week rebate. What effect does this have on Seth's hours of work?

7. Use the theory of labor supply to answer the following question. Assume a student's grade in a course depends on the amount of time spent studying. Assume a professor, perhaps in an attempt to "buy" better course evaluations, "dumbs down" a course, making it easier (achieving any particular grade will require less studying). Does that necessarily mean that students will end up receiving higher grades?

NOTES

1. The value of that worker's marginal product is what the worker's marginal product can be sold for in the marketplace. MRP works here also. It is the marginal revenue from the last worker's product. MVP seems to make less intuitive sense, in my opinion at least.

2. This is a point that frequently confuses students needlessly. It really does not matter if the firm hires labor until VMP = W or stops hiring one worker before that point. To make your life easier, simply learn that the firm will maximize profits if it hires where VMP = W.

3. There is one minor complication here. If the marginal product of labor initially rises due to specialization and division of labor, the VMP schedule could have a short upward sloping segment. This is not part of the demand curve. More precisely, the firm's demand curve for labor is the negatively sloped segment of the VMP schedule.

4. An outward, rightward, and upward shift are all the same movement. Likewise with inward, leftward, and downward. How you choose to describe the movement is entirely up to you. But realize other people might use different words and mean exactly the same thing.

5. The demand for a normal good increases as the consumer's income increases.

6. A logically complete analysis would look at the case where leisure is an inferior good. Since that appears to have little relevance to the real world, it will be passed over.

7. These names should allow for every two-person possibility.

4 The Slices of Capital, Land, and Entrepreneurship

INTRODUCTION

This chapter will analyze the markets for the remaining factors of production: capital, land, and entrepreneurship. Once completed, we will have the pieces we need for a theory of the functional distribution of income. The demand and supply approach that was so useful in the analysis of labor markets will prove equally useful here, but this chapter is not just Chapters 2 and 3 recycled with some names changed. Each factor has a special consideration that merits comment. In the cases of capital and land, the special consideration is that for both an additional market merits comment. Not only are there markets in which the services of both are traded, but there are also markets in which ownership rights to both factors are traded. In the case of entrepreneurship, the residual nature of the returns to entrepreneurship, as opposed to the "guaranteed" nature of the returns to the other factors, is significant and worthy of note. (Readers whose time is especially scarce may bypass this chapter without significant loss of continuity.)

THE MARKETS FOR CAPITAL

A hallmark of a capitalistic economy is that machinery, factories, and tools (and economists limit their meaning of the word *capital* to these and similar items) can be the private property of individuals. The owners of capital can be called capitalists, although to be a true capitalist, the ownership of capital must be combined with an entrepreneurial role. On their personal balance sheet, the value of the capital is listed in the assets column. Capitalists have several options regarding how they use their assets. One option is to employ them in their own business to produce goods and services. A second option is to rent them out for use by other businesses. Both of these options generate a flow of income known either as the rent on capital or, simply, interest. (To be precise, interest is the return on lending money, but that return comes from the return on using capital.) A third option is to sell ownership rights to another party. On the personal balance sheet, this transaction simply reduces capital and increases money assets by the same amount. Of course, capitalists can also buy an ownership stake in capital from another person. This raises capital and lowers money assets by the same amount.

What this implies is there are two markets for capital. In the first, capital services are rented. Individual B might rent from individual A the right to use a piece of capital for a period of time, even though A remains the rightful owner of the capital. If A uses it in her own business, then we say A rents the capital to herself. In the second, ownership rights to capital are bought and sold.

The demand and supply model can be used to analyze both markets. Capital's share only emerges from the first market where demand and supply determine the rental price and quantity of capital employed. The product of those two terms gives us capital's slice of the pie. The second market gives us the value of capital as an asset.

THE MARKET FOR CAPITAL SERVICES

The analysis that follows could be virtually identical to the analysis of the labor market in Chapters 2 and 3. To avoid the boredom inherent in doing the same thing twice, this section will offer a streamlined analysis. If you are not confident in your understanding of the theory of demand and supply, do not read the rest of this section until you have fully understood the previous chapters. The approach used in this section will reverse the approach used for the analysis of the labor market by starting at the level of the firm and working toward the market.

The Demand for Capital

We will work with the simple model of the firm presented in Chapter 3. The firm is a competitor in the product market and a profit maximizer. It produces output using a specific type of labor and a specific type of capital. Both factors can be hired in competitive markets. We are in the short run, with capital the fixed factor.

Figure 3.3 from the previous chapter shows the VMP schedule of labor, the wage line, and the equilibrium level of employment. How does the factor of production capital fare in equilibrium? Since there are only two factors of production—labor and capital—the entire revenue of the firm must go to those factors. If we know the firm's revenue and how much is paid out to labor, what is left must be the return to capital. The firm's total revenue can be computed by adding the contribution of each worker. The first worker adds $1,500, the second $1,650, the third $1,500, the fourth $1,350, and the fifth $1,200. Adding those values together gives $7,200 (= $1,500 + $1,650 + $1,500 + $1,350 + $1,200). The wage bill equals $6,000 (5 workers × $1,200 per worker). The difference between $7,200 and $6,000 is $1,200, the amount available to capital. This amount is called quasi rent. Quasi rent is the return to a factor fixed in the short run.

Why do we call the $1,200 a quasi rent and not the value of the marginal product of capital? Because it is not the value of the marginal product. Since capital is fixed in the short run, it cannot have a marginal product. Consequently it cannot have a value of the marginal product.

Now we can analyze the firm's decision with respect to its use of capital in the long run. The firm needs to compare the quasi rent it receives with what it could have received if the capital had been employed for some other purpose or in some other industry. If the quasi rent received exceeds alternative possibilities, the firm will attempt to use more capital services and expand in the long run. It will expand as long

Figure 4.1 **The Firm's Demand Curve for Capital**

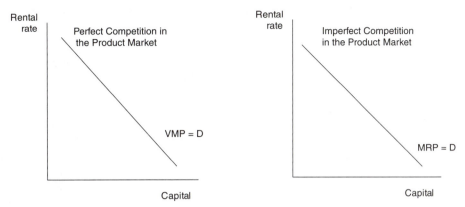

as the additional capital generates more revenue than it costs. If the quasi rent is less than the capital could earn elsewhere, capital will be withdrawn from the industry.

What determines a firm's demand curve for capital? Arguing by analogy with the demand curve for labor, a firm would want to hire additional units of capital as long as the revenue generated exceeded the rental cost of the capital. Given diminishing returns, the increases in revenue are likely to decline as employment of capital increases. In the case of perfect competition (Figure 4.1, left panel), capital's value of the marginal product schedule is the firm's demand curve for capital. In the case of imperfect competition (Figure 4.1, right panel), the relevant demand curve would be the marginal revenue product schedule.

The demand curve for capital can shift for reasons similar to those that explain why the demand curve for labor can shift. Anything that changes the VMP (or MRP, as the case may be) of capital will cause a shift in the curve. An increase in the price of the final product will increase the demand for capital. A decrease in the price of the final product will decrease the demand for capital. Anything that changes the productivity of capital, such as hiring more labor, and technological and managerial changes can shift the demand curve.

The firm demand curves can be aggregated into a market demand curve. As in the case of the market demand curve for labor, the aggregating process is not a simple horizontal summation of the firm demand curves.

The elasticity of demand is given by the following formula: $E_d = |\,\%\Delta Q_d / \%\Delta r\,|$ where E_d is elasticity of demand, Q_d is quantity demanded, r is the rental rate, and the symbol Δ means "change in." Please note the absolute value symbol. If $E_d > 1$, we say demand is elastic. If $0 < E_d < 1$, then demand is inelastic. We can also talk about perfectly elastic, perfectly inelastic, and unit elastic.

The Supply of Capital

Essentially, there are two things people can do with their income. They can consume or save. If they save, the money is typically deposited in checking or savings accounts;

placed in certificates of deposit; used to buy stocks, bonds, or mutual fund shares; or used to pay insurance premiums. There are several more exotic uses of savings, as well. Savings are ultimately lent to households, businesses, and government to be used to finance capital accumulation. To make a long story short, the act of savings is equivalent to supplying capital. Consequently we can analyze the supply of capital by looking at how people make savings decisions.[1]

To explain savings decisions, we will make use of what is called the *intertemporal choice model*. The word *intertemporal* means "over time." The intertemporal choice model is used to explain how rational consumers make consumption and saving decisions over several time periods stretching into the future. To make the model easier to understand, we will study the two-period variant of the model. This model assumes that the consumer only lives two periods and then leaves the scene. More realistic multiperiod models have been developed, but the results of these models cannot be easily shown in graphical form and the key results do not differ much from those of the two-period model. Not much would be gained from the added complexity.

The Intertemporal Budget Constraint. Assume we are at the beginning of time period t. Assume also that the consumer will live during time period t and time period t + 1, but will then leave the scene, and the consumer knows what her income will be during those two time periods. Assume the consumer's income will be $100,000 during period t and $120,000 during period t + 1.

Figure 4.2 graphs the consumer's consumption (C) during both time periods. Point A represents the situation where the consumer spends all her income each period. In period t she uses the entire $100,000 for consumption and saves $0. In period t + 1 she uses the entire $120,000 for consumption.

Consuming her entire income each period is not her only option. If she wants to, she can save some of her income in period t, invest it at rate of interest i and in period t + 1 have $120,000 plus the amount saved plus the interest earned to spend. Or, she can borrow in period t so she can consume $100,000 plus what she borrowed. Of course, money borrowed must be paid back. In period t + 1 her ability to consume will be reduced by the principal and interest she has to pay back.

Assume we have perfect capital markets. This means that the interest rate you earn on your savings is equal to the interest rate you pay on borrowed money.[2] Let i = 5 percent. If the consumer chooses to consume only $90,000 in period t, that means $10,000 is saved and $10,000 * 0.05 = $500 is earned in interest. In period t + 1, the consumer will be able to consume $120,000 + $10,000 + $500 = $130,500. That gives point B in Figure 4.2.

If the consumer borrows $10,000 in period t, the consumer will be able to consume $110,000. Next period she will have to pay back the $10,000 at 5 percent interest. In other words, she will have to pay back $10,500. This money comes out of her period t + 1 income leaving her with only $109,500 to spend. This gives point C in Figure 4.2.

Connecting points A, B, and C and all the points representing different amounts of saving and borrowing will give the intertemporal budget constraint depicted in Figure 4.2. If income in period t is represented by Y_t and income in period t + 1 is represented

Figure 4.2   **The Intertemporal Budget Constraint**

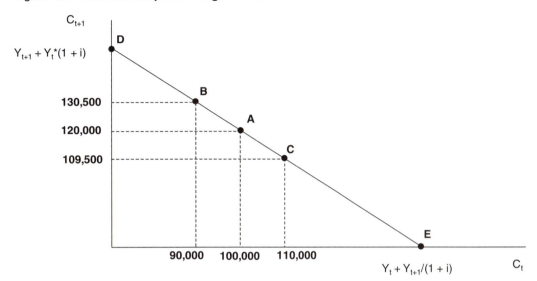

by Y_{t+1}, then point A is (Y_t, Y_{t+1}). The horizontal axis intercept is $Y_t + Y_{t+1}/(1 + i)$. This means that in period t we could consume our entire period t income plus $Y_{t+1}/(1 + i)$. The second term is the most we could borrow in period t. The most we could borrow is an amount that our second period income would permit us to pay back.[3] The vertical axis intercept is $Y_t(1 + i) + Y_{t+1}$. If we consumed nothing in period t, we would be able to save our entire income and earn interest on it. This is the term $Y_t(1 + i)$. We could add that to the period t+1 income to get potential consumption.

The slope of the budget constraint will be $-(1 + i)$. The interpretation of the budget constraint is fairly straightforward. It says that each dollar of period t consumption will cost us 1+i dollars of period t+1 consumption. If we consume the dollar in period t, we will not be able to consume that dollar or the interest it can earn in period t+1.

The budget constraint can shift and rotate. An increase in income in any period can cause the constraint to shift out parallel to itself. In Figure 4.3, the initial budget constraint is the line through A. Now let Y_t increase to Y_t'. This leads to point A'. The budget constraint will run through A', but be parallel to the initial constraint because nothing has happened to change its slope (which is determined by i).

If the rate of interest changes, then the budget constraint will rotate. In Figure 4.4 the initial budget constraint is BAD, where A represents the point where the consumer spends all her income each period. Now let i rise. Regardless of what happens to i, the consumer will still be able to obtain point A. But a higher interest rate will allow her to spend more in t + 1 if she saves in period t, and will limit how much she can borrow in period t + 1. The end result is the new budget constraint EAF.

Intertemporal Indifference Curves. The consumer has preferences regarding consumption in periods t and t + 1. These preferences are represented by intertemporal indifference curves. In Figure 4.5, point R represents one possible combination of

Figure 4.3 **The Intertemporal Budget Constraint and an Increase in Income**

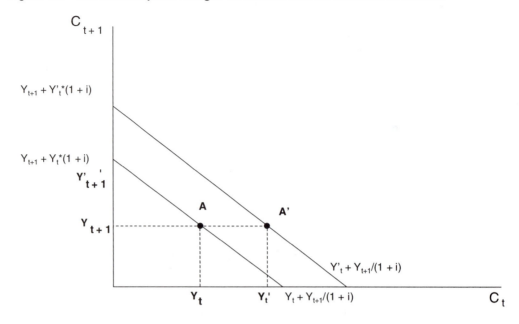

Figure 4.4 **The Intertemporal Budget Constraint and a Change in the Rate of Interest**

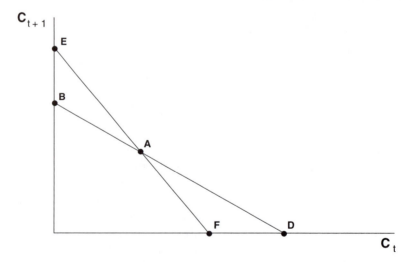

period t and period t + 1 consumption. This combination yields a certain level of utility. Every other point on the indifference curve containing point R yields the same level of utility. For example, point S represents higher current consumption and lower future consumption, but is equally desirable to point R. The indifference curve containing point T lies above the curve containing R. Every point on the curve containing T yields a higher level of utility than on the curve containing R.

The negative of the slope of an intertemporal indifference curve is the marginal

Figure 4.5 **Intertemporal Indifference Curves**

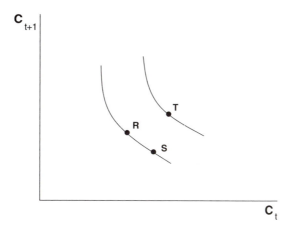

rate of time preference. Your rate of time preference measures the reward you require to abstain from consumption today. If you do not consume today, you are sacrificing. What you are sacrificing is the utility you would get today. People will sometimes abstain, but only if there is a reward. The reward is additional consumption in the future. If you will not abstain from $1 of consumption today unless you are able to consume $1.10 one year in the future, your marginal rate of time preference is 10 percent. You require a 10 percent reward to sacrifice today. If you only require a 5 percent reward you have a lower marginal rate of time preference. What a lower rate means is that you are future-oriented. You are willing to abstain today for only a tiny reward in the future. People with low marginal rates of time preference are also said to be patient. They are willing to wait for rewards. People with high marginal rates of time preference are present-oriented or impatient. They enjoy consuming today so much that they will not abstain unless the reward is quite generous.

Different people will have different marginal rates of time preference. Some are patient and some are impatient. This might be learned behavior or (less likely) it might be genetic in origin. People's marginal rate of time preference also depends on how much consumption they are currently enjoying in the present. Due to the law of diminishing marginal utility, if the person is already enjoying a great deal of consumption an additional dollar would not be very highly valued. What this means is that a person's marginal rate of time preference falls as they consume more today. The marginal rate of time preference is lower at S than at R.

Figure 4.6 shows two indifference curves, U_A and U_B. Since they intersect, they cannot be the indifference curves of the same person. Rather they are indifference curves for two individuals—persons A and B. The difference is that at the point of intersection person A has a lower marginal rate of time preference than person B. Consequently we can say person A is more patient than person B.

Equilibrium. Figure 4.7 shows an intertemporal budget constraint (DBACE). Point A is the combination of consumption where the consumer spends all her income each

Figure 4.6 **Indifference Curves for People with Different Tastes for Saving**

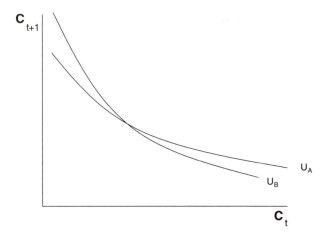

Figure 4.7 **Intertemporal Equilibrium**

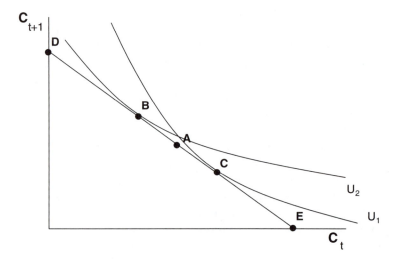

period. Indifference curve U_1 is the indifference curve of a relatively patient individual. This indifference curve is tangent to the budget constraint at point B. This consumer will maximize utility by saving in period t and enjoying additional consumption in period t + 1. The indifference curve U_2 belongs to someone more impatient. This person will maximize utility at point C where she will consume more than her income in period t by borrowing, but then have to pay back the borrowing in period t + 1.

Changes in the Interest Rate. An important exercise is what would happen if the rate of interest were to rise (Figure 4.8). The initial budget constraint is BAD, where A is the point where the consumer consumes all her income in both periods. The consumer chooses point C and is a first-period saver. An increase in the interest rate will rotate the budget constraint clockwise around A, leading to EAF. What would happen to

Figure 4.8 **A Change in the Rate of Interest**

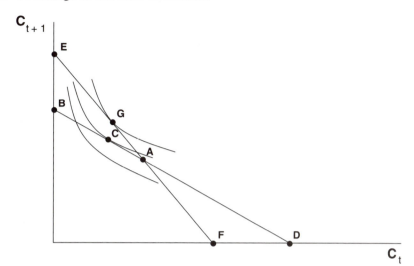

the amount of consumption and saving in period 1? In this example, the consumer ends up saving less in period 1. This is not a general result. An interest rate change has income and substitution effects similar to those encountered from a wage rate change in the case of labor supply.

Think of the income effect this way: if the rate of interest rises, you can achieve the same target level of savings by saving less.[4] The substitution effect says that if the rate of interest rises, it becomes more expensive to consume today. You end up sacrificing more of tomorrow's consumption. This would lead you to save more. Therefore the income effect would cause you to save less, the substitution effect would cause you to save more, and the net effect of an increase in the rate of interest depends on which effect is stronger.

Figure 4.9 shows two savings schedules. The one on the left is the savings schedule when the substitution effect dominates. The one on the right shows the savings schedule when the income effect dominates.

What does the empirical evidence say about the effect of changes in the interest rate on the rate of savings? As in the case of labor supply, research in this area is motivated by interest in the effect of taxes on saving. Because of a variety of conceptual and econometric issues (Rosen and Gayer 2008, 430), a strong consensus cannot be said to exist. Rosen and Gayer cite B. Douglas Bernheim, who concluded that changes in the after-tax rates of return to saving have virtually no impact on the rate of saving (Bernheim 2002). In other words, the substitution and income effects would appear to just about cancel each other out.

What does this all have to do with the supply of capital in our simple two-factor model? Saving in the intertemporal choice model is supplying capital in the two-factor model. In the intertemporal choice model the reward for saving is the interest rate, a payment for the use of money for a specified period of time. In the two-factor model, the reward for supplying capital is the rental rate, a payment for the use of

Figure 4.9 **Two Savings Schedules**

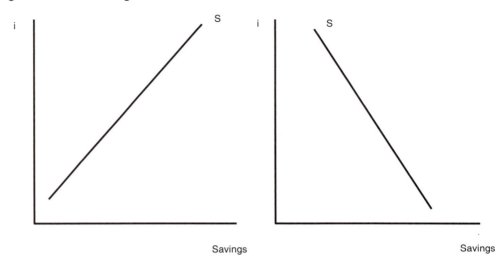

Figure 4.10 **The Supply of Capital Schedule**

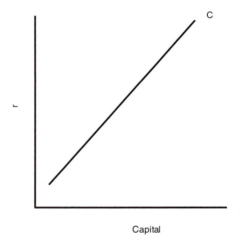

capital for a specified period of time. The interest rate can be transformed into a rental rate and vice versa. The basic logic of the intertemporal choice model holds for the two-factor model. People respond to incentives when it comes to making decisions about saving. The quantity of capital supplied will depend on the rental rate. In Figure 4.10, the horizontal axis measures the quantity of capital. The vertical axis measures the rental rate. The supply of capital schedule (S) is drawn with a positive slope indicating that the substitution effect of an increase in the rental rate is stronger than the income effect.

The market supply curves of both savings and capital is the simple horizontal sum of the individual supply curves.

The elasticity of supply is given by this formula $E_s = \%\Delta Q_s / \%\Delta r$, where E_S is

Figure 4.11 **The Market for Capital**

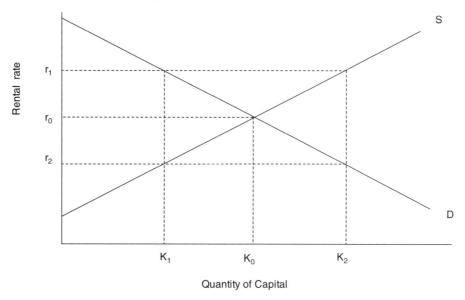

Quantity of Capital

elasticity of supply and Q_S is the quantity supplied. Here an absolute value symbol is not used. If $E_S > 1$, then supply is elastic. If $0 < E_S < 1$, then supply is inelastic. We can also talk about perfectly elastic, perfectly inelastic, and unit elastic.

Equilibrium in the Capital Market

Arguing by analogy with the labor market, in Figure 4.11 D is the demand curve for capital and S the supply curve. In equilibrium, the rental rate will be r_0 and the quantity of capital bought and sold will be K_0. If there is an excess supply of or excess demand for capital, market forces will move the market toward equilibrium. As in the case of labor, there will be full employment of capital.

Shifts in the Demand and Supply Curves. Figure 4.12 shows three demand curves, D_0, D_1, and D_2. Compared to D_0, D_2 represents an increase in demand. At any rental rate, the quantity of capital demanded will be greater along D_2 than D_0. For example, at r_0, the quantity demanded of capital is K_0 with demand curve D_0, and K_2 with demand curve D_2.

An increase in the demand for capital can occur for two reasons. One, conditions in the product market may have changed allowing firms to sell more goods and services. To produce the additional goods and services, they will need to demand more capital. Two, the productivity of capital may have changed. This could be because capital now has more of the other factors to work with. For example, a larger workforce would raise the productivity of the firm's capital stock.

Compared to D_0, demand curve D_1 represents a decrease in demand, which results from the opposite of the events mentioned in the previous paragraph.

Figure 4.12   **Shifts in the Demand and Supply Curves of Capital**

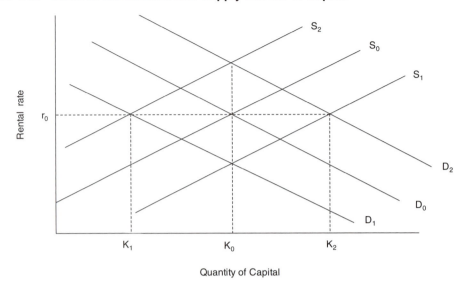

Quantity of Capital

Figure 4.12 also shows three supply curves, S_0, S_1, and S_2. Compared to S, S_1 represents an increase in supply. This could result from increased thriftiness on the part of consumers or be the result of tax or monetary policies that stimulate saving. Compared to S_0, supply curve S_2 represents a decrease in supply resulting from decreased thriftiness or tax and monetary policies that discourage saving.

Using the Model

The capital market model can be used to analyze a variety of events in a similar manner to the labor market model.

Changes in the Demand for Capital. Figure 4.13 shows the capital market in equilibrium with demand curve D_0 and supply curve S intersecting at quantity K_0 and rental rate r_0. As in the case of labor, an increased demand for goods and services will necessitate that firms will use more capital. The demand curve shifts to D_2, resulting in a higher rental rate and higher quantity of capital. What will happen is that the increased demand for capital will initially create a shortage of capital causing the rental rate to rise. This will create an incentive for people to save and a greater quantity of capital goods will eventually be supplied. That the capital market may take some time to achieve the new equilibrium should be self-evident. A decrease in the demand for capital, represented by a shift to D_1, will reduce the rental rate and the quantity of capital, as the graph plainly shows.

Improvements in Technology. Improvements in technology will raise the productivity of capital goods. An example of this is the modern cash register. Attached to scanners, they increase the speed with which customers can be serviced. The cash register

Figure 4.13 **Changes in the Demand for Capital**

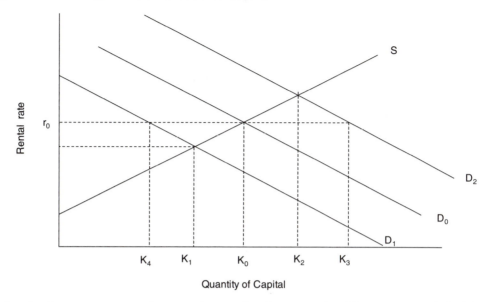

today is also a computer that can be used to keep track of inventory and decide on the coupons to offer customers.

Improved technology will shift the capital demand curve outward. The graphical analysis is identical to Figure 4.13.

A Decrease in the Supply of Capital Goods. A decrease in the supply of capital goods will increase the equilibrium rental rate while decreasing the equilibrium quantity. In Figure 4.14, a decreased supply is represented by a shift in the supply curve from S_0 to S_2. Decreases in the supply of capital goods could be caused by several factors. One is a reduction in the thriftiness of households. A second would be tax policy that reduced the incentive to save. A third would be if inflation reduced the return to saving.

How One Market Affects Another

In this economy, the markets for labor and capital are not separate and independent of each other. Events in one market will lead to a response in the other market. Two examples follow:

Increase in the Supply of Capital. The left panel in Figure 4.15 shows the market for labor. The right panel is the market for capital. Both markets are in equilibrium. D^L and S^L are the demand for and supply of labor. D^K and S^K are the demand for and supply of capital. Let some event increase the supply of capital. Perhaps people choose to become thriftier. This will shift the supply curve to S_1^K, reducing the rental rate and increasing the quantity of capital employed. The greater supply of capital will increase the productivity of labor, shifting that demand curve to D_1^L. The final result is higher wages and more employment for labor.

Figure 4.14   **A Decrease in the Supply of Capital Goods**

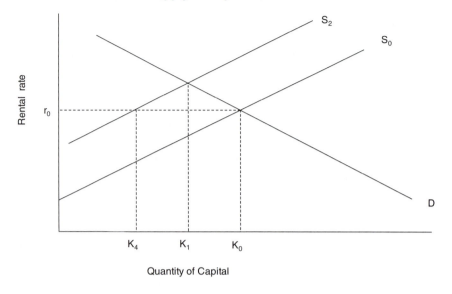

Figure 4.15   **How One Market Affects Another: Increase in the Supply of Capital**

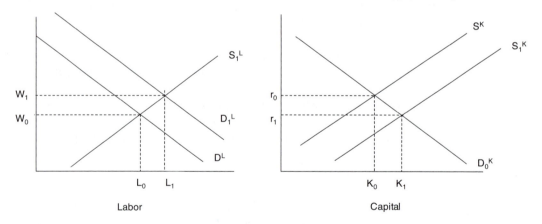

Increase in the Supply of Labor. An increased supply of labor has similar effects as an increased supply of capital. In Figure 4.16, both markets are in equilibrium. Let the supply of labor increase. The increase could come about for a number of reasons, including natural population growth, increased labor force participation, or increased immigration. Regardless, the increased supply of labor will make capital more productive. Each machine can produce more output if tended by more workers. The increased productivity of capital is represented graphically by an outward shift of the demand curve to D_1^K. The impact of this is the increase the equilibrium rental rate to r_1 and quantity of capital to K_1.

Figure 4.16 **How One Market Affects Another: Increase in the Supply of Labor**

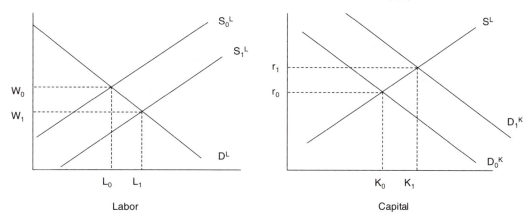

Labor   Capital

THE MARKET FOR CAPITAL

Capital is durable. It can be used over and over again until it eventually wears out or becomes obsolete. Consequently, potential buyers of capital must take into account not only how productive the capital is today, but how productive it is likely to be over its useful life.

Present Value

What would you rather choose—for me to give you $100 now or for me to give you $100 one year in the future? If you are rational (and sane) you would take the $100 now. Even disregarding the risk (I might be nowhere to be found in a year), the money in your hands right now can be put to work now and start earning now. It could be invested and earn interest. The money you need to wait for cannot do anything for you now. This example shows that money in the future is not worth the same as money today. Rather, money in the future in worth less than money today. In other words, the present value of money in the future is less than the present value of money today. The present value of $100 one year in the future is less than the present value of $100 today.

What is $100 one year in the future worth today? Your *internal rate of time preference* is a measure of the reward you require to postpone consumption. If you would postpone $100 in consumption today only if you were given $110 in consumption next year, your internal rate of time preference is 10 percent [= (110–100)/100]. People are likely to differ in their internal rate of time preference. People with high internal rates of time preference are frequently called impatient, present-oriented or, more pejoratively, unable to defer gratification. These are people who are so eager to consume now that they demand a large reward for abstaining. People with low rates of time preference are patient or future-oriented, or able to defer gratification.

Your internal rate of time preference helps determine the present value of future money. If your internal rate of time preference is p, then \$X today is equivalent to \$X*(1 + p) one year in the future: \$X today = \$X(1 + p) in one year. To get what \$X in one year is worth today, divide both sides of that expression by (1 + p). Therefore: \$X/(1 + p) today = \$X in one year .

Using numbers, if your internal rate of time preference is 8 percent, then \$100 in one year is worth \$92.59 = \$100/(1.08) today. The process of converting a future value into a present value is sometimes called *discounting* and the internal rate of time preference is sometimes called the *discount rate*.

What is the present value of \$100 two years in the future? With an internal rate of time preference of p, you expect a p percent reward for waiting one year and will expect an additional p percent for the second year. So \$X today is equivalent to \$X(1 + p)(1 + p) in two years: \$X today = \$X(1 + p)(1 + p) in two years. Therefore: \$X/(1 + p)^2 today = \$X in two years. At an 8 percent rate of time preference, \$100 in two years in worth \$85.73 today.

What is the present value of \$100 three years in the future? With an internal rate of time preference of p, you expect a p percent reward for waiting one year, an additional p percent for waiting the second year, and p percent more for the third year. So \$X today is equivalent to \$X(1 + p)(1 + p)(1 + p) in three years: \$X today = \$X(1 + p)(1 + p)(1 + p) in three years. Therefore: \$X/(1 + p)^3 today = \$X in three years. At an 8 percent rate of time preference, \$100 in three years is worth \$79.38 today.

Are you starting to see a pattern? The present value of \$X in n years is equal to \$X/(1 + p)^n.

The present value of a stream of money can easily be calculated following this model. Assume you are fortunate enough to win \$1,000,000 in a lottery that pays its prizes in \$50,000 annual increments over a twenty-year period. You really do not win \$1,000,000 because the present value of your winnings (assuming an 8 percent rate of time preference) is: PV = \$50,000 + \$50,000/(1 + .08) + \$50,000/(1 + .08)^2 + . . . + \$50,000/(1 + .08)^{19} = \$530,180. Since you receive your first payment right away (when you rush on down to the lottery office to claim your prize), it is not discounted. The remaining payments are then paid out over nineteen years.[5]

An important complication arises from the fact that people's rate of time preference is not a constant, but rather changes with their level of consumption. The more you consume today, the less valuable an additional dollar of consumption becomes. This is simply the law of diminishing marginal utility in action. From the standpoint of time preference, this means the more you consume now, the less impatient you become. Your rate of time preference declines as you consume more today.

There is an important implication of this. People's saving and consumption is influenced by their rate of time preference and the market rate of interest. If the interest rate on savings is less than your rate of time preference, you will consume now rather than save, simply because the market reward for saving is insufficient. Conversely, people whose rate of time preference is less than the market rate of interest will save now because they receive a larger reward than they require. But the rate of time preference of the consumers will fall and the rate of time preference of the savers will rise. In equilibrium everyone's rate of time preference will equal the market rate of interest.

Consequently, in calculations of present value, an appropriate rate of interest can be used instead of a separate rate of time preference for each person.[6]

Investments in Capital

How does a capitalist decide whether to buy or sell a piece of capital? Assume the capitalist is seeking to buy and the capital in question is a factory. The factory can be used to produce a good or service that can be sold. The factory carries a price tag of $P. The capitalist believes the factory to have a useful life of five years. The revenue stream generated will be $R_1, R_2, \ldots, R_5$. The cost stream will be $C_1, C_2, \ldots, C_5$. Annual profits will be $\pi_t = R_t - C_t$. The capitalist's rate of time preference is p and will be constant over the next five years. If the capitalist buys the factory it will be worth the present value of the future stream of profits, or: $PV = \pi_1 / (1 + p) + \pi_2 / (1 + p)^2 + \ldots + \pi_5 / (1 + p)^5$. The capitalist will then compare PV to $P, and purchase if $PV \geq \$P$.

There is an alternative way to analyze this choice. It requires the computation of the internal rate of return of the factory. The internal rate of return (r) is the value of r that causes the present value equation to equal 0: $PV = \pi_1 / (1 + r) + \pi_2 / (1 + r)^2 + \ldots + \pi_5 / (1 + r)^5$. The math necessary to solve this problem is not pretty, but the problem can be solved by most electronic spreadsheet programs. If $r > i$ (where i is the internal rate of return on the best alternative investments), buy the capital.

In most cases the decision of the present value approach will be the same as the decision of the internal rate of return approach. In a few cases they might conflict, but these cases are unlikely to be significant in actual practice. Computing the internal rate of return is the preferred approach, but, to repeat, the math is not pretty.

Where does the demand curve for capital equipment come from? Determining the present value of capital is no mean feat. It requires forecasting values that cannot be known with certainty, including the life of the factory, the revenues, the costs, and the rate of time preference. In short, nothing in the present value equation can be known for sure except the form of the equation and the exponents. It follows that different capitalists will have different expectations. Optimists will forecast a high present value. Pessimists will forecast a low present value. At low values of $P, both the optimists and pessimists would be willing to buy. At high $P, only the optimists remain in the market. The result is a negatively sloping demand curve for capital.

We will quickly dispose of the supply curve of capital issue. The sellers of capital (construction and machine tool firms) will compare the price they can sell the capital for with the cost of production and make a decision. *Ceteris paribus,* the higher $P, the more capital will be supplied to the market.

A Numerical Example. Consider the following numerical example. Assume a machine will last three years and generate a revenue stream of $10,000, $15,000, and $12,000. Costs of operating the machine will be $5,000, $6,000, and $7,000. As an additional wrinkle, assume the machine has a scrap value of $500. That means after its useful productive life is over, it can be sold, perhaps for parts. If the investor's rate of time preference is 5 percent, the problem can be set up this way: $PV = (\$10,000 - \$5,000)/$

$(1.05) + (\$15,000 - \$6,000)/(1.05)^2 + (\$12,000 - \$7,000)/(1.05)^3 + \$500/(1.05)^3 = \$17,676.28$. If the machine was priced at \$17,000.00, it would be a good buy.

If the rate of time preference was 10 percent, then $PV = (\$10,000 - \$5,000)/(1.1) + (\$15,000 - \$6,000)/(1.1)^2 + (\$12,000 - \$7,000)/(1.1)^3 + \$500/(1.1)^3 = \$16,115.70$. This would not be a good buy at a price of \$17,000.

THE MARKETS FOR LAND

This will be a short section because the analysis of the market for land is similar to the analysis of the market for capital. In principle, it does not much matter whether the item in question is a factory or a plot of land. It is still a factor of production that has a long life. Like capital, there are markets for both the services of land and the ownership of land. Demand and supply works with both, but the land services market generates the share of income going to landowners.

The graphical analysis of the market for the services of land is represented by Figure 4.17. The horizontal axis measures the quantity of land services while the vertical axis measures the price paid, called a rent. The demand schedule for land is D. The schedule measures the VMP of different quantities of land services. What gives the market for land its unique character is a feature of land long noted, namely, "they ain't making any more of it." For all intents and purposes, the supply curve of land is perfectly inelastic and can be represented by a vertical line.

The intersection of demand and supply determines the equilibrium price, which we are calling a rent. Rent has a generic meaning—simply the price paid to use

Figure 4.17 **The Market for Land**

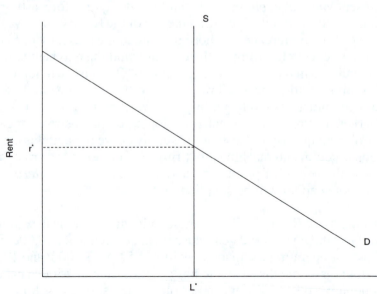

Quantity of Land Services

land—and an economic meaning—the payment to a factor in excess of what would be required to get that quantity supplied. A vertical supply curve means that quantity of land services would be offered even if the rent was 0. What else are you going to do with it? Since there are competing uses of land services, its rent is bid up to r*, but r* exceeds the reservation price of land services, which is 0.

THE MARKET FOR ENTREPRENEURSHIP

In one sense, entrepreneurship is a specialized type of labor, but simply lumping it into the labor category does not do it justice. Entrepreneurs manage the other factors of production, but, more importantly, they provide creative vision. Entrepreneurs dream of things that never were and make them a reality. Of course, there is a danger of over-romanticizing things here. What entrepreneurs dream about are new products (for example, cell phones and Flickr, but also kitty litter and super-sizing) and new methods of production (for example, air-conditioned cabs on tractors and CAD/CAM, but also the assembly line and the sweat shop). What sets the entrepreneur apart is not just vision, but moxie. Bringing that new product to market or introducing that new production method takes guts and perseverance.

The payment for entrepreneurial services is typically called profit. What sets profit apart from the other factor payments is that it is a residual. All the other factor payments are specified by contract. Entrepreneurs can lay claim to profit only after the claims of all the other factors of production have been satisfied. If the other factor payments exceed the firm's revenue, then the difference comes out of the entrepreneur's hide, or else the entrepreneur declares bankruptcy.[7] Entrepreneurs must have a high tolerance for risk.

If, against all odds, the entrepreneur manages to eke out a profit, the entrepreneur can hardly be comforted by the realization that, in most instances, periods of profitability are only temporary. If barriers to entry into the industry are low, the existence of profit will coax in new competitors to whittle away that profit. New profit streams require successful innovation or the willingness to continue to shoulder unusual risk. Only if an entrepreneur finds a protected niche in the marketplace, an industry with high barriers to entry, could short-term profits extend over a longer period of time, but even in those instances the ability to continue to reap profits is fragile. Entrepreneurs are always dependent on fickle consumer tastes. The resources that must be expended in rent-seeking activities (the legal, barely legal, and blatantly illegal tactics involved in persuading legislators and bureaucrats to issue laws and rulings that allow the entrepreneur to retain a protected market niche) frequently exhaust the profits they were intended to protect.

The role of profit is wildly misunderstood by many in our society. Many view profits as a surplus, something left over after the costs of production have been paid. Consequently, profit is not an essential part of the economic system, and something that can be redistributed by society without adverse consequences. But properly viewed, profit is a factor payment. It is the payment required to induce people to shoulder the burdens associated with supplying entrepreneurial services. Excessive redistribution of profit runs the danger of stifling creative, inventive, and risk-taking activities.

THE FACTOR MARKETS AND THE FUNCTIONAL DISTRIBUTION OF INCOME

We know from the theory of general equilibrium that all markets in the economy can be in equilibrium simultaneously (Arrow and Debreu 1954). We also know (assuming constant returns) the entire output produced by the factors will be exhausted in factor payments (Robinson 1971).

In a four-factor economy, with homogeneous land (N), labor (L), capital (K), and entrepreneurship (E), in general equilibrium the markets for each of the factors of production can be in equilibrium simultaneously. Total income in the economy (the economy's GDP) is simply $r_N*N + w*L + r*K + \pi*E$, where r_N is the rent on land and π is the rate of profit. The amount that goes to land is r_N*N and land's share is $r_N * N / (r_N * N + w * L + r * K + \pi * E)$, the amount going to labor is $w*L$ and labor's share is $w*L / (r_N * N + w*L + r* K + \pi * E)$, the amount going to capital is $r*K$ and capital's share is $r* K / (r_N * N + w*L + r* K + \pi * E)$, and the amount going to entrepreneurs is $\pi*E$ and entrepreneur's share is $\pi* E / (r_N * N + w*L + r* K + \pi * E)$.

The personal income (PI) of any person i is given by the expression $PI_i = r_N*N_i + w*L_i + r*K_i + \pi*E_i$, where N_i, L_i, K_i, and E_i are respectively the land, labor, capital, and entrepreneurial resources owned by person i.

The impact of a variety of events on the functional distribution can be analyzed using demand and supply, although precise outcomes are difficult to come by because of their sensitivity to demand and supply elasticities.

Assume the supply of labor increases. What we can predict unambiguously is that national income will rise. Not only is there more labor, but the increased labor will make the other factors more productive. A problem is encountered with predicting what will happen to the functional distribution. The increased supply of labor should reduce wages, but the level of employment will rise. If the demand curve is highly elastic, increased employment will offset lower wages and labor's income will rise. If not, it will fall.

The income of the other factors of production will rise or fall depending on whether they are substitutes or complements to labor and the relevant elasticities. Without numerical values for the various parameters associated with the model, the exact outcome cannot be determined.

Figure 4.18 shows factor shares in the United States over the time period 1929–2007. The data is from the Bureau of Economic Analysis (BEA) of the Department of Commerce. BEA's charge, among other things, is to collect that data needed to compute the nation's GDP and related measures of income. One measure of income computed is national income, which can be broken down into compensation of employees, proprietor's income, rental income, corporate profits, net interest, taxes on production and imports less subsidies, business transfer payments, and the surplus of government enterprises. A word of caution is that these categories only roughly measure the concepts discussed in Chapters 2–4. To construct the figure, compensation of employees was taken as a measure of labor's share. Labor's share has fluctuated over time from a low of 54.25 percent in 1929 to a high of 67.72 percent in 1980. In 2007 it was 64.43 percent. The share of entrepreneurs was the sum of proprietor's income and corporate profits. Proprietor's income is the income of businesses that are not corporations. The share of entrepreneurs fluctuated between 9.57 percent in

Figure 4.18 **The Functional Distribution of Income in the United States, 1929–2007**

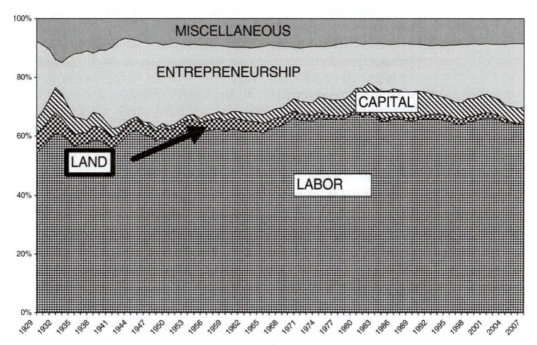

Source: Bureau of Economic Analysis, Table 1.12, National Income by Type of Income

1932 and 29.41 percent in 1942, and in 2007 it was 21.58 percent. This category is very problematic. Since many proprietors work in their own businesses, it is likely that some of proprietor's income is really labor income in disguise. Land's share is taken to be rental income and capital's share is net interest. The remaining categories were combined into the miscellaneous category.

CONCLUSION

This was a highly technical chapter with limited policy applications. It completes the discussion of the functional distribution of income by showing how demand and supply analysis can be applied to the markets for capital, land, and entrepreneurship. Given the earlier discussion of how individual portfolios contain mixtures of factors of production, the importance of government tax and transfer policies, and the impact of discrimination, the functional distribution of income tells us very little about how the pie is sliced in our economy. Nonetheless, it is a crucial ingredient in beginning the discussion because, as noted in Chapter 2, money does not grow on trees.

QUESTIONS FOR REVIEW AND PRACTICE

1. A consumer earns income of $90,000 and $100,000 in periods 1 and 2, respectively. If the interest rate is 10 percent, draw the intertemporal budget

constraint. Assume that income for period 2 rises to $110,000. Draw the new intertemporal budget constraint assuming the interest rate stays at 10 percent.

2. You win the lottery (great day!). Although it was advertised as a $2,000,000 jackpot, you discover that your winnings will be paid to you in twenty annual installments of $100,000 each. You will get your first check upon presentation of your lottery ticket to the lottery officials, the second check will be received one year from that date, the third check will be received two years from that date, and so on. Assuming no inflation over the next nineteen years, what is the actual value of what you have won? Assume an interest rate of 5 percent.

3. A capitalist owns a machine that will last for two more years. The good the machine helps produce will yield revenue of $50,000 and $40,000 with costs of $35,000 and $39,000. It will have no scrap value. The capitalist has been offered $15,000 to sell the machine. If the capitalist's rate of time preference is 5 percent, will the capitalist sell the machine? Does the answer change if the capitalist's rate of time preference is 10 percent?

4. The annual rent on a parcel of land is $2,700. The land will generate this rent from now until the end of time. What is the maximum amount you would be willing to pay to become the owner of the land? Your rate of time preference is 10 percent. Helpful hint: instead of using the present value formula with an infinite number of terms, you can use the following formula for the present value of a sum of money (M) that will be earned annually forever: $PV = M/i$.

5. Explain how profit is the value of the marginal product of an entrepreneur.

NOTES

1. Business and government are also savers. An analysis of how they make saving decisions would be interesting, but ultimately not essential for our purposes.

2. While unrealistic, in this context this simplifying assumption does not distort any result.

3. Let X be the amount borrowed. $X(1 + i)$ is the amount we would have to pay back. The most we could possibly pay back was Y_{t+1}. That gives $X(1 + i) = Y_{t+1}$. Therefore $X = Y_{t+1}/(1 + i)$.

4. This assumes saving is a normal good, which seems reasonable.

5. Today many lotteries offer the winner a lump sum in lieu of payments stretched out over a long time. The lump sum is not $1,000,000. Rather it is the present value of the stream of payments discounted at some interest rate.

6. Which market rate of interest is appropriate to use is a matter of considerable debate, but beyond the scope of this book. It is an issue likely to be studied in courses on public finance.

7. The other factor payments are not guaranteed. If an entrepreneur is forced to declare bankruptcy, some of the other factors may end up not being fully compensated for the services they provided. Bankruptcy laws specify what happens in great detail. Regardless, the entrepreneur is always last in line to share in the revenues.

5 | Labor Markets That Do Not Clear

INTRODUCTION

The labor market model introduced and used in Chapters 2 and 3 is one in which the labor market always "cleared." In Figure 5.1 at wage rate W_0, L_0 workers want jobs and L_0 vacancies are available. There is a worker for every job and vice versa. You might say that every unemployed worker and job vacancy has been cleared (or removed) from the market. This chapter looks at models where markets do not clear. Although market clearing models are adequate for many purposes, there are several rules, institutions, and practices that can keep labor markets from clearing for extended periods of time. Their ubiquity means that these factors play an important role in real world labor markets and the analysis of inequality, discrimination, poverty, and mobility.

WAGE CEILINGS AND FLOORS

Economists use the word *equilibrium* so often that it is easy to fall into thinking that equilibrium is automatically a good thing. There are some good aspects of equilibrium, to be sure. For one thing, at equilibrium we have no idle workers or unfilled jobs. Another thing is that at equilibrium workers are allocated among industries in a way that maximizes total output.

To demonstrate the latter point, see Figure 5.2. Assume there are two industries in the economy, Industry A and B. The figure shows the labor markets for both industries. Demand and supply conditions are identical in each. The supply curves are drawn as vertical lines just to simplify the analysis. (If they were drawn with their typical positive slope, the outcome would be the same, but it would be harder to see.) In a free-market equilibrium, each industry would hire 5 workers and pay a wage of 6. Total output in industry A would be the sum of the value of the marginal product of each worker employed. That would be $10 + 9 + 8 + 7 + 6 = 40$. The same would be true in industry B. Total output for the economy would be $40 + 40 = 80$.

Now assume that industry A is prevented from paying a wage less than 7. Industry A would then hire 4 workers and the market would not clear because at a wage of 7 the quantity supplied of labor would be 5. Industry A would produce 10

Figure 5.1 **Equilibrium in the Labor Market**

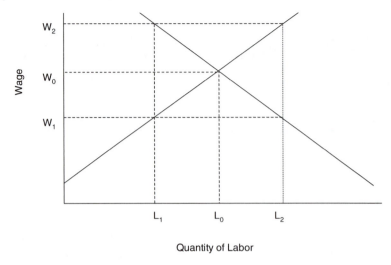

Figure 5.2 **Efficiency of Equilibrium**

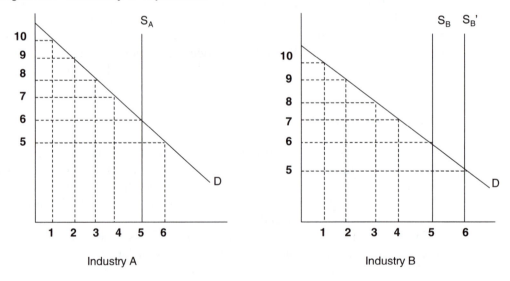

+ 9 + 8 + 7 = 34. The unemployed worker would then be forced into industry B. This would shift the supply curve to S_B', the new equilibrium wage would be 5, and the level of employment would be 6. Output in industry B would be 10 + 9 + 8 + 7 + 6 + 5 = 45. Total output in the economy would be 34 + 45 = 79. In other words, if a market-clearing equilibrium could not be achieved in one industry, total output would fall. Labor would be misallocated. There would be too little labor in the industry where labor was more productive and too much in the industry where labor was less productive.

   In short, an equilibrium wage is an efficient wage, which is a good thing. However, there is nothing about an equilibrium wage that implies that the wage is "just" or "fair," which is also a good thing. The equilibrium wage does not have to be high enough to be a "living" wage nor low enough to allow employers to achieve reasonable costs of production. An efficient wage that is not judged "just" or "fair" cannot be considered a good thing.

   From time to time, when society judges market-determined wages to be unjust or unfair, society will attempt to adjust wages by legislating wage ceilings or floors. A wage ceiling is a wage rate that sets an upper limit on the wage. A wage floor is a lower limit on the wage. We can use demand and supply to analyze the impact of wage ceilings and floors.

Wage Ceilings

Assume the labor market in Figure 5.1 is the market for plumbers. In a free market, plumbers would earn W_0 and L_0 would ply the trade. Now assume society gets fed up paying plumbers W_0 and enacts legislation that puts a ceiling on the wage plumbers can earn. Let W_1 be that ceiling. What would happen? At wage W_1 plumbers would be more affordable than before, leading to an increase in the quantity demanded to L_2. In effect, instead of doing their own small jobs on their own, homeowners would call plumbers. However, at W_1 fewer people would want to ply the trade. Maybe some plumbers leave the occupation and become carpenters. Whatever the case, the quantity supplied would decrease to L_1 and there would be a shortage of plumbers equal to $L_2 - L_1$. In short, if you employed a plumber you would not pay as much as before, but it would be much harder to find a plumber.

   Other consequences of this policy can easily be imagined. With a shortage, plumbers might find themselves so busy they are pressured to do sloppy work. Or maybe less qualified plumbers, persons whose skill level is so low they would be happy to work at W_1, would enter the occupation and do poor quality work. Another possibility is that homeowners desperate for a plumber might violate the law and agree to pay plumbers more than the wage ceiling, perhaps by "under-the-table" payments.

   Are there any examples of wage ceilings in action? Wage ceilings are not common, but are used occasionally. The following two examples are from the market for physicians. Admittedly, the market for physicians is not an especially competitive one, but the consequences of the policy under consideration are similar to what would happen if the market were competitive. Another advantage of the examples is they are contemporary.

   Under Canadian Medicare—Canada's national health insurance system—doctors bill the provincial governments for patient visits. Presumably to prevent "gaming the system," the law places an upper limit on total payments to any one doctor. That leads to a common joke in Canada, "What is the best place to find a doctor in Canada in December?" "Miami." Because many doctors reach their payment limit prior to the end of the year and object to working without pay, they simply take a vacation in sunny Miami.

   In the United States, reimbursement rates for doctors who treat Medicaid and

Medicare patients are dictated by government policy. There is a considerable number of doctors who have stopped accepting those types of patients because the reimbursement rates are not considered adequate.

WAGE FLOORS

Alternatively, what if society felt W_0 was not a fair wage for the men and women who plumb our nation's pipes? Then society might legislate a wage floor equal to W_2. This would mandate that plumbers must receive at least W_2. The effect of this is easy to see on the graph (Figure 5.1). At W_2, L_2 people would want to work as plumbers, but only L_1 plumbers would be demanded. There would be a surplus of plumbers equal to $L_2 - L_1$.

Again, additional consequences are easy to imagine. Maybe unemployed plumbers will become so desperate to work that they offer to work for less than W_2. Or maybe plumbers will be willing to put up with inadequate working conditions.

The major real world example of price floors in action is the minimum wage. This extraordinarily interesting policy will be discussed in detail in the next section.

Few societies can resist the temptation to fiddle with markets in an attempt to confront inequality and poverty problems. What is all too often overlooked is that there are unintended consequences of doing so, and many of these unintended consequences are undesirable. The case of the minimum wage is the best example of this.

THE MINIMUM WAGE: A TALE OF TWO SUPPLY CURVES

Never far from any discussion of policies to reduce inequality and poverty is the minimum wage. The inconvenient truth is that there are many people whose earning ability is extremely limited. Absent a trust fund, these people end up with very low incomes. A substantial majority of Americans (but not economists) believe government should enact legislation to ensure that these workers are paid "decent" wages.[1]

As of this writing, the federal minimum wage in the United States is $5.85 per hour. It is scheduled to rise to $7.25 per hour shortly. Because Federal laws apply to any worker engaged in interstate commerce and because most workers are engaged in jobs that are related to interstate commerce,[2] most workers are covered by the federal minimum. Most states also have minimum wage laws that apply where federal law does not.[3] Simple arithmetic shows that the federal minimum does not go very far. If a worker works 40 hours a week for 50 weeks during the year earning minimum wage, total earnings will be 40*50*5.85 = $11,700. This would put a single individual barely above the poverty line.[4] If the worker was sole support of a two-person family, the family's income would fall short of the poverty line by $1800. The gap would be greater for larger families. In short, it would be hard to argue that even earning the minimum wage provides a "decent" standard of living. Imagine trying to live on less than the minimum.

While to many people the existence of a minimum wage law seems like simple justice, to economists the issue is a bit more complicated.

The Conventional Argument Against Raising the Minimum Wage

Many economists are strongly opposed to any minimum wage, much less attempts to increase it. The main reasons are that (1) the minimum wage is poorly targeted to its intended beneficiaries, (2) it is a job killer, fringe benefit killer, and training killer, among other things, and (3) there are much superior alternative policies.

The Targeting of the Minimum Wage. With respect to the first reason, minimum wage employment is not that widespread. In 2007 approximately 12 million workers in the United States earned between the then existing minimum wage of $5.85 per hour and the proposed minimum of $7.25 per hour (Dahl et al. 2007). This was approximately 8 percent of total employment. More importantly, only about 18 percent of those minimum wage workers came from families living below the poverty line.

The Unintended Consequences of the Minimum Wage. With respect to the second reason, opposition to the minimum wage would seem to follow logically from the most straightforward application of the simplest of economic principles. Most undergraduates in their first few weeks of Principles of Economics are likely to have been exposed to a wage floor analysis like the one above (see Mankiw 2007, 120–23 for a best-selling example).

Is the minimum wage a good policy? Here it will be useful to make a distinction between positive and normative economics. *Positive economics* is the economics of what is. It is the scientific element in economics. It represents using economic methodology to predict the impact of various policies. The analysis in the preceding paragraph is an example of positive economics. The way to tell if an analysis is positive is to ask whether the statements made can be proven true or false. The conventional analysis of the minimum wage predicts that an increase in the minimum wage will raise wages for some workers and cause others to lose their jobs. In principle, both claims can be determined to be true or false by looking at the evidence. Admittedly, looking at the evidence is not a simple thing to do. You will explore these difficulties in your statistics and econometrics courses, but they will not be detailed here.

Normative economics is the economics of what should be. It attempts to prescribe and argue for particular policies. Normative economics is based on positive economics, with the economist's own values brought into the mix. With respect to the minimum wage, a positive analysis of the policy will identify winners and losers. Winners will be workers who retain their jobs at the higher wage. Other winners might include workers who previously were employed at a wage above the minimum, but who receive a raise after the minimum has been increased to maintain the differential with the unskilled workers. Losers are those workers who had jobs, but have lost them, workers who have been induced to seek jobs but have been unsuccessful, employers who have to pay higher wages, and consumers who end up paying higher prices for goods and services that are now more costly to produce.

If the economist concludes that the gains to the winners exceed the losses to the losers, then that economist will likely advocate a minimum wage increase. Whether gains to anyone outweigh losses to anyone is a proposition that can never be proven true or false by any means. What it does reflect is that economist's values regarding who is deserving or who is not.

The textbook analysis is couched in terms of money wages, employment and unemployment. The conventional analysis can easily be extended to take in other aspects of the employment relationship.

To attract workers, employers do not just offer money wages. They offer money wages plus additional compensations, which might include fringe benefits, training opportunities, how much supervision a worker faces, how respectfully a worker is treated by his supervisor, and even the temperature the air conditioner is set at in the workplace. This could be called a compensation package. Each of these items has value to the worker, and the worker can trade-off one item for another. For example, workers may be willing to accept lower wages in exchange for fringe benefits or training opportunities. Also, each of these items is costly for the employer to provide.

If employers are required to raise the money wage they pay as a result of minimum wage legislation, their costs of production will rise in the absence of any other change. Since many employers of low wage workers operate in highly competitive product markets, they cannot allow their costs to escalate. Consequently wage increases may be offset by reductions in other items in the compensation package. Look at it this way, employers undoubtedly are very concerned about the total cost of employing labor. They are less likely to be concerned about the specific forms that compensation takes, and, in fact, may be eager to provide workers with the package they most desire. Doing so will minimize the cost of hiring the desired quantity of labor.

As a result, employers might be able to manage the cost impact of a minimum wage increase and this will act to minimize layoffs. But, from the standpoint of the worker, the job has become less desirable. Employers have had to substitute money wages for other items in the package, but the reason these other items were there in the first place was because the workers valued them more than money wages. In other words, the minimum wage increase causes employers to reduce what workers value more and provide more of what workers value less.

Of course, there are some jobs where workers are not likely to be very productive and where the compensation package is likely to be low in the first place. In those cases where employers do not have much flexibility in making adjustments, workers might end up being laid off. It would seem then that workers in the worst jobs would be impacted most negatively by the minimum wage increase.

Alternative Policies. With respect to the third reason, many economists argue that a better long-run approach is the institution of policies that enhance the productivity of workers, such as improved education and skill training. In the short run, a policy like the Earned Income Tax Credit achieves the same ends with much reduced costs. A more complete discussion of the earned income tax credit can be found in Chapter 13.

The Case Against the Conventional Argument

The conventional analysis of wage floors, even with extensions, seems simple and neat. Finding empirical evidence supporting the conventional predictions ought to be a "slam dunk." There certainly has been no shortage of minimum wage studies; well over 200 studies have been done in the last 60 years or so (see Brown, Gilroy, and Kohen 1982; McKenzie 1999; and Neumark and Wascher 2007). While most of the conclusions of these studies have been supportive of the conventional view that the minimum wage reduces jobs, fringe benefits, and training opportunities for the least-skilled workers, a significant minority have not been. And some of the studies in this minority have been so widely publicized that laypeople could easily get the impression that the thinking of economists on this issue has been completely transformed. Is there anything to it?

The New Economics of the Minimum Wage. In 1995 David Card and Alan Krueger published *Myth and Measurement: The New Economics of the Minimum Wage* (Card and Krueger 1995), a thorough reanalysis of the minimum wage issue. They acknowledged that most economists accepted some form of the conventional model and that most of the previous empirical work has supported its predictions. But things change. And some of the most recent evidence tells a very different story.

Card and Krueger studied the minimum wage using a number of different methodologies, but one study in particular has come to represent their message—an analysis of the 1992 increase in the minimum wage in New Jersey (Card and Krueger 1994, 1995).

The background to the study was this: The federal minimum wage was raised to $4.25 per hour in 1991. New Jersey decided to raise its minimum to $5.05, effective in 1992. Right next door to New Jersey, Pennsylvania had tied its minimum wage to the federal level.

This created nearly ideal conditions for a natural experiment. A natural experiment is a situation where actual conditions allow the equivalent of a laboratory experiment. New Jersey and the eastern region of Pennsylvania were so close to each other that they could be considered part of the same general market area. Overall economic conditions were similar in the two areas. The only major difference was that New Jersey raised its minimum wage to a level higher than that of Pennsylvania.

Card and Krueger's team looked at 410 fast food restaurants located in the two states.[5] Several months before New Jersey's minimum wage increase, they called each restaurant and obtained information on employment levels, prices, and working conditions. Several months after the increase, they did the same thing.

The key finding was that while employment declined somewhat in Pennsylvania (probably as a result of a worsening macroeconomy), employment actually rose in New Jersey! Conceivably, employers could have reacted as described in the conventional view, raising prices or reducing other elements of the compensation package. Card and Krueger attempted to anticipate this by gathering relevant data. They found that prices did not rise dramatically in New Jersey. The major fringe benefit offered fast food workers, reduced price or free meals, was actually improved. The restaurants did not make major changes in how many hours per day they were open or the number of cash registers. The restaurants also did not change appreciably the time period until an employee's first raise or the usual amount of the raise. Unfortunately, they did not have data on supervision styles or temperature in the work area.

Figure 5.3 **Monopsony**

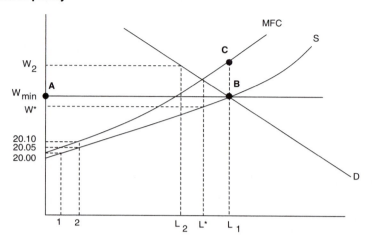

What could have explained that unexpected result? Card and Krueger as good economists used a standard economic model, namely, the monopsony model. Figure 5.3 shows a graph of a monopsony. The firm faces an upward sloping supply curve of labor. This means it can only hire more labor by offering to pay a higher wage. If the labor supply curve is upward sloping, that implies that the cost of hiring additional labor—the marginal factor cost—also slopes upward and lies above the labor supply curve. Think of it this way; referring to Figure 5.3, notice that at a wage of $20, only one worker will seek employment. To get a second worker requires that the wage be raised to $20.05. What is the marginal cost of hiring the second worker? You have to pay that worker $20.05 but that is not the entire cost because the first worker will have to be paid $20.05 also. The marginal factor cost for the second worker is $20.10, the $20.05 the employer pays the second worker plus the $.05 raise given the first worker. The analysis is similar for every other worker.

An employer will decide how many workers to hire by comparing the value of the marginal product/marginal revenue product of each worker with marginal factor cost. The profit-maximizing level of employment will be L*. What wage will be offered? While it is natural to find a point of intersection and then go vertically down and horizontally across, in this case the wage will be w*. The employer will pay the lowest wage needed to induce L* workers to work.

What if w* is considered "too low," and a minimum wage of w^{min} is enacted? At w^{min}, L_1 workers will want jobs. Since each worker up to L_1 can be hired at the same wage, namely w^{min}, the marginal factor cost of hiring labor is constant at w^{min}. The first worker hired costs w^{min}. The second worker hired will have to be paid w^{min}, but a raise does not have to be offered to the first worker, so the marginal cost of hiring the second worker is simply w^{min}. This is true until L_1 workers have been hired. Therefore the MFC is horizontal line AB up until L_1 workers. After that w^{min} will not do. Offered wages must increase and the MFC curve will jump up to the previous level.

What does this imply for employment? With w^{min} the employer will, as before, compare value of the marginal product/marginal revenue product to MFC. The desired level of employment will be L_1! Employment can actually increase with a minimum wage.

Of course, this does not mean that "the sky's the limit." If the minimum wage were set at level w_2, then employment would actually decrease below the initial equilibrium.

How realistic is the monopsony model? For decades the monopsony model has been viewed as a curiosity, a possible but highly unlikely situation (Manning 2003, 3–11). The reason is that the term *monopsony* has been defined literally. Monopsony means one buyer. Markets where there is literally only one buyer of labor would seem to be few and far between, particularly in our modern economy.

What is fundamental here is not the presence of a single buyer, but rather that the supply curve of labor should be positively sloped. Regardless of whether the firm is a fast food restaurant or a car wash, how likely is it that every employee would quit immediately if the employer reduced the wage by a penny? It would appear to be an unlikely occurrence when we recognize the existence of certain frictions in the labor market. Workers might be unlikely to quit if they are unaware of other job opportunities and do not want to take the time to search, are aware of other job opportunities but do not want to pay a higher bus fare to travel to those sites, or simply enjoy their current job. If employers do not lose everyone when they cut the wage a bit, the labor supply curve is positively sloped and we have the economic equivalent of the monopsony of Figure 5.3.

An interesting footnote to Card and Krueger's research is that their team gathered data by actually calling the fast food restaurants and asking the manager or assistant manager about employment levels. A few years later Neumark and Wascher (Neumark and Wascher 2000) reinvestigated the impact of the New Jersey minimum wage increase. For their study they used administrative payroll records from restaurants of the same chains located in the same geographic area. While their sample was not exactly the same as Card and Krueger's, it stands to reason that there was substantial overlap. What Neumark and Wascher found was that, contrary to Card and Krueger, the minimum wage increase actually reduced employment in New Jersey. While in principle there could be several explanations for the discrepancy in results, the explanation Neumark and Wascher favor is that the question asked over the phone—"How many full-time and part-time workers are employed in your restaurant, excluding managers and assistant managers?"—was not terribly precise (Neumark and Wascher 2000, 1372). The respondent might have answered on the basis of anything from the current shift to the payroll period, which may have been as long as two weeks. Also, there was no guarantee that the respondent was the same each time the restaurant was called. Different managers and assistant managers could very easily have interpreted the question differently. In short, the answers given over the telephone may very well have been less valid than those gleaned from the administrative payroll records.

As indicated, the majority of the economic research on the minimum wage, both before and after Card and Krueger, has supported the traditional view that the minimum wage is a job, fringe benefit, and training killer, among other bad things. Unfortunately, most people do not follow economics research results very closely. Most people, it seems, are highly suspicious of the marketplace in general (Caplan

2007). The result is that less thoughtful people have had no reason to change their thinking and thoughtful people have at least some reason to keep hope alive. Higher minimum wages have not yet been stamped out as a policy alternative.

Why Do We Have a Minimum Wage?

If the minimum wage is not well targeted, has undesirable unintended side effects, and there are superior alternatives, why do we even have a minimum wage in the first place? As a general rule, there are always two reasons for bad policies. One is ignorance; the other is self-interest.

To be fair to minimum wage supporters, the evidence against the minimum wage is not that overwhelming. Even under the worst-case scenario, modest minimum wage increases only do modest damage so that minimum wage increases can be supported as a symbolic action to show our concern for the poor.

The self-interest argument is a bit more cynical. Figure 5.4 depicts both the unskilled and skilled labor markets. While unskilled workers cannot do the exact jobs that skilled workers do, they can be viewed as substitutes for skilled workers once we realize that goods and services can be produced using a variety of different technologies. Consider a very basic service, namely, a car wash. Cars can be washed several different ways using different combinations of labor and capital. At one extreme, cars can be washed using a bunch of unskilled workers with washcloths and water pails. This technology is pretty common among high school and college students who are trying to raise funds. At the other extreme, cars can be washed in totally automated systems (where you put your car's front wheel in a guide and remain in the car as it is pulled through the wash). Here no unskilled workers are needed, but skilled workers might be required to keep the system working. The technology used ultimately

Figure 5.4 **Effect of a Minimum Wage Law in the Skilled Labor Market**

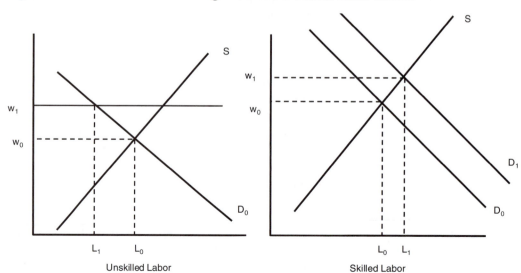

Unskilled Labor   Skilled Labor

depends on the relative prices of labor and capital. When labor is cheap, the former technology is employed. When labor is expensive, the later is chosen. At different wage levels, unskilled labor substitutes for skilled labor.

An increase in the minimum wage means that technologies that require unskilled labor are less likely to be used. This is bad for unskilled labor, but good for skilled labor. In a demand and supply context, an increase in the wage of unskilled labor increases the demand for skilled labor. Is it any surprise that labor unions and other organizations of relatively skilled workers are big supporters of legislation to raise the wages of workers who earn far below what their members earn?

The Living Wage Movement

Over the past 15 years or so, approximately 100 cities and counties in the United States have enacted so-called living wage ordinances. Notable examples include Baltimore, Maryland (which inaugurated the movement in 1994); Chicago, Illinois; Detroit, Michigan; the county of Miami-Dade, Florida; Oakland, California; Philadelphia, Pennsylvania; the city and county of San Francisco, California; and San Jose, California. Half of the twenty largest cities in the nation have such ordinances, and 40 percent of the population in cities with populations exceeding 100,000 live under these laws (Adams and Neumark 2005, 2). Maryland was the first state to enact a statewide living wage ordinance in 2007 (Waltman 2008). In essence, these ordinances require government contractors (essentially private companies doing business with the city or county governments) and/or firms receiving "business assistance" (firms receiving tax abatements, grants, low-interest loans, and many other types of financial assistance from government) to pay their employees a "living wage" as a condition of continuing to do business with or receive assistance from the government. Typically the living wage is set at a level that would allow the recipient's family an income higher than the poverty line. Living wage levels often far exceed the legislated minimum wage. College students have frequently participated in campaigns to get living wages for the employees at their own institutions.

What has been the impact of living wage legislation? In a careful study, Adams and Neumark concluded that living wage laws achieve their primary goal, which is to raise the wages of low-paid workers in firms targeted by the legislation (Adams and Neumark 2005, 5–6). However the analysis of the policy cannot stop at that point. From an economic standpoint, there is not much difference between a living wage program and a minimum wage. Both seek to set the wage rate at a level above the market clearing level, and, consequently, we need to be aware of the types of unintended consequences associated with minimum wage laws. Adams and Neumark investigated employment effects and found disemployment of the least-skilled workers along with increases in employment of higher skilled workers (Adams and Neumark 2005, 6–7). Employers are apparently substituting higher- for lower-skilled workers. Among the poor, though, the net effect of these changes seems to be to reduce the poverty rate, although this positive effect is much more likely for those who were close to the poverty line to begin with (Adams and Neumark 2005, 18). The most disadvantaged, however, are likely to be hurt by these laws (Adams and Neumark 2005, 10), because disemployment effects are so significant for this group.

OTHER REASONS WHY LABOR MARKETS MIGHT NOT CLEAR

Government policies are not the only reason why labor markets might not clear. Under several highly plausible circumstances, firms may voluntarily offer above-market wages. The social nature of the labor market—the fact that the commodity being offered for sale is a human being and not an artichoke—may also act to keep wages above the market clearing level.

EFFICIENCY WAGE THEORY

Efficiency wage theory says that some employers will voluntarily pay higher-than-equilibrium wages. We know from Figure 5.1 and our discussion of wage floors that such a policy will lead to labor surpluses. Why would employers do this if they could hire perfectly adequate labor at the equilibrium wage W_0?

The rationale that forms the basis of efficiency wage theory is that the payment of higher-than-equilibrium wages does not cost the employer anything because workers are induced to be more productive. There are four reasons why workers might be more productive.

1. A higher wage might allow the worker to purchase a more nutritious diet, which will cause the worker to be stronger and hence more productive. While this argument does not appear to be particularly compelling in contemporary America, it likely carries some weight in less developed countries.
2. There are many jobs where workers are expected to work without direct supervision. In some cases this is because the worker possesses a degree of expertise that a supervisor could not hope to match. In other cases, it is because workers work by themselves out in the field. Consider the case of a sales force out on the road. Would it make any economic sense to send out one supervisor with each salesperson? In such instances, how do you ensure that the workers in the field are giving their all? What will reduce the probability of shirking on the part of the worker?

    Perhaps the occupation has professional standards that influence work ethic or the worker is a true believer in the cause. Staffers on Capitol Hill work prodigious hours but are not very well paid simply because they are passionate about what they do. Where neither of these tactics is likely to work, a logical alternative is to simply pay people more. If people are paid more than the equilibrium wage, the desirability of the job is enhanced. Who would want to lose a job that provides such great compensation? Consequently, the worker might work extra hard just to protect against being fired.
3. Paying a higher wage reduces turnover. Firms dislike turnover for two reasons: First, recruiting and screening new employees is a costly activity. Second, training new employees is also costly. If firms can avoid the costs associated with replacing workers by paying a wage in excess of equilibrium, they may actually end up more profitable.
4. Paying a higher-than-equilibrium wage will create a surplus of labor. This

allows the employer to be picky about whom he or she chooses. The result is higher quality workers. Note that the assumption of homogeneous labor has been surreptitiously relaxed. Employers could not benefit from being picky unless some workers were "better" than others.

Is there any evidence to support the efficiency wage hypothesis? Direct evidence is hard to come by, but history provides us a very interesting case study.

In the early part of the twentieth century, the Ford Motor Company was a leader in the fledgling automobile industry and an innovator in manufacturing methods.[6] Prior to 1908, automobiles by and large were constructed using craft methods. With the introduction of the Model T, Henry Ford shifted to the assembly line method of production. The assembly line method was more productive than craft methods, but there was a down side. The jobs were boring. Standing on the assembly line all day long doing one repetitive operation was more than many people could stand. Consequently, Ford's workers did not stay long. In 1913, turnover at Ford's River Rouge plant in Detroit was 913 percent. That meant that three workers had to be hired for every position.

In 1913 Ford shut down his plant and fired everyone. Then he made an announcement that was heard all over the United States. When he opened again, he would begin paying $5 per day. Now $5 per day might not sound like much, but in those days it was twice the going wage for labor of that type. People heard of this and headed to Detroit from all over the United States. Of course, there were some catches. The main one was that in order to be eligible for the $5 per day wage, a worker had to be approved by Ford's Sociological Department. What this meant was that the worker had to be supporting a family and his home life had to be in order. The Sociological Department visited the homes of employees to certify their eligibility. Today this seems like a paternalistic policy, and it was, but Ford did have a reason that made sense to him. He hired many immigrants and he wanted them to shed their old world ways and become Americanized.

What effect did this policy have? Over the next several years turnover fell, costs of production fell, and prices of Model T's fell to one-fifth their 1913 level. The Model T became the biggest selling car in the world and Ford's production methods triumphed and were emulated by many.

Was the $5 per day an efficiency wage? The alternative is that Ford offered more than the going rate out of the goodness of his heart. But, as anyone who knew him would say, Ford was no bleeding heart. He was a hardheaded businessman, and his methods worked.

RECIPROCITY

The norm of reciprocity can be explained this way: if you do something nice for me, I'll do something nice for you. What if both employers and employees subscribe to the notions of fairness and reciprocity? Employers may offer an above-equilibrium wage because they believe it is the fair thing to do. Alternatively, once a nominal wage level has been established employers may be loath to lower it even though labor market conditions have changed due to concerns with fairness. Regardless, workers may feel that if the employer is offering such a generous wage, they have a responsibility to reciprocate by working harder.

Establishing that employers pay higher-than-equilibrium wages is in principle relatively easy. All we have to determine is whether there is an excess supply of qualified labor. Establishing why employers do this is much more difficult.[7] Is fairness or fear of punishment at work here?

A relatively new field within the discipline of economics is experimental economics. In this field economists perform laboratory experiments as a means to test economic theories. The virtue of performing experiments in the lab is that the researcher has control over the conditions of the experiment. The problem is that it is difficult to replicate the real world in a laboratory setting.

An interesting experiment on point was performed by Ernst Fehr, Georg Kirchsteiger, and Arno Riedl (Fehr, Kirchsteiger, and Riedl 1993). Using student volunteers, they set up a labor market in their laboratory. Five employers were placed in one room. Eight workers were placed in another. The employers were given the production function for their good and the price it could be sold at and told to maximize profits. To produce they needed to hire one unit of labor. To hire the labor they made a wage offer that was carried to the other room.

The workers had a reservation wage. When wage offers were posted the first worker to respond would get that job. After the worker was hired, each worker would then decide on an amount of effort to put forth on the job. Effort was costly to the workers. The more effort provided, the lower the net gain from working at that job. This effort level was then conveyed to the appropriate employer and that information helped determine the profit earned.

A key element of this game was this: employers and workers never made face-to-face contact and employers never knew which worker was hired each period. If both sides had been completely rational, the following would have been observed: employers would have offered the lowest possible wage that was approximately equal to the reservation wage. Why? The workers had no choice. There were more workers than jobs. Once hired, a rational worker would have offered the lowest level of effort possible. Why? Effort was costly and no one would ever know who slacked off.

What happened? In numerous replications, employers offered a wage in excess of the equilibrium level and workers provided effort in excess of the minimum. The interpretation seems fairly straightforward. Employers offered a high wage in hopes of eliciting extra effort. Workers provided extra effort to reciprocate for the high wage. In short, fairness considerations seem extant in the labor market.

PUBLIC AND NONPROFIT SECTOR LABOR MARKETS

How do the public and nonprofit sectors fit into this model? Even in a society as market-oriented as the United States, both sectors are significant in size. Approximately 22 million people, 15 percent of the workforce, are employed by federal, state, or local government. Approximately 11 million people, 7.1 percent of the workforce, are employed by the nonprofit sector (Anheier 2005). Are workers in these sectors paid the value of their marginal product?

It is unlikely that workers are paid less than the value of their marginal product. While it is true that government agencies and nonprofit organizations typically do not sell a good or service and are not profit maximizers, they still must compete in the marketplace for the available labor. To entice a worker to spurn a private sector job (at which they are being paid the value of their marginal product), they have to offer an employment opportunity at least as good. This is not to deny that workers may seek employment at specific government agencies or nonprofit organizations because they support the mission of the agency or organization and are willing to accept lower than the going monetary wage for the specific type of labor they supply. Congressional and White House staffers and the employees and volunteers of nonprofit organizations seeking to feed the homeless, protect the victims of domestic abuse or sexual assault, or save the whales are clear evidence of this. However, those cases can be rationalized by pointing out that the utility of working for certain types of causes may substitute for monetary reward.[8] The total compensation for the job (money plus utility) should be equivalent to the total compensation for the rejected private sector job.[9]

If public and nonprofit sector workers are not paid less than the value of their marginal product, might they be paid more? There would appear to be a simple test of this. Are there surpluses of applicants for jobs in these sectors? If there are, then it is logical to conclude that these jobs are viewed as superior to private sector jobs. On the basis of casual empiricism, it would appear that surpluses of applicants is not a general condition in these sectors, although it can arise from time to time for specific agencies or organizations in particular parts of the country.[10] These instances may simply represent temporary disequilibrium.

What would cause government or the nonprofit sector to pay more than they needed to in order to recruit suitable labor? In the case of government, there is a significant principal-agent problem. Generally speaking, a principal is someone who wants something done, but, because of lack of expertise or time, is unable to accomplish it and therefore hires an agent to complete the task. The problem is that the incentives of the two parties are not always the same. The principal wants the job done quickly and cheaply. The agent wants to be paid generously, but not have to work too hard. How does the principal structure the "contract" with the agent to minimize the amount of "shirking" the agent does?

In this context, the ultimate principal is "we, the people." We want our children taught and the garbage picked up as cheaply as possible. We do not have the time to monitor all of these employees and certainly lack the expertise to judge how well many of these tasks are being performed. The agents of "we, the people" are the politicians we elect, but the politicians have only a partial incentive to keep pay down, particularly since public employees are frequently a decisive voting bloc and "we, the people" may find it difficult to discern the direct connection between the taxes they pay and the salaries and benefits of their public servants.

Of course, the principal-agent problem gets even stickier because most politicians are not experts at managing government agencies. Consequently, they become principals hiring professional managers as their agents. While the politicians may have some incentive to keep the cost of government down, the city managers and agency heads that they hire may want large paychecks, big offices, and large fiefdoms to lord over. It may not be in the interest of the politicians to monitor closely the behavior of their agents because if their agents become disgruntled, public services will suffer and the politician will pay the ultimate price.

If the public employees are unionized, the matter is further complicated.[11] In fact, public sector unions remain a growth area for organized labor while organized labor appears to be getting weaker.

CONCLUSION

Situations where markets do not clear are not mere curiosities. They are a significant part of our economic life. Fortunately, the market clearing model of Chapters 2 and 3 does not have to be scrapped. Its hallmark is flexibility. It can handle these situations while barely breaking a sweat.

With the discussion of the minimum wage, we have begun investigating policies to deal with inequality. We will have to hold off on more extensive policy analysis until we have made our way through the next chapter's explanation of the existence and persistence of wage differentials in our economy. Once we have done that, we will be ready for a bigger policy orientation. Chapter 7 will review some of the most emblematic government policies that deal with inequality in the distribution of income. What does economics have to teach us about the impact of these policies?

QUESTIONS FOR REVIEW AND PRACTICE

1. Figure 5.5 shows the market for bank tellers.
   a. If a price ceiling of $8.50 was imposed on the market, how many bank tellers would be hired?
   b. If a price ceiling of $11.50 was imposed on the market, how many bank tellers would be hired?
   c. If a price floor of $11.50 was imposed on the market, how many bank tellers would be hired?
   c. If a price floor of $8.50 was imposed on the market, how many bank tellers would be hired?
2. If labor is hired in a monopsonistic market, a minimum wage will always guarantee employment will increase. True or false? Explain.
3. Could an objective scholar make a convincing argument in favor of a higher minimum wage if the scholar believed the evidence supported the conclusion that the minimum wage was a job killer, fringe benefit killer, and training killer? How would that argument go?
4. Are workers and employers who practice reciprocity irrational?
5. In an analysis of globalization, two sociologists write:

   . . . Not surprisingly, business people and their political allies respond to attempts to raise the floor under the lowest-paid workers with claims that increasing the minimum wage will inevitably augment inflationary pressures and job losses can cause grave damage to global competitiveness.

Figure 5.5 **The Market for Bank Tellers**

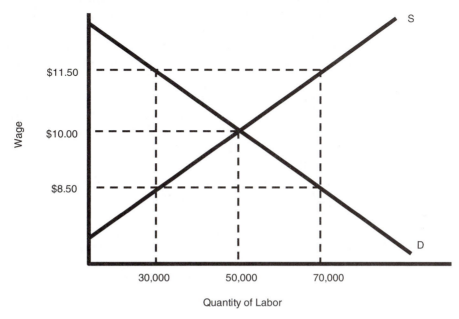

To combat these arguments, proponents of a "living wage" make the simple point that anyone working full time should earn enough to support a family at least at the poverty line (Hytrek and Zentgraf 2008, 153–54).

Does the argument in the second paragraph, "combat" the argument in the first paragraph? Can a scholar ever ignore the arguments made by the opposing side in a debate?

NOTES

1. In a November 2006 Gallup Poll, 83 percent of Americans were in favor of "Congress passing legislation that would raise the minimum wage." Only 14 percent were opposed to such legislation (Jones 2006). Economists are not as favorably disposed. In a 2003 survey of members of the American Economic Association (the leading professional society for economists), respondents were asked whether they supported a minimum wage increase. The five-point response scale ran from 1, support strongly, to 5, oppose strongly, with 3 representing "have mixed feelings." The mean response was 2.83 (Klein and Stern 2007).

2. The interpretation of what is meant by interstate commerce has been a point of contention throughout much of American history. Briefly, while there is a certain logic to arguing that being involved in interstate commerce refers only to jobs in industries devoted to carting and hauling—like trucking, shipping, and airlines, an alternative logic is that any industry that is touched in any

way by interstate commerce should be included. The latter definition includes not only the carters and haulers, but also the senders and recipients of any goods that are carted and hauled. In a highly specialized economy like that of the United States, this definition has a broad scope indeed. The Supreme Court found the latter view more to its liking in *NLRB v. Jones & Laughlin Steel Corp.* (United States Supreme Court 1937), and that appeared to settle the matter for a long time. Of course, the broader the definition of interstate commerce is, the greater the impact of the federal government over our economic affairs. Conservatives tend to like a narrower definition; liberals tend to prefer the broader definition.

3. See Minimum Wage Laws in the States for an up-to-date listing of state minimum wage laws (United States Department of Labor 2007). Fourteen states simply use the federal level. Thirty states use a higher minimum. Kansas has a minimum wage below the federal level. Five states (South Carolina, Tennessee, Alabama, Arkansas, and Louisiana) do not have a minimum wage law.
4. The poverty line for a single individual in 2006 was $10,488. The poverty line for a two-person household without children was $13,500. It was higher if there was a child in the picture. See Chapter 12 for a discussion of the poverty line.
5. The restaurants were part of the Burger King, KFC, Wendy's, and Roy Rogers chains.
6. The material in this section is from Raff and Summers (1987).
7. And to many economists this is not particularly relevant. To most economists, determining how people behave is the crux of the matter. The motives behind that behavior are typically mysterious and are not essential to know.
8. In the lingo of economics, what is being discussed here is what is known as compensating differentials. This concept will be developed at length in the next chapter.
9. Of course, private sector jobs can have nonmonetary attractive or repulsive features as well.
10. Sharon P. Smith claimed that federal government jobs were superior to private sector jobs in the 1970s (1976). Since that time federal government raises have been modest, so that condition may have "corrected" itself. As a citizen reviewer for the Rappahannock United Way, I have seen plenty of agency grant applications requesting additional funds so that they could hold on to their employees.
11. Wellington and Winter believe that certain characteristics of the public sector act to give public employee unions disproportionate power to the detriment of the public interest (Wellington and Winter 1971).

6 Slicing the Pie in a Nondiscriminatory Pure Market Economy

INTRODUCTION

According to the data cited in Chapter 1, in 2006 there was enough money income to allow nearly $184,000 for every four-person household, which represents a fairly comfortable standard of living. Of course, every household did not receive $184,000 in money income. Most received less, and among those households receiving less, some received so little that they were considered poor. Among those households that received more, some were extraordinarily affluent, either as the result of containing a "superstar" earner or inheriting and/or accumulating great wealth.

This chapter uses the factor market theory developed in Chapters 2 through 4 to begin explaining differences in income among people—the personal distribution of income. I say "begin explaining" because this chapter will only explain the personal distribution in a pure market economy. The impact of government redistribution policies and discrimination will appear in later chapters. Please note that the models in this chapter will be static in nature. They will explain the distribution of income at a particular point in time, not how it evolves over time. That element of slicing the pie will also be addressed in a later chapter.

From Chapter 4, an expression for the personal income of person i is $PI_i = r_N*N_i + w*L_i + r*K_i + \pi*E_i$. This chapter extends that discussion by explaining why people supply different amounts of the various factors and why the returns to the different factors might differ among people.

DIFFERENCES IN LABOR EARNINGS

There are great differences in the labor earnings of people and households. This is explained by wage differentials and differences in the number of work hours supplied to the labor market. This section will address both issues.

LONG-RUN WAGE DIFFERENTIALS

Harking back to the *Parade* magazine gallery of working Americans referenced in Chapter 1 and your own personal experience, it is obvious that different people earn

Figure 6.1   **Elimination of Long Run Wage Differentials by Mobility**

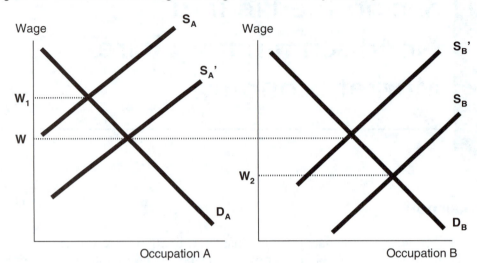

Occupation A   Occupation B

different wages. It is equally obvious from perusing previous issues of *Parade*'s "What Do People Earn" feature and from your own knowledge of how the world works that wage differentials between different classes of jobs can persist for long periods of time. The next section explains why.

Wage Inequality and Labor Immobility

Refer to Figure 6.1. Assume there are two occupations, A and B, and the jobs require identical skills, working conditions are the same, and all workers have identical skills and tastes. Initially there is a wage differential. Demand (D_A) and supply (S_A) conditions in occupation A set the equilibrium wage at w_1. Demand (D_B) and supply (S_B) conditions in occupation B lead to an equilibrium wage of w_2. w_1 is higher than w_2.

What is likely to happen? Given our assumptions, only one outcome is possible. Workers in occupation B will notice that workers in occupation A are earning more than they are. They will also notice that they possess adequate skills to do the job and the working conditions are exactly the same. Workers in B will quit their jobs and flock to occupation A. As this happens the supply of labor decreases in B and increases in A. S_B shifts inward and S_A shifts outward.

Where would the new equilibrium be? Workers change jobs as long as one occupation pays more than the other. Job shifting will cease when both occupations pay the exact same wage. In Figure 6.1, a new equilibrium will be achieved when the supply curve of labor to A becomes S_A', the supply curve of labor to B becomes S_B', and the wage rate in both occupations is w.

Based on this analysis we can say the following: If a wage differential between A and B persists over time, that must mean that there is some factor preventing workers from leaving the low-wage occupation and entering the high wage occupation.

Figure 6.2   **Equilibrium Long Run Wage Differentials**

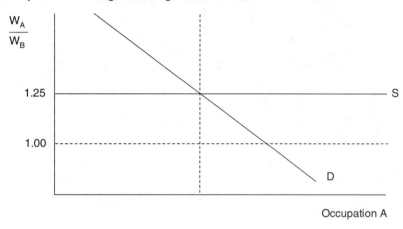

Occupation A

Compensating Differentials

What might prevent workers from leaving low-paid jobs and seeking employment in higher-paid jobs? One factor that has been recognized for centuries is the various nonwage characteristics of jobs. Nonwage characteristics are exactly what their name implies. They include all features of jobs other than the wage rate paid, including fringe benefits, working conditions, riskiness of the job, and the social status associated with the job. That this factor has been recognized for a long time is seen from this quote from the grandmaster himself, Adam Smith. Smith argued that "The whole of the advantages and disadvantages of the different employments of labour and stock must, in the same neighbourhood, be either perfectly equal or tending to equality" (Smith 1991, 88).

Assume occupations A and B differ in the following way: Occupation A is what everyone agrees is a "dirty job." Workers are required to work in the hot sun and end up each day caked in dust, and there is not even a shower provided. Occupation B is a "clean job." Workers work all day in a spotless, air-conditioned facility. Assume further that everyone feels the same way about this nonwage characteristic, that is, everyone hates with the same degree of passion the idea of working at the dirty job and loves with the same degree of passion the idea of working at the clean job.

Figure 6.2 refers to occupation A and is constructed a bit differently from the occupation A graph in Figure 6.1. The main difference is that the vertical axis is not the wage in occupation A. Rather it is the wage ratio w_A/w_B. The wage ratio 1.0 indicates complete equality of wages between the two occupations. At wage ratios greater than 1.00, the wage in A exceeds the wage in B. For example, at 1.25 the wage in A exceeds the wage in B by 25 percent. If the wage in B was $400 per week, the wage in A would be $500 per week. Let D be the demand curve and let S be the supply curve of labor. The D curve needs no further discussion. The S curve does. What S says is that no one will offer to work in occupation A unless the wage is at least 25 percent higher than the wage in B. The reason, of course, is because A is such a dirty job.

Figure 6.3 **Long Run Wage Differentials Where there are Differences in Tastes**

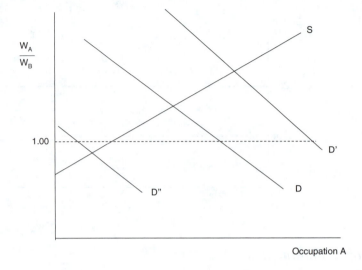

Workers require a reward—a compensating differential—to induce them to take on such dirty work. But, since everyone feels exactly the same about dirty/clean work, a 25 percent differential is all that is required. If the differential was 26 percent, then everyone would want to work in the dirty job. Under our assumption, the supply of labor to occupation A is perfectly elastic at the wage ratio 1.25. The demand for labor then determines the level of employment in occupation A.

Figure 6.3 is more realistic. Here the supply curve of labor is positively sloped. What this means is that workers differ in how passionately they hate dirt and love cleanliness. The way it is drawn here, there are actually some workers who prefer dirtiness to cleanliness as indicated by the fact that some workers would choose occupation A even if it paid less than occupation B! (There is no accounting for taste.) Some workers dislike dirt a little. Others dislike dirt a lot. These differences in tastes are captured by the positive slope of the supply curve. To hire more workers, occupation A must offer ever-higher wages to compensate those workers who dislike dirt more passionately.

The interesting result here is this: The demand curve for labor determines not only the number of workers hired but also the wage ratio. If the demand for labor was low enough (say D"), the dirty job might actually have a lower wage than the clean job!

A similar analysis applies to any other nonwage characteristic. Take the case of the riskiness of the job. During the Iraq War, the job of supplying U.S. military bases was contracted out to civilian firms. From supply depots in friendly border countries like Kuwait, caravans of trucks would head out to the various military bases in-country. Despite receiving protection from the U.S. military, these convoys were constantly in danger of attack from "insurgent" elements. In September 2004 approximately 25 percent of the convoys on the road were attacked daily, and casualties among the truck drivers were not uncommon (Glanz 2004).

To lure American civilian truck drivers to accept these risks, contractors paid salaries that were 2 to 3 times what the truckers earned in the United States (Glanz 2004). One trucker who earned $30,000 a year in the United States was able to earn more than $80,000 in Iraq (Glanz 2004). And a feature of the tax law allowed truckers who remained in the conflict zone for over 330 days to receive a sizable tax break.

The additional compensation constituted a compensating differential for the risk to life and limb. As Figure 6.3 shows, the risk of the job by itself does not guarantee that the truck drivers will earn more in Iraq than elsewhere. If there was a large enough risk-loving group, the equilibrium wage might actually be less. They would accept a lower wage in order to experience the thrill of getting shot at. That was certainly not the case in Iraq. According to Charles McDaniel, a civilian convoy commander, "My wife, she doesn't like it, . . . My mother, she doesn't like it. My kids don't like it" (Glanz 2004). But the money and the camaraderie were so good that he would not leave anytime soon (Glanz 2004).

Other examples include the prestige of the job. Some workers might be willing to accept less pay in order to work in a job considered socially prestigious. Of course, people could conceivably differ on how they view the prestige of jobs. Some people are eager to join the Peace Corps. Others would not touch it. Variability of income is a characteristic that could be important. Some jobs, like accountant, offer fairly steady work and pay. Others, like actor, provide only intermittent work and pay (at least if you are not a superstar).

These differentials are not immutable. Changes in tastes can increase or decrease the wage gaps. Consider the dirty job example. If over time people's tastes change so that the dirty job becomes less desirable to everyone, the supply curve on the graph would shift inward. If everything else held constant, the wage differential for the dirty job would increase. Of course, changes in tastes are likely to evolve over long periods of time.

Changes in technology can also play a role. If technological developments make truck transportation in a war zone safer—for example, perhaps better armor can be developed—that would influence the differential between truck driving in a war versus a peace zone. Again, technological developments are something that take place in the long run.

Cost of Acquiring Skills

Many jobs require that their holders have certain skills. Often these skills can only be acquired through training, an activity that is frequently both time-consuming and costly. For example, to become a brain surgeon an individual needs to complete high school, college, medical school, an internship, and a residency at the bare minimum. The costs include tuition, fees, books, equipment (your own stethoscope, scalpel, and lab coat), and, because training interferes with holding another job, lost earnings. [1] These costs can help create wage differentials for the simple reason that workers need some compensation to induce them to incur these costs.

Figure 6.4 looks similar to Figure 6.3 with the exception that the vertical intercept of the supply curve is at a wage ratio greater than 1.0. The positive slope of

Figure 6.4 **Long Run Wage Differentials and the Cost of Acquiring Skills**

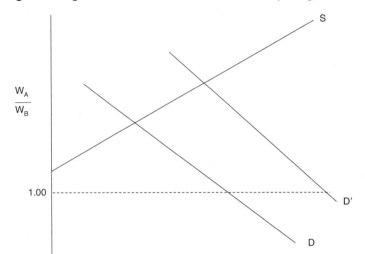

this curve needs some explaining. One reason for the positive slope is that the cost of acquiring skills is likely to differ for different workers. Some workers are able to progress through the training programs faster than others. Some particularly precocious students can skip grades. Students from wealthy families can more easily attend prestigious training institutions. Students from wealthy families do not have to work during the summer and can advance their course of study through summer classes.

Another factor is the internal rate of time preference. (If you did not read Chapter 4, read the rest of the paragraph. If you did, you can skip to the next paragraph.) Roughly speaking, the internal rate of time preference is a measure of the reward you require for waiting. For example, what sort of reward would you require in order to postpone consuming $100 right now? If you would postpone $100 now in return for $110 in one year, your internal rate of time preference is roughly 10 percent. You require a 10 percent reward in order to postpone consumption for a year. The acquisition of training requires that you postpone consumption. The tuition, fees, books and equipment is certainly money that you could have used for partying. The same is true for the money you could have made by taking a job instead of devoting your time to the training program. Some people will require a larger reward than others to postpone consumption. These sorts of folks will require a large wage differential in order to undertake the training. People who do require a large reward are sometimes called "impatient" or "present-oriented" and are said to be unable to "defer gratification."

Regardless of the causes, the end result is that demand determines the number employed in occupation A and the wage ratio. The costs of acquiring skills can act as a barrier to movement from low-paid to higher-paid occupations.

Winner-Take-All Markets

In 2004 the actress Lindsay Lohan earned $10 million (Brenner 2005). This was 909 times more than Julie Lentes, a 43-year-old merchandiser from Huntington, Indiana who earned $11,000 (Brenner 2005). What could possibly explain such a huge gap? Lindsay's job certainly is not dirtier, riskier, or less socially prestigious than Julie's. Although Lindsay's job requires talent (and looks), these things were not acquired through years of rigorous training. She is only a high school graduate. Could this possibly be just demand and supply at work or is there something more going on? One explanation is that some people do their work in what are called winner-take-all markets (Frank and Cook 1995).

For our purposes, the key distinguishing characteristic of a winner-take-all market is that the top performers receive a disproportionately large share of the total rewards.[2] There are numerous high-profile examples of these markets. In the acting profession, Lindsay Lohan and a handful of other top rank stars are paid multimillion-dollar amounts per movie while most actors have to wait tables or drive cabs to make ends meet. The top musicians sell millions of CDs, have their songs downloaded millions of times, and sell out large venues for live performances while most of the rest just scrape by. The average salary in the NBA exceeds two million dollars per year, but there are only 400 roster slots. Of course, what makes these markets interesting is the fact that the winners partake in enormous rewards. Not all winners are so favored. Brian Luke was the 2003 U.S. Traditional Longbow (an archery event) champion, but that did not allow him to live the high life. Likewise for Jennifer Schmitt, the 2004 national female Singles handball champion.

What leads to the high earnings of the top performers? It is a combination of demand- and supply-side factors. On the demand side, some activities are just more popular. These are called "mass" winner-take-all markets. Basketball is more popular than handball. Rock-and-roll is more popular than polka music. In other markets there may be a small number of buyers, but these buyers pack such financial clout and are so intensely interested in the product that large incomes can result. An example of these "deep-pocket" markets is the market for art or top defense attorneys. Another demand side factor is network economies. Some goods become more valuable as more consumers use it. One telephone is not very useful to anyone, including the person who owns it. Many telephones are useful to many people.

As a product gains a toehold in a market, its advantages can increase simply because it is ahead of the game. An example from the Stone Age is the competition between the VHS and Beta formats for VCRs. In the early days of VCRs, there were two formats for the machines and tapes. To many videophiles, Beta was actually the superior format because video quality was higher. However, its Achilles heel was that the earliest versions of Beta tapes could only hold about two hours worth of programming. This meant many of the most popular movies could not be shown in Beta format unless they were sold as multiple tapes. The earliest versions of VHS could hold up to six hours of programming. Consequently, video rental stores were more likely to stock VHS than Beta tapes and as a result people turned to VHS machines. After a few years, VHS triumphed and Beta became a relic. Recently, a similar competition raged in the high-definition DVD world between the Blu-ray and HD-DVD formats. Blu-ray has emerged triumphant, presumably because of some small advantage.

Similar to this is the lock-in through learning or investment effect. "Technologies that are more widely used in the early stages thus tend to attract a disproportionate share of R&D efforts, and this in turn leads to even more widespread adoption" (Frank and Cook 1995, 35). There are many processes that exhibit similar strong positive feedback effects. In essence, "success breeds success" (Frank and Cook 1995, 36). Why has Duke University's basketball team been so successful for so long? Part of it has to do with Coach K, to be sure, but much of it has to do with past success. A program that develops a winning reputation can more easily stay on top because it has an easier time recruiting top-ranked prospects who want to succeed at the highest level.

Frank and Cook identify several other demand-side reasons why rewards are likely to be disproportionately visited on a few top performers (Frank and Cook 1995, 37–44).

- Decision leverage: As we move up the ranks in any organization, the consequences of a decision maker's actions get greater and greater. If the supervisor of the mailroom makes a mistake someone gets their mail a day late, if the CEO makes a mistake the whole corporation could collapse. "Thus, if the top contenders for the CEO position are distinguishable with respect to the quality of the decisions they are likely to make in office, then the competitively determined salary of the best candidate can be dramatically higher than for the second best, even when the estimated difference in their talent is very small" (Frank and Cook 1995, 37).
- Natural limits on the size of the agenda: There is psychological evidence that people have only a limited ability to process large amounts of information (Miller 1956). One implication in this context is that people are likely to remember the names of only a few top performers. Quick, name the top actors of your generation. Although there are many talented actors, you probably can only come up with the names of six or seven without too much strain. What this implies is that these six or seven will dominate their industry and earn disproportionate rewards even though they may only be a little bit better than everyone else.
- Habit formation and acquired tastes: Our demand for some goods and services increases with repeated exposure. During the 1960s, although the Beatles were my favorite band, I was always a bit disappointed with my first listen to their newest album. However, given their track record, I would always give the album a second listen. Usually by the end of the first side (we are talking records here) I had concluded that the album was really great, and I have never changed my mind since. If they were an obscure band, they would not have been given a second chance.
- Purely positional concerns: Face it, many of us like to impress our friends and neighbors. We buy some goods simply because of the status they confer. When possible we wear Manolo Blahnik[3] instead of Payless shoes. We like the best and are willing to pay more for it, even if it is not objectively that much better.

- Avoidance of regret: If you are a large corporation defending yourself in a several hundred million dollar lawsuit, "who ya gonna call," the best lawyer on the planet or the second best? Not wanting to second-guess yourself ("Darn, I should have hired X!") is a powerful motive that leads to concentration of earnings.

Probably the most important supply-side factor is production cloning. In some industries the services of the best performers can easily be distributed to the mass market. Take the case of musicians. Once a musician's performance is recorded, it is a simple matter to stamp out millions of CDs at very low cost and even easier to distribute the songs via the Internet. The same is true with movies. Lindsay Lohan's *Mean Girls* is easy to reproduce and distribute to literally millions around the world (*Mean Girls* 2004). In contrast, the *Mean Girls* of the pre-movie era age could only have been done on the stage, and only several hundred people could have seen each performance.

SHORT-RUN WAGE DIFFERENTIALS

At any particular point in time, long-run wage differences can be disrupted by disequilibrium in labor markets. Some workers are fortunate enough to be associated with expanding industries while others are unfortunately tied to contracting industries (at least for the time being until they abandon ship or are tossed overboard).

Let us assume that two jobs are identical in all respects except that one is dirtier than the other and as a consequence carries a 15 percent wage premium. What if demand changes so that there is an increase in demand in those industries that use the dirty labor and a decrease in demand in those industries that use the clean labor? This should increase the demand for dirty labor and decrease the demand for clean labor[4] and cause the dirty labor wage premium to increase, say to 20 percent. This 20 percent differential is only a temporary, short-run phenomenon because workers would leave the clean job for the dirty job until the wage premium was reduced back to the original 15 percent.

The Cobweb Theorem

An interesting digression is to consider the cobweb theorem. There are some markets, especially for highly trained professionals, that seem to exhibit systematic periods of boom and bust. The markets for engineers, physicists, and lawyers have been alleged to have these characteristics (Freeman 1975a; 1975b; 1976). A model sometimes used to explain these fluctuations is the cobweb theorem,[5] which is potentially applicable when an occupation requires a lengthy training period. What it shows is that there can be some interesting wage dynamics as the labor market searches for equilibrium.

In Figure 6.5, let the initial demand curve be D_0 and the long-run supply curve be S_{LR}. The long-run supply curve shows the quantity of labor supplied at each wage assuming enough time is allowed for workers to obtain the requisite skills. Equilibrium exists at wage w_0 and quantity L_0.

Figure 6.5 **The Cobweb Model**

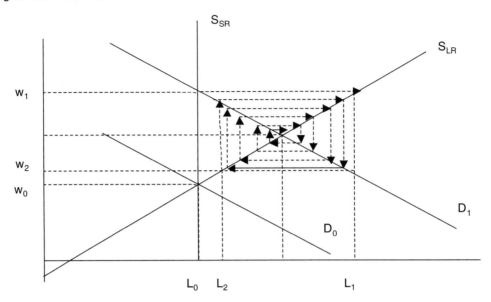

Now assume an increase in demand to D_1. If there is no reserve army of workers with the necessary skills and the skills take a long time to acquire, the market will not be able to move up along the supply curve S_{LR}. Rather, if we assume there are no workers with the needed skills immediately available, then in the short run S_{SR} is the relevant supply curve. The increase in demand will cause wages to jump upward to w_1. In response to w_1, workers will seek training. The result is that in the long run, L_1 workers will acquire those skills. Unfortunately for them, L_1 workers cannot find employment at w_1. Rather, the wage will be driven down to w_2 (remember, in the short run there will be a vertical supply curve at L_1), but at that wage the number of workers seeking work in that occupation will contract back to the long-run supply curve (point not indicated). But the shortage of workers will cause the wage to rise to the demand curve (again point not noted). The higher wage will then cause another long-run increase in supply, leading to a decrease in wage, leading to a decrease in quantity supplied, leading to an increase in wage, and so on. The arrows show the path the market takes to a new equilibrium. The reason the model is called a cobweb should be obvious from the appearance of the graph.

The cobweb model is vulnerable to some fairly telling criticisms (McConnell, Brue, and Macpherson 2006, 202). The first is that it makes some fairly naïve assumptions about how workers form expectations. Surely workers would come to expect these boom-and-bust cycles and plan accordingly? The second is the assumption that workers respond only to starting salaries in an occupation. It may be more realistic to assume that workers make their career choices on the basis of lifetime salaries, which may not fluctuate as much as starting salaries.

LONG-RUN LABOR SUPPLY

For any individual i, labor earnings depend on the quantity of labor supplied as represented by the L term in the personal income identity. As the discussion in Chapter 3 showed, for any individual, the number of hours of labor supplied depends on a whole host of personal idiosyncratic factors (i.e., tastes), but also the wage rate. Theoretically, the effect of the wage rate is ambiguous. The income and substitution effects pull in opposite directions. Empirically, in recent decades it appears that the substitution effect has predominated. Individuals earning higher wages have tended to work longer hours.[6] The explanation for this finding is not altogether clear but may have something to do with the fact that higher-wage workers tend to have more education. It may be that more educated workers simply have a stronger "taste" for work. If employers invest more in recruiting, hiring, and training more highly educated workers, they may insist on longer hours. Since the jobs held by more educated workers tend to be cleaner, less physically demanding, and more "fulfilling" jobs, there may be less resistance on their part to longer workweeks (McConnell, Brue and MacPherson 2006, 78–79). The bottom line is that higher-wage workers tend to supply more labor, further increasing the inequality of personal incomes although not necessarily inequality of utility.

DIFFERENCES IN CAPITAL EARNINGS

Differences in the earnings of the owners of capital (paradoxically called unearned income in our statistics) arise from differences in rental rates and the quantity of capital supplied. This section will discuss these factors briefly.

LONG-RUN RENTAL RATE DIFFERENTIALS

In the simple model, in short-run equilibrium quasi rents are likely to differ from industry to industry. However, in the long run, assuming perfect competition and freedom of entry and exit, rental rates ought to be equal. Capital will be pulled out of industries earning low quasi rents and invested in industries earning high quasi-rents. The equilibrating process will cease only when rental rates are the same in all industries.

If rental rates do not equalize, then the following factors may be at work.

- There may be lack of competition within industries and limited mobility between industries. For example, the return to capital in a monopoly industry may be higher than in a competitive industry.[7] Barriers to entry into an industry may be created a number of ways. In some industries there are significant economies of scale that impede the entrance of new firms. In others, government franchises, charters, or patents may prevent entrance of new firms.
- While machinery, factories, and tools may not have preferences regarding the characteristics of the industries they work in, their human owners might. Humans may be, for example, attracted by the glamour of the movie industry and turned off by the dirt of the garbage-hauling industry. (Of course, some may

have preferences in the other direction. Tony Soprano liked garbage hauling for the opportunities it provided to shelter income.) In other words, there may be compensating differentials to capital investment in different industries. We can make a similar argument with respect to risk. Using the movie business/garbage hauling example above, we would probably reverse the result. Movies are a relatively risky investment. Who can predict the tastes of the movie-going public? Garbage hauling is probably less risky because everyone generates garbage and needs it removed.

• Large investors find it easier to diversify. Small investors must take a plunge and can either score big or be destroyed.

There is empirical evidence that rates of return for individuals are positively related to their level of wealth (Bardham, Bowles, and Gintis 2000; Yitzhaki 1987).

THE SUPPLY OF CAPITAL SERVICES

Wealth is distributed unequally in the United States. In fact, the distribution of wealth is much more unequal than the distribution of income. A more detailed discussion of the distribution of wealth is presented Chapter 16.

DIFFERENCES IN LAND AND ENTREPRENEURIAL EARNINGS

Differences in the earnings of land owners can arise for various reasons. Clearly an important reason is because land is heterogeneous. Land differs in terms of its fertility, location, weather conditions, and whether there are valuable natural resources located on (trees, flowers, deer), beneath (coal and oil deposits), or above (great views of the universe or birds congregating above) it. An interesting thing to contemplate is the element of luck involved. Often people who acquire land do not know for sure how valuable it is. For millennia, land sitting on top of oil pools had no special value until technological developments turned oil into something prized. *The Beverly Hillbillies* hunted their land for decades before discovering "black gold."

With respect to the quantity of entrepreneurial services supplied, many are called and few are chosen. What makes one person a successful entrepreneur and another a mediocrity is difficult to determine after the fact and impossible to predict beforehand.

CONTROVERSY: WHAT'S BEHIND THE RISE IN WAGE INEQUALITY IN THE UNITED STATES?

Income inequality has been on the increase in the United States over the past three decades. Table 6.1 shows the distribution of household income in 1973 and 2006. Every quintile except the highest had a lower share in 2006 than in 1973.

A major reason for the increase in income inequality is that earnings (the major component of income) inequality has been on the rise. Figure 6.6 shows earnings for white males at the 90th, 50th, and 10th percentile from 1963 to 1997.[8] In addition

Table 6.1

Distribution of Household Income, 1973 and 2006

	1973 Share of Income (%)	2006 Share of Income (%)
Lowest fifth	4.2	3.4
Second fifth	10.5	8.6
Third fifth	17.1	14.5
Fourth fifth	29.6	22.9
Highest fifth	43.9	50.6

Figure 6.6   **Changes in the Indexed Value of the 90th, 50th and 10th Percentiles of the Wage Distribution for White Males (1963 values normalized to 100). Data from March CPSs.**

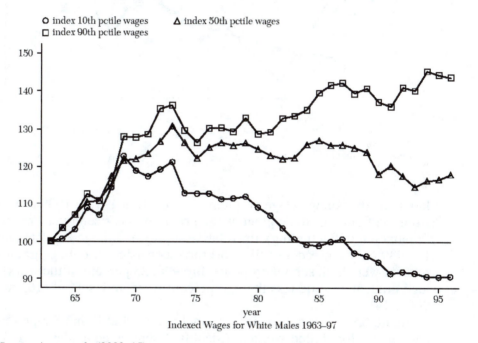

Source: Acemooglu (2002, 15)

to the increasing spread between wages at the high and low ends, it is also true that earnings for workers at the 10th percentile has fallen significantly while earnings at the 50th percentile are a bit lower than they were at their peak. So actually there are two significant phenomena to explain—rising inequality and decreasing real earnings at the low end.

An interesting model that addresses the issue is that of Daron Acemoglu (Acemoglu 2002). The Acemoglu model is an application of the theory of demand and supply with a twist. Figure 6.7 shows the relative supply of college-educated

Figure 6.7   **The Behavior of the (log) College Premium and Relative Supply of College Skills (weeks worked by college equivalents divided by weeks worked of noncollege equivalents) between 1939 and 1996. Data from March CPSs and 1940, 1950, and 1960 Censuses.**

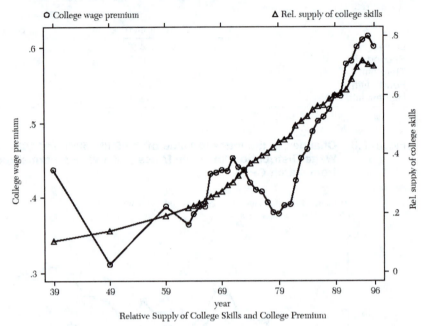

Source: Acemoglu (2002, 16).

labor and the college wage premium over the time period 1939 to 1996. As is clear from the figure, as the college wage premium has risen over time (albeit doing a fair amount of fluctuating), the relative supply of college-educated labor has risen. In 1939 only 6 percent of the workforce consisted of college graduates while 68 percent were high school dropouts. In 1996, 28 percent of the workforce was college graduates while less than 10 percent were high school dropouts (Acemoglu 2002, 14).

Figure 6.8 shows a demand and supply graph. Let D and S represent the demand and supply for skilled workers (identified here as equivalent to college-educated workers) at an early date. S' represents the increased supply of skilled workers. The only way that the wage premium could increase along with increased employment is if the demand curve shifted out by more than the supply curve did. That is represented by D'.

What could cause this dramatic increase in demand? According to Acemoglu, there has been accelerating skill-biased technological change. What this means is that the technological change that has taken place has increased the demand for highly skilled labor and decreased the demand for low-skilled labor.

Robert Reich, former secretary of labor in the Clinton administration, has put a human face on this phenomenon (Reich 1989). Reich contends that the key area

Figure 6.8 **Demand and Supply Analysis of Increasing Wage Inequality**

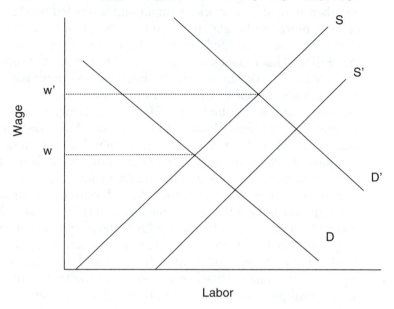

of technological change in recent years has been in the so-called information technologies (computers and telecommunications). As firms have come to increasingly rely on these technologies, they have had to hire workforces that could use them. By and large that had meant a skilled workforce. Skilled workers are more likely to work with computers and other information technologies, than unskilled workers (Krueger 1993; Autor, Katz, and Krueger 1998). This simple theory explains both rising inequality and why wages on the low end have fallen.

The twist Acemoglu gives to the model is the recognition that technological change of a specific type does not just fall out of the sky. It is not just luck that the type of technological change we have been experiencing has tended to favor skilled workers. Rather, the expansion of the number of skilled workers stimulated the skill-biased technological change that occurred.

His theory of endogenous skilled-biased technological change is based on the intuitively plausible notion that innovation will respond to profit incentives. Since a key determinant of profitability is market size, the development of skill-biased technologies will be more profitable when there are more skilled workers.

The nature of technological change today differs from earlier eras. In the 19th century, technological change was biased toward unskilled workers. During that time traditional craft methods of production that required skilled workers gave way to factory methods of production that made use of semiskilled and unskilled workers.

Of course, technological change was not the only factor at work. Acemoglu recognized several other factors that have contributed to increasing inequality. They include:

- Organizational change: Old-style firms had skilled and unskilled workers working together, with skilled workers managing unskilled workers. As skilled workers become more productive, they have an incentive to form teams that work separately from the unskilled because the unskilled pull down the productivity of the skilled. This reduces productivity of low-skill workers who had previously benefited from working with high-skill workers. However, Acemoglu argues that this accounts for only a small part of the story.
- Decline in unions: In the United States today, only about 7.6 percent of workers are members of unions. Unions have been in relative decline since the mid-1950s when nearly 1/3 of the labor force were members. Technological change may in fact have played some role in the decline in unions. Regardless, weaker unions have a harder time protecting the wages of low-skill workers.
- Decline in value of minimum wage: In real terms the minimum wage has declined fairly significantly. All told, the decline in minimum wage is not likely to be the major factor influencing inequality. Only about 8 percent of workers earn minimum wage and it is unlikely to have much impact on workers above the median.
- Trade: Traditionally the United States has had a comparative advantage in high-skill products. This is true today but the increasing volume of trade has put upward pressure on wages of the skilled and downward pressure on wages of low-skill workers.
- Immigration: Low-skill immigrants have dominated the current wave of immigrants. Low-skill immigrants compete with low-skill American citizens for jobs. The low-skill immigrants are also complements to the labor of high-skill workers and this has raised the productivity of high-skill Americans.

CONCLUSION

This chapter has reviewed factors that would cause differences in labor, capital, land, and entrepreneurial earnings in a pure market economy. Explanations for why people get different size slices that emphasize one or a few factors should be looked at with suspicion. The factors that cause differences are many and varied, and that many factors contribute to an explanation should be assumed to be the norm.

The reasons for differences in labor earnings discussed in this chapter largely reflect matters of taste and choice. Individual attitudes toward getting dirty on the job, risk, social status, willingness to undergo expensive training, and the preferred number of hours in a workweek all contribute to differences in labor earnings. Some of these considerations are also relevant to explanations of differences in capital, land, and entrepreneurial earnings, although the existence of barriers and just plain luck may play a larger role.

What are the normative aspects of this approach to inequality? Individuals have virtually no influence over the factor prices they receive. These factor prices are determined in impersonal, competitive markets where individuals are essentially "price-takers." Individuals have only partial influence over the amount of labor, capital, land, and entrepreneurial services they supply. Certainly individuals can decide how many hours to work (although they are limited to no more than 24 hours per day) and how hard to work each day. Similarly, individuals can decide how much to save (with the constraint that they need to consume enough to survive), how much land to supply and how much effort to devote to entrepreneurial activities. However, and these aspects were certainly not highlighted but would be difficult to deny, the amount of labor, capital, land, and entrepreneurial services each person can supply will depend on how much they were endowed with.

The idea of endowment may be easiest to understand with respect to capital. Some people are born lucky and inherit large sums of capital. A similar process works with respect to labor. Undoubtedly there is some element of genetic inheritance. Some people receive genes that allow them, given a supportive environment, to be bigger, stronger, and, probably, smarter than others. Bigger, stronger, and smarter people can supply more labor than others. Also, some people by the accident of birth may be raised in advantageous circumstances. Their parents' positions may give them "connections," or the neighborhood they are raised in may have better schools, peers, and role models. The result is that people who were raised in better circumstances may have more labor to supply.

The bottom line here is that even in the simplest model, the equity of the distribution of income cannot be taken for granted. Subsequent chapters will add more to the explanation of income differences.

QUESTIONS FOR REVIEW AND PRACTICE

1. One could argue that a long commute to work is an undesirable characteristic of any job. If most people live in the suburbs, what would the theory of compensating wage differentials predict about the relative wages of jobs in the suburbs versus wages in jobs located downtown (*ceteris paribus*)? Explain. What if some people especially loved working downtown and did not mind the commute? Explain.
2. Digging ditches is a dirty, low-prestige job. The fact that it is low-paying serves to disprove the theory of compensating differentials. Discuss.
3. Some cobweb models "explode," that is, they move further and further away from equilibrium. Under what conditions will a cobweb model "explode?" (Hint: look at the slopes of the demand and supply curves.)
4. Explain what factors might cause long-run differences in the returns to entrepreneurial ability.

NOTES

1. A more complete discussion of these issues, namely, investment in human capital, is found in Chapter 14.

2. A second characteristic is that payoffs are primarily determined by relative rather than absolute performance. For example, the income of a tennis player does not depend on how good she is in absolute terms. Rather it depends on how many rivals she can beat. If you can beat everyone, you are number one. Since the significance of this characteristic has mainly to do with the efficiency of these markets, it will not be emphasized in the subsequent discussion (Frank and Cook 1995, 25).

3. Manolos are high-end, trendy shoes (for those of you who have never watched *Sex and the City*).

4. The demand for labor is a derived demand. It is derived from the demand for the product the labor helps produce.

5. The cobweb theorem is not THE model for these types of markets. The applicability of the cobweb theorem is a matter of some debate. Regardless of the merits of the debate, the cobweb theorem is pretty neat and you will enjoy learning about it.

6. See Schor (1991). Schor's conclusions have been challenged by several economists. See Rones, Ilg, and Gardner (1997), Bluestone and Rose (1997), and Robinson and Godbey (1997).

7. Having a monopoly does not guarantee excess profits. You could have a monopoly of a product no one wants.

8. The focus on white males is simply to remove the confounding influence of race, ethnicity, and gender. Graphs for other race, ethnic, and gender groups would tell a similar story.

7 Equalizing the Slices

INTRODUCTION

The United States does not have a pure market economy. While most of our output is produced by private, profit-seeking firms, government plays a significant role taxing, spending, and regulating. While redistribution of income is not the explicit goal of most of what government does—the explicit goal of most government activity is to provide goods and services that the private sector would undersupply (examples include national defense, national parks, roads, and schools), establish rules and use financial incentives to encourage socially beneficial behavior (examples include mandatory school attendance and tax deductions for homeowners), discourage socially harmful behavior (examples include pollution and maximum work hours), and fight inflation and unemployment—redistribution is the effect of everything government does. This chapter attempts to explain how government policies can redistribute income.

The line of division between government policies that purport to redistribute income and those that fight poverty is not clear. Virtually any policy that redistributes income from rich to poor will also have some effect on poverty, and virtually any policy to fight poverty will change the distribution of income. Many of the topics in this chapter and Chapter 13 on policies to fight poverty could be interchanged without significant confusion resulting.

Consistent with the economic approach to everything, the analysis that follows will emphasize not only the impact of the policy on the size of the slices distributed to everyone, but also the potential trade-offs involved. The size of the slices may bear some relation to the size of the entire pie. Mainstream opinion within the economics profession holds that attempts to equalize the size of the slices may lead to a reduction in the size of the pie. "According to this common view, increasing government intervention in markets leads to more fairness at the cost of less efficiency" (Miller 1994, 2). The universality of this conclusion has been disputed (Haveman 1988).

TAXES AND TRANSFERS

If the rich have "too much" and the poor "too little," what could be simpler than the Robin Hood solution—take from the rich and give to the poor? Of course in modern times we do not have Robin and his Merry Men literally stealing from the rich and giving to the poor (although some people seem to think we do). Rather society does it democratically by empowering the government to tax the rich and use the proceeds to benefit the poor. The normative aspect of redistributing income by these means is a controversial issue, and will be addressed in Chapter 8. This section will concentrate on the positive economics of redistributing income by these means. If we cut the pie differently than the market does, how does that affect the ultimate size of the pie? How will the rich respond to having their "hard-earned income" taxed away? How will the poor respond to having their income augmented by receiving transfer payments from the government?

ECONOMIC ANALYSIS OF TAXES AND TRANSFERS

Positive economic analysis can address two aspects of taxes and transfers, namely their incidence and impact on incentives.

Tax Incidence

In 1991 the federal government enacted what was known as the "luxury tax." This tax was an excise tax on a number of luxury items, such as exotic sports cars, personal jets, yachts, and the highest-end stereo systems. The primary purpose of the tax was to raise revenue to reduce the budget deficit (then at record levels). The secondary purpose was to achieve the primary purpose by "soaking the rich," a group whose income and wealth gains relative to the rest of society had become embarrassingly noticeable. What could be better than raising needed revenue by "sticking it" to the people who buy expensive, frivolous items?

Within a year, the tax was repealed. It was not repealed because the deficit had disappeared. Rather it was repealed because it became evident that the rich had reduced their quantity demanded of luxury items and the result was lay-offs of the people who produced luxury items (Bryant 1992; Nordheimer 1993). Furthermore, many of the people who produced sports cars, jets, yachts, and stereo components were decidedly not rich. The moral of the story from our standpoint is that taxes do not just affect the people they are placed on. They sometimes affect innocent bystanders.

The *statutory incidence* of a tax refers to who is expected to write the check to the government. The *economic incidence* refers to whose real income is reduced by the tax. What the theory of tax incidence teaches us is that the two are not always the same.

Theory of Tax Incidence. Figure 7.1 shows demand (D) and supply (S) in the market for cigarettes. Assume there are no taxes and the quantity axis measures packs of cigarettes. The equilibrium price is $6. This means the consumer pays $6 a pack and the producer receives $6 a pack.

Now assume the government enacts an excise tax of $2 a pack and places it on the producer. In other words, the cigarette manufacturer is required to send $2 to the government for each pack of cigarettes sold. Graphically, this will shift the supply curve vertically by $2 because the cost of producing cigarettes has just

Figure 7.1 **Tax Incidence in the Market for Cigarettes–Tax Placed on Producer**

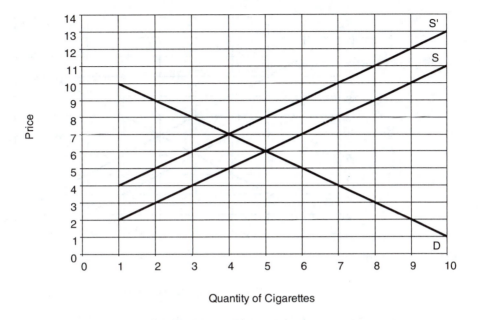

Quantity of Cigarettes

risen by $2 (essentially the tax is an additional cost of production). The supply curve S' lies $2 above S at every quantity. The new equilibrium is $7. This means consumers pay $7, but producers receive $5 a pack (remember $2 has to be sent to the government).

The end result is that the producers are sending checks to the government—$2 for each pack sold. Compared to the initial equilibrium, however, the producer is only receiving $1 less ($5 compared to $6). The consumer is paying $1 more ($7 instead of $6). The producer only ends up paying half of the $2 tax. The consumer also pays half the tax because $1 of it has been "shifted" onto the consumer.

Now consider Figure 7.2. The initial equilibrium is the same as in the first example. In this case, though, the $2 tax is placed on the consumer. Consumers will be charged an additional $2 for each pack of cigarettes they buy. How will that affect the market? The presence of a tax will not increase the consumer's willingness to pay. The consumer's demand curve (D) will stay put. D shows the maximum amount the consumer will pay for any quantity. Since the amount paid must include the $2 tax, a new demand curve must be drawn that is shifted vertically downward $2 from D. The demand curve (D') shows the maximum price the consumer will pay in addition to the tax. The consumer is willing to pay $7 at the quantity of 4. This $7 will consist of the $2 tax plus a maximum of 5 additional dollars.

The intersection of D' with the supply curve will establish the new equilibrium. There consumers are paying $7 and producers are receiving $5. This outcome is exactly the same as the previous one. The $2 tax is equally split between consumer and producer. An important conclusion is that the economic incidence of a tax is

Figure 7.2   **Tax Incidence in the Market for Cigarettes–Tax Placed on Consumer**

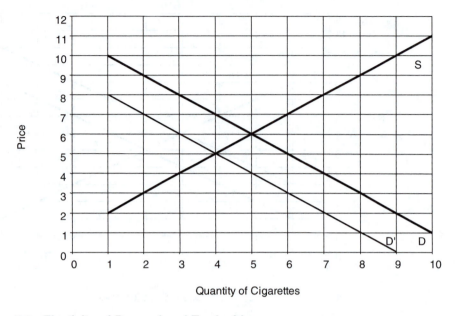

Quantity of Cigarettes

Figure 7.3   **Elasticity of Demand and Tax Incidence**

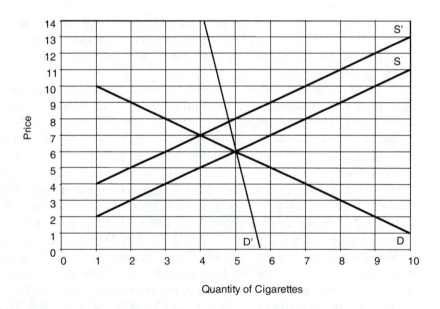

Quantity of Cigarettes

independent of its statutory incidence. The economic incidence will be the same whether the tax is placed on the consumer or the producer.

This 50/50 split is only an artifact of the specific model used. Figure 7.3 shows demand curve D' that is considerably less elastic than D (at the equilibrium point). If the demand curve was D', much more of the incidence of the tax would be shifted

Figure 7.4 **Elasticity of Supply and Tax Incidence**

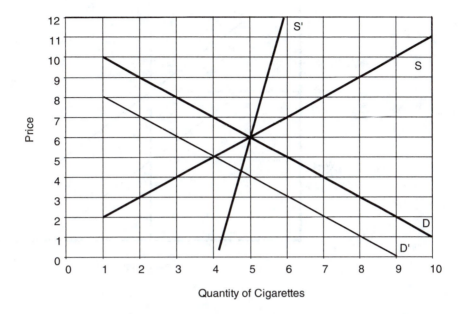

onto consumers. In that case consumers would end up paying approximately $7.80, as opposed to $7 in the first case. The conclusion is that the more inelastic the demand for a good, the more the consumer ends up paying (which makes sense!).

Figure 7.4 shows the case of a tax on the consumer (remember, it does not matter whether the tax is on the consumer or producer). Supply curve (S') is much less elastic than S. If the supply curve is less elastic, the bulk of the incidence of the tax falls on the producer.

Ultimately, the incidence of a tax depends on both the elasticities of demand and supply. The side of the market that is more inelastic ends up paying relatively more of the tax.

The Social Security Tax. Social Security is funded by the Federal Insurance Contributions Act (FICA) tax, also known as the payroll tax. In a statutory sense, both the worker and the employer are taxed. The worker pays a tax of 6.2 percent on the first $102,000 of earnings each year.[1] The employer pays a tax of 6.2 percent on the first $102,000 of the worker's earnings. So if a worker made $50,000 one year, the worker would have $3,100 taken from his paycheck ($50,000 * 0.062), and the employer would be obligated to contribute $3,100 to be credited to that worker.

The theory of tax incidence just reviewed should caution us to not accept statutory claims of tax incidence at face value. The fact that employers are taxed for Social Security raises the cost of hiring labor and should decrease the demand for labor. Assuming everything else is held constant, the impact of this is to reduce the wage paid to labor and, consequently, at least some of the employer's tax burden is passed on to the employee.

Figure 7.5 **Incidence of the Social Security Tax**

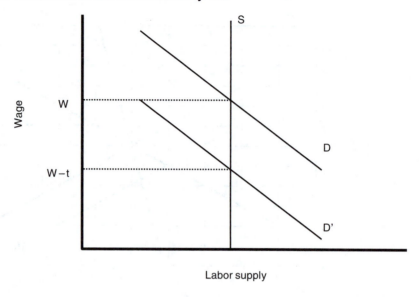

But there is the other side of the market to consider. The fact that employees must pay Social Security tax reduces the reward from working. If the substitution effect dominates, this will decrease the supply of labor, and, everything else held constant, raise wages and, consequently, pass some of the employee's burden on to the employer.

Of course, the end result crucially depends on the elasticity of demand and supply. For most groups on the labor market, labor supply is relatively inelastic. In Figure 7.5, let the labor supply curve (S) be vertical. The initial demand curve is (D). The imposition of a tax on the employer shifts the demand curve to D'. The end result is that the employer still pays a tax, but has been able to shift the burden to the employee by paying proportionately lower wages. The employee suffers the entire burden of the tax placed on him because he is committed to the labor market no matter the wage. The employee ends up paying a payroll tax of 12.4 percent on the first $102,000 made. That the employee shoulders the entire burden is the usual assumption made in analyses of the payroll tax.

The Corporate Income Tax. Many people strongly support the continued use of a corporate income tax because they think the tax is on "those rich corporations" and not on them. The first thing to remember is that all taxes are ultimately on people. We cannot tax a corporation without taxing people. Which people end up being taxed when a corporation is taxed? One possibility is the owners of the corporation because the tax reduces profits. Since corporate stock is disproportionately owned by the rich, this result might very well be what many people hope. There are other possibilities. The tax might get shifted forward to consumers in the form of higher prices. Or it might get shifted backward to workers in the form of lower wages, managers in the form of lower salaries, or suppliers in the form of lower prices.

Consider the following model: Assume the only factors of production are labor and capital. Also assume that capital is perfectly mobile internationally, but labor is not. That means capital will seek its highest return anywhere on the globe. In this case, a tax on corporations will initially reduce the return to capital. This will cause capital to emigrate seeking higher returns. The reduced stock of capital in the taxing country will decrease the productivity of labor causing wages to fall. The net result is the corporate tax gets shifted completely to labor!

Of course, different assumptions about the relative mobility of factors will lead to very different results. The empirical work on this issue is extensive, but has yet to reach a consensus.

Incentive Issues—Taxes

The incentive issue is essentially the impact of taxes on work, saving, and investment.

Taxes on Labor. Consider the simplest form of tax-and-spend redistribution. The government will impose a tax on labor income and use the money raised to send "welfare" checks to the poorest citizens. The impact on labor supply for the people paying the taxes and receiving the benefits can be analyzed using the labor supply model from Chapter 3.

Assume a month consists of 30 days or 720 hours (= 30*24). A representative individual (Pat) earns a wage of $20 per hour and there are no taxes. In Figure 7.6, AB shows Pat's budget constraint under those conditions. One of Pat's indifference curves is depicted, allowing us to determine that Pat will work 176 hours during the month and will earn $3520.

Now let government enact a tax on labor earnings. The tax requires everyone to pay 25 percent of their earnings to the government. The effect of the tax is to rotate the budget constraint inward around the horizontal intercept. The government cannot reduce the number of hours in the day so there are still 720 hours available, but the tax does reduce the amount of take-home pay. If Pat worked all 720 hours, he would be able to take home only $10,800, an amount that is 75 percent of what he could take home if there was no tax. The new budget constraint would be AD.

The important question from the standpoint of positive economics is what impact does this tax have on Pat's willingness to work? On the basis of the discussion in Chapter 3, we know this is not an easy question to answer because of the income and substitution effects. On the basis of the income effect, Pat would be expected to work more hours. Since Pat takes home less money, Pat would have to work more hours to achieve a target level of income. On the basis of the substitution effect, Pat would be expected to work fewer hours. Since the reward for working has been reduced (Pat's take-home pay for each hour of work has been reduced), Pat would cut back on work hours. The net effect depends on the relative strength of the income and substitution effects.

What is true for Pat is not necessarily true for the marketplace as a whole. We need to remember that the income lost by all individuals as a result of the tax is replaced when the government subsequently spends the money.[2] Therefore there is no

Figure 7.6 **Impact of a 25 Percent Tax on Labor Income**

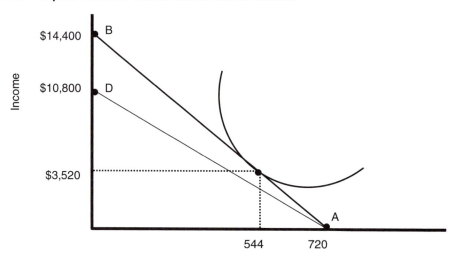

net income effect for society as a whole. There is, however, a substitution effect for every individual. Consequently, we can conclude that imposing this simple tax will probably lead to a reduction in work hours. Critics of using tax-based redistribution have a point. The size of the pie will be reduced, but by how much is unknown. While there is likely to be a reduction in work hours, there is no reason to presuppose that the reduction will be a large one. It is ultimately an empirical issue.

Taxes on Interest. Figure 7.7 shows the budget constraint CAB for an individual in a two-period intertemporal model. (Review the exposition of this model in Chapter 4 if you feel the need.) Assume the individual earns Y_1 in period 1, Y_2 in period 2, there are no taxes, and the interest rate is i. If the individual saves every dollar earned in period 1, he will be able to consume $Y_1(1 + i) + Y_2$ in period 2 which serves as the vertical intercept of the constraint. If the individual borrows against period 2 earnings in period 1, the maximum he will be able to consume is $Y_1 + Y_2/(1 + i)$. Place an imaginary indifference curve on the graph and find the individual's intertemporal allocation of consumption.

Now assume that a tax of t percent is placed on interest earnings. This means each dollar saved will earn (1-t)i percent compared to i percent previously. For example, if the interest rate was 4 percent and the tax rate was 25 percent, each dollar saved would earn a 3 percent after-tax return. Further assume that any interest paid on borrowed money is deductible from the standpoint of the income tax. This means money borrowed at i percent interest will actually cost (1-t)i. For example, if you borrow $100 at 4 percent interest you pay $4 in interest each year. If the interest is deductible and your tax rate is 25 percent, the interest payment will reduce your taxable income by $4 and your tax payment by 25 percent of that, or $1. The $1 saved on taxes offsets

Figure 7.7 **Taxes on Interest**

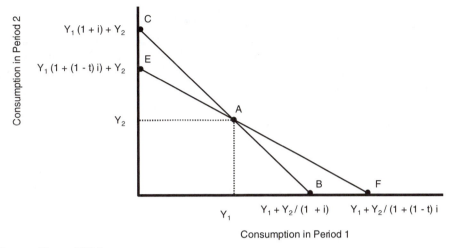

Source: Chang (1994)

the $4 paid in interest for a net payment of $3, which is an effective interest rate of $(1-t)i$. This means the maximum you could borrow in period 1 is $Y_2/(1+(1-t)i)$.

The effect of the new tax policy will be to rotate the budget constraint. The new budget constraint will still pass through point A because the individual can always consume all his income each period and not worry about taxes. The vertical intercept would change to $Y_1(1+(1-t)i) + Y_2$ and the horizontal intercept would become $Y_1 + Y_2/(1+(1-t)i)$. In Figure 7.7, the new budget constraint would be line EAF.

What effect would this have on the level of saving? From the individual standpoint, the outcome is ambiguous because of the competing influences of the income and substitution effects. From the standpoint of the economy, the negative income effect of the tax is offset in the aggregate by the positive income effect associated with spending the money so raised. What is left is the substitution effect, which is likely to lead to lower saving. The empirical magnitude of that, however, has never been shown to be large.

What if interest payments were not deductible? In essence, line segment AF in Figure 7.7 should be eliminated so the new budget constraint becomes the kinked line EAB. If the individual was a period 1 borrower, there is unlikely to be any effect on the intertemporal allocation of consumption. If the person was a period 1 saver, then a net substitution effect is likely.

The Capital Gains Tax. The capital gains tax is a tax on the changed value of assets. For example, if you buy a stock for $100 in year 1 and sell it for $120 in year 2, you have enjoyed a capital gain of $20. Under our tax system, that gain must be declared as income in the year it is received and tax must be paid on that income.[3] For quite some time, there has been debate in the United States about the appropriate capital gains tax rate. Some, mainly conservatives, have argued for lower capital gains tax rates. They reason that lower rates would make people more willing to save and invest to the benefit of all by virtue of the impact of saving and investing on the size of the pie. Critics of the policy have pointed out that lower capital gains taxes would redound to the benefit of the already rich primarily because the rich own a disproportionate share of the assets. Conservatives have had the upper hand in recent years because capital gains tax rates have been reduced to a maximum of 15 percent, which is less than the rate that people pay on the money they earn by the "sweat of their brow." What is often overlooked is the simple fact that there still is no persuasive evidence that a reduction in the capital gains tax rate will have a significant impact on saving and investing (Rosen and Gayer 2008, 388).

Estate and Gift Taxes. The incentive effect of estate and gift taxes, particularly the incentive to accumulate wealth and supply labor, has been an especially controversial issue in the United States in recent years. See Chapter 16 for a discussion.

Incentive Issues: Transfers

Just as there are incentive issues with the collection of tax revenue, there are incentive issues regarding the distribution of the money collected.

Straight Transfers. Assume tax money (a disproportionate amount of which will come from the rich in a progressive system) is simply distributed to poor people as a lump-sum cash payment with no strings attached. The policy just described is not like any policy our government has ever used. Probably the most similar real world counterpart was the old Aid to Families with Dependent Children program.

Figure 7.8 shows Jill's budget constraint (AB). Jill has fairly modest earning power. She is only able to command $5 per hour in the marketplace. Here Jill chooses to work 80 hours per month and earn $400.

Under the welfare program, Jill becomes eligible to receive a transfer payment of $200 per month. On the graph, that transfer would be represented by budget constraint DEA. Note that DEA is parallel to AB because Jill's earning potential has not changed. The horizontal intercept cannot change, however, since there is no way to manufacture more hours in the month. The budget constraint has a discontinuity from point E to A. The discontinuity says if Jill worked 0 hours during the month, she would still have an income of $200.

How does Jill react to this? What we have here is a pure income effect. Jill's income has increased, but there has been no change in her earning power. Under the reasonable assumption that leisure is a normal good, Jill will use the additional income to purchase more leisure, which implies less work. The less work can come about through a variety of means. Shown is the outcome where Jill moves to point F. Her hours of work are reduced to 60, but her income still rises to $500. Another possible outcome is that she moves to point E (indifference curve not shown). Here Jill would rather sacrifice income because she regards work as especially onerous.

So the policy will reduce hours of work among recipients. Again, how much remains an empirical matter.

Figure 7.8 **The Incentive Effect of Transfers**

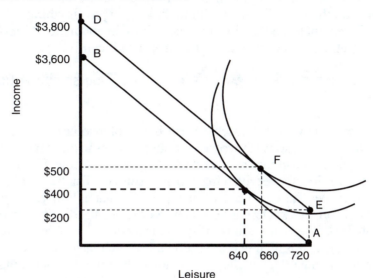

The Spectrum of Incentives

Up to this point, the discussion in this section has come straight from the mainstream of economic analysis. It focuses on the financial incentives that economists know and love. Financial incentives are not all there is, however. The grand spectrum of incentives also includes moral and social incentives. Moral incentives reflect the fundamental beliefs that people have about right and wrong. Many will do what they believe is right and avoid doing what they believe is wrong—even if the private costs and benefits do not exactly align. Social incentives refer to the power of society to shape our actions. Many people will take or avoid certain actions simply to win social acclaim or avoid social approbation—even if the private costs and benefits do not exactly align.

Levitt and Dubner provide an interesting example of how the various incentives can collide with each other (Levitt and Dubner 2005, 19–24). An Israeli daycare center was concerned about parents who arrived late to pick up their children. They imposed a modest financial fine of $3 for each late pickup and discovered the problem increased. The economists studying the issue reasoned that prior to the institution of the fine, moral and social considerations governed the behavior of the parents. The parents who picked their children up on time (the vast majority) did so because they considered it wrong to impose on the daycare center and were concerned with how other people would view their tardiness. Once the fine was imposed, the moral and social stigma associated with tardiness simply evaporated. The fine was interpreted as saying that being late was "acceptable" behavior because it was just another thing you could pay for. Of course, the fact that the fine was modest was also significant. If the fine had been $100 very different behavior likely would have followed. Interestingly enough, the fine was later removed, but the problem continued at the new higher level. The stigma had been erased permanently, and now the parents could pick up their children late without having to pay anything.

The point is not that financial incentives do not matter. *Ceteris paribus,* they clearly do. Rather, the construction of appropriate incentives is a very complicated matter.

EMPIRICAL EVIDENCE ON THE IMPACT OF TAXES AND TRANSFERS ON EQUALITY AND EFFICIENCY

Table 1.3 showed the household distribution of income in the United States in 2006 using different definitions of income. For our purposes in this chapter, the two most important definitions of income are market and disposable income. Simplifying greatly, the former measures income received from market sources. The latter adjusts that income for government benefits received and taxes paid. No matter how you look at the data, whether in a table format, Lorenz curve, or Gini coefficient, the distribution of market income is less equal than the distribution of disposable income. However, as the discussion in Chapter 1 cautioned, this finding is not irrefutable proof that government taxes and transfers have an equalizing effect on the distribution of income. For one thing, disposable income is not a comprehensive measure of the impact of government policy on the distribution of income. Several policies with great impact are simply not measured—such as the benefits flowing to different segments of society from the provision of public goods, such as national defense and public education, and from various tax expenditures,[4] such as the deduction for home mortgage interest. Second, the market/disposable income comparison does not take into account the impact that existing government benefits and taxes have had on the incentive to earn market income. The appropriate comparison is between the existing distribution of income (assuming we can put monetary values on everything) and what the distribution of income would have been if the only source of income was via the market. What we actually compare is the existing distribution of income against the market incomes earned in an environment in which significant government benefits and taxes exist. The conclusion that government policy leads to a more equally sliced pie is based more on faith than hard evidence.

This is also true with respect to the impact of taxes and transfers on efficiency. The theoretical literature on the impact of taxes and transfers on efficiency is extensive (Rosen and Gayer 2008). The empirical literature is large, but not particularly fulfilling. Individual policies, such as the impact of tax incentives on work, saving, and investment, appear to have modest effects (Danziger, Haveman, and Plotnick 1981). The cumulative effect of these policies on the size of the pie is not clear. As in the case of the distribution of income, the appropriate comparison is between the actual size of the pie and what it would be if there were no government benefits and taxes. It would be an act of hubris to claim to know what the precise extent of the inefficiency is. "Tax policy analysis is more of an art than a science" (Bruce 2001, 383).

MANDATING BENEFITS

Government is often tempted to require employers to provide workers with particular benefits. In the United States, examples of mandated benefits include the requirement of premium pay for work over 40 hours each week, the Occupational Safety and Health Administration (OSHA) regulations on workplace safety, and the requirement that health insurance packages include pregnancy benefits.[5] In Europe it is not uncommon for government to mandate the length of workers' vacations. The desirability of mandating benefits is highly controversial among economists. It is not that the benefits themselves are not desirable. In every instance the benefit itself is a "good thing." The controversy is over the extent of the trade-offs involved. Many economists take the position that there is "no such thing as a free lunch" and that any benefit provided carries a cost in terms of other benefits that could have been provided. Instead of government deciding what the compensation package should contain, it is always better to let the parties directly involved make their own decisions. Other economists think that in some instances government initiative can eliminate a market failure so that the benefits of mandating particular benefits can exceed the cost.

In this section we will provide a positive analysis of hypothetical legislation in which employers provide their employees with health insurance, although we could substitute any benefit in place of health insurance and the analysis would work the same. Some of the analysis may sound similar to the minimum wage analysis from Chapter 5. That is because the minimum wage is simply another instance of a mandated benefit.

THE HEALTH INSURANCE PROBLEM IN THE UNITED STATES

The limited extent of health insurance coverage in the United States is a national problem that has been recognized for quite some time. In 2006 nearly 47 million Americans (approximately 15.8 percent of the population) had no health insurance (United States Bureau of the Census 2007c, 18). This issue is important mainly because of the potential financial burden imposed by health-care problems. Americans spend more than $4,000 per person per year on health care. Since most people are healthy and spend comparatively little, the burden on those unlucky enough to encounter health problems can be huge. The average cost of a day in the hospital is $1,128 (OECD 2007). A visit to a doctor can cost between $100 and $200. The cost of a kidney transplant is $89,939 the first year and $16,043 per year thereafter (The University of Maryland Medical Center 1999). A significant health problem can be financial Armageddon to most people.

In the United States, most people (approximately 75 percent) obtain health insurance as part of the compensation package offered by their employer. The importance of employer-based insurance owes much to the generous tax subsidy provided by the government. Contributions that employers make for health insurance in the name of their employees are not taxed even though those contributions are clearly "income" to the employee. This type of financing is prominent as a result of historical circumstances. In the 1930s and 1940s health insurance of any type was the exception rather than the rule. During World War II wages were controlled by the War Stabilization Board in the interests of national security. To provide some additional compensation to workers who were working long and stressful hours to provide the resources needed for the war effort, the War Stabilization Board authorized firms to provide a tax-free health insurance benefit. Worker demand for this benefit mushroomed in the postwar years. Today health insurance benefits are widely available at large, established firms. Smaller firms are much less likely to make the benefit available. The self-employed also face great difficulty obtaining affordable health insurance.

It is a natural step to propose that employers be required to provide health insurance for their employees. In fact, that was a major component of the President Clinton's health insurance reform plan that was launched with such fanfare in 1993 but crashed and burned soon after. What about mandating that employers provide health insurance as one of the benefits provided to employees?

THE CASE AGAINST MANDATED HEALTH INSURANCE

Just as there is "no such thing as a free lunch," there is no such thing as a free mandated benefit. In a competitive labor market with rational, perfectly informed decision makers and no barriers to mobility, mandated benefits are not only unnecessary but they actually reduce workers' standard of living.

Consider a labor market in equilibrium. The compensation package (the mix of money wages, fringe benefits, working conditions, and so on) offered can be looked at from the standpoint of the cost to the employer and the value to the worker. From the standpoint of the employer, its cost cannot exceed the value of the marginal product of the last worker hired. From the standpoint of the worker, its value must be the highest possible at that cost.

Consider the following example: Compensation package A consists of a $15/hour money wage and two weeks vacation. Compensation package B has a $13.50/hour money wage, health insurance, and one week of vacation. Both packages cost the exact same amount. If workers prefer A to B, then firms offering B will be unable to hire anyone. They will be forced to offer A or else go out of business. If there is an even better package, it is in the best interest of some firms to discover it and begin offering it. The other firms will then have to match it or die. If there is not a better package, then workers are already receiving the highest value possible.

What if government attempts to mandate benefits? Assume the equilibrium package was A, but now government requires firms to include health insurance. Firms in competition cannot simply increase the value of some benefit. Doing so would raise their costs of production. They would then be forced to reduce some other elements of the package. If the firm reduced wages to $13.50/hour and cut back vacation time to one week, they could afford to provide insurance. Are workers better off? Previously they could have had package B, but they preferred package A. The bottom line is that by mandating benefits, government's actions have actually had a negative impact on workers.

THE CASE FOR MANDATED HEALTH INSURANCE

The case against mandated health insurance depends on some fairly stringent assumptions about the nature of workers and labor markets. If these assumptions do not hold—if the labor market is not competitive with perfectly informed, rational workers and no barriers to mobility—then there is no presumption that the market is optimally efficient and government involvement is suboptimal. If so, then a case can be made that mandated benefits might actually increase efficiency.[6]

For example, if workers are shortsighted and think they are going to live forever in perfect health, they might not buy insurance. By mandating insurance, government avoids this situation. Of course, you might wonder who could be that dumb. In my first job after college at age 22, I was on the verge of rejecting health insurance until my office manager "convinced" me that I wanted it. So I could be that dumb!

Even if people are perfectly informed, they are unlikely to purchase the socially optimal level of health care. Clearly, I benefit by being able to visit a doctor when I feel sick. You benefit too because (in the case of contagious diseases) if I am healthy you are less likely to become sick. The benefit to society of me going to the doctor is the benefit to me plus the benefit to you. Unfortunately, I do not care about you. I just care about me. I only take into account the benefit to me and hence I underconsume health care. With health insurance, this externality effect is significantly reduced.

Another problem with health insurance is adverse selection. This means that private health insurance might not be provided in optimal amounts because the people most likely to want to buy it are those most likely to have to use it. Therefore premiums would have to be high, which would discourage its use. If employers are required to provide health insurance, then many healthy individuals will be covered, which will reduce the average cost of providing it.

STRENGTHENING LABOR UNIONS

How often have you heard someone say that "what those workers really need is a union"? This statement reflects the well-founded belief that unionized workers have better compensation and working conditions than nonunion workers (Lewis 1963; Freeman and Medoff 1984). If unions are good for workers, would stronger unions and more widespread unionization be better?

WHAT DO UNIONS DO?

Labor unions are complicated organizations and nearly everything about them is contested. Even the meaning of the term "labor union" is mildly contested. For our purposes, we will define a labor union as an organization whose members are "employees" and whose main focus is to improve compensation and working conditions for its members. This definition includes organizations such as the United Brotherhood of Carpenters and Joiners (United Brotherhood of Carpenters and Joiners 2007), the International Brotherhood of Teamsters (International Brotherhood of Teamsters 2007), and the United Autoworkers (UAW; United Autoworkers 2007), but excludes the American Medical Association (American Medical Association 2007). The latter is excluded because while the AMA's pursuit of its agenda frequently redounds to its members' bottom lines, many of its members are not employees and the organization itself does not represent doctors in contract negotiations with an employer. The AMA is better thought of as a professional association, which is a horse of a different color.

Figure 7.9 **Collective Bargaining**

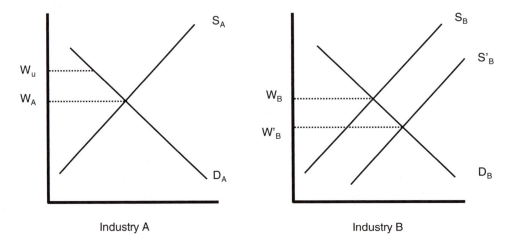

But some people, including the late highly respected Nobel laureate Milton Friedman, would not make this distinction (Friedman and Friedman 1979).

Unions promote the interests of their membership in a variety of ways. The most obvious is by the process of collective bargaining. Under collective bargaining the union acts as the representative of its members.[7] It bargains on behalf of its members with the employer over the terms and conditions of employment. Once a contract is signed, the union will then oversee and administer the contract for its duration. Collective bargaining needs to be distinguished from individual bargaining where each individual worker bargains with the employer over the terms and conditions that will apply to his or her employment.

Refer to the left panel of Figure 7.9. Let D_A and S_A be demand and supply of labor in industry A. In the absence of a union, the equilibrium wage would be w_A. Workers would not need a union to be paid this wage. Employers would voluntarily offer it. Workers would need a union to get a wage higher than the equilibrium, like w_U. This would be the goal of collective bargaining.

This points out the importance of the word *collective* in that term. Employers would not willingly offer wage w_U. They need to be coerced into doing so. The major power that unions possess is the force of numbers. By bargaining as a group, they can threaten to withhold the labor of the group (in other words, strike) unless the employer gives in. An individual threatening to withhold his or her labor would not have that clout, especially in a competitive labor market. Of course, employers have some leverage, too. If employers can hold out for a long time or bring in replacement workers (known as scabs),[8] workers may be reluctant to risk a strike. Ultimately what it comes down to is relative bargaining power. The stronger the union is, the higher wage it is likely to achieve.

Unions have other ways to promote their members' interests. A second way is by controlling supply to an industry. In Figure 7.10, D and S are demand and supply in the industry prior to the union. The equilibrium wage is w and equilibrium quantity

Figure 7.10 **Controlling Supply**

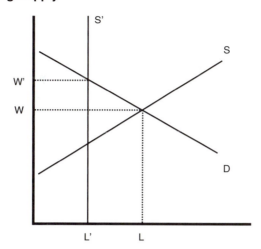

hired is L. Assume a union is able to gain control of the supply of labor to an industry. It might do this by being the sole source of training for the skills needed to work the job. Union-run apprenticeship programs are an example of this. Another strategy available to unions is the concept of a *closed shop*. A closed shop is an arrangement under which employers can be compelled to hire only union members.[9] Unions control supply by controlling membership in the union. Regardless of how it is done, if the union is able to limit supply to L', the equilibrium wage rises to w'.

A third way to promote member interests is by controlling demand, either aggregate demand or demand in a particular industry. In Figure 7.11, let D and S be demand and supply prior to the union. The equilibrium wage is w and equilibrium quantity is L. If the union is able to raise demand for its type of labor by shifting D to D', then both the equilibrium wage and the quantity hired could increase. There are several ways unions work to increase demand. Unions act individually as well as through federations, such as the AFL-CIO and Change to Win, to support "full employment" policies. They tend to support a high level of government spending and low interest rates. Unions actively lobby for policies that help their own industry. Unions are major supporters of protectionist trade policies that shield domestic industry from foreign competition.

In addition to fighting for the economic interests of their members, unions also provide political representation. Unions support political candidates[10] and engage in lobbying activities at all levels of government. Admittedly, much of this political representation ultimately affects the ability of their members to prevail in collective bargaining, but unions are also involved in political activities that do not have a direct impact on the bottom line. For example, unions provide strong support for civil and voting rights legislation.

Although to a much lesser extent than in earlier times, unions are also a source of social support for their members. They sponsor Christmas and July 4th parties, provide college scholarships for members' children, and, in some cases, provide death benefits.

Figure 7.11   **Controlling Demand**

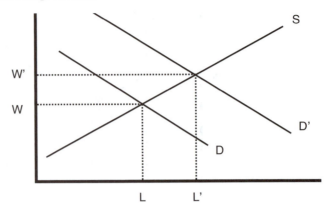

THE EXTENT OF UNIONIZATION

Union membership in the United States has been on the decline for a long time. In 2006 the percentage of the labor force unionized was 12.0 percent, down from 20.1 percent in 1983, and down from nearly one-third of the labor force in the mid-1950s.[11] The absolute number of union members in 2006 was 15.4 million, down from 17.7 million in 1983 (United States Department of Labor. Bureau of Labor Statistics 2007c).

The decline in union membership has, not surprisingly, been associated with a decline in union clout. The indicators of declining clout are everywhere. Unions have been less successful in bargaining for wage gains. In fact, givebacks have become common. Often, unionized workers continue working without a contract. Obtaining the first contract with an employer after a new union has been organized has become especially difficult to come by. The level of strike activity today is quite low by historical standards.

Once upon a time important labor leaders such as AFL-CIO President George Meany and UAW President Walter Reuther were household names. Who knows the name of the AFL-CIO President today? (As of this writing, it is John Sweeney.) Even the rogues are less colorful. Who today could possibly compare to Jimmy Hoffa?[12]

The trends in the United States are similar to those in some countries like the United Kingdom and Australia, but unlike those in many other countries. Canada's unions are still strong.

What accounts for the decline in unions in the United States? Part of it may be the result of long-term economic and demographic trends. The economy has moved from a manufacturing orientation to a service orientation, and unions have traditionally been weaker in the service sector. Women make up a larger proportion of the labor force, and women have traditionally been less likely to join unions. But these facts do not really constitute a complete explanation. What is preventing the service sector and women from organizing? Closer analysis suggests that American employers are much more resistant to union organizing drives today than in the past. In fact, employers are much more willing to break the law to keep unions out (Freeman and Medoff 1984). The reason for this may well have to do with the rapid pace of technological change and increasing globalization of the economy. In a more competitive economic environment, unions may well be an impediment that employers can do without.

THE UNION "WAGE" EFFECT

How do we measure the impact of unions on wages? In 2006, the median weekly earnings of a union member were $781 versus $612 for nonunion workers (United States Department of Labor. Bureau of Labor Statistics 2007c). Can we say that the act of joining a union will cause a raise of 27.6 percent $[(781 - 612) / 612 = 0.276]$? The answer is no. We cannot simply take a random union member and compare to a random nonunion worker because there are many factors that influence a worker's productivity—schooling, training, experience, and so on—and union members do not have the same characteristics as nonunion workers. To measure the impact of unionization on wages, we need to hold constant these other factors.

There have been many careful analyses over the years. Currently the union wage effect is thought to be about 15 percent (Cleveland, Gunderson, and Hyatt 2003, 302). The wage effect varies by industry and country, and over the business cycle.

CONTROVERSY OVER THE IMPACT OF UNIONS

We can all agree that unionized workers are better compensated than workers who are not union members. Does it follow that inequality and poverty can be reduced simply by strengthening unions and expanding union membership?

Before we jump to conclusions, we need to wade through some rather interesting analysis and controversy.

The traditional analysis suggests we need to look at the big picture when it comes to the impact of unions, and the big picture is fairly indistinct. Begin by referring back to Figure 7.9 and look at the entire picture, not just the left panel. The demand and supply curves are the same in both industries leading to the same equilibrium wage $(W_A = W_B)$. Now assume a union enters and organizes all the workers in industry A. The union then enters into collective bargaining with all the employers in the industry eventually winning wage W_u. At this wage, firms in the industry will have to lay off some workers. What do these workers do? In the absence of government programs supporting unemployed workers, they will have to find alternative employment. The workers enter industry B. This shifts the supply curve to S' and forces down the wage to W_B'. Consequently, even if the workers themselves are quite similar in terms of their tastes, the existence of a union can create wage differences among them.

Now refer to Figure 7.12. Assume no union, demand and supply in both industries is D and S, and both have an equilibrium wage of 5 and quantity of labor of 5. (The labor supply curves are drawn as vertical lines to simplify the analysis.) From the graph we can determine that output in industry A is 35. This is computed by adding up the VMP of each worker hired $(9 + 8 + 7 + 6 + 5 = 35)$. The same is true in industry

Figure 7.12 **Unions and Economic Efficiency**

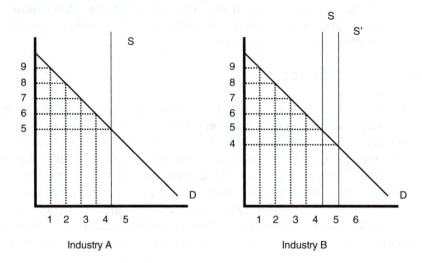

Industry A   Industry B

B for total output in both industries of 70. (Hopefully this analysis looks similar to Figure 5.2 in Chapter 5.)

Now let a union organize industry A and win a wage of 6. The industry will be forced to lay off one worker so total employment falls to 4 and output in industry A falls to 30. Interestingly, prior to unionization, industry A hired 5 workers and produced 35. The average productivity of labor was 7 (= 35/7). After unionization, the industry hired 4 workers and produced 30. The average productivity of labor actually rose to 7.5 (= 30/4). So unions can raise productivity by organizing an industry.[13] But focusing on what happens in industry A is an example of looking at the little picture.

The worker laid off from industry A needs to find a job and naturally drifts to industry B. This shifts the supply curve to S' and the new equilibrium wage will be 4. Industry B will now be producing 39. What is the impact of total production in the two industries? Industry A produces 30 and industry B produces 39. Total production is 69, which is less than previously. Despite the rise in productivity in industry A, total productivity in the two industries falls. Average labor productivity in B falls from 7 to 6.5. Labor unions, while potentially raising productivity in the industries they organize, cause a misallocation of resources leading to a decline in total productivity. Using a metaphor previously introduced, in the traditional analysis labor unions can increase the share of the pie going to their members but at the expense of the reduced slice for others and a smaller pie!

The traditional analysis, while influential with many economists, is not without opposition (Freeman and Medoff 1984). Among the points made by critics of the traditional analysis are the following:

- Contrary to Figure 7.9, nonunion industries will not necessarily end up paying lower wages. Rather, to prevent being unionized themselves they will try to pay comparable wages. This is called the union threat effect.

The results of this chapter may surprise readers who believe that union wage gains come at the expense of nonunion workers—a position espoused in years past by such notable economists as Henry Simons and Milton Friedman. The evidence does not support this simplistic view but rather presents a more mixed picture. Some nonunion workers gain from unionism, notably those in large nonunion firms and in firms threatened by organizations that choose to combat unionism with "positive labor relations." Other nonunion workers, notably less-skilled "secondary" workers, appear to lose from unionism. The net effect on the entire nonunion workforce is unclear (Freeman and Medoff 1984, 160–61).

- That unions will increase the degree of wage inequality does not necessarily follow from the analysis above. The model clearly predicts that unions will increase inequality between union members and nonunion workers. However, union/nonunion wage dispersion is not the only dimension of inequality. Overall inequality is influenced along other dimensions as well. A long-time goal of unions has been reduction of management's discretion over wage setting. Attaching wages to jobs rather than workers is one way to do this. Almost universally, union contracts establish wages for particular categories of jobs. Anyone who holds that job gets that wage, regardless of the individual level of productivity. Management cannot reward its favorites with higher wages. The effect of this is to reduce wage dispersion among union members at the same firm or establishment. Unions also strive to reduce wage dispersion among union members at different firms and establishments. A long-standing goal of unions is to "take labor out of competition," to prevent firms from using lower labor costs to gain competitive advantages. Unions also raise the wages of their members relative to that of managerial employees. Since managerial employees tend to be higher paid, this also reduces the overall level of inequality. There is some empirical evidence that the total impact of unions is actually to reduce the overall level of inequality (Freeman and Medoff 1984, 90–3).
- With respect to efficiency, empirical studies support the conclusion that there is a loss in output due to the misallocation of labor resulting from the union wage effect as demonstrated in Figure 7.12. However, estimated losses have never been found to be large. In 1963, Rees concluded that the social cost of monopoly wage gains was approximately 0.2–0.4 percent of the GDP (Rees 1963). Freeman and Medoff reached the same conclusion two decades later (Freeman and Medoff 1984, 57). To provide some perspective, at the 2006 level of GDP ($13.1 trillion), the loss would equal between $26 billion and $53 billion. Allocated equally over the approximately 300 million Americans, that would work out to a loss of between $88 and $176 per person per year.

More recent analyses have pointed out that unions have an impact on efficiency that goes well beyond any misallocation of labor caused by union wage gains. Unions, by improving wages and working conditions, reduce turnover and the costs associated with recruitment and training. Unions also serve as the voice of and protection for workers when complaints are made about working conditions. If management is willing to work constructively with unions and workers, a more satisfied and, consequently, more productive workplace could be the result.[14] Freeman and Medoff and Belman all report empirical evidence supportive of this view (Freeman and Medoff 1984, 165–169, 176–180; Belman 1992). "What have we learned from a decade of quantitative research? *First,* contrary to the fears of neo-classical economists, unions do not of themselves lower productivity. The majority of studies find that unions are associated with higher productivity. Of those which have not found positive effects, there is typically either no effect or a negative effect associated with a poor labor relations climate" (Belman 1992, 70).

Freeman and Medoff also find no empirical support for a negative (or a positive) impact of unions on productivity growth (Freeman and Medoff 1984, 169–71). During the peak of union strength in the 1950s, the economy grew at a very rapid rate in historical terms. Economists have started calling that period the Golden Age. The period of union decline has been associated with slower productivity growth.

There is also no conclusive evidence that unions always hinder technological change (Keefe 1992).

- Of course, if the preceding points are correct, why would employers oppose unions? An obvious reason would be if unions reduce profitability. On that issue the empirical evidence seems solid that unions do reduce profitability, often substantially (Freeman and Medoff 1984, 181–90; Belman 1992).

The answer to the question posed at the beginning of this section—If unions are good for workers, would stronger unions and more widespread unionization be better?—remains open.

"Beneficial to organized workers, almost always; beneficial to the economy, in many ways; but harmful to the bottom line of company balance sheets: this is the paradox of American trade unionism, which underlies some of the ambivalence of our national policies toward the institution" (Freeman and Medoff 1984, 190).

ECONOMIC INEQUALITY AND ECONOMIC GROWTH

What is the relationship between the size of the slices and how rapidly the size of the pie expands? Or, dropping the metaphorical approach, what is the relationship between economic inequality and economic growth?

The mainstream economic view is that some inequality is essential for growth. The onerous working, saving, and investing that has to be done in order for an economy to grow will not be forthcoming without the incentive provided by differential reward. This point of view provides the theoretical basis for the supply-side economics approach to economic policy that has been so influential in recent decades. A key tenet of supply-side economic policy has been reductions in marginal tax rates. These reductions will increase the individual reward to work, saving, and investment and stimulate more of each.

The alternative point of view is that a highly unequal society will face obstacles that will prevent it from growing rapidly. This point of view can be rationalized a couple of ways; by invoking political factors, for example. It may be that there is so much unrest in highly unequal societies that economic growth may be stifled. Even

Figure 7.13 **Income Distribution and Long-Run Growth**

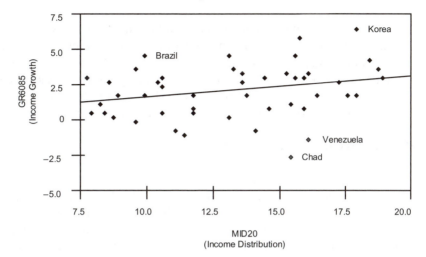

in stable, democratic societies, inequality may be detrimental to growth. If income is distributed log-normally, the society is likely to have a majority of the population with income below the mean. This majority may then use its voting power to impose high taxes on the rich to the detriment of long-run growth (Chang 1994, 6). Another rationalization might emphasize financial imperfections. In a highly unequal society, the poor may be unable to make the sorts of investments in labor skills necessary to raise social productivity.[15]

Obtaining empirical support for either point of view is surprisingly difficult. Roberto Chang constructed a sample of data on income distribution (measured by the share of income earned by the middle 20 percent of its population) and long-run growth rates (the 1960–1985 average annual growth rate of per capita GDP) for 48 countries (Chang 1994). Figure 7.13 shows a scatter diagram with a regression line fitted to the data.

What is easily observable is the mild positive relationship between the degree of equality and the rate of economic growth. Torsten Persson and Guido Tabellini concur with Chang (Persson and Tabellini 1994). The problem is that finding this result multiple times is not definitive evidence of a causal relationship between equality and growth. It may, however, be evidence of a causal relationship between growth and equality. It could be that as a society gets richer, the marginal utility of private goods and services falls and attention is therefore focused on policies leading to greater equality (Friedman 2005). Of course, a third conclusion is also possible. Maybe both growth and equality are the outcome of other factors. Using sophisticated statistical techniques, Lundberg and Squire concluded that there are several factors that can simultaneously increase growth and equality (Lundberg and Squire 2003). For example, expanded education, land distribution policies, and trade openness operate in this manner.

How you view this issue today is more a matter of faith than evidence.

CONCLUSION

This chapter has taken great pains to point out the trade-offs associated with policies to redistribute income. The fact that there are inefficiencies is not in any way conclusive proof that these policies should not be considered. Society may very well be willing to pay an efficiency cost to achieve an equity goal. But society may also find it useful to think creatively about policies to slice the pie more equally. Are there ways to achieve our equity goals while minimizing our efficiency costs?

QUESTIONS FOR REVIEW AND PRACTICE

1. Under U.S. law, employers are required to grant new mothers or fathers 6 weeks of unpaid leave upon the birth of a child. The employee can come back to work with no loss of benefits or position. Who bears the cost of this legislation?
2. Jed is able to earn $8 per hour on the job. Draw his budget constraint assuming 480 possible work hours per month, and Jed receives no other income. Sketch in an indifference curve showing Jed working 160 hours during the month. Congress passes a law establishing a "guaranteed monthly income" of $1,200. Draw Jed's new budget constraint. What is likely to happen to Jed's work hours? (Give your answer in terms of increases or decreases in hours, not an exact number.)
3. What impact would a system of unemployment compensation have on a union's ability to win wage increases for its members?
4. The National Hockey League, with the support of the player's union, requires that players wear helmets while on the ice. Why does the league have to mandate the wearing of helmets for such a dangerous game? Does mandating helmet use increase or decrease the utility of the league's players?

NOTES

1. The cap on earnings is typically increased each year to reflect changes in the cost of living.

2. Of course, not every individual gets back exactly what he or she pays in taxes. That would destroy the rationale for the policy, which is to redistribute income. But the total amount of income taxed will be spent.

3. If the asset is held and not sold, there still is a capital gain, but these "unrealized gains" are not taxable. To a certain extent, capital losses can be used to offset capital gains. The precise rules are complicated, but, fortunately, not essential to our analysis.

4. A *tax expenditure* is a provision in the tax code that confers a benefit on somebody. Any deduction could easily enough be called a tax expenditure. The impact of tax expenditures is equivalent to government spending that benefits someone.

5. Although employers are not required to provide any health insurance.

6. The case for mandated health insurance is not the same thing as saying mandating employer provision is the best way of providing the good. If society thinks workers ought to have health insurance, government could provide health insurance. This could be provided by a system of national health insurance, or workers could be given economic incentive to buy insurance on their own by providing tax credits for insurance premiums, or workers could simply be required to purchase insurance on their own as a prerequisite to holding a job. The best approach is the one with the highest benefit-cost ratio.

7. Under the principle of exclusive representation in the United States, a union represents all members of a bargaining unit whether they are members of the union or not.

8. The origin of the picket line was to prevent the replacement of striking workers.

9. In the United States, closed shop agreements are illegal. However, there can be union shop agreements that permit the employer to hire whomever he pleases, but the worker must eventually agree to join the union. Some states have "right-to-work" laws which outlaw the union shop and replace it with the open shop. Under an open shop, employers can hire whomever they please and the worker is not compelled to join the union.

10. Under election laws in the United States, unions cannot provide direct financial support to particular candidates, but they can provide indirect support (for example, unions cannot make direct financial contributions to candidates, but they can fund "issue-oriented" advertising advocating certain positions) and they can endorse candidates.

11. The 1983 and 2004 statistics are from U.S. Bureau of Labor Statistics (2007c). The data from the mid-1950s was constructed using different definitions of what constituted a labor union and hence is not comparable to the later data, but the point it conveys is essentially correct.

12. There are many excellent biographies of Jimmy Hoffa. Two of the best recent works are by Arthur A. Sloane (1991) and Thaddeus Russell (2001). Hoffa's fabled life has also been the stuff of Hollywood films, such Jack Nicholson and Danny DeVito's *Hoffa* (*Hoffa* 1992) and Sylvester Stallone's *F.I.S.T.* (*F.I.S.T.* 1978).

13. This analysis ignores the potential effect on productivity of union work rules and strikes.

14. Because unions protect workers from management reprisals, there is probably more grousing in a unionized workplace. Paradoxically, more grousing is a good thing (Freeman and Medoff 1984, 136–49).

15. See Chang, page 7. The importance of investments in labor skills is discussed in detail in Chapter 14.

8 How Big a Slice Do We Deserve?

INTRODUCTION

We have seen the factors influencing how the pie was sliced (or at least one version of that story). This chapter asks how the pie *should* be sliced. Several philosophical approaches to this all-important issue are reviewed. The chapter does not conclude with THE ANSWER being revealed; for reasons to be explored, there is no scientifically objective answer. Philosophers have discussed this topic for literally centuries, and they have come up with many valuable insights that should help you to reach your own answer.

How the pie should be sliced is a fundamentally normative question. Recall the distinction between positive and normative economics from Chapter 5. The two statements "Greater immigration of low-skill workers will increase the degree of inequality in the United States" and "We should restrict immigration by low-skill workers" illustrate the divide. The former statement is an example of positive economics. It could (in principle) be proven right or wrong using appropriate evidence and techniques. Positive economics describes how the economy works and is the scientific, objective part of economics. The latter statement is an example of normative economics. It describes a desirable state of affairs or prescribes a specific policy. Normative statements cannot be verified as either right or wrong because their "correctness" depends in part on individual values. Immigration by unskilled workers has a variety of impacts on different groups of people. If we take the positive statement to be correct (and all normative economics relies on positive economics), we can say that immigration harms low-skill American workers, but it is probably beneficial to the low-skill immigrants themselves as well as high-skill Americans. Whether this is a good policy or not depends on how you weigh the benefits to the "winners" versus the costs to the "losers," and this will reflect your personal values. I might think the benefits to immigrants and high-skill Americans exceed the losses to the low-skill Americans, and that would be a fundamentally just outcome. You might think the exact opposite. My view of the situation cannot be proven right or wrong; nor can yours.

With respect to the big issue at hand in this chapter, I might think that I deserve virtually the entire pie, leaving only a few crumbs for you. You might not think much of that opinion. You might think I am being very selfish. In fact, the vast majority of all people might think I am being incredibly selfish. That does not make my opinion

Table 8.1

Total and Marginal Utility from Glasses of Water

Glass	Total Utility	Marginal Utility
1	5	5
2	9	4
3	12	3
4	14	2
5	15	1

wrong, and there is no way to scientifically prove it wrong. Your only hope is to convince enough people I am wrong and make sure I am out-voted.

UTILITARIANISM

The utilitarian school of thought was influential in the seventeenth and eighteenth centuries. Two of the most prominent utilitarians were Jeremy Bentham and John Stuart Mill. You might notice that the word utility fits inside utilitarianism. As economists use the term, *utility* refers to a feeling of happiness, well-being, or satisfaction. The utilitarian philosophy is concerned with happiness, well-being, or satisfaction. In particular, utilitarians believe the well-being of society as a whole depends on the utility of all members of that society. Mathematically, $W = f(U_1, U_2, ..., U_n)$, where W is society's well-being and U_i is the utility of person i. .

The simplest way to describe the utilitarian point of view is by its support of policies that create "the greatest good for the greatest number." Utilitarians are interested in the happiness of society as a whole, and are willing to weigh the happiness of one person against that of another.

An important element of the utilitarian philosophy (although they used different language than we do today) is the law of diminishing marginal utility. Marginal utility is defined as the increase in a person's utility from consuming one more unit of a good. Table 8.1 shows the utility and marginal utility one person receives from consuming water. The second column shows total utility. It is explained this way. The person receives 5 utils (the unit in which utility is measured) of utility from drinking one glass of water. The person will receive 9 utils from drinking two glasses, and so on. The third column shows marginal utility. As defined, it measures the increase in total utility from consuming additional glasses of water. Under the reasonable assumption that the person gets 0 utility from consuming 0 glasses of water, the first glass consumed increases the person's utility by 5. The second glass causes total utility to rise from 5 to 9. Consequently, the marginal utility of the second glass is 4.

Figure 8.1 shows a graph of marginal utility. Notice the negative slope of the graph, which is indicative of the law of diminishing marginal utility. According to the law of diminishing marginal utility, as you consume more of one good, eventually the increases in total utility will get smaller and smaller. In other words, marginal utility will eventually decline. An intuitive explanation seems fairly straightforward. Assume

Figure 8.1 **Graph of Marginal Utility**

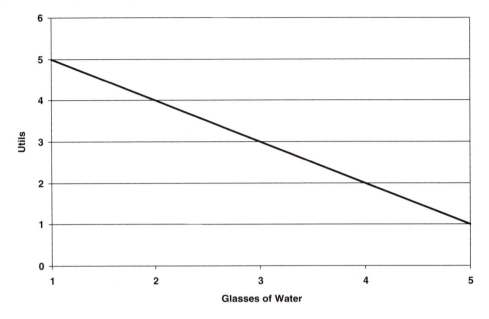

a hot day and you are thirsty. That first glass of water tastes great and is just the thing you need. A second glass right after the first glass might be good, but probably not as satisfying. If you keep drinking glass after glass of water eventually your stomach will be filled and the water will become annoying, not satisfying.

Logic suggests that what is true of water is probably true of most goods and services. The utilitarians thought the law of diminishing marginal utility also applied to income and wealth. Figure 8.2 shows a marginal utility schedule for income. Assume Nerdy Bill (the richest person in the world) had income Y_B. The graph shows that the dollar represented by Y_B provided Nerdy Bill with 10 utils of utility.[1] Let Destitute Delores be the poorest person in the world and have income Y_D. The marginal utility of the dollar represented by Y_D is 1,000.

Now take 1 dollar from Nerdy Bill and gave it to Destitute Delores. Nerdy Bill's income would fall to $Y_B - 1$ and he would lose 10 utils of utility. The money given to Destitute Delores would raise her income to $Y_D + 1$ and her utility would rise by 999 utils. What would happen to the total utility of society? Since Nerdy Bill loses 10 and Destitute Delores gains 999, society's total utility increases by 989. Should we do it? Utilitarians believe in the greatest good for the greatest number, and this policy certainly accomplishes this, so utilitarians would support this redistribution.

Where would it end? Total social utility would be maximized when Nerdy Bill's income was so reduced and Destitute Delores's was so increased that they became equal. In other words, utilitarian philosophy can be used to rationalize redistribution with the goal of achieving greater equality of income and wealth.

Can we level any criticism at this argument? There are two prominent long-standing criticisms, one logical but probably frivolous and the other logical and potentially

Figure 8.2 **The Marginal Utility of Income**

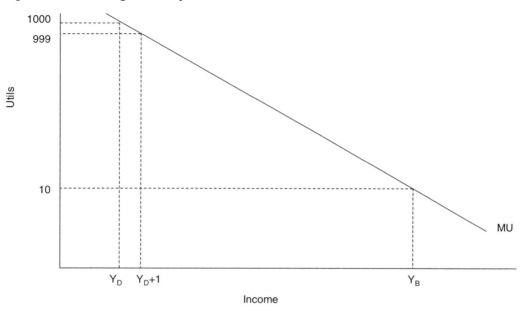

devastating. The first criticism finds fault in our assumption that both Nerdy Bill and Destitute Delores have the same marginal utility of income curve. Maybe Nerdy Bill loves money so much that his marginal utility of income curve lies above the poor person. Maybe Nerdy Bill would feel he lost more utility from losing the Y_B dollar than Destitute Delores received from getting that dollar. Maybe.[2] But it is unlikely.

The second criticism can best be explained using a metaphor.[3] Assume the money taken from Nerdy Bill is placed in a bucket and carried to Destitute Delores. Unfortunately, the bucket has a leak in it and dollars are lost as it is carried. If we take $1,000,000 from Nerdy Bill, maybe only $500,000 reaches Destitute Delores. Is the policy a good idea under those circumstances? Maybe yes, maybe no. It would depend on how much utility Nerdy Bill lost from giving up $1,000,000 and how much utility Destitute Delores gained from getting $500,000. What if $999,999 leaked out so that only $1 reached Destitute Delores? Then Nerdy Bill's lost utility may very well exceed Destitute Delores's gain.

What causes the leak? It is a combination of two things: disincentives and administrative costs. Disincentives result from the impact of the redistribution policy on the behavior of both Nerdy Bill and Destitute Delores. Maybe Nerdy Bill resents being taxed so severely, and thinks that the return to him has been compromised so severely, that the work effort and risks he had been taking are no longer worth it. A rational Nerdy Bill will respond by not working as hard and earning as much money. Destitute Delores also faces a disincentive. If she is simply given money, what is her incentive to work? Either way, the policy may have the effect of reducing the size of the pie.

Administrative costs include the resources devoted to running an agency that collects money from rich people and redistributes it to poor people (i.e., the costs of running the Internal Revenue Service and welfare agencies). Every bureaucrat engaged in this activity is not available to produce other goods and services.

In both cases, an attempt to slice the pie more equally may end up reducing the size of the pie. There is a trade-off between the goals of efficiency and equity.

As statistics to be introduced in Chapter 12 will show, the poor tend to get less education and work and save less than the rest of the population. This behavior is difficult to reconcile with the law of diminishing marginal utility. People with very little to begin with are likely to receive large increments in utility from even small increases in consumption, and studying, working and saving are ultimately avenues to raise consumption. Of course, this behavior can be reconciled with rational behavior by blaming the disincentives built into government transfer programs.

A recent contribution rationalizes this behavior in a different way using some of these concepts (Karelis 2007). This alternative approach holds that for many basic goods and services marginal utility does not diminish for the poor. Rather marginal utility rises. The argument rests on a recategorization of goods and services. The traditional view states that all goods and services either provide pleasure (call them pleasers) or relieve pain (call them relievers), and the provision of pleasure is simply the reciprocal of the relief of pain. Take the case of the drinking water in Figure 8.1. The "normal" case already discussed is that of the reasonably well-hydrated individual who chooses to drink water for pleasure and discovers diminishing marginal utility. Contrast that to the case of the seriously dehydrated individual. This person might be in pain, and the dehydration problem will only be alleviated with several glasses of water. In that case, simply drinking one glass of water would not alleviate much pain. In fact, it may barely be noticed. The person needs to drink several glasses of water before the cells are sufficiently rehydrated.[4] In this case, the marginal utility of the first glass may be very low, but additional glasses add greater and greater increments of utility until the pain has been eliminated. Only then will the law of diminishing marginal utility kick in. For the seriously dehydrated, water may initially be a reliever, but will turn into a pleaser when a certain level of hydration is reached.

Karelis argues many of the poor are so poor that they live lives of misery. Consequently many of the basic goods and services they consume are relievers, not pleasers. Consuming tiny additional amounts of these relievers provides little in the way of utility. If the poor assess that the additional consumption they attain through studying, working, and saving is modest, they may rationally opt out of that lifestyle and remain poor.[5]

A clear policy implication of this approach is that large-scale, "no strings attached" redistribution from rich to poor can be justified on both equity and efficiency grounds. Massive transfers to the poor that alleviate misery will give the poor large increments of utility at a low cost of lost utility to the rich. In addition, the transfers to the poor will actually make studying, working, and saving a rational choice.

LIBERALISM

The philosophy of liberalism is most closely identified with the writings of John Rawls (Rawls 1969). To understand the Rawlsian approach you need to think at a fairly abstract level.

Assume we are part of a group of people that is going to establish a society. Every society needs a set of rules that governs how it works. Some of these rules will be written laws. For example, the laws might spell out what property rights are. Other rules are implicit, such as the understanding that able-bodied people should surrender their seats on the subway to the weak and frail. Nonetheless these rules will be well understood by every member of the society, even if not everyone likes or adheres to every rule all the time. In the language of Rawls, if we lack a set of rules, then we are in the Original Position.

Let us assume that the rules are determined democratically. Every member of the group has an equal say in what the rules would be. What rules will this incipient society establish? Here Rawls sets up another condition: Assume everyone operates "behind the veil of ignorance." This means is that no one knows what their talents are and consequently has no idea whether they will thrive or fail in this new society. That knowledge obviously presents a problem. If you knew what your talents were, then you would obviously favor rules that favor your talents. For example, if you were 7 feet tall and could play basketball, you might favor rules that allow good basketball players to earn huge incomes. But you do not know that, or anything approaching it. What do you do?

According to Rawls, the strategy everyone would favor is known as the *maximin*. This means everyone would favor a set of rules that would provide the maximum benefits to the least among them. In other words, people would favor a set of rules that would provide a generous safety net, preventing everyone from falling too low. People would feel this way because they would not want to take the chance that they would be the least capable person. Remember, no one knows what he or she will become so why take any chances?

In this type of society, no inequality would be tolerated unless it worked to the advantage of the least well-off. Rawls called this the Difference Principle. The clear belief here is that a good society is a highly equal society. The range of allowable policies would seem to be quite limited because they are restricted to those that benefit the person at the bottom. This sort of society would endeavor to establish a generous "safety net" for all.

Obviously we do not redistribute income on the scale Rawls proposes. Why not? The Rawlsian explanation would seem to be related to the Golden Rule—"he who has the gold makes the rules." Real-world societies were put together by dominant individuals who established rules that perpetuated their dominance. This, of course, is unfair. The only fair way to establish rules is to use the method Rawls suggested, and that would lead to everyone trying to protect their own interests.

A criticism of Rawls is his assumption of extreme risk aversion on the part of everyone. Is it really true that everyone is so concerned that they will be the least that they would oppose any rule that created an opportunity for someone to win big?

LIBERTARIANISM

Robert Nozick is the name frequently associated with the philosophical libertarian position (Nozick 1974), although there are many others who have made the libertarian case splendidly. Nozick's position states that society does not create income; people do. People are entitled to the "fruits of their own labor." Consequently, society has no right to redistribute income. People can give away their own income if they choose to, but there is no justification for society coming in and taking it from them. Doing so is simply theft.

An important implication of this is the following. How do we judge an equitable society? According to Nozick, a society is fair if its rules are fair. Everyone having an equal chance to carve out the largest slice of pie possible is the hallmark of a fair society. Everyone ending up with the exact same size slice is not an appropriate goal. Metaphorically speaking, as long as we all start at the same starting line, society is fair. How we finish is our own responsibility.

At first glance, it might seem as if Nozick is taking an extreme conservative position and opposing all efforts at redistribution, but that is not necessarily the case. Nozick could very easily be interpreted to support taxation of people with high incomes and the provision of benefits to people with low incomes to the extent that it created equality of opportunity.

PARETO EFFICIENT INCOME REDISTRIBUTION

Up to this point, the analysis assumes individuals receive utility only from the consumption of goods and services. This equation shows this relationship mathematically: $U_i = f(X_1, X_2, ..., X_n)$. In this case redistribution is bound to reduce the utility of the giver since redistribution must necessarily reduce the amount of one or more X's consumed. The Pareto efficient income redistribution view argues that redistribution could actually raise the utility of society if the giver gets utility from the utility of the recipient. The Pareto mentioned here is Vilfredo Pareto (1848-1923) an Italian economist who made important contributions to the study of economic efficiency. According to Pareto's definition, an efficient outcome is one where no one can be made better off without making someone worse off. Redistribution in the utilitarian framework is automatically inefficient because every act of redistribution helps someone (the recipient) but hurts someone else (the giver). In the Pareto efficient income redistribution scheme some degree of redistribution is efficient because it helps both the recipient and the giver.

Consider this alternative specification of an individual's utility function. Let U_i depend not just on goods and services consumed, but also on the utility of everyone else: $U = f(X_1, X_2, ..., X_n, U_1, U_2, ..., U_m)$. This equation shows that people care about the well-being of others. They are sad when others are suffering and happy when others feel joy. It implies that redistribution may actually raise the utility of the individual giver. While the giver loses the ability to consume X_i, this may be more than offset by the increased utility of the recipients of the charity. This suggests that there may not be a pronounced trade-off between efficiency and equity.

Along similar lines we can make these additional arguments. Even if people do not actually get utility from the well-being of others, redistribution might be a self-interested policy. Any system of redistribution establishes a social safety net. People might view paying taxes as the equivalent of paying the premiums on an insurance policy—in this case an insurance policy against being really poor. Furthermore, the existence of a safety net might increase social stability. If people are protected against being really poor, they might be less likely to try to steal from the rich. If the rich do not have to worry about being attacked, they can live much more enjoyable lives.

Of course, that leads to the following consideration. If people actually benefit by transferring part of their income and/or wealth to others, why does government need to be involved? Part of the explanation may have to do with the public good nature of redistribution.

We can categorize goods on the basis of certain characteristics. One characteristic is rivalry. A good is rival when the amount I consume of it reduces the amount you can consume. A hamburger is a rival good because if I take a bite out of it, that bite is no longer available to you (or if I transfer that bite from my mouth to yours, it loses some of its appeal, but we do not want to go there). The opposite of rival is nonrival. A good is nonrival when the amount I consume does not reduce the amount you consume. National defense is an example of a nonrival good. The amount of national defense I consume does not reduce in any way the amount you can consume. There is not a missile that defends me and a battalion that defends you. Rather we both are protected by the entire system of national defense.

Another characteristic of goods is exclusivity. A good is exclusive if nonpayers can be prevented from consuming the good. A hamburger is also an example of an exclusive good. McDonald's will not give you a hamburger unless you first plunk down your money. The opposite of exclusive is nonexclusive, defined as a good that can be consumed by nonpayers. National defense fits this characteristic. Once a system of national defense is in place, everyone is protected, even if they did not pay anything toward it. There are not little gaps in the sky so that missiles might fall on the nonpayers but not on anyone else.

If a good is both rival and exclusive, it is a private good. A good that is nonrival and nonexclusive is a public good.[6] Private goods can be adequately supplied by the private market. Obtaining an adequate supply of a public good frequently requires government activity for two reasons: First, the nonrival characteristic means that each additional consumer can be supplied at 0 marginal cost. From basic microeconomics, the efficient amount of a good is obtained when price equals marginal cost. But in the case of a public good, a firm could not make any money selling it at marginal cost. Second, because of nonexclusivity, people get to consume the good even if they do not pay. What is their incentive to pay? People actually face the incentive to free ride, to avoid paying but benefiting from the payments of others. This means there is no guarantee that enough money can be raised through voluntary payments to fully fund the activity.[7]

Into the breach steps government. Government can fully fund the good and provide it at a low cost or for free because government has a power that no private firm has, namely, it can compel payment because it has the power to tax (and to put you in jail if you refuse to pay your taxes).

What does all this have to do with redistribution? A case can easily be made that redistribution is a public good. Certainly it is nonrival. The value of redistribution— the warm, fuzzy feeling you get when you know unfortunates are being helped—can be shared by everyone. And redistribution is nonexclusive. You can get that warm, fuzzy feeling even if you did not contribute anything toward it. People do have an incentive to free ride on charity. Consequently, government may have to be brought into the mix to create an adequate level of redistribution.[8]

There are other reasons why government might need to get involved. Maybe you live in Grosse Pointe, Michigan, and have never even seen a poor person except on television. Government can help identify poor people and provide them with aid. Also there might be economies of scale in charity. One big organization might be able to pinpoint funds more precisely then many individuals working on their own.

Commodity Equalitarianism

Commodity equalitarianism is the idea that there are some goods and services that are so important that they should be distributed equally regardless of a person's ability to pay. Of course, what exactly those goods and services are is a matter of pointed debate. In the United States certain aspects of citizenship would seem to fall into this category. Freedom of speech and the right to vote are both distributed equally. But food, shelter, and health care are not. Whether they should be is a question that might usefully be entertained.

Intergenerational Equity

What obligations do generations have to each other?[9] This is a fairly tricky issue because different generations coexist. Assume there are two generations—the older generation and the younger generation. At any point in time, the older generation is likely to be richer than the younger generation. If you believe redistribution is a priority, then transfers from the older to the younger generation are mandated. However, due to economic growth, the total lifetime wealth of the younger generation is likely to be higher than that of the older generation. That suggests transfers in the opposite direction.

These issues will have to be faced front-and-center in the Social Security crises that are plaguing the United States and several other countries.[10]

If you are of the younger generation, you will have the immense pleasure of living through the Social Security crisis. Some brief background about the workings of the Social Security system is in order here.

Social Security provides a monthly money income to individuals who have reached a certain age and are retired.[11] To finance these benefits, the United States has adopted a pay-as-you-go system. This means current workers are taxed (the FICA tax) to provide the benefits for current retirees. Of course, this means the taxes paid by current workers are not invested in an investment fund in that worker's name. When that worker retires, his or her benefits can only be financed by a tax on that time period's workers.

Largely due to demographics and technology, a squeeze is coming. The demographic problem results from the relative size of generations. The baby boom generation has just begun to retire and members of that generation will be living in retirement for roughly the next half century. Since the baby boomers are a much larger generation than those that followed, financing their benefits will place quite a tax burden on the younger generations. The technological problem results from advances in medical technology and the subsequent lengthening of the life span. People will live in retirement for much longer periods of time.

Over two decades ago in anticipation of this, Congress modified the Social Security financing rules. Tax rates were raised on working baby boomers and the funds were deposited in the Social Security trust fund. When the boomers retired, part of the funds for their retirement were to come from this trust fund, which was, of course, their money. But things are a bit more complicated than that. The money in the trust fund was not put in a "lock box." Rather, it was lent to the government to help finance general spending. Therefore, when the government begins to draw on the trust fund, that money will come in the form of repayment of the previous loans, and the money for that will either come from increases in tax revenue or decreases in government spending. Either way, future generations will have to bear a disproportionate burden of financing the retirement of the baby boomers.

Is any of this fair? Baby boomers certainly have a legitimate claim. They paid their taxes while they were working to pay for the retirement of their parents and grandparents. In fact, they paid relatively more to help build up the balance in the trust fund. When their time comes, do they not have a right to expect the working generation to live up to the implicit promise that the baby boomers lived up to? Since the baby boomers brought into the world, raised, and put up with the antics of their children—the younger generation—does this not mean the younger generation owes something in return? Also, since the younger generation is likely to be richer than the older generation, is it not simple justice that they share some of their wealth?

On the other hand, the current working generation is being asked to fund the retirement of an existing generation that is far more wealthy than they are and is likely to live in retirement for many more years than any previous generation in human history. Television ads showing retirees riding motorcycles does not help the situation. The current working generation probably has less to look forward to when it retires. Planned increases in the retirement age means this group will have to work longer and be retired for a shorter period of time. Benefit cuts may be in the offing.

The resolution of this problem awaits a skillful and brave politician. It is not for nothing that Social Security has been called "the third-rail of American politics." Touch it and you die.

Equality of Opportunity versus Equality of Results

Two terms that are frequently batted about in discussions of how the pie is sliced are equality of opportunity and equality of result. And, at least in the American context, equality of opportunity is generally accorded a great deal of respect while equality of result is disrespected.

Most people believe they know the difference between the two terms. Using metaphor again, view life as a race with the order in which you cross the finish line determining the size of the slice of pie you receive. Equality of opportunity then means everyone starts from the same starting line at the same time and are on their own from that point forward, assuming no dirty tricks are played on anyone while they are running. Equality of result means the race is rigged so that we all reach the finish line at the same time and end up with the same size slice.

The reason equality of opportunity is given so much respect has to do with its association with personal responsibility (Roemer 1995). Americans, in particular, believe people have a natural right to individual freedom, but with rights come responsibilities. The right to freedom comes with the responsibility to use that freedom responsibly. People who fail to behave responsibly ought to suffer the consequences. If society invests the resources to place everyone at the same starting line, then everyone has the responsibility to make the best of that opportunity. Once the starter's gun is fired, how well you do depends on your own personal skill, ingenuity, and fortitude. You have no one to blame but yourself.

By way of contrast, why would we ever want to ensure that everyone crosses the finish line at the same time? If individual freedom is an illusion, then people cannot make choices. And if people cannot make choices, how can they be held responsible for the conditions they find themselves in? The only moral response would be to offset differences in outcome. The large slices of pie for the winners are as unjustified as the small slices for the losers.

Therefore it largely comes down to the degree of personal autonomy you believe people possess. If you judge the degree of personal autonomy to be great, a belief in equality of results would be inconsistent. Equality of result essentially excuses people from the consequences of their own bad behavior, which is both morally wrong and economically disastrous.

However, the ambiguities associated with the meaning of the term *equality of opportunity* are often not appreciated. As described earlier, it means everyone starts from the same starting line at the same time. As a frequent (albeit slow) participant in local road races (everything from 4 miles to 10K), I know something about starting lines. I have never seen a starting line wide enough to accommodate all the participants. Some people start on the line, but most of us start way back. My position is usually the midway point. Half the runners start ahead of me and half start behind. I have been in races where it literally has taken me from 30 seconds to a minute just to reach the starting line.[12] Generally, the faster, more competitive runners stake out their position right on the line, although it is often not a struggle for them to do so because us slow folks simply accept our status and voluntarily migrate to the back. In a very important sense, I do not have equality of opportunity in these races. But even if I could start on the line, my chances of winning are nonexistent. I am too old, my legs are too short, the muscles in my legs are too weak, and I might be carrying too many pounds to be really competitive. Would not equality of opportunity mean that I ought to have a half-mile or three-minute head start on the fast runners? Or maybe I should be given a motorcycle.

In the 2008 Los Angeles Marathon, women runners were given a twenty-minute head start on the men hoping to make the finish especially exciting. As it turned out, the top woman, Tatiana Aryasova, finished in 2:29:09, which meant she crossed the finish line well ahead of the top male, Laban Moiben, who finished in 2:13:50. Although no claim was made that Tatiana had actually "won" the race, she did receive extra television coverage as the first to "break the tape," and a casual observer could easily have been fooled.

The point is this. A common view is that equality of opportunity means that government has to provide equal resources to everyone—equal access to schooling, equal access to skill training, an equal shot at getting hired in any particular job, and so on. But another plausible point of view is that government is actually obligated to give unequal amounts of resources to people. Weaker participants ought to be given extra amounts of resources to compensate them for their weaknesses. How is that fair? They could not compete otherwise. When you consider that people are born with different genetic endowments and are raised in different types of households in different types of neighborhoods in different parts of the country at different times in our country's history, the scope of compensatory government action is potentially enormous just to achieve equality of opportunity.

It is often thought that equality of opportunity is a conservative position because it contemplates limited government involvement in the economy, while equality of results is more liberal in its requirement for large-scale government involvement. This is not necessarily the case.

CONCLUSION

How big a slice do we deserve? Where you stand on this issue probably has little or nothing to do with the fundamental logic of the philosophies surveyed. Rather, it would appear to be related more to where one comes down on a centuries-old, probably irresolvable issue of how responsible are we for our own fate in life? Can we do anything we have the imagination or energy to achieve, or are some of us so irredeemably handicapped by the burdens placed on us by our "identities,"—our class, gender, race, ethnicity, nationality, sexual orientation, weight, height, looks and so on—that our place in the pecking order is largely preordained? If you are a fan of the former view, then you are likely to be attracted to more libertarian philosophies that make equality of opportunity a leading value, but do not shed tears for those who subsequently falter along the way. They had their shot, but failed to make the most of it, and have no one to blame but themselves. If you are a fan of the latter view, then simple justice demands wholesale redistribution and eternal vigilance against any new inequalities that might crop up. High achievers are lucky and low achievers have everybody to blame except themselves.

QUESTIONS FOR REVIEW AND PRACTICE

1. Presumably as the economy grows over time, it becomes easier for everyone to have their "basic needs" met. Does the utilitarian argument lose its force in an economy where everyone's basic needs are met?
2. Tax policy raises $X from the rich to redistribute to the poor, but there is a leak in the bucket. How big a leak do you think should be tolerated in the effort to redistribute income?

3. What are the basic preconditions for equality of opportunity to prevail?
4. Rank the philosophies discussed—utilitarianism, liberalism, libertarianism, Pareto efficient income redistribution, and commodity egalitarianism—in terms of their commitment to equality of opportunity and equality of results. Explain your ranking in both cases.

NOTES

1. If you are uncomfortable using symbols, let us use a numerical example. Assume the richest person's income is $1,000,000 (a week? a day?). The point a refers to the 1,000,000th dollar (the dollar right after $999,999). The 1,000,000th dollar provides 10 utils of utility. The 999,999th dollar provides a bit more utility, although the exact amount is hard to read from the graph.

2. Any connection between Nerdy Bill and Bill Gates is purely coincidental. By all accounts Bill Gates is an extremely generous man. He has already given $25 billion to the Bill and Melinda Gates Foundation.

3. The metaphor was first used by Arthur Okun (Okun 1975).

4. Actually reviving a seriously dehydrated person is a bit more complicated than that, but we need not get bogged down in the biological details.

5. Karelis would also add avoiding alcohol and drug abuse and staying out of trouble with the law to this list (Karelis 2007).

6. There are other combinations such as rival and nonexclusive or nonrival and exclusive, but discussion of that is not needed here.

7. Actually, any number of public goods experiments have established that not everyone free rides (Andreoni 1995). Nonetheless, enough do so that funding public goods exclusively by voluntary contributions would be problematic.

8. Whether we do in fact redistribute enough remains an open question. The point is that we would not redistribute nearly as much as we do without government involvement.

9. Define a generation as a group of people born at about the same time.

10. Unfortunately, many countries, including the United States, are trying to avoid facing these issues.

11. For more detail, see Harvey S. Rosen and Ted Gayer (2008, 228–255).

12. And the clock is ticking all the time. A new innovation in road races is the wearing of a computer chip on your running shoe. Since these chips do not start keeping time until you cross over the starting line, they are likely to be a boon to the times of slower runners.

Part II

Discrimination

9 Does the Slice We Receive Depend on Our Race, Gender, Ethnicity, or Other "Irrelevant" Personal Characteristics?

INTRODUCTION

In the United States, average wages (and many other indicators of economic success) differ by education, job market experience, hours worked, the possession of special skills, and English-speaking ability. They also differ by race, ethnicity, gender, weight, beauty, religion, skin tone within a race, national origin, national origin within a race, and sexual orientation. Many, not all, would consider the former differences legitimate because these characteristics are thought to be related to productivity and are costly to acquire. Most would not consider the latter differences legitimate because there is no direct connection between any of them and ability to do a job, and many of these characteristics are things you are born with and cannot change. These later differences are often attributed to discrimination.

This chapter provides an introduction to the economic analysis of discrimination. After defining some key terms, four important mainstream economic models of discrimination are reviewed. The key implications of these models are often misunderstood by economists and laymen alike.

DEFINING TERMS

There are three terms we need to focus on—prejudice, segregation, and discrimination. *Prejudice* is a dislike of, distaste for, or misperception of some person, place, or thing. If person A prefers B to C, then A can be said to be prejudiced against C.[1] What substitutes in place of B and C? One possibility is that B is apple juice and C is grape juice. In that case, A's prejudice against grape juice might express itself in terms of not being willing to pay the same price for grape juice as apple juice. This form of prejudice is typically viewed as benign even though A's tastes are ultimately harmful to grape juice producers. Another possibility, more germane to this chapter, is that B represents the members of a particular race, ethnic group, nationality, gender, or other unit; and C represents the members of another group. For example, B might be whites and C Hispanics. A's prejudice might be expressed in terms of unwillingness to pay C the same wage as B despite C being as productive as B, or A might be less willing to hire or promote or more eager to lay off C than B. This form of prejudice is thought of as socially undesirable. Here A's tastes would seem to be harmful to C's interests. Interestingly enough, in this case A's tastes may even be viewed as harmful to A since A may end up overlooking some C's who are highly productive.

Segregation is the separation of people, places, or things based on their characteristics. If a firm only hires B workers for the front office and C workers for the factory, then the workforce of the firm is segregated. If Bs only live in one neighborhood while Cs only live in another, then there are segregated neighborhoods.

What is *discrimination*? Following Gary Becker (Becker 1971) economists have tended to define discrimination as a situation in which people who are "the same" are treated differently. In the context of the labor market, discrimination exists when workers who are equally productive receive different rewards, such as wages, fringe benefits, promotion opportunities, and protection against layoff, among other things. In the context of financial markets, discrimination exists when families with the same income and wealth have differential access to financial market instruments, such as mortgages and other types of loans. In the context of schooling, discrimination exists when students who have the same academic ability and are similarly well-behaved receive different services from the schools, such as access to advanced classes, and receive different punishments for transgressions of the rules.

One thing this definition implies is that differences between people and/or groups are not themselves evidence of discrimination. While "all men are created equal,"[2] it seems preposterous to believe that all "men" really are equal. Human beings differ in terms of skills, tastes regarding labor versus leisure, tastes regarding consumption versus saving, and tolerance of risk, among other things. Consequently, even in the fairest society imaginable, they are likely to differ in measures of economic success (at least before taxes and transfers). What is true for individuals is likely true for groups of individuals clustered in any arbitrary way, for example by race, ethnicity, gender, weight, beauty, religion, skin color within a race, national origin, national origin within a race, and sexual orientation, among other things.

A complication here is that this definition of discrimination does not always apply to how the term is used in everyday speech, or even by some economists. "It is hard to see that discrimination can have any meaning other than a 'taste' of others that one does not share" (Friedman 1962, 110). Here the word is used in the same way I used prejudice above. As we will see in the upcoming sections, it makes sense to distinguish between prejudice and discrimination because prejudice does not always lead to discrimination and discrimination can occur without prejudice.

The Becker definition recognizes that we need to keep track of the various spheres of life in which people operate and recognize that how people are treated in one sphere spills over to the other spheres. People can be treated "fairly" in one sphere yet not be successful simply because they were victims of discrimination in other spheres. Labor market discrimination exists when individuals who have the same productivity receive unequal rewards. But the absence of labor market discrimination does not mean everyone is given an equal chance of success in the labor market. If people have been discriminated against in the acquisition of human capital, they cannot enter the labor market with the same productivity. And if people have been discriminated against with respect to access to homes in "good neighborhoods," they might not be able to acquire the same human capital, even if there is no substantial discrimination in that sphere.

The locus of discrimination is vitally important from the standpoint of policy. For example, if discrimination takes place in the acquisition of human capital, but not the labor market, workers from different groups will end up earning different wages. Imposing draconian measures on employers requiring group quotas in hiring is likely to be both inefficient and inequitable, but imposing similar draconian measures on schools may ultimately bear more fruit. Just as in the medical profession, where doctors are taught to treat the disease and not the symptom, antidiscrimination policy is unlikely to be successful unless it treats discrimination where it arises and not just where it manifests itself.

The legal definition of discrimination in the United States is not fully consistent with the Becker view. There are two standards. One standard is called "disparate treatment." Under disparate treatment, "any economic agent who applies different rules to people in protected groups is practicing discrimination" (Yinger 1998, 25). The second discriminatory standard in our law is "disparate impact." This refers to practices that appear to be neutral, but have the effect of imposing disadvantage on one group more than on others. Because society feels that rules based on race, ethnic or national origin, gender, or other characteristics are particularly troublesome, the thrust of the law is to minimize their usage as much as possible. The only defense employers have is "business necessity," a requirement that is very difficult to meet. Employers are pushed to use "rules of thumb" that do not make use of membership in particular groups.

Models of Discrimination

Economic theory can be used to analyze discrimination. In many contexts, to analyze something means to explain why it exists and what its effects are. Most economic approaches (such as those here) do the latter but ignore the former. Most economic approaches start with the existence of discrimination, but do not attempt to explain why people have "a taste for discrimination." This omission is not made because this is unimportant. Rather it is outside the area of expertise of economists. Economists are still waiting for our brother and sister social scientists in other disciplines to complete this task satisfactorily.

In fact, in the context of the discipline of economics, there is nothing unusual about this. In most economic theory, tastes are treated as a given.[3] In the standard theory of the consumer, we might begin by assuming people prefer pizza to pierogi, but do not attempt to explain why.

To say economic theory can be used to analyze discrimination is a bit misleading in the sense that it could be construed to mean there is a single, unified theory of discrimination. This is not true. Rather, there are several approaches. At certain points these approaches complement each other. At other points they conflict. Each approach yields useful insights and is worth studying.

That an economic theory of discrimination even exists comes as a surprise to many people. Discrimination is often viewed as a vile and irrational practice that defies analysis. But in reality, discrimination is a result of choices we make, all choices have benefits and costs, and there is no discipline better suited to analyzing choices and the benefits and costs than economics.

That we could possibly learn anything from such an analysis comes as an even bigger surprise. To many the problem is as simple as it is troublesome and can be neatly summarized in three statements:

1. All differences in economic outcomes based on race, ethnicity, gender, and so on are the result of discrimination.
2. All discrimination benefits the perpetrator and all similar individuals, and hurts the victim and all similar individuals.
3. Any differential treatment that is correlated with race, ethnicity, gender, and so on should be immediately banned.

What could economics possibly add to this?

As we will see, using economic theory is valuable because it shows that both the problem and the solutions are not nearly that simple.

THE PERSONAL PREJUDICE MODEL

The economists most closely associated with the development of the personal prejudice model of discrimination are Nobel laureates Gary Becker (1971) and Kenneth Arrow (Arrow 1972). The model assumes people have a "taste for discrimination" against certain groups. Of course, since different people can be expected to have different tastes, the degree of animosity toward various groups will differ from person to person. The theory then makes use of the standard mainstream setup, namely, rational utility-maximizing individuals and competitive, profit-maximizing firms. The model then analyzes four types of discrimination: employer, employee, customer, and government discrimination.

The Employer Discrimination Model

Assume two groups of workers in the labor market: the Violets (V) and the Teals (T). V and T are equally productive. This means the value of the marginal product schedule for both is identical ($VMP_V = VMP_T = VMP$). Employers have a taste for discrimination against T.[4]

How will profit-maximizing employers act? Following the theory of the demand for labor, V will be hired as long as its VMP exceeds its wage rate. Short-run equilibrium will be achieved when $VMP = W_V$, where W_i is the wage of group i.

What about T? The employers' taste for discrimination can be represented by a discrimination coefficient (d). The discrimination coefficient can be thought of as a measure of the disutility to employers from associating with T. From the standpoint of hiring, employers compare the productivity of T workers with their wage rate, but their taste for discrimination causes them to devalue the productivity of T workers. Symbolically, employers will hire T until $VMP - d = W_T$. This means employers act as if T were less productive than V, and hire fewer T than V at the same wage.

This relationship can be rearranged to $VMP = W_T + d$, and interpreted as employers believing Ts are more expensive. Not only do employers have to pay T workers

Figure 9.1   **The Cost of Employer Discrimination**

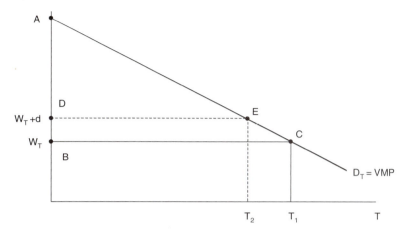

money wages of W_T, but they are also forced to endure the disutility that comes with association. Therefore it feels as if T workers are more expensive.

Since VMP is the same for both groups of workers, it follows that in short-run equilibrium $W_V = W_T + d$. The wage of V exceeds T by the discrimination coefficient d. In this equilibrium there is *discrimination* as economists use the term because two groups of workers who are identical in terms of productivity receive unequal rewards.

Assume that the employer produces output using the inputs labor and entrepreneurship. Figure 9.1 shows the demand curve for T (D_T = VMP). If the employer is not prejudiced (has a discrimination coefficient of 0), then the employer will take W_T as the wage rate, hire T_1 worker Ts, and earn profits of ABC.[5] A prejudiced employer with discrimination coefficient d would treat the cost of hiring T as $W_T + d$. That would lead to T_2 worker Ts hired and, more importantly, profits of ADE, which are obviously less than ABC.

The message here is clear. Employers with a taste for discrimination will pay a price in terms of lost profits. The intuition behind this conclusion is simple. Prejudiced employers will, because of their taste for discrimination, fail to hire workers whose productivity exceeds what they have to be paid. The obvious consequence is lost profits.

This counterintuitive conclusion is interesting in its own right. It also shows the value of theories of discrimination. Conventional wisdom appears to be that someone who is able to discriminate benefits from doing so while their victim loses. The latter is the case here, but the former is not.

The employer model can be used to analyze other aspects of discrimination. We showed that in short-run equilibrium W_V would exceed W_T. What determines the size of the wage gap? Figure 9.2 shows the market for T, but unlike Figure 9.1 the vertical axis measures the ratio of the wage of T to V. At 1.0, the wages of V and T are equal to each other.

The demand curve D shows how many T will be demanded at each wage ratio. Note the horizontal segment. This means there are some employers who will hire T even if

Figure 9.2 **The Wage Gap Between V and T**

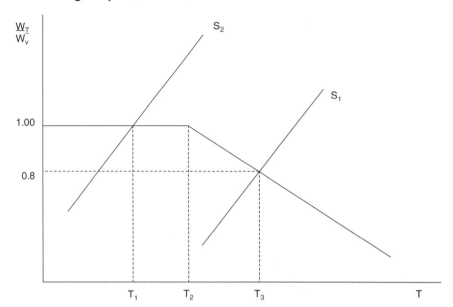

their wage is equal to that of V. These are the nonprejudiced employers (with $d = 0$). However, beyond T_2 workers the curve slopes downward. This means the only way additional T will be hired is if their wage is less than that of V. This is because any additional employers will come from the ranks of $d > 0$. Because they are prejudiced, they will not hire T unless they can pay a lower wage. As more prejudiced employers enter the mix, the wage ratio must decrease.

Let S_1 be the supply curve of T workers. It crosses the D curve at wage ratio 0.80. This means that in order for T_3 workers to be hired, the wage ratio must fall to 0.80. If it were any higher than that, T_3 workers would not be hired because not enough employers could stand to do it at a higher wage ratio.

From this graph we can see that the wage ratio between T and V is not a fixed number. Rather it depends on a number of market factors. One factor is the relative supply of T. If there were few Ts (supply curve of S_2), there would not be a wage gap because this many workers could be accommodated by nonprejudiced employers. Another factor (not shown on the graph) is the number of nonprejudiced employers. If the number of nonprejudiced employers were larger, there would be a longer horizontal segment to the demand schedule. The intersection with the supply curve would be at a higher wage ratio. A third factor is the degree of prejudice. If there were still prejudiced employers, but each was less prejudiced (had lower values for d), the negatively sloped portion of the curve would be flatter, again leading to a higher wage ratio.

Another interesting implication of the model is that workforces are likely to be segregated in the sense that employers will have either all V or all T workforces, not mixtures of both. The reason is fairly simple. In equilibrium the wage paid to V workers will exceed the wage paid to T workers by d. Employers whose discrimination coefficient exceeds d would not hire T workers because they are viewed as too expensive. Their workforces then would consist entirely of V. Employers whose discrimination coefficient was less than d would hire only T workers because they would be viewed as relatively cheap.

Now consider what happens in the long run. The firms that hire T workers will be more profitable than firms that hire Vs because Ts are just as productive, but are paid a lower wage. These firms will be able to expand, increasing the demand for T workers. In addition, nonprejudiced employers can enter the industry and earn higher profits by using Ts, further increasing the demand for Ts. Along with the increased demand for Ts will come a decreased demand for Vs. In long-run equilibrium, the wages of Ts and Vs will become equal. There likely will still be prejudiced employers in business, but since the workforces will be almost completely segregated, their prejudice no longer works to the detriment of Ts. The bottom line is that there may not be discrimination even though prejudice still flourishes.

The preceding paragraph is one of the most misunderstood aspects of the employer discrimination model. Does it imply discrimination already died out a long time ago? Not necessarily, if the market environment was not adequately competitive. More importantly, the prediction is only in regard to employer discrimination. Other types of discrimination analyzed below could still work to restrict Ts relative to Vs even if employers had clean hands.

The Employee Discrimination Model

Employees can have tastes for discrimination. Let all the assumptions from the previous model hold except that employers are not prejudiced. Now assume V workers do not like T workers. That means V workers will not work with T workers unless they receive compensation in the form of a higher wage. Employers, who are not the bad guys in this scenario, are faced with the following choices. They can hire all Vs and pay them a wage equal to the value of their marginal product. They can hire all Ts and pay them a wage equal to the value of their marginal product. Since Vs and Ts have the same productivity, the wage bill will be the same in either case. The third option is that they can hire both Vs and Ts. In this case, they have to pay Ts the value of their marginal product, but Vs will have to be compensated at a higher rate because of their distaste for Ts. This means Vs are being paid more than the value of their marginal product, which would reduce the employer's profit. The third option then does not make any economic sense and will not be chosen. The end result is segregated workforces, but both types of workers will be paid the value of their marginal product. The bottom line here is that while there is prejudice, there will not be discrimination.

The Customer Discrimination Model

For this third model, assume neither employers nor employees have a prejudiced bone in their bodies, but customers do.[6] This means customers prefer being served by Vs rather than Ts. Probably the easiest way to think about this is to imagine the situation of the waitstaff at a restaurant. Prejudice means that customers prefer V waitpersons to T waitpersons. The disutility of interacting with a T during a transaction raises the real cost of the transaction to the customer. If the price of the good or service is P, then the cost to a prejudiced customer is P + d.

Proprietors of establishments then have a problem. If they hire Ts to wait on customers, their sales will fall. From an economic standpoint, it will only make sense to hire Ts if Ts can be hired at a lower wage, if Ts are more productive, or if Ts are hired only in jobs that do not require interaction with customers.

The Government Discrimination Model

The fourth type of discrimination is on the part of government. Here government does not give T citizens the same access to government services that V citizens have. The clearest example of this is the *de jure* segregated school systems in the South. These systems were outlawed by the famous *Brown v Board of Education* (United States Supreme Court 1954) U.S. Supreme Court decision in 1954. However it was not until several years later that these systems were actually eliminated. Policies this noxious are a thing of the past. A more contemporary example is a 1999 settlement reached between a group of African-American farmers and the U.S. Department of Agriculture (Firestone 1999). The farmers claimed they had been discriminated against in the receipt of loans and subsidies, and the agriculture department, although not admitting to having discriminated, agreed to make restitution and change its practices.

One of the implications of government discrimination is that our assumption that V and T are equally productive is likely to be untenable because government is a key provider of labor market skills.

STATISTICAL DISCRIMINATION

The statistical discrimination model raises a number of vexing issues, most notably about whether premeditation is necessary for discrimination to be said to exist. The elements of statistical discrimination can best be explained using a made up but fairly concrete example.

Assume a nonprejudiced employer is trying to fill a job. There is no way to determine the productivity of each applicant, but the employer knows the distribution of productivities of the applicants. Not knowing individual productivity beforehand seems a relatively innocuous assumption. Assume the job is that of office manager. To be a good office manager requires a whole variety of "people skills" that are likely to be difficult to detect from a resume or even a face-to-face interview. Knowing the distribution of productivities is a less innocuous assumption, but may be squared with reality if the employer relies on past experience with employees in that job category.

In Figure 9.3 let the rectangle labeled T represent the distribution of productivities of applicants for the job (ignore the box labeled V for the time being). Productivity is uniformly distributed and runs from 10 to 40 with a mean value of 25.

What wage should the employer offer? If the employer knew each worker's productivity, the employer would simply offer a wage equal to the worker's productiv-

Figure 9.3   **Distribution of Productivities of Applicants for Office Manager's Job**

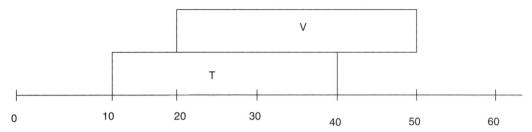

ity. To offer less would lead to the worker refusing the job. To offer more would be to "overpay" the worker. If individual productivity is unknown, however, the best strategy is to pay a wage equal to the expected value of an applicant's productivity. This wage will minimize the likelihood of having offers rejected due to an inadequate wage and of overpaying due to an overly generous wage. Here a wage offer of 25 would make the most sense.

Let the employer get applications from both Ts and Vs. Now work with both rectangles in Figure 9.3. Rectangle V shows the distribution of productivities of V applicants. V productivities are distributed uniformly and run from 20 to 50 with a mean value of 35. Rectangle T shows the distribution of productivities of T applicants. T productivities are distributed uniformly and run from 10 to 40 with a mean of 25. On average, Vs are more productive than Ts, but there are plenty of Ts who are more productive than Vs.

What if a test existed to predict the productivity of applicants, but it was an imperfect test? Assume the test is correct half the time and completely useless the other half of the time. In that case the best strategy for the employer would be to use a weighted average of the test score and the expected value of a group's productivity to determine a wage offer. In this case, the weights would be 0.5 on the test score and 0.5 on the group's average productivity since the test is correct only half the time. For example, if a T applicant scored 20 on the test, the best wage offer would be $0.5(20) + 0.5(25) = 22.5$. A V applicant with the same score would be offered $0.5(20) + 0.5(35) = 27.5$. The end result is that two workers with the exact same test score will receive very different wage offers.

This example is the essence of statistical discrimination. People are being judged not just on their own merits, but also on the basis of typical characteristics of the group to which they belong. If the employer acts this way, has discrimination occurred? In one very important sense it certainly has. The employer treats two applicants with the exact same test score differently. In another sense, things are not that clear-cut. The employer certainly has no intention to discriminate, and is just making a hardheaded business decision that will be the correct one more often than not.

Going one step further, the statistical discrimination model cannot be used to rationalize beliefs that are contrary to fact. If employers believe Vs come from a group that is more productive on average than Ts, then it makes sense to select Vs. What if employers are wrong about this? What if employers, blinded by racism, sexism, or some other kind of -ism, consider Ts to be less productive on average than Vs even when that is not the case? If they are wrong about relative group productivity then

Figure 9.4 **he Crowding Hypothesis**

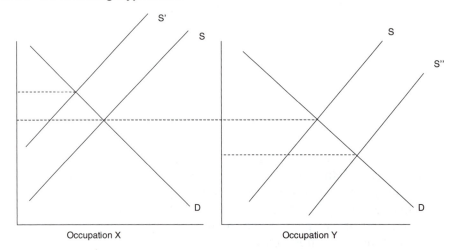

they will make many bad choices and suffer the consequences. In the long run they must adjust their thinking to get it approximately right. Any remaining differences between groups will then have to reflect true differences in productivity.

The Crowding Hypothesis

The crowding hypothesis is frequently called upon to rationalize occupational segregation and wage differentials. Its major use has been in the analysis of gender differentials (Bergmann 1971), but there is no reason why it has to be exclusively confined to that issue.

Figure 9.4 shows the labor market for two occupations, X and Y. The labor force consists of V and T, and both are equally productive in both occupations. As a benchmark, assume the demand curve is D and the supply curve is S in both occupations, leading to the same wage for both, and that V and T are found in both occupations. Also assume that no one is discriminating against anyone. Now assume employers in occupation X develop a distaste for a certain type of worker, say the hapless Ts. If these employers then refuse to hire Ts, the following will happen: Ts already in the industry will lose their jobs. This will reduce supply in occupation X to S'. The now jobless Ts will move to occupation Y in search of a job. This increases the supply of labor to S''. The impact on wages in both markets is obvious. Wages rise in occupation X and fall in Y. The end result is a wage differential between equally productive workers, an outcome economists call discrimination.

Self-Confirming Expectations

The fourth model can be thought of as part of the statistical discrimination family of models, but it incorporates several interesting extensions (Coate and Loury 1993a; Loury 1992). Assume two types of workers, V and T, and two types of jobs, skilled

Table 9.1

Probability of Outcome for Each Type of Worker

Outcome	Untrained	Trained
Worker can do skilled job	0	.4
Ambiguous result	.4	.6
Worker cannot do skilled job	.6	0

and unskilled. To do the skilled job, a worker must have been trained. Any worker can do the unskilled job. To make the analysis a bit less abstract, assume a set of numerical values to represent various outcomes.[7] A trained worker in a skilled job produces 20. An untrained worker in a skilled job will produce 0. Any worker, trained or untrained, will produce 10 in an unskilled job.

Employers are unable to determine whether a worker has obtained the training necessary to do the skilled job, but can administer a test that attempts to determine that information. The test has three possible outcomes. It can either establish that the worker can or cannot do the skilled job, or it can yield an ambiguous result. Let Table 9.1 show the probability of each outcome for trained and untrained workers. The table can be read this way: There is no chance an untrained worker can do well enough on the test to convince the employer that he or she could do the skilled job. Sixty percent of the time the untrained worker will perform so poorly that it will be obvious he or she cannot do the skilled job. Forty percent of the time the untrained worker's test score will put him or her in the ambiguous zone. For trained workers, there is no chance they will do so poorly the employer will be convinced that they cannot do the skilled job, but there is only a 40 percent chance he or she will do well enough to erase all doubt. Sixty percent of the time, the test result will be ambiguous.

How do employers deal with the ambiguous cases? Classify an employer as an optimist if the employer believes that a worker who scores in the ambiguous zone has actually received training. The employer is liberal toward a group if the employer assigns ambiguous scorers to the skilled job. An employer is a pessimist if the employer believes that ambiguous scorers have not received training. The employer is conservative toward a group if ambiguous scorers are assigned to the unskilled job. Employers tend to be liberal toward groups they are optimistic about and conservative towards groups they are pessimistic about (Loury 1992, 24). Assume employers are optimists about Vs and pessimists about Ts. Why do employers feel this way? It could be prejudice or it could be an inference based on previous experience. Regardless, the employer will be liberal toward Vs if they present an ambiguous score and conservative toward Ts who have the very same score—a result few would deny constitutes discrimination.

How do workers respond to this? Workers have to decide whether to obtain training or not. Training costs 5, and workers will obtain training only if it is good investment.

Look at the problem from the standpoint of V workers. If untrained, they would get the lowest score on the test 60 percent of the time and get an ambiguous score 40 percent of the time. In other words, 60 percent of the time they would be assigned to the unskilled job and get a wage of 10 and 40 percent of the time they would be assigned to the skilled job and get a wage of 20. As untrained workers, their expected wage $[E(w_V)]$ would be $E(w_V) = 0.60*(10) + 0.40*(20) = 14$. As trained workers, every single V would score high enough to be assigned to the skilled job and earn a wage of 20. Therefore $E(w_V)$ for skilled Vs would be 20. A V would incur a cost of training of 5, but that would raise the expected wage by 6. Every V would consider training to be a good investment and every V would be trained. The expectation that employers had would in fact be true.

The problem looks very different from the standpoint of Ts. Untrained Ts would always be assigned to the unskilled job since they would never score at the top on the test and, consequently, would receive a wage of 10. Would obtaining training be worthwhile? Since employers are pessimistic about Ts, a T would be assigned to the skilled job only if he or she scored at the top, and the probability of that is only 40 percent. Consequently, the expected wage of a T $[E(w_T)]$ is $0.4*(20) + 0.6*(10) = 14$. Obtaining training will only raise the expected wage of a T from 10 to 14, which, with training costs of 5, is not a good investment. It would not make sense for any T to obtain training, thus confirming the expectation that employers originally had.

What policies would be appropriate in this instance? Policies to subsidize the training of Ts may work. If training costs could be lowered below 4, then Ts would find it worthwhile to become trained.

Another policy is to vigorously enforce antidiscrimination laws so employers treat Vs and Ts with ambiguous test scores exactly the same. The practical problems associated with enforcing this policy might be enormous. To prove a discrimination case in court, each and every litigant would have to be able to establish the qualifications of every job applicant and the decision made by the employer with regard to every applicant (Coate and Loury 1993b, 95).

A third alternative is affirmative action. In the context of this model, think of affirmative action as a policy requiring employers to achieve a certain proportional representation of Ts in skilled jobs.[8] For example, if Vs were 90 percent of the labor force and Ts were 10 percent, then an affirmative action program might require that 90 percent of the skilled workers be Vs and 10 percent be Ts. Of course, immediately mandating that skilled jobs employ Ts in the same exact proportion as their representation in the population is only an easily grasped example. If Ts are significantly less trained than Vs, such a goal might not be realistic and a lower goal might be substituted. As we will see, using a lower goal does not necessarily confine Ts to "second-class" status forever. Achieving the lower goal in the short term might be achievable while attaining the higher goal is impossible. Attainment of the short-term goal might then serve as a springboard for attaining a subsequent higher goal.

A semantic game still being played in the United States is whether setting goals in terms of proportional representation actually constitutes a quota—where a quota is thought to be a bad thing. Let us say the government sets X percent as the goal for T representation in skilled jobs. X percent is a quota if the employer is required to achieve that level of representation—or else. There can be no excuse for not achieving X percent representation. X percent is a goal if an employer's failure to achieve it can be excused when the employer can prove "good faith" efforts on its behalf.

Initially, since more Vs than Ts are obtaining training, Vs are being disproportionately assigned to the skilled job. To meet the affirmative action goal, the employer can either assign more Ts to the skilled job or fewer Vs. Either way, the employer's profits will fall. If more Ts are assigned to the skilled job, then workers who are unskilled are being allowed to perform the skilled job. Unskilled workers have a productivity of 0 in the skilled job, but will be paid 20. If fewer Vs are assigned to the skilled job, then workers who are skilled are not permitted to perform the skilled job. Workers who have a productivity of 20 in the skilled job are assigned to a job in which their productivity is 10. Which course the employer chooses depends on what will reduce profits the least.

To simplify greatly, the course the employer will follow will be the one that minimizes the number of unprofitable assignments, and this will depend on the relative number of Vs and Ts in the labor force. If Ts are scarce, then the employer is likely to increase the assignments of Ts to skilled jobs. If Vs are scarce then the employer is likely to reduce the assignments of Vs to skilled jobs.

Consider the case where Ts are scarce, Ts are Y percent of the labor force, and the initial goal is X percent, where X percent < Y percent. Employers will want to increase the representation of Ts in skilled jobs, but this goal may be rather simply achieved just by becoming liberal toward Ts. The long-run implication of this is likely to be positive. As employers become liberal toward Ts, the Ts find their incentive to invest in training has increased. As more Ts become trained, the goal can be increased upward until in long-run equilibrium Ts are as trained as Vs and affirmative action can wither away.

If Ts are scarce, but the goal is set unrealistically high, then problems are created. If employers cannot achieve the goal from among Ts who score in the ambiguous zone, then they will also have to assign to the skilled job some Ts who fail the test. Assigning Ts who fail to the skilled job is called patronizing behavior on the part of employers (Loury 1992, 27). The degree of patronization is the proportion of Ts with failing scores assigned to skilled jobs.

Patronization will enable achievement of the goal in the short run, but is likely to have undesirable long-run features. The degree of patronization affects the incentive Ts have to invest. Since patronization increases the probability that an untrained T can get a skilled job, it reduces the incentive to invest in training on the part of all Ts. Why invest in training when you can get a skilled job anyway? As Ts cut back on training, employers must increase the degree of patronization and a vicious cycle occurs.

The affirmative action program does eliminate discrimination, but at a cost. Ts end up less productive. In addition, since Vs still have to get training while Ts do not, V resentment against Ts may increase.

CONCLUSION

Although four models of discrimination were presented in this chapter, the models essentially represent two distinct and contrasting approaches to the analysis of the problem. One approach, exemplified by the personal prejudice and crowding hypothesis models, looks at discrimination as a "taste-based" phenomenon. The behavior of the dominant group is largely driven by bigotry (Harford 2008, 136). While reprehensible, the bigots do not emerge unscathed. "In other words, taste-based discrimination is not only miserable for the victims, it is expensive for the bigots" (Harford 2008, 137).

The second approach, exemplified by the statistical discrimination and self-confirming expectations models, looks at discrimination as a rational phenomenon. The dominant group's treatment of the victim group is simply a consequence of profit-maximizing behavior. Malice need not be intended in order for it to occur. This makes solutions harder to achieve since the dominant group is less likely to perceive its actions as something that ought to change, and because change will always be damaging to the dominant group.

Theories of discrimination are explanations for why discrimination exists and what impact it has, and suggest, at least in a very general way, policies to combat it. They are not proof of anything. Chapter 10 investigates how economists have attempted to document and measure the extent of discrimination in contemporary society.

QUESTIONS FOR REVIEW AND PRACTICE

1. On the basis of the personal prejudice model of employer discrimination, would discrimination be more widespread in competitive or monopolistic industries? Explain.
2. Is statistical discrimination "worse" than personal prejudice? Investigate this question in all its ramifications.
3. Is the discrimination in the crowding hypothesis model rational or irrational? Explain your answer.
4. How are the predictions of the self-confirming expectations model influenced by differences in productivity, the accuracy of the test, and training costs?
5. Jason is a member of group J, who are less productive on average than group M, Mario's group. The average productivity of group J is 15, while the average productivity of group M is 30. Jason and Mario take a skills test that is accurate 25 percent of the time and receive identical scores of 25.
   a. If the firm is a profit maximizer, what wage offer will Jason receive?
   b. If the firm is a profit maximizer, what wage offer will Mario receive?
   c. Would the firm offer Jason a wage of $25 if this test was accurate 75 percent of the time?
   d. Explain why J workers have less incentive to obtain costly training than M workers.
   e. Imagine the government imposes an affirmative action policy upon all firms requiring them to employ an equal percentage of J and M workers. What effect does this have on the incentive to obtain training for J workers? And for M workers?

NOTES

1. Of course, there is a flip side here that is sometimes overlooked. A's prejudice against C can also be viewed as a prejudice in favor of B. For an analysis of the flip side, see Peggy McIntosh (1988).

2. In this context, consider the word *men* to mean all humans—men and women. The use of the word *men* in this way is archaic, but that is the way it was once used.

3. An important relevant exception to that will be discussed in Chapter 15.

4. What employers are is immaterial. They are probably V, but they could easily be Mauves and Chartreuses. It is unlikely they are T.

5. Actually area ABC is a quasi rent, but since it goes to entrepreneurship, we could just as well call it profit.

6. We will ignore the complication that all employers and employees must also be customers at least some of the time.

7. The parameters used in this particular example come from Kevin Lang (2007, 277–80).

8. Actual affirmative action is a bit more complicated than this. See the discussion in Chapter 11.

10 Detecting and Measuring Discrimination

INTRODUCTION

As indicated in Chapter 9, wages (and many other indicators of economic success) differ by education, job market experience, hours worked, the possession of special skills, and English-speaking ability because each of these factors influences a worker's productivity. Wages also differ by race, ethnicity, gender, weight, beauty, religion, skin tone within a race, national origin, national origin within a race, and sexual orientation. The former differences are often viewed as "legitimate," while the latter differences are inherently suspect. If wages differ on the basis of race, ethnicity, and other "irrelevant" personal characteristics among workers with the same productivity, we label the difference discrimination. This suggests a strategy for detecting and measuring the extent of discrimination: select workers of equal productivity who differ by race, ethnicity, and so on, and measure what differences in wages (and other indicators of economic success) remain.

This is easier said than done. This chapter investigates the controversies arising over how to interpret the voluminous empirical record on the detection and measurement of the extent of discrimination. There are three main empirical strategies economists and others use, and each has flaws. As a consequence, after a half century of sophisticated empirical studies some economists would seem to believe that discrimination is almost extinct, while others continue to believe it runs rampant. Can this gap be bridged? If only numbers could tell a simple story, but they cannot.

The three main empirical strategies are:

- Regression studies
- Audit studies
- Laboratory experiments

The following sections will discuss these strategies, the controversies over what the results mean, and the significance of these results for public policy. Reading this chapter will not turn you into an empirical economist—you will need several heavy-duty quantitative analysis courses for that—but it will make you a skeptic, which is a healthy attitude to have toward empirical work.

Figure 10.1 **Regression Analysis**

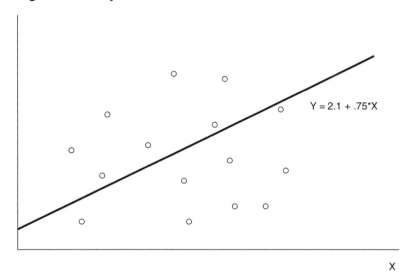

REGRESSION STUDIES

DOING A REGRESSION STUDY

A regression equation shows the quantitative relationship between a dependent variable and one or more independent variables. Assume economic theory posits that there is a causal relationship between variable X and variable Y. Changes in variable X are thought to "cause" changes in variable Y. For example, X could be the price of some product and Y could be quantity demanded. Or, X could be disposable income and Y could be consumption spending. Or, X could be a person's years of schooling and Y could be the person's wage rate. Assume further that the relationship can be described by the linear equation Y = a + bX. In this equation X is the independent variable, Y is the dependent variable (because its value depends on the value of X), and a and b are coefficients. If the equation was graphed with values of X measured along the horizontal axis and values of Y measured along the vertical axis, it would graph as a straight line. Coefficient a would be the vertical intercept of the line. Coefficient b would be the slope of the line. Essentially the goal of regression analysis is to "estimate" numerical values for a and b.

The estimated coefficients can be used for three purposes. One purpose is hypothesis testing. What if we thought there was a negative relationship between price and quantity demanded? That would imply that in a regression of quantity demanded on price, the coefficient b should be a negative number. A second purpose is forecasting. The estimated equation can be used to forecast future values of Y. The third purpose is policy analysis. The estimated equation can be used to predict the impact on Y of different values of X.

To estimate the coefficients of a regression equation, obtain a sample of data on X and Y. Figure 10.1 is a scatter plot of the values of X and their associated values of

Y. In regression, the goal is to find the line that best "fits" the scatter of data. The best fitting line goes through the middle of the data coming as close to each point as possible.[1] Assume that the equation of the best fitting line is $Y = 2.1 + .75*X$. The value 2.1 is an estimate of coefficient a. The value .75 is an estimate of the coefficient b.

The interpretation of the line is this: the intercept term shows the value of Y if X = 0. The interpretation of intercept terms is usually not important in regression analyses. Of more importance is the slope term. The value 0.75 says that if X rises by one unit, Y will rise by 0.75 units. It establishes (subject to what is contained in the next two paragraphs) that there is a positive relationship between X and Y.

One more issue that needs to be touched on is statistical significance. Because you typically have access to only a sample of data, there is no presumption that the values of the coefficients are their "true" values. Rather, they are estimates of their true values, and, because they are estimates, you could conceivably get a positive (or negative value) for a coefficient even if its true value is 0. Statistical significance refers to whether on the basis of the estimate you can conclude the "true" value of the coefficient is not equal to zero. Is the coefficient positive (or negative) enough not to be the result of chance? To make a very long story short, there is a simple test of statistical significance known as the t test. Frequently coefficients will be displayed with a t statistic attached. The rule of thumb is that if the t score exceeds 2.0 in absolute value, the coefficient is statistically significant. If not, then you have not established a relationship between X and Y.[2]

Sometimes, instead of a t statistic, an economist will display the standard error of the coefficient. The standard error is an estimate of how far the estimated coefficient is likely to be from its true value. In those cases, if you divide the coefficient by its standard error you will get the t statistic.

The equation $Y = a + bX$ is a simple regression equation because there is only one independent variable. What if you believed that Y was influenced by more than one variable? For example, in the case of quantity demanded, every student learns in Principles of Economics that quantity demanded is influenced by a number of variables in addition to price, including income, prices of substitutes, prices of complements, and so on. A relationship like this can be estimated using a multiple regression equation. A multiple regression equation has two or more independent variables. For example $Y = a + b_1X_1 + b_2X_2 + \ldots + b_nX_n$ is a multiple regression equation where Y depends on $X_1, X_2, \ldots, X_n$.

Conceptually, a multiple regression equation is estimated just as a simple regression equation is done. Of course, it is a bit more complicated because it involves fitting a hyperplane to an n-dimensional space, but those are details better left to a computer. The interpretation of a multiple regression equation is the following: Each coefficient shows the impact of a one-unit change in its independent variable on Y, assuming all the other variables are held constant. For example, if the model is a demand curve and Y is quantity demanded, X_1 is price, X_2 is income, and X_3 is the price of a substitute, the coefficient b_1 shows the impact of a \$1 increase in price on quantity demanded assuming income and the price of substitutes are held constant. T statistics and standard errors can also be computed and used with a multiple regression equation.

How do we use regression analysis to analyze discrimination? To illustrate, take the example of a wage equation based on human capital theory (to be discussed in more detail in Chapter 14). Human capital is the productive skills a person has acquired through education, training, or by some other means. *Ceteris paribus,* people with more human capital are more productive, and will be paid a higher wage. Consequently, a wage equation based on human capital theory would have wage as the dependent variable and many of the independent variables would be measures of human capital such as education and job market experience. Of course, there is a variety of other factors that also influence wages. The structure of the industry in which the person works may be a factor. Geographic factors may be important, such as the region of the country in which the person resides or whether they work in the city or country. Whether the person is married or not may also play a role. And, personal character-istics such as race, gender, ethnicity, and so on may influence wages.

Assume, for the sake of simplicity, that the only human capital element is years of schooling, and that industry structure, geographic factors, and marital status are unimportant. If discrimination was not an issue, then our wage equation could be written as $w = a + bS$, where w = wage and S = years of schooling.

Of course, discrimination *is* an issue. The existence and extent of discrimination is what we are trying to measure. Ignore all forms of discrimination except discrimi-nation on the basis of gender. To measure discrimination on the basis of gender in a regression equation we could add a dummy variable. A dummy usually takes on the value of 0 or 1 based on whether the person is male or female.[3] Assume females are assigned the value 1. Then the regression equation can be written this way: $Y = a + bS_1 + cG$, where G is the dummy variable for gender.

Obtaining data on the wages, schooling, and gender of a sample of individuals will enable us to estimate the regression equation. If there is discrimination against females, then the coefficient on G should be a negative number and statistically significant. The interpretation is that if you had a male and a female with the same level of schooling, the female would have a lower wage, with the coefficient on G measuring the extent of discrimination. The coefficient on G represents an "unexplained" residual. It is what is left over after we control for schooling.

Refer to Figure 10.2. If the person is a male, the term $c*G$ drops out of the equation (because $G = 0$), and the line $w = a + b*S$ shows the relationship between S and w for males. If the person is a female, the term $c*G$ stays in the equation (because $G = 1$), and the line $w = a + b*S + c$ shows the relationship between S and w for females. What you can see graphically is that for any level of S, males will receive a higher wage than females, which is what would happen if there was discrimination on the basis of gender in the labor market. The dummy variable in use here is called an intercept dummy because it shifts the intercept of the equation (from a to $a + c$).

There are other ways to use dummy variables to measure discrimination. Maybe you believe that discrimination against women lowers the return to education for them. Including a slope dummy will measure that. Write the wage equation this way: $w = a + b*S + c*(S*G)$. Here $S*G$ is called an *interaction term*. If there is discrimination, the coefficient c should return as a negative number. The impact of this can best be seen graphically in Figure 10.2. If the individual is a male, the equation graphs as $w = a + b*S$. If the person is a female, the equation graphs as $w = a + b*S + c*S$ or $w = a + (b+c)*S$.

Figure 10.2 **Regression Analysis Using the Residual Method**

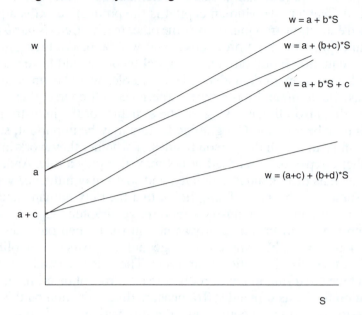

If there is discrimination against females, the slope of the equation will be flatter for females, and, at every level of S, female wages will be lower than male wages.

Finally, we can add both intercept and slope dummy variables. In the equation $w = a + b*S + c*G + d*(S*G)$ discrimination against females should cause c and d to be negative. Referring to Figure 10.2, if the person is male the equation graphs as $w = a + b*S$. If the person is female, the equation graphs as $w = (a+c) + (b+d)*S$. Females have an equation in which the intercept is shifted down and the slope is flatter, and females with the same level of S as males will receive a lower wage.

This is not the only way to detect and measure discrimination, just the most intuitively obvious. A popular alternative is to use the Blinder-Oaxacca decomposition (Blinder 1973; Oaxacca 1973). Although it is not especially complicated, discussion of this technique is beyond the scope of this chapter.

WHAT HAVE WE LEARNED FROM REGRESSION STUDIES?

Economists have done hundreds (if not more) regression studies of discrimination. An accessible example of the technique in action is James E. Long and Albert N. Link's study of the wages of mature men (aged 45–59) (Long and Link 1983). The question that led them to do the study in the first place was not racial discrimination, but rather the impact of the structure of the product market in which a firm operated (how concentrated the industry was and whether it was government regulated) on the wages of its employees. To do a proper job, they had to specify their model correctly, and this yielded an estimate of discrimination against nonwhite men.

The data consisted of 1514 observations of individual men. For each man, they had data on his human capital (represented by EDUC = years of education, TRAIN = participation in a training program, and EXP and EXP^2 for years of experience[4]), market structure of the industry he worked in (represented by C = concentration ratio in the industry, REG = a regulated firm, and LGFIRM = whether the worker is employed in a large firm or not), whether the worker was a member of a union or not (U = member of union), his marital status (represented by MSP = married, spouse present), and his geographic location (represented by dummy variables for SOUTH and WEST). The race of the worker was captured by a dummy variable (WHITE = 1 if white and 0 if nonwhite). The dependent variable was not the wage rate, but rather the natural log of the wage rate [represented by ln(w)]. This is important because mathematically it means the coefficients of the independent variables measure the percentage change in wage resulting from a one-unit change in the independent variable.

Table 10.1 shows the estimated equation. T statistics are in parentheses beneath each coefficient. Every coefficient had the expected sign, and nearly every coefficient was statistically significant at either the 0.01 or 0.05 level (roughly speaking, this means the chances of being wrong are 1 percent and 5 percent, respectively). Key results include a positive coefficient on C indicating wages are about 0.4 percent higher for every additional point of concentration in an industry, and a negative coefficient on REG indicating that if the industry is regulated wages are about 2 percent lower. Each additional year of education added about 4 percent to the wage, each additional month in a training program added 0.2 percent to the wage, being married with spouse present added 9 percent to the wage, and living in the South reduced wages about 15 percent. The coefficient on WHITE of 0.15275 can be interpreted as saying that *ceteris paribus,* white workers earn slightly over 15 percent more than nonwhite workers. The R^2 statistic measures what percentage of the variation in the data was captured by the equation. An R^2 of 0.4250 is good for the type of data they used.

To summarize, the authors of the study controlled for a wide variety of factors that influence an individual's wage. They found if you selected two individuals who had the same human capital, worked in the same type of industry, had the same union membership status, lived in the same part of the country, and had the same marital status, but who differed by race, the white individual would earn 15 percent more. A simplistic interpretation of these results is that there is significant discrimination against nonwhites, at least among mature men. However, we must be careful about simplistic interpretations.

Using Long and Link as an example of how these studies are done, how can we summarize what we have learned from the voluminous regression study record? (Please note that most of the studies referenced identify discrimination using a more complex procedure than the dummy variable method described earlier. In all cases, though, they hold constant "legitimate" differences, and identify discrimination as the residual.) A summary yields three key points:

We Discriminate Against Each Other in Many Different Ways

In addition to racial discrimination, clever economists using regression analysis have detected and measured several other types of discrimination, some types that quickly

Table 10.1

Racial Discrimination in a Sample of Mature Men

ln(w) =	4.57168	+	.00445C	−	.00012EXP²	−	.00005(U*C)	−	.09119MSP	+	.01804REG	+	.00436U
	(50.50)*		(3.06)**		(−1.78)		(−2.41)*		(2.92)**		(−.60)		(3.39)*
+	.33277LGFIRM	+	.01216EXP										
	(2.36)*		(4.72)*										
+	.04275EDUC	+	.00202TRAIN	−	.14971SOUTH				.14187WEST				
	(14.72)*		(3.50)**		(−6.89)**				(5.25)**				
+	.15275WHITE												
	(6.90)**												
	R² = .4250												

Source: Long and Link (1983), copyright Cornell University.

*Significant at the 0.05 level in a two-tailed test.

**Significant at the 0.01 level in a two-tailed test.

leap to mind and others that do not. Some examples of the other types of discrimination identified include the following:

Gender discrimination. Green and Ferber estimated a wage equation for the faculty at a large, research-oriented university (Green and Ferber 1984). The equation controlled for various aspects of professor productivity, including highest degree obtained, experience, publications of various types, and grants received.[5] It also controlled for the gender of the faculty member. They concluded that after controlling for productivity, male faculty members earned $1647.36 more than female faculty members.

In professional horse racing, horses can be ridden by either male or female jockeys. This makes it one of the few major professional sports where males and females compete directly against each other (auto racing is another). (Male horses competing against female horses is another matter.) Total winnings of female jockeys are considerably less than those of male jockeys. To win money, jockeys must get mounts, and female jockeys have many fewer mounts than males. What Ray and Grimes found was that among jockeys with the same performance and experience, female jockeys secured significantly fewer mounts, leading them to conclude that female earnings were restricted by discrimination (Ray and Grimes 1993).

Ethnic Discrimination. Darity, Dietrich, and Guilkey estimated an equation explaining an individual's Duncan Socioeconomic Index score (a measure of occupational status) as a function of various productive and personal characteristics, including human capital, marital status, residence, whether the person was born in the United States or not, and how assimilated they were to U.S. society (Darity Jr., Dietrich, and Guilkey 1997). They then looked for "unexplained" differences in socioeconomic index score among several race and ethnic groups in the United States. Holding productive and personal characteristics constant, they found lower socioeconomic index scores for Mexicans, Native Americans, blacks, and Americans (persons born in the United States who had parents born in the United States and were white); and higher socioeconomic index scores for Chinese, Japanese, English, Germans, Irish, Italians, Norwegians, Polish, Russians, and Scots. Interestingly enough, taking the long view by estimating their equation at different points along a time span of more than a century, they found that while discrimination coefficients declined for every group, they declined at different rates for different groups. For some groups, such as Mexicans, Native Americans, and blacks, the decline has been modest. For other groups, the declines have been dramatic. In fact several groups have gone from discrimination working against them to discrimination working in their favor.

Discrimination on the basis of ethnicity is not just a feature of the American landscape. Pendakur and Pendakur found that in Canada, aboriginals and visible minorities suffer from a significant wage disadvantage (Pendakur and Pendakur 1998).

Skin Tone Discrimination. Keith and Herring sampled a group of people who would all be identified as members of the black community (Keith and Herring 1991). As part of the data-gathering process, the interviewers made a judgment as to the skin tone—very dark, dark brown, medium brown, light brown, and very light—of each member of the sample. They found that people with darker skin tones did less well with respect to educational attainment, occupation, personal income, and family income after holding family background, gender, residence, age, marital status, education (where relevant), and occupation (where relevant) constant.

This type of discrimination does not just affect blacks. Among persons of Mexican descent, people with darker skin tones were again at a disadvantage (Mason 2001).

Sexual Orientation. Badgett has found that being gay, lesbian, or bisexual (GLB) results in a wage disadvantage, but the differential is only statistically significant in the case of males (Badgett 1995).

Beauty. It is quite common for people to complain that others receive various "goodies" in life because of their looks. Is there anything to this econometrically? The first issue to be addressed is whether there is a common standard of beauty. If "beauty is in the eye of the beholder," then we are wasting our time trying to study the issue scientifically. Interestingly enough, it turns out that within a culture there is a surprising degree of agreement about what constitutes beauty (Hamermesh and Biddle 1994). One of the ways we know this is because groups of people have been asked to rank individuals on the basis of their beauty, and there is a high correlation in the rankings. Consequently, we can proceed with the study.

Hamermesh and Biddle collected data on a sample of people using interviews. In addition to the standard productive and personal characteristics, their interviewers scored the looks of every subject on a scale of 1 to 5. They found that, holding productive and other personal characteristics constant, above-average-looking people tended to earn about 5 percent more and below-average-looking people tended to earn about 5 percent less than average-looking people.

Weight. Averett and Korenman found that obesity affects earnings. Using a person's body mass index (BMI),[6] they found that, *ceteris paribus,* obese women suffered a wage penalty of 15 percent and obese men suffered a wage penalty that exceeded 20 percent (Averett and Korenman 1996). Underweight men also suffered a penalty, but not underweight women.

Religion. Chiswick has concluded that after controlling for human capital, region, and ethnicity, Jews earned relatively more than non-Jews (Chiswick 1983).

The Extent of Discrimination Varies From Study to Study

A frustrating truth is that a finding from one study is difficult to replicate in another study. In one example, Jarrell and Stanley reviewed 49 studies of gender discrimination, and found that while the average gender wage gap equaled 29 percent, the range ran from −5 percent to +77 percent (Jarrell and Stanley 2004). In other words, there were results that could be cited by those that believe gender discrimination is pretty much a relic of the past and those who think it still continues to run rampant.

In another example, Shackett and Trapani studied racial discrimination among men using a richer data set than Long and Link had, and found that almost none of the race terms were statistically significant (Shackett and Trapani 1987).

This is not uncommon in science (and here I include positive economics as a scientific endeavor), and it may be a more severe problem in economics and other social sciences, which deal with people, than in the physical sciences, which deal with molecules, plants, animals, and planets. The findings of every empirical study are sensitive to data, model, and methodology. A finding of discrimination in one data set using one model (for example, the human capital model) and one particular methodology (for example, a specific estimating technique) may not be repeated if the data, model, methodology, or any combination of those three change. (The minimum wage issue discussed earlier is another example of this.) What is the conscientious economist to do? Presumably economists should take into account the preponderance of results, the quality of particular studies, maybe the reputation of the economist doing the study, and the "smell test" (does that result really make sense?). How to weigh these factors is unclear. The lesson here is to beware of people who render strong policy prescriptions using as evidence only one or a small number of studies.

Be Skeptical of the Technique

The previous section argued that you should be reluctant to fully embrace the results of any single regression study because the next study's conclusion may be exactly the opposite. This section argues that economists have become more reluctant to accept the results of any regression study, so many things have to go right for a regression study to be useful.

For one thing, regression studies are highly sensitive to a problem known as specification bias. One important dimension of specification bias is what variables are included in or omitted from the equation. Regression equations should include all factors that influence an individual's productivity. Anything missing could invalidate your results. Referring back to Table 10.1, the Long and Link model contained an impressive number of independent variables, but it would be easy to think of factors that have been left out of the equation. For example, they have included years of schooling but not any indication of the quality of school attended, how well the individual did, and what type of academic program the individual followed. They measured experience by years since graduation from school, but different occupations offer different types of training opportunities, and what about individuals who spent significant amounts of time outside the labor force? We could go on and on with shortcomings of this model. The point is this: Does the coefficient on WHITE just measure discrimination or does it also reflect factors influencing productivity that are correlated with race, but are left out of the equation? It should be recognized these potential problems are not mistakes by Long and Link, but rather shortcomings of the available data.

Green and Ferber's study of discrimination against female faculty can be subjected to a similar criticism. While they hold constant the possession of a PhD, there is no variable representing a faculty member's field. If men disproportionately take PhDs in fields where there are lucrative outside opportunities (such as accounting, engineering, and computer science) and women disproportionately take PhDs in fields where outside opportunities are more limited (education, art, and languages), that would explain at least part of the residual.

Note also there is no variable included reflecting family issues, but family issues would seem to be problematic with respect to gender. Waldfogel found that in several countries around the world, the female/male earnings gap was larger for married men and women than for singletons (Waldfogel 1998). Marriage would seem to place women at a distinct disadvantage in the labor market. This likely reflects the greater responsibilities women have traditionally had toward child care and housekeeping. Is anyone surprised by this? If workers develop a significant amount of the skills they need to be successful while on the job, women who frequently leave the labor force for child-care reasons are bound to be at a disadvantage. Henrekson and Dreber argue the significantly lower share of Swedish women in intermediate or higher executive positions compared to women in the United States (11.2 percent versus 23.6 percent) can be associated with Sweden's much more generous family leave policy (Henrekson and Dreber 2007). In Sweden, a parent can take 420 days of leave at 80 percent of their pay.[7] In the United States, a parent can take 12 weeks of unpaid leave. A Swedish woman with two children could conceivably have spent approximately two and a half years out of the labor force during probably the most crucial period of skill development. It is not surprising that this has implications for the ability to reach the top.

In addition, since women bear most of the child-care responsibilities in our society, having children reduces the flexibility women might have regarding their jobs. Jobs with long hours, variable shifts, and extensive travel are frequently not considered even though they may have high earning potential.

Is motherhood a burden? In one sense it is, but how many mothers consider it more a burden than a blessing? Is housework a burden? Almost certainly. Should men do more housework? Maybe, but how do we get that done? Maybe women should be ready to accept dirtier houses.

Part of the gender dummy variable might reflect characteristics of males that lead to higher earnings. In 2006 men made up about 54 percent of the labor force, but accounted for a little more than 92 percent of job-related deaths (United States Department of Labor, Bureau of Labor Statistics 2007a). This suggests that men disproportionately hold dangerous jobs (or are more careless). But dangerous jobs are frequently well-paid. Does the lack of women in these jobs represent exclusion or choice?

With respect to the ethnicity results, what is being captured by the residual is not obvious. Pure employer discrimination is a candidate. But there are other factors that could be correlated with both productivity and ethnicity. One factor might be language skills. To be successful at higher-paying jobs in the American labor market requires some facility with English. Poor verbal skills or a heavy accent may act as a barrier. Also there could be cultural differences regarding work, saving, and investment that influences labor market outcomes.[8]

What do the sexual orientation results really mean? A simplistic interpretation would be that GLB are victims of discrimination. However, unlike race, gender, and ethnicity, GLB status is not easily observable. How can discrimination occur if individuals cannot easily be classified? Is it possible the GLB status is a proxy for other aspects of productivity? If so, what aspects of productivity?

Are the beauty results the end result of pure discrimination? Many less-than-beautiful people probably think so. Is it possible that beautiful people are in fact more productive? It is easy to imagine they might be in certain circumstances. Certainly beautiful actors and actresses sell more movie tickets. A beautiful receptionist might put clients more at ease. There is some evidence that beautiful people perform better in school, even after you remove the possibility that their instructor could have been influenced by their looks in awarding the grade.[9] Another possibility is that beauty is simply a proxy for other types of abilities. Most people are not just born beautiful. They have to work at it. They have to exercise, eat right, and take the time to learn about and apply all sorts of beauty aids. Maybe the dedication required for this regimen spills over into other types of activities.

What are we to make of the religion finding? Does U.S. society discriminate in favor of Jews? If we simplistically interpret the residual, then we might reach that conclusion, but this does not square very well with even a cursory reading of history. While animosity toward Jews was never as virulent in the United States as in the rest of the world (witness pogroms in Russia and the Holocaust), it existed fairly close to the surface.[10] Yet it does not appear to have placed Jews as a group at a significant disadvantage. Are there elements of the Jewish religion and culture that increase productivity?

Other important dimensions of specification bias, such as the functional form of the equation (for example, linear versus nonlinear) and the form of the equation's error term (ask your econometrics instructor) will not be discussed here.

This has been a long and probably pretty confusing section. The message would appear to be that regression studies cannot be viewed as conclusive. It is impossible to find a data set rich enough to allow us to hold constant all possible sources of productivity differences. As a result, other techniques are receiving more attention.

Audit studies

There have been a number of quite interesting research projects that have actually used human subjects and a bit of deception to obtain results. The studies frequently use fake resumes or actors to see how employers will react.

In one study, the research team created resumes and submitted them in response to ads for sales, administrative support, clerical, and customer service jobs (Bertrand and Mullainathan 2004). Some resumes depicted high-skill individuals. Others represented low-skill individuals. The resumes were then randomly assigned "white" and "African-American" names.

What constitutes a white or African-American name? The researchers looked at birth records and found names that were disproportionately selected by mothers of the different races. Among the "white" names were Allison, Anne, Carrie, Emily, Jill, Laurie, Kristen, Meredith, Sarah, Brad, Brendan, Geoffrey, Greg, Brett, Jay, Matthew, Neil, and Todd. The "African-American" names used were Aisha, Ebony,

Keisha, Kenya, Lakisha, Latonya, Tamika, Tanisha, Darnell, Hakim, Jamal, Jermaine, Kareem, Leroy, Rasheed, Tremayne, and Tyrone. To see whether public perception of the names was consistent with the statistics, a random sample of individuals was asked whether they thought these names were identifiable with one or the other race. Interestingly enough, while from a statistical standpoint, Maurice and Jerome are African-American names, the public does not perceive them that way so these names were not used.

What was found was that after holding skills constant, resumes with "white" names got 50 percent more callbacks, even from employers who advertised themselves as equal opportunity employers.

This might at first appear to be compelling evidence of discrimination, but things may not be what they seem. It is not really clear whether the names are picking up race/ethnicity factors or something else. What if the white names included such monikers as Joe Bob or Cletus?[11] Would employers have been as eager to employ them as they were Brendan and Todd? Maybe what employers were reacting to was not race/ethnicity differences, but rather class differences. Perhaps employers believe that workers from the lower classes are less capable. The African-American names are certainly not all that common among middle-class African-Americans.

Of course, getting a callback does not guarantee that an individual will get the job. In another study, trained actors were sent out to interview for jobs (Fix and Struyk 1993). A white and black actor were paired and given a similar fake resume. The fifteen pairs interviewed for 583 jobs. In most cases, neither person was offered the job. In 10 percent of the cases, both actors were offered the job. In 72 cases only the white actor was offered the job. In 35 cases only the black actor was offered the job.

These results, while also fairly compelling, have also been criticized. One problem is that it is difficult to find people who are exactly the same. The actors may be carrying very similar resumes, but their behavior during the interview may be decisive (Heckman 1998). Another problem is that the actors might be so gung-ho that they act in ways that lead to the result they want to prove.

Audit studies do not always rely on fake resumes or applicants. Goldin and Rouse conducted a study of gender discrimination with respect to orchestras (Goldin and Rouse 2000). In the past, orchestras auditioned musicians in a nonblind manner. This meant the judges could see the musicians who were playing. During the late 1960s, many orchestras began to adopt blind auditions. Musicians would play behind a screen so the judges could not see them. Generally speaking, women tended to fare better in blind auditions.

Another interesting issue, but only tangentially relevant to the preceding material, is why do black parents give their children distinctively "black" names if it will work to their detriment in the labor market? Levitt and Fryer argue that it is not the name itself that is harmful (Fryer and Levitt 2004; Levitt and Dubner 2005). Rather it is who bestows the name. The distinctively black names tend to be favored by parents (typically the mother because the father is often absent) who come from "lower-class" backgrounds. Employers are not responding to the name or the race, but rather the baggage the people from lower-class backgrounds may carry with them.

LABORATORY EXPERIMENTS

Laboratory experiments have not been a major tool in economic research, but their use is becoming more common. In an early experiment, elementary schoolchildren were divided into two groups: the "red" and "blue" group (Vaughn, Tajfel, and Williams, 1981). While the group assignments were based on expressed preferences for a set of paintings there was no status assigned to either group. Neither group was designated as "superior" to the other. Which group each child was a member of was known to everyone. Then each of the children was given the task of dividing "some pennies" between a red and blue child. The child making the division knew that he or she would receive pennies based on a decision made by another child in the exact same way. In their divisions, the children exhibited "in-group bias," that is, they consistently gave more money to members of their own group. The same result was achieved when group membership was explicitly determined in a completely random manner (Billig and Tajfel, 1973).

There seems to be some basis for concluding that "pure" discrimination exists, but experiments have demonstrated that economic incentives may dull the impact of discrimination. Ball and Eckel (1996; 1998) analyzed a bargaining situation known as the ultimatum game. The ultimatum game is widely used in the experimental literature to demonstrate a number of concepts. In it, two participants are paired. One is designated the proposer and the other the responder. The proposer is given a quantity of some good (money, candy, etc.) and told to propose a split of this good with the responder. If the responder accepts the split, then both parties receive what was proposed. If the responder rejects the split, then neither party receives anything. For example, the proposer might be given $10 and propose that he or she keep $8 and that $2 be given to the responder. If the responder accepts that proposal then the results are as indicated. If not, then both proposer and responder go away empty-handed. Presumably if both parties are rational, then the proposer should propose to keep $9.99 and give $0.01 to the responder and the responder should accept that. From the responder's standpoint, getting $0.01 is better than nothing and the proposer has no reason to offer any more than the absolute bare minimum. The interesting finding, though, is that it seldom works out that way. Proposers typically offer much more even splits and responders typically reject splits that are not close to even (Roth 1995).

Regardless, in the Ball and Eckel experiment, participants were randomly assigned to be "stars" and "nonstars." Stars received their status in a special ceremony where the stars were given special seats and the nonstars were instructed to applaud the stars. They found that when the ultimatum game was played with candies, both star and nonstar proposers offered more candies to stars. However, when the prize to be divided was $10, there was no difference in the split offered to stars and nonstars. A logical conclusion is that the proposers were less likely to discriminate in favor of stars and against nonstars when the prize was something anyone would want (namely, money).

Fershtman and Gneezy employed a modified version of the ultimatum game and participants who actually differed on the basis of ethnic background (Fershtman and Gneezy 2001). They played what is called the "trust" game. The proposer starts with a sum of money. The proposer then decides how much of that money to pass on to the responder. The money passed on is then increased by a predetermined fraction. The responder then decides how much of the money to keep and how much to return to the proposer. For example, assume the starting amount is $10 and the fraction is 10 percent. If the proposer sends $9 to the responder, that amount will be augmented by 10 percent to become $9.90. Then the responder decides how much money to keep and how much to return. The trust aspect is how much the proposer trusts the responder. If the level of trust is high, then the proposer forwards a large sum of money and expects to receive a large amount in return. The authors found when the responders were men of Eastern origin, the level of trust was especially low.

Was this pure bias against Eastern men or fear that Eastern men would not send much back? To test this, the dictator game was employed. In the dictator game, the proposer simply decides how to split the sum of money and that is that. They found that in a dictator game the amount of the split was not influenced by the ethnic background of the responder. This implies that it was fear that Eastern men would not be very generous that motivated the lack of trust in the initial game, not pure bias.

Statistical discrimination theory has also provided the basis for interesting experiments. Anderson and Haupert divided a group of subjects into two groups of workers, designating one as "green" and the other as "yellow" (Anderson and Haupert 1999). Each worker was given an appropriately colored index card with a productivity level written on the back. Employers were asked to hire a specific number of workers and given an incentive to choose the most highly productive workers. The distribution of productivities for each color was known, but the specific productivity of any individual worker was only known to that worker. If the employer wanted to know, then the employer would have to pay to "interview" the worker. They found clear evidence of statistical discrimination. When average productivity was lower for one group than another and interview costs were high, employers tended to hire fewer workers from the lower productivity group. When interview costs were low, however, discrimination against workers from the low productivity group was much less.

Of course, the experiment just reported had exogenously determined levels of productivity. Fryer, Goeree, and Holt set up a labor market that had the characteristics of the Coate and Loury model discussed in the previous chapter, which determines productivity endogenously (Fryer, Goeree, and Holt 2005). In the experiment, workers were either purple or green. At the beginning of each period, they had to decide whether or not to invest. Employers could not observe the worker's actual productivity, but could administer a test that would provide a prediction that was erroneous in many instances. Unbeknownst to the participants, at the beginning of the experiment, greens were given lower costs of investment. Consequently, they invested more and were hired more often. However, later investment costs were equalized. There was not one typical result. There were sessions where investment and hiring rates increased for purples, but purples continued to lag behind greens. But there was also a session where purple investment rates surged so much and green investment rates sagged so much that the two groups actually reversed their position in the labor market.

Experimental studies, still in their infancy, would appear to confirm that identifying discrimination is not an easy task.

CONCLUSION

What policy implications can we derive from these results? Not surprisingly, liberals and conservatives come away with very different understandings.

Philosophically, liberals have always been skeptical of the equity of the market economy and are major supporters of using government policy to counteract inequity. In addition to using the full range of government actions to raise the incomes of the poor, reduce the inequality in the distribution of income, and increase the rate of mobility, liberals take the discrimination results as proof that discrimination remains a huge problem and needs to be confronted head-on. Liberals believe not only in strict antidiscrimination laws, but also affirmative action policies to rapidly increase the representation of minorities in highly paid jobs. Many liberals would not object to the use of quotas in hiring (or goals, as they prefer to call them). Liberal economist Barbara Bergmann has written approvingly about requiring goals for the employment of the Irish and Jews in some regions of contemporary America if the Irish and Jews could be shown to be "underrepresented" in certain occupations, and if there was a past history of exclusion.

> Consider, however, the situation of a New England law firm that employs forty lawyers and has no partners or associates of Irish or Jewish extraction. There are many people of Irish extraction in New England and a considerable number of Jews as well. In the past these groups were commonly denied access to jobs reserved for upper-crust males of British extraction. Many lawyers of Irish and Jewish extraction now have elite legal credentials, and if a firm of that size has no such lawyers on its staff, it is likely that some aspects of the recruitment process are keeping them from being hired. Our guidelines suggest that having a goal for hiring lawyers of Irish and Jewish ancestry would be desirable for this firm. On the other hand, in other parts of the country, and in some occupation in which being of Irish or Jewish ancestry has not recently been a substantial disadvantage, goals for such people, even when they are underrepresented, would be unnecessary and undesirable (Bergmann 1996, 95–96).

The United States elected an Irish-American president (John F. Kennedy) nearly fifty years ago. The impact of being Jewish on earnings was discussed earlier in the chapter.

Far from being drenched in discrimination, conservatives believe that discrimination has withered away as a factor that explains labor market outcomes. That employers discriminate over an extended period of time is inconsistent with fundamental economic logic. Accordingly, it is not surprising that the empirical evidence, like that cited earlier, does not tell a clear and convincing story. Also, there are the lessons of history, which seem to suggest that prejudice and discrimination are not an absolute bar to economic success. For example, in addition to the evidence on Jews cited earlier, blacks of West Indian origin in the United States have earnings near average and considerably above those of blacks born in the United States, and Japanese- and Chinese-Americans have incomes well above the average despite being of a different color than most Americans and having been the victims of discrimination in the past (Sowell 1981). And in 2008, voters in the United States elected a black president.

QUESTIONS FOR REVIEW AND PRACTICE

1. Explain how economists use regression analysis to measure discrimination. Is a significant coefficient on the attribute (e.g., race/gender/ethnicity/sexual orientation/beauty/height/weight/color/religion) variable proof of the existence of discrimination? What else could it be?

2. American men of Russian ancestry earn 57 percent more than the U.S. average. Does this mean that there is no discrimination against Russians in the United States? If not, how could such discrimination be measured?

3. Should the results of audit studies and laboratory experiments be more or less trusted than the results of regression studies?

4. The Jarrell and Stanley study cited earlier found that the gender wage gap in several studies ranged from −5 to +77 percent (Jarrell and Stanley 2004). What could account for such a wide variation in results? How are economists supposed to reach a conclusion?

5. Estimate a regression equation with the following results:

$$w = 12 + 1*S - 0.40*R + 0.5*EXP$$
$$(2.2) \quad (-1.2) \quad (2.3)$$

   where w is hourly wage rate, S is years of schooling, EXP is years of labor market experience, and R is a dummy variable taking the value 0 if the person is white and 1 if the person is nonwhite. T statistics are in parentheses below the estimated coefficients.

   a. Which variable(s) is (are) dependent and independent?

   b. If S = 16, EXP = 20, and D = 0, what is the predicted wage rate? If S = 16, EXP = 20, and R = 1, what is the predicted wage rate? What interpretation should be given to the coefficient on R?

   c. Which variables, if any, are statistically significant using the rule of thumb from the chapter?

   d. What can you conclude about discrimination from the results?

NOTES

1. You will learn exactly how this is done in your econometrics courses. Not here.

2. Please refer to any econometrics textbook for a more complete discussion.

3. It does not matter which gender is assigned the value of 1.

4. Including the squared experience term was an attempt to capture diminishing returns to years of experience.

5. Note that there is no direct measure of teaching performance, which pretty much represents the priorities at large, research-oriented universities, at least as they were in the 1980s.

6. BMI = (weight in pounds/height in inches^2)*703. A BMI < 18.5 is underweight. BMI in the range 18.5–24.9 is normal. BMI in the range 25.0–29.9

is overweight. A BMI of 30.0 or greater is obese. Although widely used and informative, it is not a flawless statistic. Every player in the National Basketball Association is obese on the basis of BMI.

6. To be precise, the parents can share 480 days of leave with 60 days being reserved for each parent.

7. In addition to Anglos and blacks, the sample includes Mexican or Chicano, Puerto Rican, Cuban, Central or South American, and other Spanish (Carliner 1976).

8. Thomas Sowell is an economist who has written extensively about the economic implications of cultural differences between ethnic groups (Sowell 1981, 1983, 1994, 1998a).

9. See Giam Pietro Cipriani and Angelo Zago (2007). This study looked at college students. It may very well have been the case that good-looking college students may have been good looking when they were younger students and therefore had benefited from all sorts of teacher favoritism.

10. It is generally agreed that there was a "Jewish quota" at Harvard for many decades.

11. Admittedly those names are much more likely in my part of the country than Boston or Chicago. I wish to thank a student of mine, Christopher Hines, for making this argument.

Reducing the Impact of Discrimination on How the Pie is Sliced

INTRODUCTION

Despite the difficulties associated with detecting and measuring the extent of labor market discrimination, the continuing existence of several types of discrimination in the labor market in our society is not seriously questioned. In a just society, steps are taken to reduce the impact of this discrimination on how the pie is sliced. The most effective steps in terms of equity and efficiency are seldom obvious. Consequently, policies to fight labor market discrimination are almost always highly controversial.

This chapter will review three high-profile approaches to fighting labor market discrimination. The first approach is via the so-called antidiscrimination statutes. Do the statutes and their interpretation lead us closer to the achievement of a just society? Do they make economic sense? The second approach is the murky area known as affirmative action. What does the term *affirmative action* mean, and does it lead to efficient and equitable outcomes? The third approach is an attempt to change how the labor market works using a policy known as comparable worth.

AN OVERVIEW OF ANTIDISCRIMINATION LAW

That discrimination in employment should be illegal is relatively noncontroversial.[1] In fact, laws that address this issue directly have been around for more than four decades. However, the passage of a law seldom settles anything. By its very nature, written legislation tends to be ambiguous. Legislators cannot possibly anticipate every conceivable situation. For example, it is easy to write that employers should not discriminate on the basis of gender, but some of the implications might be surprising. What if it is a state requirement for prison guards in maximum security prisons to weigh at least 120 pounds and be 5' 2" tall? Many more women would be excluded by that requirement than men. Is that discrimination on the basis of gender, or just common sense?[2]

This then is one of the major roles of the legal system. We call upon courts, juries, and the wise judges presiding over them to adjudicate these knotty controversies. The decisions then become the precedents that define what the law really means. It should come as no surprise that while attempting to clarify, judges sometimes create deep thickets of controversy. From a judicial standpoint, when a law is ambiguous any decision runs the risk of being charged with being in conflict with the "original intent" of the law. From an economic standpoint, questions may then be raised about whether the meaning given to the law fits well with the achievement of efficiency and equity.

KEY LAWS

The body of law that represents our approach to combating discrimination consists of several statutes. The four essential statutes are as follows.

Equal Pay Act of 1963 (United States Code 1963)–The Equal Pay Act was an amendment to the Fair Labor Standards Act.[3] The purpose of the act was to overturn various state "protective" labor laws by requiring "equal pay for equal work." To be specific, it prohibited an employer from paying one gender lower wages than the other for equal work in the same establishment on jobs requiring equal skill, effort, and responsibility, performed under the same working conditions. There were four exceptions to this standard. Unequal wages could be justified if they were the result of a seniority system, a merit pay system, a payment system based on quality or quantity, or if they were the result of any factor other than gender.

The Equal Pay Act is a good example of the role that courts play in defining precisely what the words of the legislation mean. Many people might look at the act and think that equal pay for equal work means the exact same type of work. They would be wrong. The courts have interpreted equal work to mean "substantially equal work."

Shultz v. Wheaton Glass Co. involved the following controversy (United States Court of Appeals 1970): Wheaton Glass Co. produced glass containers of various types. One job classification at the factory was that of selector-packer. As finished glass pieces appeared, selector-packers would inspect and package the good pieces and discard the bad pieces. Both men and women were hired as selector-packers, but the men were paid $2.355 per hour while the women were paid $2.14. According to the company, the reason for the wage differential was that in addition to selector-packer responsibilities, the male selector-packers were required to spend some of their time working as "snap-up boys." The snap-up boy job classification involved crating and moving bottles, sweeping, cleaning, and other unskilled tasks. Employees who worked exclusively as snap-up boys were paid $2.16 per hour. No women worked as snap-up boys because the collective bargaining agreement had set limits on the weight women could be required to lift. This restriction on the jobs women could do was not addressed by the Equal Pay Act and was therefore not an issue in the case.

The glass-making ovens did not continuously produce pieces. Frequently there was downtime between the end of one customer's order and the beginning of the next customer's order. During those times both male and female selector-packers were sent to the "Resort" area where all the females and some of the males inspected and packed rejected glassware. The remaining male selector-packers were required to do snap-up boy tasks during these times. Not all male selector-packers did snap-up boy tasks, and those who did spent a relatively small amount of time on them.

Women employees brought suit claiming a violation of the Equal Pay Act. The company won in the lower court because the court reasoned that the male selector-packers did substantially different work from females, and the fact that male selector-packers also worked as snap-up boys was a significant economic benefit to the firm because of the flexibility it gave the firm.

The U.S. Court of Appeals overruled the lower court (the case never did make it to the Supreme Court). The appeals court found that the jobs were not substantially different. For one thing, not every male did snap-up boy work. Secondly, the court could not understand why paying full-time snap-up boys $0.02 more per hour than female selector-packers justified paying male selector-packers $0.185 more per hour. The flexibility argument was similarly flawed. How could the flexibility created by males doing a job that paid just a little bit more than the females were earning justify the actual wage gap? In short, the court found the "disproportionate" wage gap difficult to justify. The court also noted there was no proof that all females could not do the snap-up boy job.

The use of the "substantially equal" rule allows courts to exercise some judgment with respect to job classifications. Real differences between jobs could justify gender pay differentials. Artificial differences could not.

Title VII of the Civil Rights Act of 1964 (United States Code 1964)–The Civil Rights Act of 1964 was a landmark piece of legislation that outlawed discrimination in many areas of American society. The prohibition against employment discrimination was placed in Title VII. The law stated that it was unlawful for any employer, union, or employment agency "to refuse to hire or discharge any individual, or otherwise to discriminate against any individual with respect to his compensation, terms, conditions, or privileges of employment, because of such individual's race, color, religion or national origin [Section 703(a), 78 Stat. 255, as amended, 86 Stat. 109, 42 U.S.C. §2000–2(a)]." There were three exceptions allowed. Differential treatment was not unlawful in situations where religion, sex, or national origin is a bona fide[4] occupational qualification reasonably necessary to the normal operation of the business, where it is the result of a bona fide seniority system, and no employer would be required to grant preferential treatment to any group because of existing imbalances.

An interesting anecdote has to do with the inclusion of sex in the list of protected characteristics (Whalen and Whalen 1985). Sex was not in the original bill and was still not part of it as it neared final passage. Congressman Howard W. Smith (D-Virginia), an opponent of the bill and chair of the powerful Rules Committee, worked to add sex to the list in an attempt to peel away votes in favor of the bill. His strategy ultimately failed; but not before causing some consternation in the ranks of bill supporters. For example, there were organizations like the AFL-CIO that would have willingly gone forth on the Civil Rights Act without the inclusion of the prohibition against discrimination on the basis of sex.

Age Discrimination in Employment Act (United States Code 1967, amended 1978, and 1986)–This act prohibits discrimination on the basis of age. The minimum age at which protection kicks in is forty years. The maximum age has been increased through time as society's values have evolved. In 1968, the maximum age for protection was set at sixty-five. In 1978 the maximum age was raised to seventy. In 1986, the maximum age provision was entirely abolished, although there are some occupational restrictions, for example the case of airline pilots.

There are some exceptions to the law's protections. The law does not provide absolute job security for older workers. They may still be fired for cause. A bona fide seniority system will provide protection against the act. Also, in some situations age can be a bona fide occupational requirement.

Americans with Disabilities Act (ADA; United States Code 1990)–This act protects the more than 43 million Americans with various mental and physical disabilities. The act uses a very broad definition of disability. It defines disability as (1) a physical or mental impairment that substantially limits one or more major life activities, (2) a record of such an impairment, or (3) being regarded as having such an impairment. Included among those protected are individuals with mental disabilities and those with AIDS. Excluded from protection are illegal drug users, alcohol abusers, homosexuals, bisexuals, pedophiles, transsexuals, exhibitionists, voyeurs, compulsive gamblers, kleptomaniacs, pyromaniacs, transvestites and individuals with other gender-related disorders.

This act can be differentiated from the others in a very important way. The ADA not only requires nondiscrimination but it also requires that employers make "reasonable accommodations" for their handicapped employees. For example, not only can an employer not discriminate against a worker in a wheelchair, but the employer must build ramps and provide other structural accommodations to make it easier for that worker to get to work. The reasonable accommodation requirement stops only when it would cause an undue hardship for the business.

Court interpretations of the meaning of the law have been problematic. In order to create "a demanding standard for qualifying as disabled" (United States Supreme Court 2002, 197), the U.S. Supreme Court, in a series of judgments, has ruled individuals who are able to control a disability by mitigating measures—medication, prosthetics, hearing aids and other auxiliary devices, diet and exercise, or other treatments—are not protected by the law since a major life activity (the ability to work) is not substantially limited, even if the employer discriminates against them by some action (United States Supreme Court 1999a, 1999b, 1999c). As of this writing, Congress is considering the ADA Restoration Act which would expand the protection provided by the law to those with significant disabilities, not just those whose ability to work is compromised by a disability.

ENFORCING THE LAWS

The laws are enforced in a variety of ways. The Equal Employment Opportunity Commission (EEOC) is primarily responsible for the enforcement of most of the laws mentioned (Title VII, ADEA, ADA). The EEOC is an agency of the federal government and its board members are appointed by the president and confirmed by the U.S. Senate.

An individual who believes that he or she has been a victim of discrimination is required to file a complaint with the EEOC. After investigation, if the complaint is found to have merit, the EEOC will contact the employer, union, or employment agency and attempt to settle the complaint by conciliation. For many years, there was a large backlog of unresolved complaints at the EEOC. In recent years, the backlog has been reduced significantly as a result of the commission's efforts to move cases along and clarification of the law after years of commission and court decisions.

If conciliation does not work, the EEOC can bring suit in federal court. The suit can be brought on behalf of the individual, but the EEOC is not very interested in these types of cases. It is more interested in class action suits. A class action suit occurs when a number of individuals complain of a similar injury—for example, if the employer discriminates against all black workers or all women in the plant. A class action suit can grow out of a complaint by an individual if the EEOC lawyers recognize that the injury is likely to be generally shared.

If the party charged is found guilty, then the court can fashion a "make-whole" remedy. A make-whole remedy is just what its name implies. The court tries to compensate the victim for damages incurred. In order to do that, the court has considerable leeway. It can order back pay and punitive and compensatory damages up to $600,000. To prevent the guilty party from continuing with the same practices the court may order that the employer make changes in procedures, such as those used for recruiting, hiring, and promotion.

LEGAL THEORIES

The "nuts and bolts" of how our legal system works remain a mystery to many people. Our knowledge is largely derived from grade school descriptions of the criminal justice system. There we learn that in criminal cases an individual is "innocent until proven guilty" and the burden of proof rests with the government. It does not exactly work that way in discrimination cases. In these types of cases there are "shifting burdens." The case can be considered as consisting of distinct and separate stages with the burden resting on a different party in each stage. At any point, if a party does not meet its burden, the case ends.

There are two legal theories that are used in discrimination cases. The legal theory determines the procedure the court uses in hearing the case. *Disparate treatment* is the theory used in the case of intentional discrimination against individuals. Following this theory, the complainant must first establish a *prima facie* (on the face) case of discrimination Essentially this means that the complainant must show that what happened "looked like" discrimination. Here the burden is on the plaintiff. The complainant must establish that he or she was a member of a protected group, that there was a job available, that the complainant was denied the job, and that the person charged continued to seek applicants for the job. Then it is up to the employer to state a nondiscriminatory reason for the decision. The burden is now on the employer. Then the plaintiff must show by a preponderance of evidence[5] that the employer's reason was actually a pretext for discrimination. The burden has now shifted back to the plaintiff.

Disparate impact is the theory used to deal with apparently neutral policies that have a discriminatory impact. Following this theory, the plaintiff must establish a prima facie case of discrimination (burden on plaintiff). This means that the plaintiff must show by statistics or other means that a protected group is underrepresented in the employer's workforce. Then the employer indicates the business necessity for the practice or shows job-relatedness (burden shifts to employer). Then the plaintiff shows that the practice was simply a pretext for discrimination (burden back on the plaintiff). In these cases, the effect of the policy is important, not its intent. Plaintiffs do not have to prove that the defendant wanted to discriminate, only that the practice had a differential impact on members of protected groups and it could not be justified by business necessity.

LANDMARK ANTIDISCRIMINATION LAW COURT DECISIONS

As indicated earlier, the precise meaning of a law can seldom be ascertained simply by reading the text of the law. An accumulated body of court decisions is also needed to make sense of the law. This section will review four landmark Supreme Court decisions that established precedents in the interesting and important areas of what constitutes discrimination, preferential policies, and lay-offs. The reasoning of the majority and the dissenters will be examined, as well as some outside criticisms of the decisions. Close examination of the cases shows that most of them were what an impartial observer would have to concede were tough calls. Most discrimination cases that make it to the Supreme Court are not simple morality plays. They are not just a matter of an evil villain doing something bad to an innocent victim. Often the "villain" is someone operating in good faith trying to do the right thing in an environment where standards are changing and there are no clear guidelines. And, in virtually every case, there are innocent third parties who are hurt by the decision.

Griggs et al. v. Duke Power Company (1971) (United States Supreme Court 1971): Duke Power Company was (and still is) a power-generating company located in North Carolina. This case originated at its Dan River Steam Station in Draper, North Carolina. At the time, the steam station was divided into five operating departments: labor, coal handling, operations, maintenance, and laboratory and test. The first two departments were "outside" departments; the latter three were "inside" departments. See Figure 11.1. The terms *inside* and *outside* referred to where most of the work took place.

Prior to 1955 Duke Power Company blatantly discriminated on the basis of race. It was not illegal, it was the South, and no one claimed otherwise. Blacks would only be hired in the labor department where the highest wages were below the lowest wages in every other department. In 1955 the company began requiring a high school diploma for initial assignment to coal handling or for transfer from coal handling to any inside department. During this time there were several white employees who lacked a high school diploma but worked very successfully as coal handlers and in other inside departments.

In 1965, the effective date of the Civil Rights Act of 1964, Duke again altered employment policies. For initial assignment to coal handling or any inside department or for transfer from labor to any other department, the applicant had to get a passing score on two employment tests (the Wonderlic Personnel Test, a test of general intelligence still in use today, and the Bennett Mechanical Comprehension Test) and have a high school diploma. In that part of North Carolina few blacks had high school diplomas or could achieve high scores on the employment tests. Consequently the coal handling and inside departments remained nearly all white.

Figure 11.1   **Functional View of Dan River Steam Station**

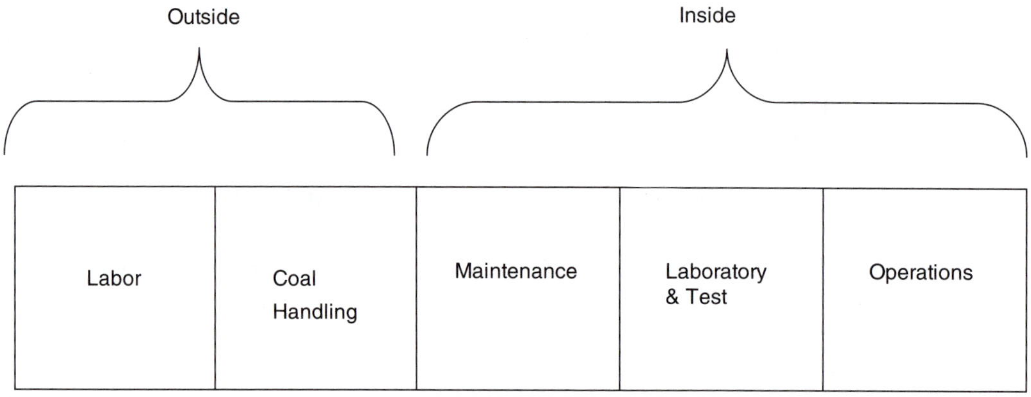

Willie S. Griggs was one of several black employees of the company who decided to test Duke Power Company's adherence to the law.[6] Despite not having high school diplomas, they applied for jobs in the coal handling and inside departments. They were denied those jobs and, as a consequence, ended up suing Duke Power Company for violation of Title VII.

Duke's defense was simple. It did not discriminate against anyone. Rather, it treated everyone the same by requiring each one to pass the same employment tests that the company considered necessary for locating the types of productive employees it needed. That the employment tests disproportionately eliminated African-American job applicants was regrettable, but incidental. Discrimination was not Duke's intention.

To make a long story short, the case wound its way through the courts until it reached the U.S. Supreme Court. In its judgment, the Court found for Griggs, and established an important precedent.[7] Any employment practice that works to the disadvantage of a particular group[8] is a violation of Title VII unless the practice can be shown to be essential to the successful operation of the business. The issue of intent is of no consequence.

Regarding intent, cynical types might regard Duke's claims as dubious. The company had to know in that section of North Carolina its employment test and the high school diploma requirement would eliminate a substantial portion of African-Americans from the labor pool, and Duke had not produced rigorous evidence that these requirements were accurate predictors of job performance. But Duke's "true" motives were not at issue because the Court did not read the prohibition against discrimination to apply only to situations where there was intent. Rather it read the prohibition to apply to any instance where a hiring requirement had a differential impact and could not be justified as a business necessity.

It is easy to imagine a company innocently adopting a seemingly innocuous employment policy. Maybe the company feels, without having done the research to back it, that high school graduates are more "reliable" than dropouts, or applicants with arrest records are "scary." According to the Court, vague feelings no longer cut it if

Figure 11.2 **Functional Structure of Kaiser Gramercy, LA Plant Prior to 1974 Agreement**

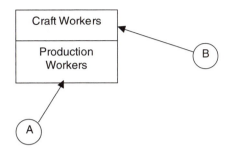

the practice has a disproportionate effect. Employers must be sensitive to the effect of all their employment practices.

In the U.S. judicial system, the Supreme Court rules on fairly abstract principles of law. The practical implementation of those rulings is left to other bodies, such as the lower courts and relevant government agencies. It fell to the EEOC to develop guidelines regarding employment tests.

Subsequently, the EEOC decided that employment tests that work to the disadvantage of a protected group are suspect unless they are professionally validated and if the selection rate for any group is less than 4/5 of the selection rate for the group with the highest rate of selection (4/5 rule of thumb). This does not mean that employment tests cannot be used. It also does not mean that bad employment tests cannot be used. Bad employment tests can be used, but only if they treat everybody equally badly.

Unlike other decisions to be discussed subsequently, the *Griggs* decision was not highly controversial. No dissents were recorded. Nevertheless, it should be recognized that absence of dissent does not mean the decision constituted a free lunch. Practically speaking, developing inexpensive tests that are accurate predictors of job performance is no mean feat. If firms are prohibited from using their own rules of thumb, which have met their needs in the past, they may simply have to resort to quota hiring. The practical importance of this criticism may, in fact, be minimal. Americans appear to have learned to live with *Griggs,* and like it.

United Steelworkers of America, AFL-CIO-CLC v. Weber et al. (1979) (United States Supreme Court 1979): The Kaiser Aluminum Company had a plant in Gramercy, Louisiana. Essentially Kaiser had two types of blue-collar jobs—production jobs and craft jobs. The production jobs were mainly low-skill and low-pay jobs. Workers from the surrounding community were recruited to fill them. They usually started at the bottom of the job ladder and worked their way up. The craft jobs were high-skill and high-pay. Since there were few workers in the local community with these skills, Kaiser recruited in the national market. There was no way for production workers at the top of the job ladder to move into the craft jobs.

Figure 11.2 depicts the structure of the plant. Locals entered at point A, but could not move from the upper rung of the production jobs to the craft job section. Craft workers were recruited in the national market represented by B.

In 1974 only 5 of the 273 craft workers were members of protected minority

Figure 11.3   **Functional Structure of Kaiser Gramercy, LA Plant After 1974 Agreement**

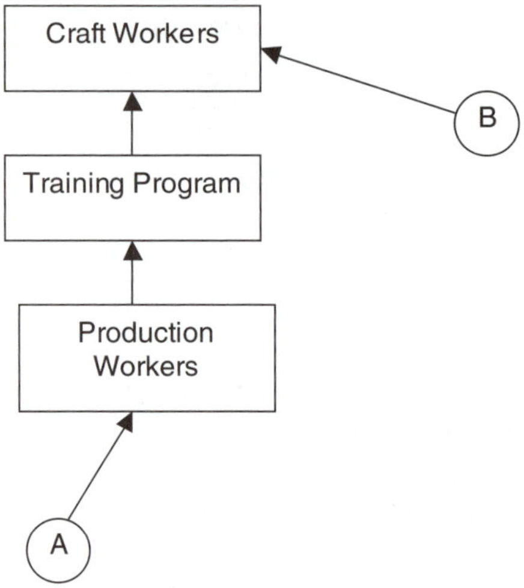

groups. As a point of comparison, 39 percent of the local community were members of these protected groups.

The lack of locals in the craft jobs had been a sore point for years. To remedy this, the 1974 agreement called for the establishment of a training program that would have allowed local production workers to obtain the skills needed to move into the craft jobs. In Figure 11.3 a training program is placed between the production and craft job segments. In this model, locals at the upper levels of the production segment could enter the training program and acquire the skills necessary to be hired for a craft job.

To increase representation of minority workers in these craft jobs (and maybe to prevent a future lawsuit), the agreement also specified that affirmative action would be applied in selecting candidates for training. In particular, the training program would enroll one minority worker for every white worker enrolled until such time as the representation of minority workers in the craft jobs approximated their percentage in the local labor force.

Brian Weber was a local boy, white, and at the upper rungs of the production worker job ladder. He very much wanted to become a craft worker and applied for a spot in the training program. He was turned down, while a black worker with fewer years of seniority was selected ahead of him. In the initial training class of thirteen, there were seven blacks and six whites, and the most senior black in the group had less seniority then several whites. Weber sued.

Essentially the case involved the issue of whether Title VII forbids voluntary affirmative action programs. In a 5–4 decision, the Court ruled against Weber and for the company and union, and gave its imprimatur to preferential treatment for protected groups.

The majority opinion was a tricky one to write. The problem was the text of the law, or what is frequently referred to as the "letter of the law." Title VII said it was unlawful for any employer, union, or employment agency "to refuse to hire or discharge any individual, or otherwise to discriminate against any individual . . . because of such individual's race, color, religion or national origin." Presumably an individual could in good faith read the prohibition against discrimination against any individual to actually mean any individual, regardless of whether he or she was a member of a protected group. The way the majority dealt with the problem was by invoking the spirit of the law. The majority reasoned the law had been passed to help improve the economic conditions of blacks and several other minorities. This program certainly did that, which provided all the justification needed. It would be a strange law indeed that protected a white male against a voluntary plan to undo the effect of centuries of discrimination. If Congress had not meant the law to be interpreted this way, it could have written "would not require or permit" racially preferential treatment. It did not.

The majority opinion provoked vigorous dissent from the Chief Justice Warren Burger and Associate Justice William Rehnquist. Rehnquist argued that the majority had misconstrued Title VII, a mystifying outcome given the clarity of the law itself, the explanations of the meaning of the law offered during the congressional debate, and previous Supreme Court decisions (United States Supreme Court 1979, 219–255). Brian Weber was excluded from the training program for no reason other than his race. No participant in the case denied that. How could that be lawful under a law that read it is unlawful "to refuse to hire . . . , or otherwise to discriminate against any individual . . . because of such individual's race, color, religion or national origin"? The words "any individual" presumably meant any individual, and that had to include Weber. During committee debate on the legislation, Senator Hubert Humphrey (D-Minnesota), one of the primary sponsors of the bill, went to great pains to emphasize that the bill would not permit discrimination of any type (United States Congress 1964, 6549). Senators Joseph Clark and Clifford Case submitted a memorandum to the Senate that read in part:

> Title VII would have no effect on established seniority rights. Its effect is prospective and not retrospective. Thus, for example, if a business has been discriminating in the past and as a result has an all-white working force, when the title comes into effect the employer's obligation would be simply to fill future vacancies on a nondiscriminatory basis. He would not be obligated—or indeed permitted—to fire whites in order to hire Negroes, or to prefer Negroes for future vacancies, or, once Negroes are hired, to give them special seniority rights at the expense of the white workers hired earlier (United States Equal Employment Opportunity Commission 1968, 3043).

Previous Supreme Court decisions in labor market discrimination cases had enshrined a color-blind approach. For example, in the Griggs case, the unanimous court opined, "[d]iscriminatory preference, for any group, minority or majority, is precisely and only what Congress had proscribed" (United States Supreme Court 1971, 431).

The gender counterpart of *Weber* is the interesting case that follows.

Johnson v Transportation Agency, Santa Clara County, California, et al. (United States Supreme Court 1987a): Twenty-two percent of the employees of the Santa Clara County Transportation Agency were women. This is compared to 36.4 percent in the area labor market. Of these employed women, 76 percent were office and clerical workers, while 22 percent were service and maintenance workers. Seven percent were agency officials and administrators, 8.6 percent were professionals, and 9.7 percent were technicians. There were no women among the 238 skilled craft workers.

In December 1978, the agency adopted an affirmative action plan. The goal of the plan was to achieve "a statistically measurable yearly improvement in hiring, training and promotion of minorities and women throughout the Agency in all major job classifications where they are underrepresented" until female representation in all jobs matched the area labor market. There were no numerical quotas specified in the plan, but race and sex were permitted to be used as factors in selecting employees for jobs.

One of the jobs was that of road dispatcher. The duties included assigning road crews, equipment and materials, and maintaining records pertaining to road maintenance jobs. It required four years of dispatch or road maintenance experience. There were twelve applicants for the job. Nine of the applicants were judged qualified. Seven of them took the second stage interview and scored 70 or more on the interview, where 70 was considered the cutoff between being qualified and unqualified. One of those applicants was Paul Johnson. Johnson had scored 75 on the interview, had over ten years of experience is similar type jobs, had been involved in road maintenance since 1977, and occasionally worked as a dispatcher. Diane Joyce was another applicant. She scored 73 on the interview and had nine years of experience working for the agency. She had been working road maintenance since 1975 and had worked occasionally as a dispatcher.

After a second interview, the agency recommended Johnson. The affirmative action officer recommended Joyce. The agency eventually selected Joyce while saying the two applicants were, essentially, equally well-qualified.

Johnson sued, claiming that he had been discriminated against on the basis of sex in clear violation of Title VII. He won at the district court level, but lost in the court of appeals. Johnson then appealed to the Supreme Court, where he ended up the loser. The Supreme Court cited the Weber case as a precedent. Voluntary affirmative action programs like this one were acceptable under the *Weber* precedent if there was a manifest imbalance, the program created no absolute bar to advancement of whites, and the program was temporary. In this case, there was a manifest imbalance. The plan set aside no positions for women and Johnson had no absolute entitlement to the position (seven applicants met the minimum requirements) and the plan intended to "attain," not "maintain," balance.

Justice Scalia issued the most pointed dissent, saying that there was no proof of sex discrimination at the agency. Usually this sort of remedy is used when there has been discrimination. The implicit goal of the plan seemed to have been to align the sex composition of each job with that of the market. In fact, supervisors would be evaluated on basis of affirmative action numbers produced. Scalia felt that was an arbitrary goal. People do differ in their tastes for certain types of jobs so there was no reason to suppose that the sex composition of any job would be precisely equal to or even approximately equal to the sex composition of the labor market. The Court was essentially giving to each and every protected racial and sexual group a governmentally determined "proper" proportion in each job category. Johnson was the leading candidate for the job. He lost out because the agency director intervened without bothering to review the interview. He did not get the job for one reason and one reason only—his sex. Essentially the plan was not directed at discrimination as practiced by the agency because the agency did not discriminate. Rather, it was being directed at a society that does not raise many little girls to aspire to be road dispatchers. Johnson ought not to be denied a job because of someone's vision of the "ideal" society. The case contrasted with Weber because the low number of black craft workers was undoubtedly the result of discrimination.

Weber and *Johnson* taken together have established a fairly strong precedent in favor of voluntary preferential treatment programs. These two rulings do not mean that anything goes. Companies cannot simply establish such programs because they think it is a "good thing to do." There must be a reason for the program—evidence the company had discriminated in the past, or a profound workplace imbalance—and the program cannot be open-ended, meaning the program will cease once the problems that led to its establishment have withered away.

The personal prejudice model in Chapter 9 pointed out that discriminatory policies are no free lunch for those doing the discriminating. Employers must sacrifice profits in the short run to sate their taste for discrimination. What the previous two cases show is that preferential policies voluntarily adopted to undo the effects of prior discrimination are also no free lunch. The Brian Webers and Paul Johnsons of the world are harmed.

Wygant et al. v Jackson Board of Education et al. (United States Supreme Court 1989b): After a period of racial unrest in the Jackson County, Michigan, schools, a plan was worked out to increase hiring of minority teachers. The school board believed that minority teachers would be positive role models for all students and would help create a better educational and social atmosphere in the schools. When economic troubles necessitating layoffs occurred, a problem arose since the minority teachers had the least seniority and consequently lost their jobs, thus defeating the purpose of the plan. So the board of education and teachers' union included a clause in the collective bargaining agreement stating that when layoffs had to be made, minority layoffs would be limited so that their proportional representation on the faculty would not be reduced. This meant more-senior white teachers would be laid off before less-senior minority teachers. A suit was brought by a group of white teachers, including Wendy Wygant, who had been laid off and claimed that the provision was illegal discrimination on the basis of race.

The case made its way to the Supreme Court where it was ruled that the layoff provision was not permissible. Any use of racial preferences is inherently suspect. Any layoff scheme that uses them can only be justified if it is "narrowly tailored" to achieve a "compelling governmental interest." The Court held that the layoff scheme was not "narrowly tailored" because layoffs impose too great a burden on the individual who had been laid off. On its face, this ruling appeared to conflict with previous rulings such as *United States v Paradise et al.* (United States Supreme Court 1987b), which said the Alabama Department of Public Safety could use a racial quota for hiring to achieve 25 percent black representation among police officers to remedy a past history of discrimination. It would also seem to be inconsistent with Weber. The Court justified its ruling by arguing that the burden of hiring or promotion preferences was broadly diffused (people who did not get hired or promoted would not necessarily have had the expectation that they would get the job), while that of layoff preferences was not (the person who was laid off had definitely lost a job). The Court also ruled that a "compelling governmental interest" could not be identified in this case. While the government certainly has an interest in ending discrimination, the school board had not established that there was discrimination in this case. It had never been the stated policy of the school board to not hire black teachers. The school board had argued that "societal discrimination" had reduced the potential supply of black teachers who were needed to provide positive role models. According to the Court, "societal discrimination" was too vague a concept to justify such drastic action.

The dissent said that contrary to the majority's assertion, there was plenty of evidence that the school board had discriminated. Further, the use of racial preferences in this case must have been "narrowly tailored" because the union and the school board had voluntarily agreed to it. Certainly the burden placed on white teachers who had been laid off was great, but the problem was caused by economic conditions, not discrimination on the basis of race.

The field of discrimination is huge. It would take some very weighty law books to do it justice. This survey of four cases looked at some of the more salient issues. Least controversial was the *Griggs* case definition of discrimination. Differential outcomes can constitute proof of discrimination if the practices causing it cannot be shown to be job-related. Voluntary preferential policies are protected if they involve hiring and promotion because the benefits are diffuse. Voluntary preferential policies are not protected if they involve layoffs because the costs are heavily concentrated on a few persons. It is hard to shake the feeling that the Court's rulings reflect an attempt to minimize howls of outrage rather than a unified conception of justice.

AFFIRMATIVE ACTION

What is affirmative action? It is a slippery term used different ways by different people and sometime in different ways by the same person at different times. It operates in multiple spheres, including the labor market and education.

It might be easier to explain what affirmative action is not. Affirmative action is not nondiscrimination. We would not need a new term to describe something that we already understood fairly well. Rather, affirmative action is a set of policies that requires we take proactive steps to eliminate differences, not just stop discriminating.

In the labor market there are two slightly different ways in which the term *affirmative action* is used. The first refers to affirmative action in government contracting. In 1967 President Lyndon Johnson issued Executive Order 11375.[9] An executive order is an edict issued by an official in the executive branch of the government, typically the president, requiring certain actions to be taken or avoided.

In this case, the order applied to any government contactor[10] with fifty or more employees or contracts worth $50,000 or more. As a condition for getting and keeping contacts the firm had to inventory the racial and gender composition of all the jobs at the firm and identify those jobs in which minorities and women were "underutilized." For those jobs, the firm had to provide a written plan specifying "goals and timetables" for remedying the underutilization. The firm must then make good faith efforts to achieve the goals and timetables. If the firm fails to make good faith efforts, then it could be disbarred[11] and made subject to a lawsuit.

The second way the term is used is in the context of remedies that courts can use when an organization has been found guilty of illegal discrimination. Courts may require "such affirmative action as may be appropriate" to undo effects of past employment practices.

The evidence we have is that affirmative action has increased the employment and wages of minorities and women, and has done the opposite for white males. However, the bottom line is what affirmative action does for efficiency and equity.

Impact of Affirmative Action on Efficiency

While discrimination is inefficient, affirmative action is not simply ending discrimination and, hence, ending the inefficiency. It is a policy with an explicit objective of reducing group differences in the labor market by using goals and timetables. As the Coate and Loury model discussed in Chapter 9 showed (Coate and Loury 1993a), logically the existence of an affirmative action program could provide the incentive for the discriminated group (the Ts) to acquire needed human capital. Just as logically, with different values of the parameters we might get a patronizing equilibrium where the incentive of the Ts would be to not invest. Of course, we get similar ambiguity with respect to the dominant group (the Vs). Under certain parameters, the Vs would continue to invest in human capital. Under other parameters, they might reduce their investment. The point is that economic theory does not provide a clear prediction of the impact of affirmative action on efficiency. When theory does not provide a clear guide, we must get empirical evidence.

Affirmative action policies have been subjected to extensive empirical testing. Economists have estimated production and cost functions and they have looked at company financial data, employee performance ratings and attitudes, and administrative costs. A consensus has not yet arisen.

An interesting approach to the analysis of the efficiency of affirmative action is the experimental evidence provided by Andrew Schotter and Keith Weigelt (Schotter and Weigelt 1992). For several decades now economists have used laboratory experiments to test hypotheses. Schotter and Weigelt set up an experiment that attempts to replicate a tournament. A group of subjects (often college students because they are what is available to economics professors) is brought into the laboratory. The subjects are paired with each other, but no one knows who their partner is. The subjects are then asked to select an integer "decision number" from 0 to 100 inclusive. Each decision number has a cost associated with it with costs increasing as the decision number increases. The experimenter then selects a random integer from −40 to +40 inclusive and adds that to the decision number. The subject whose "total number" (= decision number + random number) is higher receives winnings of $X. The other subject receives $Y, where Y < X. Then both subjects subtract their cost from their winnings to get their earnings. The game then proceeds through several rounds.

The correlation with the tournament model works like this. The decision number is the amount of individual effort each "worker" puts forth. Effort has a cost associated with it. The random number reflects unexpected events in the labor market that influence performance—maybe someone gets sick, there is a downturn in the economy, or consumer tastes change. The total number is that subject's overall performance that period. The winner in each pair is the one whose overall performance is higher, and rewards are based on relative performance, not absolute performance.

Schotter and Weigelt ran the experiment three ways. In the "baseline" tournament, both subjects had the same costs and they ended up putting forth about the same level of effort.[12] In the "uneven" tournament, one subject was given higher costs than the other. The disadvantaged subject became "discouraged" and tended to reduce effort level (in some cases even dropping out). Then an affirmative action program is instituted, where disadvantaged subjects were given bonus points. These bonus points were added to their total number. The results ultimately depended on how uneven the tournament was to begin with. If the cost asymmetry between the subjects was small, the affirmative action program increased the chances that the disadvantaged subjects would win, but it decreased overall effort levels. Disadvantaged subjects maintained their effort level while that of the advantaged subjects decreased (Schotter and Weigelt 1992, 534). From the firm's standpoint, this program would lead to a decrease in profits and affirmative action would have to be considered an economically inefficient program. If the cost asymmetry was large, things changed. Disadvantaged subjects would find their chances of winning increased, but both they and the advantaged subjects increased their effort levels. Firm profit levels would rise and the program could be considered to be economically efficient.

Experimental evidence such as this does not prove anything. It is merely suggestive. It does indicate that there are some instances in which affirmative action may actually increase efficiency while there are other instances where efficiency decreases. What is the case in the real world? It is hard to say for sure, but there is little evidence that firms will adopt these programs voluntarily.

IMPACT OF AFFIRMATIVE ACTION ON EQUITY

Is affirmative action fair? Undoubtedly each of our individual positions in life is influenced by our family history extending back many generations. Many if not most members of disadvantaged groups are probably not as well off today as they would have been if our history as a society had been very different. Correcting the wrongs of the past is an obligation we all share, and there is no better time to begin than right now. With respect to race and gender relations in the United States, some scholars speak of white and male privilege. The implication is that all whites and all males have unearned privileges today because of what happened in the past. Taking away those privileges is not unfair.

That said, an affirmative action program will always have winners and losers. The losers may come from a group that historically has been advantaged, but the individual losers themselves may very well have clean hands. In fact, it is easy to construct a model that shows that while some whites benefited from discrimination in the past, most did not.

COMPARABLE WORTH

Women and Men at Work, a prominent sociology text by Irene Padavic and Barbara Reskin, includes the following:

> Living in a culture that devalues female activities makes the practice seem natural. Consider 13-year-olds' after school jobs. A neighbor pays a boy $20 for 30 minutes' work shoveling snow and a girl $8 for an hour's baby-sitting (although these figures vary by geographic region). Why does the baby-sitter accept this pay gap? She may not realize how much less she earns per hour. But she has probably already absorbed her society's attitude that girls' jobs are worth less than boys' (Padavic and Reskin 2002, 11–12).

The analysis underlying that passage might seem strange to people steeped in the principles of economics because it would appear to be a problem easily explained by demand and supply. The higher earnings of snow shovelers are simply a compensating differential to get kids to leave the warmth of their rec rooms to do some heavy lifting in the snow and cold. The lower earnings of babysitters probably reflects the fact that, while it is undeniably an important job (after all, young children need supervision and their parents need peace of mind), it is done inside, and, when the children behave, the job offers opportunities to watch TV, talk on the phone to friends, and eat out of the parents' refrigerator. That tween boys are more eager to do the former rather than the latter and that tween girls are more eager to do the latter rather than the former partially reflects prior socialization but also is a result of differences in upper-body strength between the sexes that begin to show themselves by the later tween years.

Consider this thought experiment. If snow shovelers were paid "too much" and babysitters were paid "too little," would there not have to be surpluses of snow shovelers and shortages of babysitters? The theory of demand and supply would predict this outcome. My experience has been that snow shovelers have always been scarce on cold, snowy days, while babysitters have always been easy to find.

Regardless of what hardheaded economists say, the belief that occupational wages reflect the gender composition of an occupation and not supply-and-demand factors is fairly widespread and helps explain some of the appeal of the policy known as comparable worth.[13] Since women are not respected, the work they do is undervalued, which leads to lower wages on jobs predominantly performed by women.

The antecedents of comparable worth are the pay gap between men and women (already discussed), a continued high level of sex segregation in occupations, and the fact that lower-paid occupations are more likely to be female-dominated and higher-paid occupations are more likely to be male-dominated. Table 11.1 shows median usual weekly earnings for full-time workers for the five highest-paid and six (to account for a tie) lowest-paid detailed occupations in the United States in 2005. Women are the minority in each of the highest-paid occupations. In only one of these

Table 11.1

Median Usual Weekly Earnings of Full-Time Wage and Salary Workers by Detailed Occupation and Sex, 2005

Occupation	Median Usual Weekly Earnings (Both Sexes)	Women as a Percentage of the Occupation
Chief Executives	$1,834	24.3
Engineering Managers	$1,786	10.1
Lawyers	$1,609	33.9
Physicians and Surgeons	$1,557	48.0
Pharmacists	$1,547	33.3
Child Care Workers	$332	93.2
Host and Hostesses; restaurant, lounge and coffee shop	$332	84.4
Food Preparation Workers	$321	55.8
Combined food preparation and serving workers, including fast food	$310	74.2
Dishwashers	$296	20.6
Counter attendants; cafeteria, food concession, and coffee shop	$292	62.2

Source: U.S. Department of Labor (2006). Table 18, http://www.bls.gov/cps/wlf-table18–2006.pdf (accessed 24 June 2008)

occupations does their representation exceed their share of the labor force (about 46 percent). Women are the majority, often substantial, in each of the lowest-paid occupations with the exception of dishwasher. Consistent with the sentiment expressed above, advocates of comparable worth believe the reason these occupations are either high- or low-paying has virtually everything to do with the sex of those who do them and little to do with supply and demand.

In the early 1970s the state of Washington did a job evaluation of its workforce. Job evaluation is a procedure under which an organization brings in an outside expert (usually a trained management consultant) to study its jobs. The consultant will rate jobs on the basis of several characteristics thought to be important. In the Washington State case, jobs were rated on the basis of "knowledge and skills," "mental demands," "accountability," and "work conditions." Rated means the job was given a point score, with more points allocated to jobs that score higher along each of the dimensions. Jobs that require greater knowledge and skills, make greater mental demands on their workers, and are associated with more accountability received more points than jobs that required less knowledge and skills, made lesser mental demands, and were associated with less accountability. Jobs that had bad working conditions received more points than jobs performed in nice conditions. After each job was rated along each dimension, the points were totaled.[14] Job evaluation has been in use in industry for literally decades. A firm, often in partnership with a union, will do a job evaluation and use the resulting scores to determine relative wages for its various jobs. There are two main reasons why job evaluation is used. First, since many jobs that firms offer are idiosyncratic to the firm, there is not a market wage to guide wage setting. Second, job evaluation schemes are frequently viewed as an equitable manner in which to settle the potentially contentious issue of what wages to attach to what jobs. To keep peace in the workplace, employers agree to use job evaluation schemes. Consequently, there are management consultants who are specialists in job evaluation.

The results of the 1974 job evaluation provided some interesting grist for the mill. To take one example, a grade III secretary had a total point score of 197 compared to the 97 of a delivery truck driver, yet the truck driver was paid $76 more per week (Bergmann 1986, 178). In the state of Washington at that time the grade III secretaries were almost all female while the delivery truck drivers were predominantly male. A registered nurse received more points than either an auto mechanic or a civil engineer, but was paid less (Bergmann 1986, 178–79). Registered nurses were predominantly female while auto mechanics and civil engineers were predominantly male. Senior computer systems analysts were better paid than registered nurses and had a higher point total, but their point differential was about 9 percent while their salary differential was 34.5 percent (Bergmann 1986, 179). Guess the sex composition of senior computer systems analysts in 1974.

Comparable worth supporters believe evidence like this makes their point that female-dominated jobs are typically undervalued. They propose that all employers should be required to do job evaluations and readjust pay scales to reflect the relative point values of the different jobs. Should the pay on undervalued women's jobs be raised or the pay on overvalued men's jobs be lowered? Simple logic suggests either approach would achieve the same goal. Comparable worth supporters have always advocated the former and never the latter. Politics have always trumped logic.

Comparable worth supporters have never dirtied their hands to worry about where the money comes from to pay the higher salaries. Presumably in the government case, taxpayers will simply be handed a higher bill. In the private sector case, higher prices for consumers or lower profits for employers would be the consequence.

In the 1980s and 1990s comparable worth was a moderately hot topic and made some headway. All but five states studied their pay scales, but only a handful have actually implemented their findings. Washington and Minnesota are notable examples of the latter group. Scores of city, county, and local governments have instituted comparable worth adjustments as have had nearly 200 public colleges and universities. In Canada the province of Ontario took the lead enacting the Pay Equity Act of 1988, which required comparable worth job evaluations of all private employers of more than ten employees starting January 1, 1990. All provinces except those in the West eventually enacted similar legislation. Pay systems in Australia and Great Britain have some elements of comparable worth built in.

Many economists remain quite skeptical of comparable worth as a policy. Among the criticisms of comparable worth are the following:

- Despite the widespread use of job evaluation schemes, there should be no presumption that they are scientifically objective measures of a job's "worth." They are simply one evaluator's subjective view. There have been instances when two evaluators have evaluated the exact same jobs and reached very different conclusions (Gold 1983, 49–54).
- Since the jobs in question are already recruiting an adequate supply of labor

as it currently stands, would it not be the case that raising wages for some jobs would ultimately create surpluses of labor for some jobs and shortages for others? If you like minimum wages, you will love comparable worth because it is simply a system of minimum wages throughout the economy. The inefficiency of such a system is obvious and would be readily apparent right away. We need flexible, market-determined wages to allocate labor to where it is most needed. Comparable worth would prevent the price system from doing what it is supposed to do.

- Would raising wages of predominantly female jobs simply create an incentive for women to remain in those jobs? That would seem to be inconsistent with the presumed goal of reducing sex segregation and sex stereotyping of jobs.
- The guiding principle of comparable worth seems to be that the importance of a job to society (its worth) should govern its remuneration (but does not when women do important jobs). In that, they have it all wrong. They have made a mistake that laypeople have made for literally centuries, but that economists clarified in the nineteenth century. The problem is known as the diamond-water paradox. Which good has a higher price—diamonds or water? Which good is more important—diamonds or water? Hopefully you answered diamonds to the first question and water to the second. Water, which is so much more important to society than diamonds, is relatively cheap because water is much less scarce than diamonds. Ultimately the price of any good is determined by both demand (its worth to society) and supply (its scarcity). Neither demand nor supply is more important. That is like asking which blade of the scissors is more important in cutting the paper. Relatively speaking, since water is so plentiful, its price is low despite its great importance. In the technical language of economics, the price of a good is governed by its marginal utility, not its total utility.

The conflict in visions of how the labor market works, as represented by the quote at the beginning of this section, could not be starker.

CONCLUSION

This chapter reviewed the most important antidiscrimination laws, and discussed several interesting and significant lower and Supreme Court rulings that have defined the laws. A key lesson is that we need to remove our rose-colored glasses when thinking about the antidiscrimination laws. While discriminatory practices are a nasty business, the legal remedies available frequently harm innocent third parties. As a normative matter, these are trade-offs we may be willing make, but we should never pretend the trade-offs do not exist. The thorny thicket that is affirmative action was then investigated. Despite the fact that affirmative action has been part of the landscape for nearly four decades, conclusions about what impact affirmative action has that we can really be confident in are few.

The most controversial aspect of antidiscrimination law has been its treatment of preferential policies. The law allows voluntary preferential treatment policies as long as they are narrowly tailored and temporary. While highly controversial in the 1980s and 1990s, much of the heat these rulings generated has seemed to dissipate. We as a society have begun to make our peace with the policies.

The frontier of antidiscrimination law would seem to be greater inclusiveness, extending protection to groups previously unprotected. Protection against discrimination on the basis of sexual orientation may very well be the next wall to be breached. After that, who knows? The evidence is striking that people are treated differently on the basis of such physical characteristics as height, weight, and physical attractiveness. Are laws protecting the less-favored in these areas soon to follow?

The policy of comparable worth is difficult to reconcile with the view of the workings of labor markets that is favored by the vast majority of economists. Market-determined wages still act to clear the market, even if the wage reflects a "taste for discrimination." Artificially "perfecting" wages will inevitably create labor market shortages and surpluses in the conventional model. Comparable worth advocates have yet to address themselves to those objections. Perhaps they question whether labor supply curves have any elasticity, or else they are willing to trade off efficiency for the more equitable wage structure they believe will follow.

QUESTIONS FOR REVIEW AND PRACTICE

1. To be promoted to lieutenant, police officers in a city police department first have to pass a written aptitude test. This requirement was challenged in court by several black officers on the grounds that the test unfairly discriminated against blacks. To win the case, what did the black officers have to prove? What did the city have to prove, if anything, to be found innocent of discrimination?

2. As a matter of law and a matter of economics are the antidiscrimination laws interpreted correctly by the courts?

3. Develop a model of the effect of labor market discrimination on personal investments in education. What would your model predict about the effect of affirmative action programs (like in *Weber* or *Johnson*) on personal investments in education?

4. Review the employer discrimination case of the Personal Prejudice Model. What are the long-run predictions of this model? What are the implications of this model for the *Weber v United Steelworkers* case and affirmative action as practiced by the federal government? (Hint: The question asks you what the model says, not what your personal opinion is.)

5. What are the trade-offs involved in affirmative action? Do you consider affirmative action to be a fair policy? What efficiency loss would you be willing to tolerate for a successful affirmative action program?

6. Construct a theory of the labor market under which comparable worth is an equitable and efficient policy.

7. The Equal Pay Act of 1963 prohibited employers from paying different wages to workers who performed the same work but differed by gender. There were four exceptions to this standard. List the four exceptions and provide a contemporary example of each.

8. How has the Age Discrimination in Employment Act changed over time? Are

there any occupations that should have a mandatory retirement age? Explain your answer.

9. What was the fate of the ADA Restoration Act of 2007? What are the positive and normative economic issues involved in deciding whether that was an appropriate outcome?

NOTES

1. This is not to deny that some who view things from the libertarian perspective might argue that freedom requires that individuals should be able to use their property as they see fit, even to the extent of discriminating against some people. Most libertarians work from a model that says discriminators are only hurting themselves. Nonetheless, public opinion in the United States favors the existence of antidiscrimination laws.

2. Lest you think that was just a fanciful example, this was one of the issues faced by the United States Supreme Court in the 1977 case *Dothard v Rawlinson* (United States Supreme Court 1977). The Court ruled that the weight and height restrictions were discriminatory, but that women could be restricted from "contact" jobs as a way to help keep order. Female guards in maximum security prisons are not uncommon these days.

3. The Fair Labor Standards Act was initially enacted in 1938. It is best known for setting minimum wage and maximum hours standards.

4. *Bona fide* essentially means "in good faith."

5. A preponderance of evidence means that the evidence leans more toward one side than the other—50 percent + 1. It is a lighter burden than "beyond a reasonable doubt."

6. Since Griggs's name was the first in the alphabet, he got to enter history. The rest of the group became *et al.*

7. The precedent was briefly disrupted by the 1989 *Ward's Cove* case (United States Supreme Court 1989a), but subsequent legislation restored the precedent.

8. The opinion suggested that white males could be one of those groups. Subsequent rulings have cast doubt on that.

9. This order had been based on President John Kennedy's Executive Order 10925 issued in 1961.

10. A government contractor is a private firm that does business with the government, e.g., a clothing company that manufactured military uniforms to be sold to the Pentagon or a construction company that built a government office building. The volume of business that the government does each year with contractors is substantial.

11. Disbarment means the firm would be prohibited from receiving further government contracts.

12. The level of effort was what would have been expected given the parameters of the model. See Clive Bull, Andrew Schotter, and Keith Weigelt (1987).

13. This policy is sometimes called pay equity.

14. Various weighting schemes can be employed to reflect the relative importance of different characteristics. For example, the total points available for one characteristic might be greater than the total points available for another. Or, the same point scale might be used for each characteristic, but differential weights applied when the point totals for each characteristic were totaled. The details of specific job evaluation systems need not detain us.

PART III

POVERTY

12 A Slice Too Small

INTRODUCTION

Having a slice that is large enough to be nourishing is a prerequisite for a good life. But by the measurement standards used in the United States, tens of millions of people receive a "slice too small." Worldwide, billions of people receive a too-small slice. This chapter discusses the extent of poverty in the United States, explains how poverty is measured, wades into the debate over how poverty should be measured, attempts to describe a "typical" poor person, and looks at the wide range of opinion about why people are poor.

THE EXTENT OF POVERTY IN THE UNITED STATES

According to the United States Bureau of the Census, in 2006 36.5 million residents of the United States had incomes so low they were considered poor. That number was 12.3 percent of the population; this number is frequently called the poverty rate.

The official statistics do not tell a very happy story. Figure 12.1 shows a time trend of the number of poor and the poverty rate in the United States over the period 1959 to 2006.[1] While the number of poor people has fallen since 1959, the decrease has only been a little over 3 million. In fact, the number has actually increased since the early 1970s by over 13 million persons. While the poverty rate has fallen significantly since 1959, it is higher today than in some of the intermittent years. In 2000 the poverty rate was 11.3 percent, and three decades ago, in 1973, it was 11.1 percent.

Comparing the United States to other countries in this regard is problematic. The method the United States uses to obtain the "official" poverty statistics presented in the previous paragraph is not comparable to the methods by which any other country measures poverty rates. International comparisons will be more feasible when we discuss alternative methods of measuring poverty.

MEASURING POVERTY

The United States uses an absolute standard of poverty obtained by comparing a unit's (individual, family or household) income to a fixed and unchanging poverty threshold.

Figure 12.1 **Number in Poverty and Poverty Rate, 1959 to 2006**

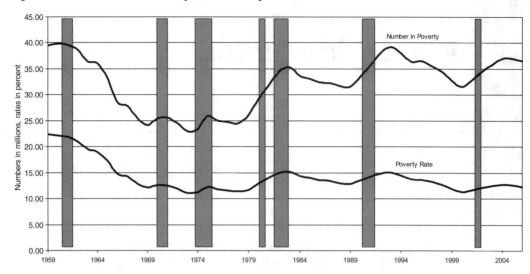

Source: U.S. Census Bureau, Current Populaton Survey, 1960 to 2007 Annual Social and Economic Supplements; NBER designated contractions in shaded areas

THE ORSHANSKY STANDARD

The U.S. Census Bureau measures poverty by using poverty thresholds based on the Orshansky standard. Table 12.1 shows the poverty thresholds in use in 2006. These thresholds are income levels defined by size of family and number of children. If a family has an income below its threshold, the family and every member of that family is defined as being poor.

The story of the origin of the poverty thresholds is both instructive and interesting. The first poverty line was arbitrarily established by the Council of Economic Advisers in 1959. The council used a poverty threshold of $3,000 for families and $1,500 for individuals. A few years later the government attempted to measure poverty more precisely, and the job was given to Mollie Orshansky, an economist with the U.S. Social Security Administration.

Orshansky began by working with the Department of Agriculture's food budgets. Earlier, the USDA had designed food budgets representing different standards of living. There were four levels—economy, low-cost, moderate-cost, and liberal; all were defined by the type and cost of food consumed.

Orshansky choose the economy budget, a budget designed for "temporary or emergency use when funds are low." Table 12.2 is an example of an economy budget.[3] The table shows the amount of various food types allowed per week for selected age and gender groups. How does this food budget compare to what you eat today? The assumption was that all this food would be prepared and consumed at home.[4] There was no allowance for meals eaten out or other food eaten away from home (like at school or work).

Table 12.1

Poverty Thresholds in 2006 by Size of Family and Number of Related Children Under 18 Years

Size of Family Unit	Related Children Under 18 Years								
	None	One	Two	Three	Four	Five	Six	Seven	Eight or More
One person under 65	10,488								
One person 65 years and older	9,669								
Two people: householder under 65 years	13,500	13,896							
Two people: householder 65 years and older	12,186	13,843							
Three people	15,769	16,227	16,242						
Four people	20,794	21,134	20,444	20,516					
Five people	25,076	25,441	24,662	24,059	23,691				
Six people	28,842	28,957	28,360	27,788	26,938	26,434			
Seven people	33,187	33,394	32,680	32,182	31,254	30,172	28,985		
Eight people	37,117	37,444	36,770	36,180	35,342	34,278	33,171	32,890	
Nine people or more	44,649	44,865	44,269	43,768	42,945	41,813	40,790	40,536	38,975

Source: U.S. Census Bureau, 2006.

Table 12.2

The Economy Budget. Suggested Intake per Week

Group	Milk, cheese, ice cream (Qt.)	Meat, poultry, fish (Lb.)	(Oz.)	Eggs (No.)	Dry beans and peas, nuts (Lb.)	(Oz.)	Flour, cereal, baked goods (Lb.)	(Oz.)	Citrus fruit, tomato (Lb.)	(Oz.)	Dark green and deep yellow vegetables (Lb.)	(Oz.)	Potatoes (Lb.)	(Oz.)	Other vegetables and fruits (Lb.)	(Oz.)	Fats, oils (Lb.)	(Oz.)	Sugars, sweets (Lb.)	(Oz.)
Children																				
7 months–1 year	5.5	0	8	4	0	0	0	12	1	0	0	4	0	8	1	0	0	1	0	1
1–3 years	5	0	12	4	0	1	1	8	1	0	0	4	1	0	2	0	0	4	0	4
4–6 years	5	1	0	4	0	4	2	4	1	4	0	4	1	8	2	0	0	6	0	6
7–9 years	5	1	8	5	0	6	2	8	1	8	0	8	2	4	3	0	0	10	0	10
10–12 years	6	1	12	5	0	8	3	4	1	12	0	8	2	12	3	4	0	10	0	12
Girls																				
13–15 years	6.5	2	0	5	0	8	3	4	1	12	0	12	3	0	3	8	0	12	0	10
16–19 years	6.5	2	0	5	0	8	3	0	1	12	0	12	2	12	3	4	0	8	0	10
Boys																				
13–15 years	6	2	0	5	0	10	4	8	2	0	0	12	3	4	3	8	0	14	0	12
16–19 years	6	2	8	5	0	12	5	8	2	0	0	12	4	12	3	8	1	0	0	14
Women																				
20–34 years	3	1	4	4	0	4	3	0	1	12	0	12	3	0	3	0	0	8	0	12
35–54 years	3	1	4	4	0	4	3	0	1	12	0	12	2	12	2	12	0	6	0	12
55–74 years	3	1	4	4	0	4	2	8	1	12	0	12	2	8	2	8	0	6	0	6
75 years and over	3	1	4	4	0	4	2	4	1	12	0	12	2	4	2	4	0	6	0	6
Pregnant	7	2	0	7	0	4	2	8	3	0	1	8	2	8	4	0	0	6	0	8
Lactating	10	2	0	6	0	4	3	4	4	0	1	8	3	12	4	8	0	10	0	12
Men																				
20–34 years	3	2	0	5	0	10	4	12	1	12	0	12	4	4	3	8	0	14	1	2
35–54 years	3	2	0	5	0	10	4	4	1	12	0	12	3	8	3	0	0	12	0	14
55–74 years	3	2	0	5	0	6	4	0	1	12	0	12	3	0	2	12	0	12	0	12
75 years and over	3	2	0	5	0	6	3	8	1	12	0	12	2	12	2	8	0	10	0	12

Source: Cofer, Grossman, and Clark, 1962.

Next Orshansky computed the cost of the various items. Then, since surveys showed that the typical American family spent about one-third of its income on food (United States Department of Agriculture 1956), she took the cost of the food budget, multiplied it by three, and derived the poverty thresholds.[5]

According to Orshansky, the thresholds were designed as an attempt to "specify the minimum money income that could support an average family of given composition at the lowest level consistent with standards prevailing in this country" (Orshansky 1965, 214). This points out that the poverty line constructed in this way was never meant to be an objective measure of poverty status. Indeed, an objective measure is impossible. "To say who is poor is to use all sorts of value judgments" (Orshansky 1969, 37). And political value judgments were employed. A consideration was that the poverty population should not seem so small that antipoverty programs would not be warranted, but should not seem so large that a solution would seem impossible. A benchmark was a line from President Franklin Delano Roosevelt's second inaugural address, "I see one-third of a nation ill-housed, ill-clad, ill-nourished" (Roosevelt 1937). If the poverty threshold had yielded a poverty rate exceeding one-third, then it would have appeared that no progress had been made since the Great Depression, which might have suggested that no progress could be made (Orshansky 1969, 37).

This exercise was performed until 1967 when the Census Bureau decided to simplify things. Since that time, the poverty thresholds for each year have been computed by taking the previous year's thresholds and increasing them by the rate of inflation.

This method of measuring poverty is said to use an absolute standard. Essentially, it establishes a standard of living defined in terms of how many goods and services people can buy. That same standard is used each year. Since it is unchanging, it is absolute.

Who Is Poor?

What are the characteristics of the typical poor person? We probably all have a mental image in our minds of what the typical poor person looks like. It would be interesting to see whether our mental picture squares with reality. Unfortunately there are two problems. As an exercise in statistics it would be possible to put together a profile of a typical poor person. For example, in 2006 if we just look at the absolute numbers that fall into each demographic characteristic we can say that the typical poor person is a native-born white female aged 18 to 64 living in a central city in the South and who did not work at all last year, had children, but did not have a husband. But emphasizing what is typical is fraught with danger. If we try to craft policies that meet the needs of the typical poor person we run the danger of not meeting the needs of nontypical people, and there are many people in all the nontypical categories. For example, there are more poor people who do not live in central cities than live in them, and more who live outside the South than in it. There are nearly as many poor married couples or no-wife families as there are poor female-headed no-husband families. While there are more poor whites, blacks are three times more likely to be poor than whites. In

Table 12.3

Families and People in Poverty by Selected Characteristics, 2005

Characteristic	Number (thousands)	Percentage
Type of Family		
Married-couple	2,944	5.1
Female householder, no husband present	4,044	28.7
Male householder, no wife present	689	13.0
Race and Hispanic Origin		
White	24,872	10.6
White, not Hispanic	16,227	8.3
Black	9,168	24.9
Asian	1,402	11.1
Hispanic origin (any race)	9,368	21.8
Age		
Under 18 years	12,896	17.6
18–64 years	20,450	11.1
65 years and older	3,803	10.1
Nativity		
Native	31,080	12.1
Foreign born	5,870	16.5
Naturalized citizen	1,441	10.4
Not a citizen	4,429	20.4
Region		
Northeast	6,103	11.3
Midwest	7,419	11.4
South	14,854	14.0
West	8,573	20.4
Metropolitan Status		
Inside metropolitan statistical areas	30,098	12.2
Inside principal cities	15,966	17.0
Outside principal cities	14,132	9.3
Outside metropolitan statistical areas	6,852	14.5
Work Experience		
All workers (16 years and older)	9,340	6.0
Worked full-time, year-round	2,894	2.8
Not full-time, year-round	6,446	12.8
Did not work at least 1 week	16,041	21.8

Source: U.S. Bureau of the Census, Current Population Survey, Annual Social and Economic Supplements, 2007.

short, looking at the typical poor person can be highly misleading. The solution to that is to simply look at the facts. See Table 12.3 for an overview of characteristics of families and people living in poverty.

1. Race: As already indicated and as Table 12.3 makes clear, most poor people in the United States are white. It is important to know this because it appears to conflict with the general public perception that most poor people are black. Martin Gilens argues that some of the blame for this misperception can be laid squarely on the doorstep of the media who have consistently overrepresented blacks among the poor in their coverage of the poverty issue (Gilens 2004).

However, here things get a bit sticky. Is poverty a "white problem" or a "black problem?" To paraphrase the words of a famous American, it depends on what the meaning of the word *problem* is. Certainly there are more poor whites than any other group, but in the United States whites make up the majority of the population. If we look at the poverty rate by race we see that it is 8.3 percent for whites and 24.9 percent for blacks. This means that if you were to select a black person at random, that person would be three times more likely to be poor than a white person selected at random. This points out that trying to put a racial face on poverty is not a very fruitful activity.

2. Type of family: Table 12.3 shows that most poor live in families, most of the families are female-headed with no husband present, and most of the poor in these families are children. Nevertheless over one quarter of the poor are single individuals and the poverty rate for singletons is approximately twice that for families. While female-headed families predominate in the poverty ranks, there are a great many married-couple families that are poor. In fact, the total number of poor married-couple families is a little over 80 percent of the number of female-headed families. Of course, poverty rates differ greatly by type of family. The married-couple poverty rate is 5.1 percent while the rate is 28.7 percent for female-headed families, which is more than five times greater.

3. Age: Here is another case of the complexities caused by numbers. Most poor people in the United States are between the ages of eighteen and sixty-four (call them adults), which is why I made the typical poor person of that age group. But most *people* in the United States are between the ages of eighteen and sixty-four. If we look at poverty rates, we see that the rate for children (less than eighteen years of age) is approximately 70 percent higher than that of adults. The lowest poverty rate is for senior citizens (over sixty-four years of age).

   The poverty rate for seniors was not always lower than that for children. From the beginning of poverty rate computation until the mid-1970s it was higher. The dramatic improvement for seniors is probably a tribute to the effectiveness of our Social Security system as much as anything. This pattern of having lower poverty rates for seniors than for children is a reversal of historical patterns that are centuries old.

4. Nativity: The fact that more native born people are poor than nonnative born is simply a reflection of the fact that most people in the country were born here. Again, the poverty rates tell the real story. People who are nonnative but naturalized citizens have lower poverty rates than the native born. This probably reflects the fact that people who are willing to uproot their lives and move to a foreign culture are likely to have unusual levels of motivation and skills and immigrants who become naturalized have lived here long enough to become accustomed to the culture. Nonnaturalized residents have very high poverty rates, which presumably reflects language and cultural adjustment difficulties.

5. Region: Most poor people are southerners, and southerners, have the highest poverty rate. This is a longstanding historical pattern, but the differences between the regions have decreased over time.

6. Metropolitan status: While officially the three categories of residence are (1) inside central city, (2) outside central city (but inside metropolitan region), and (3) outside metropolitan region; more familiar terms would be city, suburb, and country. The city is home to most of the poor and has the highest poverty rate, but rural areas are also centers of poverty.

7. Work experience: These statistics need to be treated with some care. Most poor people did no work the previous year, but since a large proportion of the poor are children or senior citizens and some poor are disabled, that statistic should not be too shocking. Perhaps more shocking is the 2.9 million people who worked full-time, year-round and did not make enough to exceed the poverty line. How is that possible? If you work full-time, year-round (approximately 2,000 hours) at the 2008 minimum wage of $5.85 per hour, you end up making only $11,700, a bit below the $12,078 needed to raise a two-person, nonelderly family above the poverty line.

WHY ARE PEOPLE POOR?

PROXIMATE, INTERMEDIATE, AND FUNDAMENTAL CAUSES

Why people are poor is obviously an important question that needs to be addressed in any discussion of poverty. Unfortunately, it is not an easy one to answer. A distinction must be made between the proximate cause, intermediate causes, and the fundamental cause of some phenomenon. The proximate cause is the "nearest" cause. In the chain of causation A → B → C → D → E → F (A causes B, B causes C, C causes D, D causes E, and E causes F), the proximate cause of F is E. The fundamental cause is the "original" cause. It is the thing that ultimately sets in motion the chain of causation. In the example just used, the fundamental cause of F is A. Factors B, C, and D are intermediate causes.

TRACING THE CAUSES OF POVERTY

Ultimately we are interested in the fundamental cause (or causes) of poverty. Finding the fundamental cause (or causes) is not just an academic exercise. If our ultimate goal is to design policies to reduce the poverty problem, we need to identify and do something about fundamental causes. Not infrequently our attempts to unravel the chain of causation stops at the proximate or intermediate causes, but attacking intermediate or proximate causes will at best provide temporary amelioration of the problem, like placing a Band-Aid on a head wound.

The proximate cause of poverty is low earning ability, a conclusion as trivial as it is uninteresting. Going back one step, the reason people have low earning ability is because they lack skills, do not work very much, or do not own much capital or other resources. Going back one more step, why do people lack skills, not work very much, and not own capital or other resources?

Here we are about to enter a thicket of intermediate causes and feedback loops from which we may never emerge. Lack of education, family dysfunction, neighborhood

Table 12.4

Educational Attainment and Poverty

	Official Poverty Measure (2000)
All Persons	11.3
Education of those aged 25+	
Less than high school	22.2
High school	9.2
Some college	5.9
College graduate +	3.2

Source: U.S. Bureau of the Census, Current Population Survey Annual Demographic Supplement data, 2001.

effects, lack of transportation, poor health, and just plain bad luck have all been cited as factors contributing to poverty.

- Lack of education: The poor tend to have fewer years of education and attend lower-quality schools. As Chapter 6 explained and Chapter 14 will make even plainer, the earning capacity of persons is positively related to their educational attainment. Table 12.4 shows the distribution of the poor (aged 25 years or older) by educational attainment in the year 2000. High school dropouts are nearly seven times more likely to be poor than college graduates. Interestingly, dropping out of high school does not condemn one to a life of poverty. Nearly 78 percent of high school dropouts were not poor.
- Family dysfunction: There is widespread belief that the characteristics of your family influence your subsequent economic success by instilling (or not instilling) traits needed for success. Did your parents provide a nurturing or chaotic home environment? Did your parents help you with your homework, encourage academic success, and provide resources in the form of books and computers?[6] Did you grow up in an intact or broken home?[7]

    Parents are important sources of information about the job market and have (or do not have) connections. They also pass along their culture, race, and ethnicity to their children.
- Neighborhood effects: There is a widespread belief that the neighborhood you grow up in (where neighborhood is defined broadly to include not just the people who live near you, but also your peer group and your cultural capital) shapes your behavior in a variety of important ways. Are your neighbors brain surgeons and rocket scientists or drug dealers and welfare recipients? Are your friends well-behaved, conscientious students or rowdy "gangstas" in training? Do you come from a culture that values education and obedience, or one where these values are less enforced? Do you live in a depressed area or one with a vibrant economy?[8]

    A leading sociologist, William Julius Wilson, has made the paradoxical argument that part of the disintegration and social chaos (crime, drug use, welfare dependency) of contemporary ghetto neighborhoods stems from the reduction of housing discrimination in the suburbs (Wilson 1987). Back in the day, housing discrimination pretty much bottled up all the members of certain racial and ethnic groups in particular neighborhoods in the city. This meant that middle-class persons lived side by side with lower-class persons. The force of middle-class values was sufficient to keep lower-class behavior in check. Some writers have waxed poetic about how even in ghetto neighborhoods doors would remain unlocked at night. The truth of these recollections of the "good old days" has not been established. As the middle class began exiting to the suburbs, the positive role model effect abated, which led to what we have today.

- Lack of transportation: Today many good blue-collar jobs—the types of jobs that would be compatible with the skills of the poor and that would allow the poor to escape their poverty—are found in the suburbs. Many good white-collar jobs are found in the central city and the holders of these jobs are denizens of the suburbs. Public transportation systems have been designed to cater to the needs of white-collar workers. These systems take workers into the city in the morning and out of the city in the evening. Poor city dwellers find it difficult, if not impossible, to get to the suburban jobs.
- Poor health: An individual's health is a factor that directly influences many economic outcomes, from the types of jobs held to potential earnings. Healthy people can work longer hours, are not restricted in the tasks they are able to do, can handle stress better, and can concentrate better.
- Just plain bad luck: Some individuals just have bad luck. Some manage to catch on with expanding industries, others choose badly. Marriages dissolve. People are involved in accidents. Most buy losing lottery tickets.

Of course all this takes place against the backdrop of macroeconomic conditions. Does a rising tide lift all boats? Look back at Figure 12.1. The shaded areas on the graph show the periods of recession in the United States since 1959. Clearly the poverty rate rose significantly during those periods while declining during the alternating periods of expansion. It also seems that the impact of economic growth on the poverty rate has declined over time. Since the early 1970s the poverty rate has fluctuated within a fairly narrow band even though that period has been one of significant increase in real GDP.

Are any of these factors a fundamental cause? To be a fundamental cause, a factor must cause events but not be caused by any of those events itself. It would be difficult to consider any of those factors fundamental because of the feedback relationships between them. Consider a simple two-way feedback loop between income and health. Bad health causes low income for the reasons mentioned above. But your income can influence your health. People with higher incomes can buy better medical care and insurance, may live in healthier environments,[9] may be able to afford a healthier diet, may work in occupations performed under safer and healthier conditions, and may be more knowledgeable about health issues in general and what constitutes a healthy lifestyle.

Consider other two-way causation loops between other factors on the list. Growing up in a "bad" neighborhood can certainly act to limit your chance to achieve economic success, but lack of economic success can consign you (and your family) to a bad neighborhood. Economic success feeds back on family stability and vice versa. Not having a car or having an unreliable car can create problems with obtaining and holding a good job, while having a good job allows you to buy a reliable car.

N-way causation mechanisms can be imagined, if described only with great difficulty. It can get very complicated very fast, but the basic point is that fighting a so-called war on poverty requires attention to the whole package of barriers facing the poor. For example, providing college scholarships to poor students will not be very effective if the family dysfunction and neighborhood effects limiting achievement in elementary school cannot be nipped in the bud.

The true story of Lisa Brooks is illustrative. Lisa Brooks was a character in David K. Shipler's *The Working Poor: Invisible in America* (Shipler 2004). Lisa was a twenty-four-year-old single mother of four in the late nineties, a time of significant economic expansion (Shipler 2004, 26–7). Lisa worked hard as a caretaker at a halfway home for mentally ill adults, but at $8.21 an hour the only housing she could afford was a damp, drafty apartment. When a son was stricken with an asthma attack, she called an ambulance to get him to the emergency room. When her insurance would not cover the ambulance charges she was left with an unpaid bill on her credit report that prevented her from obtaining better housing and a more reliable car. Of course, having a sickly child and an unreliable car was not good for her work stability and she continued to struggle to earn a "living" income.

What was the fundamental cause of Lisa's poverty? Did her low earning ability that forced her to settle for inadequate housing that exacerbated her son's health problems help keep her in poverty? Was it because her single parent status kept family income low and meant there was not another parent to share the burden of caring for her son? What responsibility did Lisa bear for the fact that she was a single parent? Did the fact that her earning power was low and her four children inhibit her ability to land a mate? Since Lisa already had four children by the age of twenty-four, it is possible she had made some bad choices as a teenager. Were her choices then ultimately to blame for what happened later? Can a teenager ever be held responsible for the bad choices she makes? What responsibility did Lisa's parents have for their failure to prevent her from making bad choices? Did Lisa's parents do everything they could, or did Lisa simply lack appropriate social support at the time when it was most needed? Would living in a better neighborhood with better housing and a support group have prevented the downward spiral of Lisa's family? Did her son's poor health cause her economic crisis, or was her economic crisis the cause of her son's poor health? Would an even stronger overall economy have made most of the problems disappear? Or was Lisa just a victim of bad luck?

THE FUNDAMENTAL CAUSE (OR CAUSES) OF POVERTY

There are essentially two schools of thought on the fundamental cause (or causes) of poverty. One school believes the fundamental cause of poverty lies with individuals. For a variety of reasons, an individual may lack "what it takes" to work their way out of poverty. A variety of "deficiencies" are cited: the poor are poor because they are not very "smart," lack motivation and drive, lack morals, lack thriftiness, or are reluctant to take risks. Unless we can find a way to eliminate these deficiencies, the poor will always be with us. The other school believes the fundamental cause of poverty lies in the institutions of society. The poor are capable, but find the institutions "stacked against" them. Unless we can find the will or a way to improve our institutions, the poor will always be with us.

Illustrative of the "the problem is people" approach is the work of Richard Herrnstein and Charles Murray (Herrnstein and Murray 1994). On the basis of extensive empirical analysis, they argue that a major factor determining economic success in the United States is "intelligence,"[10] which is largely influenced by genetic factors. Among the empirical evidence cited is a study of sibling pairs. Their sample consisted of brothers and sisters who had the same parents, grew up in the same household, lived in the same neighborhood, and came from the top 75 percent of the income distribution. One member of the pair had a "normal" (average) IQ while the other had either an exceptionally high (top quartile) or low (bottom quartile) IQ. What they found was that the high IQ sibling had an income 25 percent higher than that of the normal sibling while the low IQ sibling had an income 30 percent less than that of the normal sibling (Murray 1997). One implication of this is that the only thing that would reduce poverty is wholesale redistribution of income from rich to poor.

Another example of the "the problem is people" approach was contained in Section 104 of the Personal Responsibility and Work Opportunity Reconciliation Act of 1996, an act that is frequently referred to simply as the welfare reform law. Section 104 contains the "charitable choice" provision. Essentially, this provision allows faith-based organizations[11] to compete for government contracts to aid poor people on an equal basis with other organizations.[12] The supporters of the provision believed that faith-based organizations had already demonstrated a remarkable record of success in this area.

> Much of the impetus behind welfare reform in the United States rested on the view that poverty—at least to some extent and for some individuals—resulted from bad values. If these values could be changed and those individuals removed from the welfare rolls, then more attention and funds could be provided to those who truly needed the monies. Since the end of poverty required a change of values, the best way to accomplish that change would be by increasing the places where recipients would come into contact with people modeling the necessary values (Queen 2004, 67).

Adherents of "the problem is people" view are not all of the same mind. For example, people who support the charitable choice provisions do not necessarily believe that IQ is an important determinant of earnings, and vice versa.

Illustrative of the "the problem is institutions" approach is the dual labor market theory (Reich, Gordon, and Edwards 1973). According to the theory, the labor market can be considered to be divided into two sectors (see Figure 12.2). The primary sector consists of the "good" jobs. These jobs pay high wages, offer generous fringe benefits, and provide training and promotion opportunities. The secondary sector consists of the "bad" jobs. These jobs pay low wages, have no fringe benefits, and are dead end–type jobs. To be successful in the primary sector, workers have to pos-

Figure 12.2 **The Dual Labor Market Theory**

Labor Market

sess certain character traits. They need to be intelligent, hardworking, and willing to follow rules and submit to discipline. No one, least of all employers, expects this from secondary-sector employees. The problem is one of initial assignment. If you are unlucky enough to start in the secondary sector, you are likely to remain there the rest of your career because working secondary-sector jobs creates traits in workers that eventually make them unsuitable for primary-sector jobs. Discrimination also contributes to initial assignment. Disfavored groups such as minorities, women, and immigrants tend to be placed in the secondary sector.

"The problem is institutions" approach is not represented solely by analyses from left-wingers who are suspicious of capitalism. Right-wingers can also critique the institutions of society, although the institution they direct their fire at is government run amuck. From minimum wage laws and other attempts to mandate benefits to welfare programs that create incentives for not working or saving, they identify the barriers confronting the poor as primarily the unintended side effects of various government policies.

The negative feedback loop problem mentioned in the previous section also applies here. Yes, the poor may have deficiencies but are the deficiencies inherent in the poor or put there by the institutions of society? The poor may have low IQs, but low IQ may be a consequence of the inferior brand of schooling available to the poor. Or, perhaps the deficiencies of the poor shape the types of institutions they have access to. If the low IQ of the poor limits them to menial, low-paid labor, then perhaps the best type of schooling to offer is what prepares them for that type of work.

The conundrum of whom or what is to blame can be illustrated by the following assignment:

Society Ought to Do More for Camellia Woodruff

Shipler's book, *The Working Poor: Invisible in America*, should be read by anyone interested in studying poverty. Starting in 1997, Shipler, a journalist, spent nearly six years traveling the country chronicling the lives of a group of people who were members of the working poor. The term *working poor* refers to a group of people who make an attempt to work for a living, but fail to achieve a standard of living much above the poverty line. Their failure stems from both a lack of steady work and low wages when they do work.

One of the lessons of the book is that despite their problems in the labor market, the lives of many of the working poor are unlikely to be enhanced simply by policies directed at improving the workings of the labor market. In almost all cases, the working poor suffer from multiple deficiencies that have negative feedback effects. The Lisa Brooks example given earlier is a case in point.

A second lesson is that in virtually every case the poor contribute to their predicament through bad choices. The Camellia Woodruff story is illustrative (Shipler 2004, 123–125). Camellia was raised in a poor housing project in Los Angeles. Her mother never provided much nurturing and died of a drug overdose when Camellia was a teenager. Camellia dropped out of school in eleventh grade, fell into the "street life" and an abusive relationship, and was convicted of shoplifting. She had trouble getting jobs and even more difficulty holding them. In fact, Camellia had never held any job for more than a few months. At twenty-six years of age, Camellia was going nowhere fast. At that point Glenda Taylor of the federally funded Jobs-Plus program entered her life. Glenda came from a neighborhood similar to Camellia's, but had been able to go to college and make a success of herself. Glenda worked hard with Camellia and eventually got her an interview with a large, established department store for a job with some prospect for advancement. That Camellia would have actually gotten the job was not a foregone conclusion. The job was in the jewelry department, and Camellia's shoplifting charge was bound to have weighed heavily in the employer's decision. But the process never reached that stage because Camellia never bothered to show up for the interview. As she later told Glenda, she was ashamed of her shoplifting charge, unsure about whether she would make a good salesperson or not, and was disinclined toward indoor work. She was also unable to find the interview site, but, of course, never bothered to call.

Here is the crux of the controversy over the fundamental cause of poverty. Is Camellia to blame for failing to follow up on a potential opportunity, or is society to blame for stealing Camellia's self-esteem? In the fall of 2004 I asked students in my Poverty, Affluence, and Equality course to address this question. They were to write a short essay on the topic "Society Ought to Do More for Camellia Woodruff." Here are two of the essays.[13] See what you think.

> It would be easy to condemn someone who doesn't even go to the interviews that their caseworker arranges for them. But condemnation without looking any deeper than the surface is brash and ignorant. People tend to overlook the details of how they became the people they are at present. People minimize the strong effect of a loving family and a safe community. Camellia Woodruff had the benefit of neither of these. She was raised in one of the most violent, impoverished areas in California (the site of race riots in the '70s) and saw her mom die of a drug overdose. An individual might have the courage and strength to overcome one of these horrible happenstances in life, but two might just overburden the rest of us. Considering the odds that Camellia has been battling, I think we can do more to help her.

Camellia Woodruff has obviously lost the courage to persevere. She needs a little push to keep her fighting and her caseworker, Glenda Taylor, seems to understand that. Glenda understands the "fear" that can paralyze the underprivileged, and create the tendency, "not to want to go out there [into the working world], because you're scared, [or] you're afraid." Glenda Taylor arranged for Camellia to interview for the job at Macy's. As readers, we tend to focus on the fact that Camellia failed to take advantage of the opportunity that was presented to her. We find it easier to brush the problem aside by making the argument that even when we offer help, and pay for programs to help people, they don't take advantage of it. But think for a moment how your life would be different if, while growing up in a ghetto, you watched your mom die of a drug overdose. How would your life be different if no one was there to encourage you to study hard, encourage you pursue a college degree, or just generally love you?

We tend to take for granted the loving, nurturing, progressive households in which many of us grew up. Many people, like Camellia and her mother, are struggling to live day to day. They simply don't have the time or the foresight to understand the impact of education and money management. Our parents instilled in us that we should work hard in school because doing so would benefit us in the long-run. They taught us how to defer gratification and helped us to understand the value of a hard earned wage. Good parents are invaluable to a youth. They encourage us when we fail, and they scold us when we are wrong. A good upbringing is something that government food stamps and earned income tax credits simply can't buy. But there are other ways the government can aid Camellia Woodruff and the impoverished people of our nation.

One of the most important steps in helping people like Camellia begins with improving the school districts in which underprivileged individuals are brought up. First and foremost, we need to focus federal funding on impoverished areas. With increased funding, the school could entice better teachers to work in these communities. Currently, it is much more lucrative to work in a rich, cushy suburb than to work in an inner city where teachers are needed the most. Quite simply, pay is too low to entice workers to enter the market in those areas. Before spending money on testing students, we should provide students with teachers that can actually teach by subsidizing teachers' salaries in underprivileged communities.

With more funding, the school could also act more as a community center where parents can come to learn both how to manage finances, and how to handle child-rearing. True, it might be difficult to get some parents involved in the program, but the government could manage unwilling parents by making it mandatory, for receipt of federal funds, to attend these fiscal seminars and child-rearing programs. The school could additionally be used as a place to instruct parents in the skills necessary to get jobs. In doing some of these things you can construct the school as a focal point for the community. A place where both students and parents can come to learn. In this way you instill a culture of learning in both underprivileged adults and children.

Enforcement is a key ingredient in making sure that the underprivileged do more than just collect benefits. Caseworkers on the front lines are overburdened and they need help. Federal funding could be used both to increase the salaries of government workers and to hire additional caseworkers to reduce the loads on current workers. These measures would go a long way in seeing that people like Camellia are forced to find a way out of poverty. People are lazy. There is no question of that. But many of these people have never been taught how to succeed and so laziness becomes a sedative. They think that they are stupid and feel that they cannot achieve; this only serves to perpetuate the cycle. Additional caseworkers provide more time for individualized attention to people's problems. With continued support Camellia will be able to find herself and be able to become financially and socially stable.

Better education and a stronger emphasis on teaching adults how to get off welfare, coupled with a strong focus on mentally supporting the impoverished, should result in less people on the welfare rolls. Increasing the reward for people to work in impoverished neighborhoods will encourage the best and the brightest to help improve those communities. With a little encouragement from caseworkers and school administrators adults and children can become confident in their ability to succeed. Bureaucrats in Washington have already proven too far displaced from the problems of the impoverished and unprivileged to provide successful support. We need more dedicated people like Glenda Taylor to fight the battles against poverty in impoverished neighborhoods. Impoverished people, like Camellia Woodruff, first need to be taught that they *can* succeed before we can show them *how* to succeed.

—Derek Simpkins

The fine line dividing personal and societal responsibility is sometimes difficult to discern when dealing with the issue of poverty. How much help does society owe an individual who is equally disadvantaged by circumstance and self-destruction? As David Shipler acknowledges in his book *The Working Poor: Forgotten in America,* "it is difficult to find someone whose poverty is not somehow related to his or her unwise behavior—to drop out of school, to have a baby out of wedlock, to do drugs, to be chronically late to work." However, it is likewise "difficult to find behavior that is not somehow related to the inherited conditions of being poorly parented, poorly educated, poorly housed in neighborhoods from which no distant horizon of possibility can be seen." Camellia Woodruff, one of the individuals appearing in Shipler's book, is no exception to this rule. The daughter of a drug addict who eventually died of an overdose, she lived a life isolated from opportunity in the Los Angeles housing project where she lived. Camellia's vision barely extended past the moment in which she was living: Shipler reports that she had never considered where she wanted to be ten years out. She received help and advice from a sympathetic social worker, but could never follow through on the opportunities—however slim—offered her. It is here, despite the many nuances of disadvantage and despair to navigate in Camellia's life, that I find the answer to the question posed above. It is my view that society's obligation to Camellia Woodruff ends where she chooses to stop it, which is to say, it ends at the point where she squanders the help already being offered.

The fine line between personal and societal responsibility, then, becomes a moving target. There are elementary levels of aid already available to any individual who seeks it out, including both public and private organizations dedicated to helping people into the workforce, and ideally out of poverty. Camellia may or may not have sought out her social worker, Glenda (Shipler doesn't say), but once Glenda was involved, she pushed Camellia "relentlessly" to attend an orientation for a job at a department store whose manager Glenda had already talked to. Camellia may or may not have gotten the job, but the fact that she never attended the orientation, in my view, ends society's responsibility to offer more help. However, had she taken the initiative to help herself, more aid should be—and probably would have been—forthcoming. This is not to say that the reasons for Camellia's paralysis that Shipler explores are meaningless: fear of life outside the housing projects, feelings of worthlessness and self-loathing reinforced by years of poverty and despair—these are real problems that have real effects on those living in poverty. To a certain extent, however, their existence cannot become an excuse for an individual not to help themselves. Until Camellia, or anyone else, makes the decision to do that, any amount of aid will be ineffective, because the key ingredient is an individual's own initiative. Again, then, society has already stepped forward to help Camellia, and all that remains is for her to bridge the remaining distance.

—Elizabeth Elzer

THE DEBATE ABOUT THE OFFICIAL MEASURE OF POVERTY

As is to be expected when it comes to any sensitive economic statistic, there has been a debate about the most appropriate way to measure poverty.

TINKERING WITH THE ORSHANSKY STANDARD

With respect to the measurement of poverty, there have been several technical criticisms leveled at the Orshansky approach to the poverty thresholds.

1. Food budget: When Orshansky was initially developing the poverty line methodology, she had a choice between several food budgets. The one she used was a budget that was explicitly described as being for "temporary or emergency use only." The clear implication was that this was a budget that people could live on for only relatively short periods of time. Of course, many of the poor are poor for extended periods of time. The next cheapest budget plan was about 35 percent more expensive than the plan for "temporary or emergency use only." If the cost of the food plan was raised 35 percent, all the poverty thresholds would be raised by a similar amount, and we would count many more poor than we currently do.
2. Food budget requires time for preparation: At the time Orshansky did her work, people did not eat out as regularly as they do today and processed foods were not as readily available. The food budget reflects this. To take these items and turn them into an edible meal requires both cooking skill and preparation time. In that quaint time, it might have been reasonable to assume that virtually every female had both. That is clearly not the case today. Cooking skills aside, after a long day of work the last thing many parents want to do after arriving home is to spend a long time in the kitchen preparing a meal. The consequence is that the money allowed for food might not in fact stretch as far as it once did.[14]
3. The food budget multiplier: In the 1950s the typical family spent one-third of its income on food. Today the typical family spends one-fifth to one-sixth of its income on food. That implies a food budget multiplier of 5 or 6 with its consequent impact on the poverty thresholds. Table 12.5 shows what the thresholds would have been in 2006 if a multiplier of 5 had been used. The poverty population easily would have been much higher under the "fake" thresholds.
4. Consumer Price Index (CPI): As mentioned, since 1967 the poverty thresholds have simply been adjusted by the change in the cost of living each year. In principle, this makes sense. In practice, it may be a source of problems. As economists have recognized for quite a while, our measurement tool of the cost of living is likely to overstate changes in the cost of living. One reason is that the CPI does not take into account increases in the quality of goods. If this year's computer has the same price as last year's but has more RAM, a faster processor, and a DVD-RW drive, then you are getting more for your money, but statistics will just record that one computer has the same price as

Table 12.5

Poverty Thresholds in 2006 Using a Multiplier of 5 by Size of Family and Number of Related Children Under 18 Years

Size of Family Unit	Related Children Under 18 Years								
	None	One	Two	Three	Four	Five	Six	Seven	Eight or More
One person under 65	17,480								
One person 65 years and older	16,115								
Two people: householder under 65 years	22,500	23,160							
Two people: householder 65 years and older	20,310	23,072							
Three people	26,282	27,045	27,070						
Four people	34,657	35,223	34,073	34,193					
Five people	41,793	42,402	41,103	40,098	39,485				
Six people	48,070	48,262	47,267	46,313	44,897	44,057			
Seven people	55,312	55,657	54,467	53,637	52,090	50,287	48,308		
Eight people	61,862	62,407	61,283	60,300	58,903	57,130	55,285	54,817	
Nine people or more	74,415	74,775	73,782	72,947	71,575	69,688	67,983	67,560	64,958

Source: U.S. Bureau of the Census and author's calculation.

the previous year. Another reason is that the CPI does not take into account substitution of lower-priced goods for higher-priced goods in the consumer's budget. The CPI is constructed assuming you buy the same amount of beef and chicken each year. But if beef becomes relatively more expensive than chicken you are likely to buy more chicken and less beef. You get the same nutrition and enjoyment but the cost of doing so does not rise as much.

The consequence of this is that the poverty line increases too rapidly, meaning that too many people will be counted as poor.

5. Geographic variation: The census bureau uses the same poverty line everywhere, but, the cost of living is not the same everywhere. Fifteen thousand dollars will get you much farther in rural Mississippi than it will in San Francisco. The Committee on National Statistics of the National Research Council studied the impact of allowing for geographic variations in the cost of living.[15] Their research proxied state differences in the overall cost of living by using rental housing cost differences. Rental housing costs were found to differ by as much as 50 percent across the states. The regions with the highest cost of living were the Northeast and Pacific while the lowest-cost regions were the South and Midwest. Not surprisingly, when this adjustment was applied, poverty rates rose in the high-cost regions and fell in the low-cost regions. New York's poverty rate rose from 12.1 to 13.9 percent in 1999 while Mississippi's fell from 13.0 to 11.1 percent.

TINKERING WITH THE CURRENT POPULATION SURVEY MEASURE OF INCOME

Chapter 1 discussed how the census bureau measured income (called money income) and three alternatives (market, post-social insurance, and disposable income). The way income was measured had implications for inequality. Not surprisingly, the way income is measured has implications for the poverty rate.

Table 12.6 shows the poverty rate under the four definitions. The official poverty rate of 12.6 percent balloons to 19.9 percent when only market income is considered. A fuller accounting of government transfers and taxes reduces the poverty rate to 10.3 percent. Of course, these statistics are subject to the same caveats already mentioned about the impact of economic incentives.

Table 12.6

Number in Poverty and the Poverty Rate Under Alternative Definitions of Income, 2005

Definition of income	Number (in thousands)	Percentage
Money income	36,904	12.6
Market income	55,369	18.9
Post-social insurance income	37,306	12.7
Disposable income	30,075	10.9

Source: U.S. Bureau of the Census, Current Population Survey, Annual Social and Economic Supplement, 2006.

PRACTICAL PROBLEMS INHERENT IN MEASURING POVERTY

There are some practical problems associated with measuring income that are likely significant on the subject of poverty.

1. *Underreporting of income*: The income data that the census bureau uses to determine the poverty rate is all self-reported. This means that survey takers ask a family what their income is and accept what they are told as truth. It may not come as a big surprise to you to read that what people tell survey takers about their income is not always the truth. Sometimes it is an honest error. Believe it or not, many people simply do not remember things like that. I confess that I could not tell you within $10,000 what my income was last year, and I am an economist interested in those types of things. Other times the misreporting of income is deliberate. Oftentimes people are not willing to let even perfect strangers know the details of their life because of concerns about privacy or embarrassment because some of their income may have been gained from illegitimate sources. With respect to the latter, it could be that a family has earned some income "under the table" and does not want to report it because it might lead to a reduction in welfare benefits. In a few cases, the extra income may have been "earned" by selling dope, running numbers, or robbery. While survey takers are not obliged to report this information to the authorities, and few would, the respondents may not want to take the chance.

A more interesting pair of questions are these: While simple logic would dictate that there is misreporting of income, how do we know that there is underreporting? Also, do we have any notion of the magnitude of the underreporting? One reason we know there is underreporting is because poor families report spending nearly twice as much as they report receiving. The money they spend has got to come from somewhere. For whatever reason, families do not play their spending as "close to the vest" as their income. Another reason is that census bureau estimates of incomes from an area are always significantly lower than the income reported to the Internal Revenue Service. Presumably people do less lying to the IRS. One estimate is that reported income is about 11 percent lower than actual income (Kondratas 1984).

2. *Uncounted persons*: Today the Current Population Survey is conducted by phone. There is no survey taker knocking on the door. In today's world there is unlikely to be anyone at home anyway. To be contacted, then, a family needs to have a telephone. It has been estimated that using a phone survey ends up excluding 13 percent of the poor, including the homeless, as opposed to 6 percent of the entire population (Rector, Johnson, Youssef 1999, Table 3).

CONCEPTUAL PROBLEMS WITH MEASURING POVERTY

What does it really mean to be poor? There are different ways of looking at the issue that differ significantly from Orshansky's absolute income standard.

1. *Assets and consumer durables*: People's well-being is determined not only by their income but also their wealth. Yet in determining poverty, we measure

the former but not the latter. In principle you could have $1,000,000 in the bank (in noninterest-earning form) but still be considered poor if your income was too low. But of course you could draw on your wealth (presumably one of the reasons people acquire wealth is to have a cushion during bad times) and still live pretty comfortably. While there are probably not many millionaires classified as poor, the fact of the matter is that totally ignoring wealth provides a misleading picture of well-being.

One component of wealth is ownership of consumer durables. According to a recent survey, while the poor clearly have less than the nonpoor, what they do have can be surprising. Forty-one percent of the poor own their own homes, compared to 65 percent of all households (Rector, Johnson, Youssef 1999, Table 3). Sixty-six percent have air conditioners, compared to 75 percent of all households (Rector, Johnson, Youssef 1999, Table 3). Seventy-four percent have VCRs, compared to 88 percent of all households[16] (Rector, Johnson, Youssef 1999, Table 3). What do we make of a poor person who owns a home, air conditioner, and VCR? This does not imply that the poor live comfortable lives. Rather it shows that the nature of poverty in the United States is very different than it is in many countries around the world. It also suggests that simply looking at annual income can be very misleading in some circumstances.

2. *Long-term versus short-term poverty*: We need to be very careful about how we interpret the statistics. A 12.3 percent poverty rate does not mean that 12.3 percent of the population was poor the entire year. Rather, it means that 12.3 percent of the people contacted during the survey month in 2007 were poor. Some of those people had been poor for a long time and continued being poor for a long time. Some had been poor for a long time but left poverty status soon after they were surveyed. Others had just become poor but left poverty soon after the survey. Still others had just become poor and continued in poverty status for a long time. In other words, the people who were poor during the survey month were a combination of long-term and short-term poor.

Being poor is never a good thing. But being poor for a long period of time is certainly worse than being poor for a short period of time, and the statistics make no distinction. The fact of the matter is most of the poor people at any point in time are people who are likely to be poor for only a relatively short period of time. According to the census bureau, slightly over half (51.1 percent) of all spells of poverty last four months or less. Nearly four-fifths (79.6 percent) of all spells are over within a year. Over the course of a year, while 34.2 percent of the population falls into poverty for at least two months, only 2 percent of the population is continuously poor for forty-eight months (United States Bureau of the Census 2003, 14)

Part of the problem is optical illusion. By the official measure, the number of poor people changes by only small amounts from year to year. Since the size of the poverty population seems relatively stable, it is natural to infer that the same people are poor year after year. But that is not true. Literally millions of people leave poverty every year. Some find jobs, some remarry, some recover from illness, and some end strikes. Unfortunately, millions of people also enter poverty each year. This issue will be discussed in more detail later.

3. *A consumption standard*: For both conceptual and practical reasons, some economists argue that consumption is a much better measure of well-being than income. The conceptual reason has to do with the standard assumption in economics that consumers are utility maximizers who get utility from the consumption of goods and services. Would it not make sense to measure consumption directly rather than income? Of course, since you need income to consume, making a distinction between income and consumption might seem unnecessary, but that is where the practical reason comes in. If we could follow people throughout their entire lives, then it would not make much difference whether we measured income or consumption. Since you cannot consume more than you receive over your lifetime (ignoring inheritances and bequests that only a few people receive in any significant amount anyway), it would be a matter of indifference whether you measured lifetime consumption or income. But we do not follow people throughout their entire lives. Typically we have a one-year snapshot, and between consumption and income, consumption gives a much better picture of the individual's long-term well-being.

The reason for this is that income tends to fluctuate more than consumption.[17] Annual income is subject to any number of random factors such as unexpected layoffs, sickness, overtime, bonuses, and raises. Consumption does not fluctuate along with income, because people prefer stability.[18] Consequently, if income rises unexpectedly, instead of consuming all the increase, people will save. If income dips unexpectedly, instead of decreasing consumption proportionately, people will dip into savings or borrow to maintain the desired level of consumption. In any particular year, among high-income folks are people whose income is always high and those who have simply had a good year. Income may be an adequate indicator of well-being for the former group, but not for the latter. Among low-income folks, there are people whose income is always low and those who have suffered a temporary setback. Here too, income may be an adequate indicator of well-being for the former group, but not for the latter. The people whose income is temporarily high will not consume proportionately more and those whose income is temporarily low will not consume proportionately less. Consequently, for everyone consumption is a much better measure of long-term well-being.

What impact does a focus on consumption have on measures of inequality and poverty? A leader in research in this field is Daniel T. Slesnick of the University of Texas at Austin (Slesnick 2001). Slesnick measured inequality in terms of consumption. With respect to poverty, using consumption he found that poverty is actually about half the official estimate (Slesnick 2001, 196)

The practical impediment to measuring inequality and poverty this way is the fact that we do not have very accurate measures of family consumption from year to year. The CPS does not ask questions about consumption. We have mentioned already the difficulties people have keeping track of their income. Imagine the problems people would have keeping track of their consumption.

4. *Relative poverty measures*: The most fundamental criticism of our measure of poverty is that our measure misrepresents the nature of the problem. The "official" poverty line is a so-called absolute measure of poverty, which means that poverty is

defined as a certain standard of living, and that standard remains the same every year. The real value of the U.S. poverty thresholds is the same today as it was in 1963. The $20,794 four-person threshold in 2006 would buy the same amount of goods and services as the $3,200 four-person threshold did in 1963. In short, poverty means not having enough "stuff."

As the economy grows, presumably more and more people would be pulled above the poverty line. "A rising tide lifts all boats." At some point in the future society could be so rich that there would be no poor people.

An alternative is to use a relative measure of poverty. To take a specific example, many years ago the distinguished economist Victor Fuchs proposed that we consider as poor anyone whose income was less than one-half the national average (Fuchs 1969). Under this system, as society grew richer the amount of income needed to be considered nonpoor also rose in real terms. We could have a fabulously rich society but still have poor people if their incomes lagged behind everyone else. Under this scheme the only way to reduce poverty is to reduce the inequality of the distribution of income.

What would justify thinking about poverty in this way? This view puts forth that poverty is not just lacking enough stuff. Rather it is not having enough stuff relative to what everyone else has. The reason is that the level of income of a society helps determine its lifestyle. If people do not have enough income compared to others, they cannot live that lifestyle. They are left out of society.

Consider this situation:[19] In the late nineteenth and early twentieth century, one of the richest men in the United States was John D. Rockefeller. His wealth was fabled. There are song lyrics that mention being "rich as Rockefeller." In his heyday, he was the top.

Would you want to change places with Rockefeller? During most of his time there were no automobiles, no air conditioning, no modern medicine, no computers, no iPods, and so on. You may not have the luxuries he had—the mansions and servants and so on—but you may actually be leading a more comfortable life. This points out that what constitutes being poor and nonpoor depends on time and place. It is not an absolute standard.

We can make similar international comparisons today. Twenty thousand dollars annually means you are poor in the United States. If you had that amount of income in Rwanda (per capita GDP = $3,000) you would be considered quite well-to-do.

Far from being a new way of thinking, Americans and people around the world have consistently viewed poverty in a relative framework. For many years the Gallup Poll in the United States asked the question "What is the smallest amount of money a family of four needs to get along in this community?" The responses to the question grew nearly proportionately as community living standards grew (Rainwater 1977, 288–9). In comparative international studies, people's self-reported level of happiness was more closely related to their relative position in their society's income distribution than their absolute position (Easterlin 1973). In other words, a person in the middle of the income distribution in the United States is about as happy as someone in the middle of the income distribution in India, despite the fact that the average standard of living is dramatically higher in the United States.[20]

Table 12.7

Absolute Versus Relative Poverty, United States, Selected Years 1974–2004

Year	Official Poverty Rate (%)	Persons with Income < 50% of Median (%)
1974	11.2	15.9
1979	11.7	15.8
1986	13.6	17.8
1991	14.2	18.0
1994	14.5	17.8
1997	13.3	16.9
2000	11.3	17.0
2004	12.7	17.3

Source: U.S. Bureau of the Census, Luxembourg Income Study (LIS) Key Figures, accessed at http://www.lisproject.org/keyfigures.htm on June 24, 2008.

What impact would this way of measuring poverty have on the poverty rate? Table 12.7 shows what the poverty rate would have been using a 50 percent of the median income threshold for selected years over the time period 1974–2004. Compared to the official poverty rate, the relative standard would have yielded many more poor, and, on occasion during that time period, would have increased in years when the official poverty rate fell.

From a comparative international standpoint, because of its high degree of income inequality, a relative income poverty standard would reveal that the United States has a much higher poverty rate than that of other rich countries. Figure 12.3 shows relative poverty rates among selected countries in the recent past. The poverty threshold used is 50 percent of median adjusted disposable income.

5. *The NAS recommendations*: General dissatisfaction with the way poverty is measured has spawned several alternatives. One of the more interesting was a report issued in 1995 by the National Academy of Sciences (NAS) Committee on National Statistics (Citro and Michael 1995). Essentially, NAS recommends three changes in the way we measure poverty. First, they propose to change the way we measure income. The proposed new income measure will include an estimate of in-kind benefits but subtract various unavoidable expenses such as taxes, work expenses, child-care expenses, child support, and out-of-pocket medical expenses. Second, they propose to change the way the poverty threshold is calculated. Recall that the Orshansky index was based on the cost of food, and applied a multiplier of 3 to that. The NAS index would be based on the cost of food, clothing, and shelter and would apply a multiplier ranging from 1.15 to 1.25, would use a new equivalence scale that controls for the size and composition of families, and would allow for geographic variation. The third recommendation was to use a different survey, but this is a fairly technical issue that does not concern us.

Using the NAS approach, the official poverty rate of 12.1 percent in 2002 would have been raised to between 12.3 and 13.0 percent, depending on specific decisions

Figure 12.3 **Comparative Relative Poverty Rates**

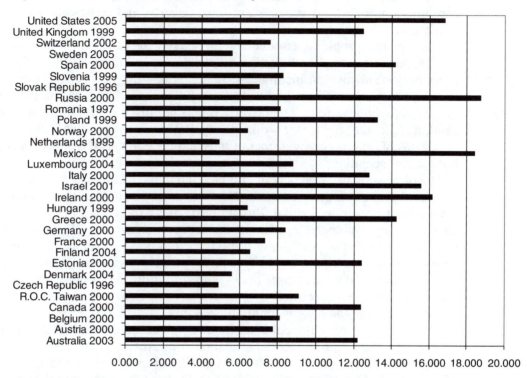

Source: Luxembourg Income Study (LIS) Key Figures, accessed at http://www.lisproject.org/keyfigures. htm on 24 June 2008.

made with respect to technical issues of measurement (United States Bureau of the Census 2003, 17)

CONCLUSION

This chapter reviewed a variety of conceptual and practical problems associated with measuring poverty, along with cataloguing the characteristics of the poor and trying to explain why people are poor. The conceptual problems appear particularly daunting. Since most of the American poor would be considered fairly well-off if they were transported, real income intact, to most of the countries in the world, that seems to be a fairly compelling reason to think of poverty in relative terms. Yet equally compelling is the argument that few of us would be willing to change places with John D. Rockefeller if it meant we had to transport ourselves back in time to the world he inhabited. Modern conveniences that we take for granted, such as air conditioning and computers, would be hard to jettison, even if it meant we could live grander than most other fellows in our society. The difficulties caused by relative versus absolute comparisons will appear again in Chapter 15, in the discussion of intragenerational mobility. The relative versus absolute conundrum is only one of the conceptual problems that have to be met head-on. The use of income versus consumption, long-term versus short-term poverty, and possession of assets are of nearly equivalent significance.

The practical problems associated with poverty measurement—how to handle in-kind income, adjusting for differences in the cost of living across the nation, counting every person and all their income, and many more—may not appeal to everyone, but are good examples of how highly technical issues can have enormous significance in the public policy arena. The poverty rate is not just a number. It is a number with clout. It colors the way we view our society. It is also a trigger that controls the release of billions of dollars of government funds and necessitates the collection of taxes to finance this spending.

The discussion of "who is poor" pointed out that constructing a profile of a typical poor person is a complicated issue. Many of us have a mental image in our mind of what a poor person looks like. Probably for many the image is of a black, ghetto-dwelling, single mother. Repetitious media depictions are largely responsible for the prominence of this image. While it might be too harsh to accuse the media of irresponsibility in this regard, it clearly is guilty of lack of subtlety. White children from the rural South and young single males who work full-time, among other stereotypes, are also prominently represented in the poverty population. Choosing one stereotype to represent all of the poor is highly misleading.

The discussion of why people are poor emphasized the multiplicity of causes of poverty and the negative feedback relationships among them. The poor do not just lack income. They lack the whole package. Fighting poverty seemingly will require a full-court press of imaginative policies. In the next chapter, we will forge ahead and provide an overview of existing antipoverty policies. Whether our current approach fits this full-court press of imaginative policies prescription remains to be seen; there are many who doubt it.

QUESTIONS FOR REVIEW AND PRACTICE

1. Is the extent of poverty measured correctly in the United States?
2. How responsible are people for their own poverty? What responsibility does the government have in the alleviation of poverty?
3. Will the poor always be with us? Examine all the issues.
4. How would you describe a typical poor person?
5. What is meant by the term *working poor*? Are the working poor better off or worse off than the nonworking poor?

NOTES

1. The year 1959 was the first year official poverty statistics were reported.

2. Comparable poverty data is not easy to come by because different countries use different definitions of poverty and not all have the resources to count it.

3. See Eloise Cofer, Evelyn Grossman, and Faith Clark (1962, Tables 5 and 10). Food plan data has been updated periodically over the years as new dietary information has become known. The data in the table is from 1959. The current food plan looks very different (Andrews et al. 2001).

4. Along with that was the implicit assumption that the household had someone with the skills and time to be able to prepare the food.

5. Actually, she used a multiplier of 3 for families but multipliers of 3.88 and 5.92 for couples and individuals, respectively. The farm poverty threshold was set at 85 percent of the nonfarm level.

6. Listening to others talk is an important way that children learn, and the children of rich parents hear more words per minute than children of poor parents. Recent research finds that the young children of college professors hear 2150 words per hour while the children of working class and welfare parents hear much fewer, 1250 and 620 respectively. (*The Economist* 2007).

7. Children growing up in single-parent homes (either as a result of divorce or because the mother never married or cohabitated) cannot receive the same quantity and quality of parental attention that children in two-parent families receive. Boys, in particular, are thought to benefit from the presence of a male in the household. The empirical significance of this effect has been questioned (Lang and Zagorsky 2000).

8. Like some of our widespread beliefs about family, the empirical support for some of the propositions is not rock solid. The census bureau defines a high-poverty neighborhood as one where 40 percent of its inhabitants are poor. That means that in several instances over half the residents of a neighborhood are not poor so it would appear that there are more than enough positive role models. Also, with modern transportation and communication, your closest friends do not have to be from your immediate neighborhood. Studies have been done in which randomly selected poor families have been able to move to "nice" neighborhoods. The Gautreaux Assistant Housing and Moving to Opportunity programs have been most often cited (Rosenbaum 1995; Office of Policy Development and Research 1996). While these programs have appeared to have positive effects on most of their participants, "Neighborhood effects are smaller than we might have anticipated" (Lang 2007, 209).

9. Compare a drafty, rat-infested apartment with lead-based paint on the walls in a crime-ridden slum area to a nice house in the peaceful suburbs.

10. The intelligence that counts most is cognitive ability, and cognitive ability can be measured by IQ or similar tests.

11. Faith-based organizations are typically associated with religious organizations. Examples would be Catholic Charities, Jewish Welfare and Family Services, and Lutheran Social Services.

12. As the mere existence of the organizations in the previous footnote demonstrates, prior to 1996 these organizations had not been excluded from social service work. There was just no guarantee that they would have the same chance to receive funding as secular organizations. The 1996 law made equal treatment of faith-based and secular organizations explicit (Queen 2004, 66).

13. I judged both of these essays to be excellent. There has been some minor editing done to both.

14. See Claire Vickery (1977) for an early attempt at measuring poverty that takes time scarcity into consideration.

15. See the discussion of this effort in Mangum, Mangum, and Sum (2003, 42–3).

16. This survey was done before DVD players become ubiquitous.

17. This explanation is based on Milton Friedman (1957).

18. Both the life cycle and permanent income theories of consumption argue that people will maximize their utility over their lifetime by smoothing out their consumption.

19. This particular example was suggested by Mankiw (2007, 554).

20. Easterlin's conclusions have become somewhat controversial. Newer research has found that a country's sense of well-being is enhanced by economic growth and that within a country a sense of well-being is not significantly related to income (Lane 1993).

13 Making Small Slices Larger

INTRODUCTION

What do we do if some people get slices that are too small? This chapter reviews the current welfare system. In one sense, the system has a program for nearly every need. There is education and training, support for a variety of family dysfunctions, housing programs addressing some aspects of neighborhood effects, health insurance, and programs that help some families deal with unexpected events. The system, however, is satisfying to no one—poor and nonpoor alike. The overall level of funding is a perennial complaint. The system also does not represent an organized, comprehensive approach to poverty. The different pieces of the system were added at different times, often reflecting diametrically opposed views as to the correct approach to fighting poverty. The pieces are often administered by different agencies using conflicting criteria. In a very real sense, we are just muddling through when it comes to fighting poverty.

This chapter describes and evaluates the existing system. Parts of several succeeding chapters will offer a variety of proposals to improve the system.

OVERVIEW OF THE CURRENT WELFARE SYSTEM

What do we mean by the term *welfare*? Virtually any government program could be considered a welfare program. Suppose the government builds a military base that provides a job for a civilian custodian and helps lift that custodian from economic dependency to economic independence. That program could be considered a welfare program even though it would be classified as military spending in the budget. Following convention, welfare programs discussed in this chapter are limited to those where participation is only for people who satisfy a means test.[1] A means test is a restriction based on financial status, usually income or wealth. Eligibility for welfare programs is limited to those whose financial means fall below a defined cutoff.

What do we mean by welfare in the United States? Welfare is not a single government program. Rather there is a welfare system, which consists of many programs. By one count, there were eighty-five federal, state, and local government programs that would fit into the category of welfare (United States Congress, 2004). Table 13.1 lists sixty-eight federal programs along with spending on each as a percentage of total federal welfare

Table 13.1

The Welfare System in the United States, 2002

Medical Aid

1	Medicaid	49.45%
2	Medical care for veterans without service-connected disability	1.57
3	State Children's Health Insurance (SCHIP)	1.03
4	General assistance (medical care component)	.95
5	Indian health services	.53
6	Consolidated health centers	.25
7	Maternal and child health services block grant	.24
8	Title X family planning services	.05
9	Medical assistance to refugees, asylees, other humanitarian cases	.01

Cash Aid

10	Supplemental Security Income	7.38
11	Earned Income Tax Credit – refundable portion only	5.33
12	Temporary Assistance for Needy Families	2.50
13	Foster care	1.65
14	Child tax credit	.97
15	General assistance (nonmedical care component)	.62
16	Pensions for needy veterans, their dependents, and survivors	.61
17	Adoption assistance	.47
18	Dependency and indemnity compensation and death compensation for parents of veterans	.02
19	General assistance to Indians	.01
20	Cash assistance to refugees, asylees, other humanitarian cases	.01

Food Aid

21	Food stamps	4.61
22	School lunch program (free and reduced price segments)	1.16
23	Special Supplemental Nutrition Program for Women, Infants, and Children (WIC)	.83
24	Child and adult care food program, lower-income components	.31
25	School breakfast program (free and reduced price segments)	.29
26	Nutrition program for the elderly	.15
27	The Emergency Food Assistance Program (TEFAP)	.07
28	Summer food service program for children	.06
29	Commodity Supplemental Food Program (CSFP)	.02
30	Food distribution program on Indian reservations	.01
31	Farmers' market nutrition program	.01
32	Special milk program (free segment)	.0002

Education Aid 2.18

33	Federal Pell grants	1.57
34	Head Start	1.44
35	Subsidized Federal Stafford loans and Stafford Ford loans	.19
36	Federal work-study programs	.16
37	Federal Trio programs	.15
38	Supplemental educational opportunity grants	.08
39	Chapter 1 migrant education program	.03
40	Perkins loans	.03
41	Leveraging educational assistance partnerships (LEAP)	.01
42	Health professions student loans and scholarships	.01

K–12

43	Fellowships for graduate and professional study	.01
44	Migrant high school equivalency program (HEP)	.004
45	College assistance migrant program (CAMP)	.003
46	Close Up fellowships	.0003

Other Services

47	Child care and development block grant	1.64

(continued)

48	TANF services	1.18
49	Social services block grant (Title XX)	.53
50	TANF child care	.44
51	Homeless assistance	.20
52	Community services block grant	.14
53	Legal services	.06
54	Social services for refugees, asylees, other humanitarian cases	.03
55	Emergency food and shelter programs	.03
Jobs and Training Aid		
56	TANF work activities	.52
57	Job Corps	.29
58	Youth activities	.19
59	Adult activities	.18
60	Senior community service employment program	.09
61	Welfare-to-Work grant programs	.08
62	Food stamp employment and training	.08
63	Foster grandparents	.03
64	Senior companions	.01
65	Targeted assistance for refugees, asylees, other humanitarian cases	.01
66	Native employment works	.002
Energy Aid		
67	Low income home energy assistance program (LIHEAP)	.34
68	Weatherization assistance	.07

Source: U.S. House of Representatives.

spending (as of 2002). Using this definition, approximately 18.6 percent of the federal government's budget is devoted to welfare programs (United States Congress, 2004).

Having detailed information about all eighty-five programs would serve little purpose. There are some programs, however, of which anyone studying poverty should be aware. The most important antipoverty programs will be described and critiqued. As indicated in Chapter 7, there is a fine line between programs that fight poverty and programs that fight inequality. That these programs are included in this chapter as opposed to Chapter 7 is largely arbitrary.

PROGRAMS TO PROVIDE MEDICAL AID

Americans finance only about 12.5 percent of their health-care costs out-of-pocket. The rest is financed by insurance (both private and government) and similar programs. It makes sense for Americans to rely on insurance. Health-care needs are unpredictable for individuals, differ dramatically from person to person, and, at today's prices, have the potential to be financially devastating. The typical risk-adverse individual is better off paying modest premiums than taking a chance of a huge loss.[2] The American system is set apart from those in most of the rest of the developed world by our heavy reliance on private insurance as opposed to government provision. This reliance reflects historical events[3] and economic inertia.[4]

Our reliance on private insurance has had important consequences for the poor. The poor are less likely to have private insurance than the nonpoor. Fewer than a quarter of the poor have private insurance as compared to nearly three-quarters of the nonpoor. The reason is because many of the poor either do not work, or else work at jobs where the compensation package is too modest to include health insurance.[5] The poor have not been left completely without a safety net, however. Government-provided insurance fills some of the gap, but not enough. Over 30 percent of poor people have no coverage whatsoever as opposed to 14 percent of the nonpoor.

Medicaid, established in 1965, is the main health insurance program for the poor. Anyone who is eligible for the various cash assistance programs described in this chapter is eligible for Medicaid. Approximately 50 percent of the poor are covered by the program. Spending for Medicaid exceeds $250 billion a year, making it the largest "welfare" program.

Medicaid will pay doctors' fees and hospital costs for a wide variety of ailments. Most services are provided free of charge to patients. The doctor or hospital simply submits the bill to government and waits to receive payment.[6]

Medicaid is a jointly funded federal-state program. States can extend coverage to other groups as long as the state foots the bill. Some states have chosen to add in groups slightly above the poverty line, the medically needy,[7] and to provide dental and eyeglasses support.

An interesting question is whether health insurance, such as that provided by Medicaid, should be considered a right. In this context, a right is a government program that must be provided fully and equally to every individual provided they meet certain criteria, for example citizenship or permanent residency status within the country. The benefits of health insurance are obvious, and the nation can certainly "afford" to pay for it. Those two facts by themselves do not necessarily make health insurance a right. What is often overlooked is that any time a right is created, a corresponding obligation is also created. If some people have a right to health insurance, it means other people have an obligation to provide it for them. Health insurance, like everything, does not just fall out of the sky like manna from heaven. It is a service that must be produced using scarce resources. Making it available for some citizens requires that resources be diverted away from others. Or, in more practical terms, does society have the right to tax you to provide health insurance for other people, most of whom you do not even know?

Alternatively, instead of entangling ourselves in a dead-end discussion of what is a right, we might look at programs like Medicaid as Pareto efficient redistribution. By helping the most disadvantaged to maintain their health, we might be ultimately contributing to their attainment of self-sufficiency. The overall burden of welfare on taxpayers may in fact end up being lower. There is no evidence to support this, but many people have strong opinions about this theory.

An anomaly of our system is that Medicaid only covers about half the poor, and most of these people are also eligible to be helped by other elements of the "welfare package" to be described later. The so-called working poor, those individuals who are not eligible for various welfare benefits and are forced to support themselves on poverty-level wages from menial jobs, receive neither government nor private insurance. It is the plight of these people that has been the primary impetus behind the drive for universal coverage in the United States. A significant number of nonpoor also do not have insurance, but, in their case, it is undoubtedly the result of ignorance and/or choice.

As an attempt to extend health insurance coverage to the children of the working poor, the federal government enacted the States Children's Health Insurance Program (SCHIP) in 1997. It allows states to cover children in families with incomes above the Medicaid income limit but below 200 percent of the poverty line or up to 50 percentage points over the state's Medicaid income limit. It has had the effect of extending health insurance coverage to an additional 2 million children.

PROGRAMS TO PROVIDE CASH AID

The Temporary Aid to Needy Families program (TANF) and its predecessor Aid to Families with Dependent Children (AFDC) are probably the programs most laypeople have in mind when they think of welfare. TANF was established in 1996 with the passage of the Personal Responsibility and Work Opportunity Reconciliation Act. The best way to understand TANF is by first considering what preceded it.

The AFDC program was created with the passage of the Social Security Act in 1935. Reflecting the values of the time, the purpose of the program was to provide government aid to families of limited means where the primary breadwinner (typically the adult male in the household) was unable to provide support due to death or incapacity. The feeling was that most families would only need support for relatively short periods of time until the female householder remarried or the breadwinner got back on his feet. AFDC was established as a joint federal and state program. Practically speaking this meant the following: The states were empowered to establish their own eligibility criteria and benefit levels within broad guidelines established by the federal government. The money to run the program came from both federal and state sources. Eligible families would receive a monthly check. Welfare benefits were considered an entitlement, a benefit that the government must provide to all who meet the eligibility criteria. You are entitled to the benefits simply because you are eligible. In the early years of the program, recipients of welfare checks had no particular responsibilities besides reporting changes in their economic circumstances. Later on, recipients had to sign up at the employment office and take suitable jobs if offered, but in reality there was no particular pressure on welfare recipients to work.

No one was particularly happy with AFDC. Conservatives blamed it for a host of "pathologies of the poor," including discouraging work, savings, and families. Liberals just thought it was not generous enough.

The establishment of TANF meant that several things changed. From an administrative standpoint, TANF remained a joint federal-state program, but the states were given greater encouragement to experiment with different ways to deliver services. Entitlement status was removed. The federal portion of the benefits were appropriated via a block grant. A block grant was a specific chunk of money dedicated to the program. If the program ran out of money before the end of the fiscal year, tough luck.

From the standpoint of the effect on recipients, TANF can best be thought of as reflecting the triumph of the conservative critique. The program consisted of two plans: the work plan and the family plan (Hays 2003).

The work plan was an attempt to enforce a work ethic among welfare recipients.

Figure 13.1   **TANF Monthly Benefits for a 1-Adult, 2-Children Family**

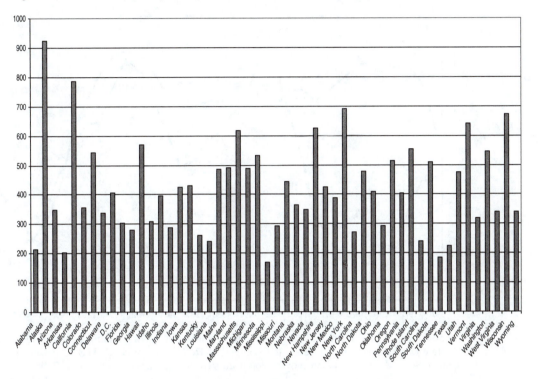

Source: The Urban Institute's Welfare Rules Database, funded by DHHS/ACF and DHHS/ASPE

Whereas under AFDC recipients were expected to pretend to seek work, TANF recipients are expected to take jobs and/or training. States are given goals with respect to the number of recipients working. What is considered work is an actual paid job with a public or private sector employer, but also some types of job training, high school attendance, and subsidized or unsubsidized community service. Work must consist of at least thirty hours per week for unmarried recipients and thirty-five hours per week for married recipients. States can exempt mothers with young children from some work requirements. This changed the culture of the welfare office. Under AFDC, the welfare office primarily determined eligibility. Under TANF, the office is a full-service provider of employment services.

States are still allowed to establish their own eligibility criteria and rules regarding the determination of monthly benefits. One consequence is that maximum benefit levels vary from state to state, often dramatically (this was also true under AFDC). Figure 13.1 shows maximum monthly benefits levels in 2006 for a family of three consisting of one adult and two children (who are not subject to a family cap, have no special needs, pay for shelter, and live in the most populated area of the state). Benefits levels ranged from $170 in Mississippi to $923 in Alaska (The Urban Institute 2006). Another consequence is an individual who is eligible in one state may not be

258   POVERTY

Figure 13.2 **The Poverty Rate and the Percentage of People on Welfare, 1970–2005**

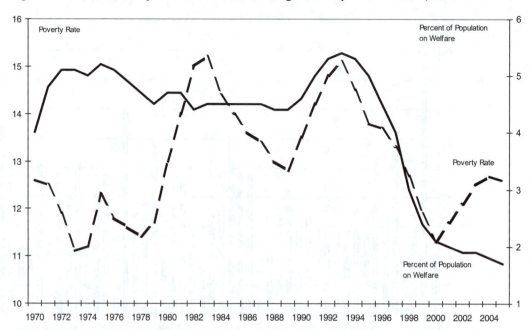

Source: U.S. Census Bureau; Office of the Assistant Secretary for Planning and Evaluation. Indicators of Welfare Dependence: Annual Report to Congress, 2007. Washington, D.C.: U.S. Department of Health and Human Services. http://aspe.hhs.gov/hsp/indicators07/index.htm, accessed 24 June 2008.

eligible in another. Other features of the law that encourage work include the Child Care and Development Block Grant and the Transitional Assistance program. The former feature provides states with enough funds to guarantee child care to any welfare recipient. The latter eases the transition from welfare to work by allowing recipients to continue their Medicaid for a period of time after beginning employment.

TANF places time limits on the receipt of welfare. No one can receive welfare benefits for more than two years in a row or more than five years in a lifetime.

The Family Plan is an attempt to encourage "family values." Marriage is not so subtly encouraged. States are given leeway to establish tougher rules regarding out-of-wedlock births and teen parents. States do not have to increase benefits to recipients who have additional children while on welfare, and teen parents can be prevented from establishing their own households while receiving benefits. Mothers must help identify the fathers of their children so the government can pressure deadbeat dads into paying their alimony.

The law also prevents immigrants from collecting benefits until they have been in the United States for at least five years.

What effect has TANF had so far? Figure 13.2 shows the percentage of people on welfare and the poverty rate from 1970 to 2005. The percentage of the population on the welfare rolls fluctuated within a narrow band and was only moderately influenced by changes in the poverty rate until the early 1990s. The decline in the welfare rolls starting in the early 1990s was associated with a decrease in the poverty rate, but the extent of the decrease was so striking (an over 65 percent decline) that something else must have been at work in addition to the healthy economy. TANF can be praised or blamed depending on your point of view. Further evidence of the importance of TANF can be seen from the behavior of both series since the year 2000. The welfare rolls have continued to decline while the poverty rate has resumed an upward movement.

Of course, the number of welfare recipients is only one measure of the effect of welfare reform. What is also important is the effect of the reform on recipients. As of this writing there is no definitive study. Generally speaking, it seems that the incomes of the now former welfare recipients have not improved much, but their self-esteem and the respect their children have for their parents has seemed to improve (Lang 2007). Blank, however, concludes that the poverty rate among less-skilled women was reduced by about two percentage points as a result of the introduction of TANF (Blank 2002). With respect to family structure, a key conservative criticism of the preceding system, there is as yet no compelling evidence that TANF has led to higher marriage and lower divorce rates (Lang 2007). Overall, TANF has not been a failure, but neither has it been a smashing success. There is no large constituency supporting either large-scale reforms or the end of TANF.

Supplemental security income (SSI) is a federal program for the indigent elderly, blind, and disabled. Since it is a federal program, benefit levels are uniform across the country. Because of its beneficiaries, SSI is a relatively uncontroversial program.

The earned income tax credit (EITC) was established in 1975. The original purpose was to help the poor offset the Social Security taxes they were expected to pay, but the program soon became a favorite with both conservatives and liberals. It was expanded modestly under the Reagan administration and dramatically under the Clinton administration. Today the EITC is a tax expenditure that costs over $30 billion a year.

The EITC works like this: Your taxes are determined by the method shown in Figure 13.3. You start by adding up your income from all sources. This is called your adjusted gross income.[8] Then you can subtract your exemptions. Exemptions are monetary amounts that represent the taxpayer and all dependents in the family. In principle, exemptions are an allowance for the cost of living, but in reality the exemption amounts allowed are too low to support a decent standard of living. You can also subtract out deductions. Deductions are expenditures that the lawmakers think should be encouraged. Examples of deductions are the interest paid on home mortgages, medical expenses, moving expenses, and charitable contributions.[9] The majority of Americans who do not have large mortgages, medical expenses, or moving expenses, and are not able to make major charitable contributions are allowed to take what is called the standard deduction.

Subtracting these two items gives taxable income. Taxable income is approximately two-thirds of adjusted gross income. Then you find the tax rate applicable to your taxable income and apply it. That gives you your tax liability. Lawmakers have established certain tax credits. These are expenditures you can subtract from your tax liability. One example is the child-care tax credit. The EITC fits here also. Based

Figure 13.3 **How to Compute Taxes**

Adjusted Gross Income
-Exemptions
-Deductions
Taxable Income
* tax rate
Tax Liability
- Credits
Tax Payment or Refund

on how much money you earn from work, you get a tax credit. The EITC credit is refundable, meaning if your credit exceeds your tax liability, the government will send you a check for the difference. Not all tax credits are refundable.

The popularity of the EITC with both liberals and conservatives stems primarily from the belief that it rewards what everyone thinks needs to be rewarded, namely work.[10] The amount of your tax credit is based on the amount of money you earn. For example, in 2006 a person with one child who earned $8500 could claim a credit of $2747. Roughly speaking, since a person earning $8500 is unlikely to have a tax liability in the first place and the credit is refundable, the $8500 becomes $11,247. It seems the equivalent of an increase in wages, and with the reward for work increased, why would people not take advantage of the program by working more? Interestingly enough, as the discussion of labor supply in Chapter 3 prepared us to see, the economics of the EITC are a bit more complicated than that.

Taking the worker with one child mentioned earlier as the example, the EITC has a complex structure that reflects a twin desire to target the benefits to the truly needy and contain costs. If the worker earns $0 she receives no credit. As she begins earning money her credit rises with her earnings. Roughly, she receives $17 in credits for every $50 earned. This is called the phase-in zone. Once the worker reaches $8050 in earnings with a credit of $2747, the credit stops increasing. Instead, it remains constant at $2747 until earnings reach $14,850. This is called the plateau zone. After $14,850 in earnings the credit begins to decrease. Roughly, it decreases $8 for every $50 earned until finally the credit vanishes at $32,050 in earnings. This is called the phase-out zone. Figure 13.4 shows a graph of the credit against earnings for individuals with no children, one child, and two or more children.

This means the income and substitution effects work differently in each zone. For individuals out of the labor force, choosing to work will carry with it the reward of the wage plus the credit. The substitution effect of the higher wage would act to encourage work. There is no income effect because the person would receive no income if she did not work. In the phase-in zone, additional earnings lead to a higher credit. The substitution effect of the credit encourages work. However, the credit also has an income effect that discourages work. The net effect of the EITC on work in this zone depends on which effect is stronger. In the plateau zone, the credit does not change over a long range of earnings. Consequently there is no substitution effect. There is still an income effect because of the credit so the net effect of the EITC on work would appear to be negative. This negative effect on earnings is even stronger

Figure 13.4 **2006 EITC Tax Credit Amounts**

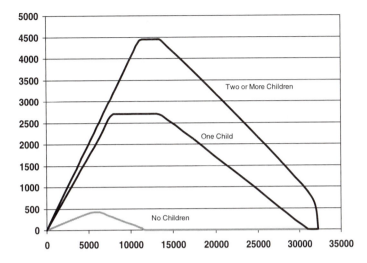

in the phase-out zone. Since the credit falls with greater earnings, there is a negative substitution effect. Coupled with the negative income effect, there should be a net negative effect on work. This effect is potentially stronger for workers who are just a little bit beyond the phase-out zone. The program may actually encourage them to reduce work hours and slip back into the phase-out zone.

That the EITC acts to encourage work is therefore not a foregone conclusion. The overall effect of the program on work will depend on how many recipients are found in each of the zones, and empirically teasing out the effect of the EITC is no mean feat. The limited evidence we have, however, seems to point to the EITC having a modest net positive effect on work (Hotz, Mullin, and Scholz 2000).

PROGRAMS THAT PROVIDE FOOD AID

The food stamps program was established in 1964. Its stated goal is to help poor families obtain food.[11] Well-nourished people can learn in school and work hard on the job. Eligible families receive a monthly allotment of food stamps. Food stamps used to be coupons that had a monetary face value. The stamps could be used in grocery stores, delicatessens, and bodegas to pay for food.[12] The seller of the food is then reimbursed by the government. Today food stamps are stored value cards, but the essentials of how they work have not changed.

The economic analysis of the food stamp program is one of the more interesting aspects of economic theory. Assume a person can consume two goods: food and nonfood. The person's income is $500 per month and food costs $1 per unit while nonfood costs $2 per unit. If the person spent all of her income on food, she could consume 500 units per month. If she spent it all on nonfood, she could consume 250 units per month. In Figure 13.5, the line running between 250 on the nonfood axis and 500 on the food axis is the budget constraint. Indifference curve U_1 is tangent

Figure 13.5 **Cash versus In-Kind Transfers: Initial Equilibrium**

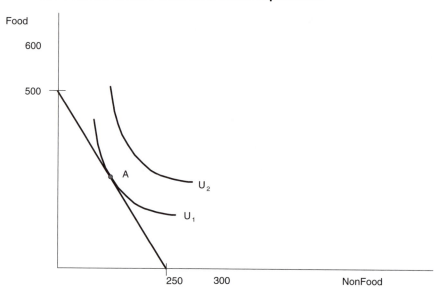

to the budget constraint at point A. This shows how much of the two goods she will choose to consume. Here she is maximizing her utility, although her utility is not all that high since $500 a month is not an ample amount to live on. U_2 is a currently unobtainable level of utility.

Now assume a food stamps program is introduced. The heroine in our story becomes eligible for $100 per month in food stamps. These stamps can be used to buy food, but are not good for anything else. Figure 13.6 shows the new budget constraint. If she spends her entire money income plus the food stamps on food, she will be able to buy the equivalent of 600 units of food. If she spends her entire money income on nonfood she can buy 250 units of nonfood, but the food stamps cannot be used to purchase nonfood so she can never obtain more than 250 units of nonfood. The food stamps, of course, can be used for food. The budget constraint ends up having a kink in it. It is shifted out and parallel to the old budget constraint up until the point of 100 units of food and 250 units of nonfood. It cannot extend to the right of 250 units of nonfood. Most people would probably respond to the food stamps by buying both more food and nonfood. The point of tangency (point B) represented by indifference curve U_2 and the new budget constraint represents that equilibrium.

Assume, for the sake of argument, that the person is a bit unusual in the sense that she does not much like food. Let her indifference curves be represented by U_3 and U_4. Prior to the food stamp program, her equilibrium would have been at point C. After the food stamp program her equilibrium would have been at point D.

Now, instead of a food stamp program, society decides to simply give every eligible person $100 in cash each month. Refer to Figure 13.7. The line QR shows her budget constraint under this scenario. Notice that the budget constraint includes combina-

Figure 13.6 **Cash versus In-Kind Transfers: Equilibrium with Food Stamps**

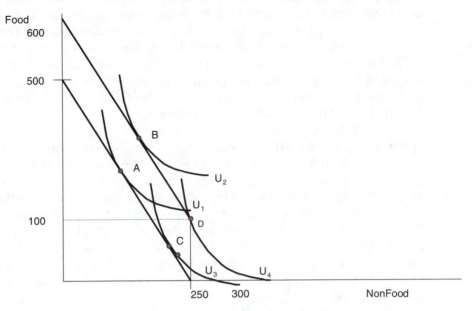

Figure 13.7 **Cash versus In-Kind Transfers: Equilibrium with Cash Transfers**

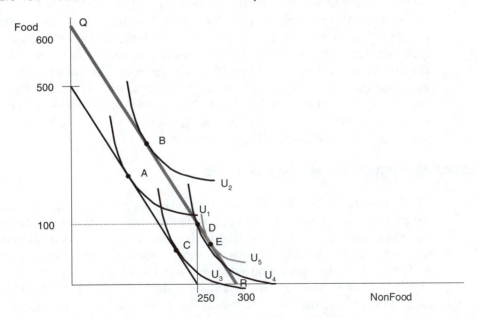

tions of goods that could not be obtained under food stamps because the cash could also be used to buy nonfood.

For a person with indifference curves U_1 and U_2, the form of the program makes no difference. Whether she receives food stamps or straight cash, it makes no difference in her consumption. For the person with indifference curves U_3, U_4, and U_5 the form of the program does make a difference. Under food stamps, she could only reach indifference curve U_4. Under the cash transfer, she could reach indifference curve U_5. This would make her better off than if she just had access to food stamps.

The intuitive explanation of this result is that if people are given cash, they can use it any way they want. If they are given food stamps, their options are a bit restricted, which means that some people will not be able to do as well as they would have if there had been no restriction on their options.

The implication is that the food stamp program is inefficient. At the same cost, simply giving people cash will create more utility. Note that this conclusion holds true for any type of in-kind transfer. For example, Medicaid should work the same way.

This conclusion has not gone unchallenged. Some argue that more choice is not necessarily better (Schwartz 2004). More options make it more difficult to choose what to purchase, simply because there is a wide selection of items. More choice is also ultimately less satisfying because of the knowledge of more alternatives forgone. The empirical significance of this conclusion is also questionable. For a poor person with an income of $1,250 per month ($15,000 a year), $100 per month in food stamps is equivalent to an increase in income of only 8 percent. It is hard to believe that none of that increase would go to food.

Other programs of note include the school breakfast and lunch programs and the Women, Infants and Children (WIC) program. The breakfast and lunch programs provide balanced and healthy meals for the children of eligible families. In the case of the breakfast program, students have to be bused to school early to take part in the program. The theory is that students can learn better with full bellies. The WIC program provides nutritional support for eligible pregnant women and for the children of eligible women for several years after they are born. The belief is that unborn babies and children will not thrive if they are not adequately nourished. Participants in the program receive vouchers that allow them to buy WIC-approved foods available at WIC-approved agencies such as hospitals, mobile clinics, community centers, schools, public housing sites, and WIC warehouses.

PROGRAMS THAT PROVIDE HOUSING AID

The Low-rent Public Housing program provides government subsidies for the construction and operation of housing units that are then run by local authorities. Currently there are about 1.3 million public housing units. The tenants of these units meet the requirements of a locally determined means test and pay below-market rents.

The public housing program does not have a particularly happy history. Begun in 1937, there have been few units built since the early 1970s. The problem is that since these units cater to the poor, individuals in the middle and upper classes have strongly opposed construction of these units in their neighborhoods. The result has been the clustering of poor people in already poor neighborhoods. The housing units, often dismissively called projects, have frequently become eyesores as their walls have become filled with graffiti, and are looked at as breeding grounds for crime. Probably the prime example of this is the Cabrini-Green complex in Chicago.[13] Paradoxically, the program has also been criticized because so few units are available compared to the poverty population of 37 million.

Another program, which currently serves about 1.4 million households, is the Section 8 Low-income Housing Assistance program. Under this program, families can attempt to locate their own housing anywhere they choose. If the unit meets certain quality standards and the rent is deemed "fair," the government subsidizes the family's rent by making payments directly to the landlord. The touted benefit is that the program expands choice for these families. Instead of being restricted to the poor side of town, families can live where they want. The problem is that freedom of choice is not absolute. There remain some restrictions on where families can live and no family in the program can spend more than 30 percent of their income on housing.

PROGRAMS TO PROVIDE EDUCATION AND TRAINING

Probably the most significant national education program is the provision of "free"[14] and universal education, which is coupled with the requirement that students start school by a certain age and remain in school until a certain age. Traditionally, schooling has been a state and local responsibility, and approximately 90 percent of current funding for the schools is generated by state and local governments.

A continuing issue is the funding of public schools. Typically, schools are funded by a combination of local, state, and federal funds, with local funds being the largest component. Averaged nationwide, local funds account for 43 percent of total school funding. This varies from state to state, with a high of 63 percent in Nevada to a low of 2 percent in Hawaii.

The primary source of the local funds is the property tax. Practically speaking, this has meant that since richer districts have higher property values, raising money has been relatively easy and the schools located in those districts have been funded relatively lavishly. The opposite is the case for schools located in poorer districts. The equity of this has been challenged. While the U.S. Supreme Court has not found this to be a violation of the Constitution, a few state supreme courts have.[15]

All states have a minimum school-leaving age; sixteen being the most common age at which students are allowed to quit school. Allowing students to leave school prior to receiving a high school diploma has been decried as a factor that puts those students at a permanent disadvantage. More practically minded people realize that there are some students who just cannot be saved and who are so disruptive and dangerous that their very presence harms the education of the other students. One commentator actually suggested the school-leaving age should be lowered to fourteen so people who inevitably would perform better at manual tasks would have the chance at a longer career (Banfield 1974, 173–78).

The economics of the school starting age is sometimes overlooked. Virtually every state requires that children start school at age five. Why not let parents decide for themselves when their children are ready to start school? Robert Frank argues that this would lead to a classic tragedy of the commons situation (Frank 2007a). Parents, realizing that their children would have a competitive advantage in school if they were a bit older than their classmates, would tend to hold their children back from starting school.

Competitive pressure among parents would lead to wholesale holding back of children until the children ended up with less education, to their detriment and the detriment of society as a whole. Therefore a regulation mandating a uniform school starting age may make some sense. Of course, there are a number of conflicting pressures at work here. Working to incentivize parents to start their children early in school is the impact of preschool programs and also the fact that there are many more families where both parents work. The school serves as a day-care center for many parents.

The federal role in primary and secondary schooling is relatively small, but not nonexistent. The Title I program provides additional federal funds to help schools that serve particularly large numbers of poor children. The No Child Left Behind Act established performance testing for schools, and offers modest funding to help schools that perform at unacceptability low levels.

The Head Start program has been around since the 1960s.[16] It is a preschool program for the children of poor families. The original goal was to offset some of the disadvantages that poor children faced that caused them to start kindergarten educationally trailing their more advantaged peers. At that time, preschool was uncommon. Over the years, though, preschool has become a generally shared experience, which has meant that poor kids have not really been given a head-start by Head Start.

Federal Pell grants provide aid at the other end of the educational spectrum. Pell grants help to pay college expenses for students of families earning less than $35,000 a year.

Public colleges and universities are an important part of the higher education landscape in the United States. While private colleges and universities are a bit more prestigious, the reality is that for every great private institution there is a similarly great public institution. For example, Harvard, Princeton, and Yale are closely matched by the University of North Carolina at Chapel Hill, the University of California at Berkeley, and the College of William and Mary. Students attending public institutions receive significant tuition subsidies. Paradoxically, students attending these institutions who receive subsidies seem to come disproportionately from the middle and upper classes. It is difficult to argue that public funding of institutions of higher education represents significant redistribution.

Government-run job training programs can be traced back to at least the Great Depression years, and probably much farther back if you are willing to accept a fairly broad definition of job training. The United States Military Academy at West Point opened in 1802 and has been providing job training to army officers ever since. Depression-era programs included such organizations as the Civilian Conservation Corps and the Works Progress Administration. These programs were more along the line of "make-work," but undoubtedly they provided valuable work experience for participants.

Government involvement in job training programs directed toward the poor began in earnest during the 1960s so-called War on Poverty. The early history of these programs was one of underachievement. With few exceptions, the results of the programs were disappointing. A large part of the problem was a failure to recognize the extent of the problem. The early programs emphasized the development of "hard" skills, but not the "soft" skills that were sometimes the biggest obstacle to employment. Often the key ingredient lacking for the poor was not just knowledge of specific industrial processes (such as how to operate a lathe), but "skills" such as the ability to get to work on time on a regular basis and to interact with their fellow workers in a civil manner.

With fits and starts, the general trend in job training has been toward programs that treat the whole person. The newest wrinkle is the Workforce Investment Act enacted in 1998. Its purpose is to make the Department of Labor a one-stop shop. The DOL will provide funding to programs that evaluate participants, refer them to the appropriate job training program, and provide help in finding jobs.

Along the same lines, TANF includes the Welfare to Work (WtW)program that funds programs that move welfare recipients to work activities.

The Job Corps program can also trace its origins back to the 1960s. Poor individuals in this program can receive job training in a variety of areas as well as help toward obtaining their high school equivalency degree if needed. What is particularly notable about the Job Corps program is that many of the training sites are in relatively remote locations that are far removed from the trainees' homes. The theory behind this was the belief that trainees needed to be removed from the "toxic" environment that had stunted their development earlier.

To make a long story short, it appears that intensive job training programs have a good return, but, of course, more intensive programs tend to be more costly and can serve fewer clients. By way of contrast, WtW serves a large proportion of the eligible poor population, but expenditures per worker are so low that the return is not very high (Lang 2007, 123).

OTHER PROGRAMS OF NOTE

One aspect of poverty that has received considerable media attention in recent years is the problem of homelessness. Although on any given night as many as 850,000 people (or 10 percent of the poverty population) (National Coalition for the Homeless 2007) might be homeless, the number of chronically homeless is probably closer to 150,000 (United States Department of Housing and Urban Development 2007). The high profile of homelessness stems from the sheer number of people affected, but also from the fact that it is an easy problem to picture and feel empathetic about—photos and videos of people sleeping on heating grates on the nation's streets and transporting their life's possessions in shopping carts have an undeniable impact.

The federal government has addressed the homelessness problem in a variety of ways, most notably through the Homeless Assistance program. This program provides financial assistance toward the operation of homeless shelters throughout the nation. But the government is not the dominant player in the homelessness arena. Local nonprofit organizations have taken and continue to hold the lead. Much of their funding comes from state and local governments.

A form of assistance to the poor that might not immediately leap to mind is the Low-income Home Energy Assistance Program (or LIHEAP). The program helps poor families modify their homes so that they use energy more efficiently, and is concerned with both heating and cooling problems. LIHEAP is relatively small in government terms; appropriations run about $1.75 billion each year. This program represents the collision of two national problems—poverty and the energy crisis.

CONCLUSION

Some ideas to carry away from this brief survey of the "welfare" system include the following:

1. When people say the government does nothing about poverty, they are greatly mistaken. Billions of dollars are spent each year in a variety of ways attacking various facets of the poverty problem. Whether we spend enough is another matter.

2. Antipoverty programs are not simple things. We do not simply bring a program into existence, spend the money, and enjoy the warm glow generated from having reduced poverty. Each program establishes complicated incentive structures that sometimes work against the goal. The classic example was the way AFDC discouraged work, saving, and family formation. An example from the current system is the theoretical discouragement of work in the plateau and phase-out regions of the EITC. A realistic view of the welfare system must include recognition of the trade-offs involved.

3. At least once per decade, economists ponder what would happen if we were to replace the crazy-quilt system of eighty-five different welfare programs with just one welfare program—a guaranteed annual income—and be done with it. Do the poor need special help buying food, obtaining medical care, and insulating their homes, or do they just need more money? Chapter 17 will explore this issue more completely.

4. How do we apportion the credit for changes in the poverty rate between economic growth and the welfare system? Rebecca M. Blank, currently a professor of economics at the University of Michigan and formerly a member of the Council of Economic Advisers in the Clinton administration, concludes "a strong macro economy matters more than anything else" (Blank 2000, 6).

She is reluctant, though, to say just how much a strong economy matters.

> While the strong economy appears to have been highly important in affecting outcomes among low-income families in the 1990s, it is difficult to measure these impacts precisely for several reasons. First, most of our economic measures reflect average economic effects, such as aggregate state unemployment rates, and do not measure the specific economic changes facing less-skilled workers. Second, the strong economy has affected not only poverty but also economic policy, and it is especially difficult to measure the magnitude of the effect on policy. For instance, the willingness of some states to enact their own earned income tax credits may be partially due to the flush situation of many state budgets in this economy. In addition, the strong economy and the availability of jobs had made it much easier for states to implement the program design and administrative changes required to reorganize their public welfare offices into work-oriented programs. Third, economists have a poor understanding of how economic growth affects some of the more informal ways in which low-income families receive income. We know little about the relationship between economic growth and the underground economy. We know little about how the willingness of absent parents or boyfriends or other family members to share incomes with single

mothers varies between good economic times and bad. There may be correlations between economic growth and family formation patterns that affect long-term economic well-being (Blank 2000, 9–10).

The ideal experiment would compare the outcomes from the world we actually live in to what the outcomes would have been if we had never instituted a welfare system in the first place. The long-term decline in poverty in the second scenario could only be attributed to economic growth. If poverty is lower in the first scenario than the second, the marginal effect can be attributed to the welfare system. Would we be shocked if poverty was higher in the first scenario than the second? This experiment is easy to talk about, but impossible to do since we only live in the first world.

QUESTIONS FOR REVIEW AND PRACTICE

1. Every year the Economics Department faculty gives its administrative assistant a holiday present consisting of a gift card to a local store. Last year the amount on the card was $125. What difference would it have made if the department simply gave the administrative assistant $125 in cash? Explain.
2. Consider the work plan and family plan aspects of TANF. Is work on the part of welfare recipients a reasonable expectation? Does government have any business getting involved in the personal lives of welfare recipients?
3. One way to extend health insurance to all Americans is to require Americans to purchase a health insurance policy. People of limited means would have their purchase of insurance subsidized. Discuss the benefits and costs of requiring people to purchase health insurance.
4. A vintage idea is a guaranteed annual income (Friedman 1962; Theobald 1965; Tobin 1968). Would guaranteeing people an annual income eliminate the need for the various welfare programs described in this chapter? Would it be a good idea?
5. What is the "pathology of the poor?" Is it accurate to use the word *pathology* in the context of talking about the poor? What does TANF do to address the "pathology of the poor?"

NOTES

1. This is essentially the definition used by the Committee on Ways and Means of the United States House of Representatives (United States Congress, House 2004, K–1).
2. The microeconomics of this need not detain us. See the material on risk and uncertainty in any intermediate microeconomics textbook, for example, Robert H. Frank's *Microeconomics and Behavior* (2008).
3. The historical record is complicated. Essentially, prior to World War II, health insurance was uncommon in the United States. Because of wartime wage controls, employers looked for other ways to deal with labor shortages. They began offering various fringe benefits, most notably health insurance.
4. Once in place, private insurance has been hard to budge. A big part of the reason is the tax treat-

ment of these benefits. Despite the fact that employer contributions for insurance are obviously part of worker compensation, workers do not pay taxes on the contributions. One estimate is that the cost of insurance is reduced 32 percent as a consequence (Gruber and Poterba 1996, 149).

5. Chapter 6 discussed the economics of mandating employers to provide health insurance.

6. There are issues here. The government does not simply pay the physician's or hospital's normal fee. Rather, the government reimburses on the basis of a set schedule per ailment per visit or per stay. The adequacy of the fee schedule is a perennial concern, but is an issue for a course in health economics.

7. The medically needy are persons whose health-care needs are so extensive that they are unable to afford treatment.

8. Actually there are some forms of income that do not need to be included, such as interest earned on state and local bonds.

9. Some people call deductions loopholes. The difference between a deduction and a loophole seems to be whether you are eligible for it or not. If you are eligible for it, it is a deduction. If your neighbor is eligible, and you are not, it is a loophole.

10. Liberals also like it because it is a comparatively generous program.

11. Some cynics have charged that another goal was to help food producers by increasing demand for their product.

12. There are strict rules about what types of items could be paid for with the stamps and which could not. Broccoli qualifies. A six-pack of beer does not.

13. At its peak, Cabrini-Green housed 15,000 mostly poor people in mid- and high-rise apartments. Gang violence was rampant and the buildings were not maintained. Most of the complex has now been demolished and the surrounding area has begun to enjoy a revival (Wikipedia, 2008).

14. We do not have to pay tuition to attend public school, but someone has to pay taxes to fund it, so education is not literally free.

15. In a series of rulings the California Supreme Court found that financing public schools by the property tax was unconstitutional (California Supreme Court 1971, 1976, 1977). The United States Supreme Court was not willing to go that far (United States Supreme Court 1973). Twenty states have had their funding schemes that rely heavily on the property tax upheld.

16. I spent a couple of happy summers working as a teacher's aid in Head Start when I was in college.

PART IV

MOBILITY

14

How the Size of a Slice Changes Over a Career

INTRODUCTION

Regardless of how you measure inequality and what the exact degree of inequality is, no one seriously questions that the distribution of income and wealth has become more unequal in the United States in recent decades. What some do question, however, is how remarkable that development is. The problem is that annual data on inequality provide a snapshot. They show the economy at one point in time. What we really want is the movie.

Consider the following situation. Assume society consists of five people: Sheila, Juan, Nancy, Barry, and Bill. Their incomes in year 1 were as listed in Table 14.1,[1] but over the next four years their incomes fluctuated for a variety of reasons. Some were employed in industries that expanded and benefited from promotions and wage increases. Some were unlucky to have been in contracting industries and may have been permanently laid off and had difficulty finding suitable new employment. Others may have received training and obtained job experience that allowed them to move up the job ladder. Some may have lost work time to illness. Others may have gotten divorced—and maybe the alimony check did not arrive regularly. At the end of the five-year period, what can we say? While income inequality was high each year, over the five-year period each person earned the exact same income![2] The high degree of income inequality was offset by a high degree of intragenerational income mobility. Even if the degree of inequality increased, it would have no effect on lifetime incomes if people continued to be mobile. Poverty is something everyone experiences, but it is only a temporary condition.

A slightly more realistic example would take into account the effects of age and experience. Refer to Table 14.2. In year 1, Sheila, Juan, Nancy, Barry, and Bill are the adults in this society. Jill, Li, Sammy, and Anna are either children or have yet to be conceived. In this society, only adults work and a career consists of five years, after which the individual leaves the scene. Sheila is in her fifth year of work, Juan his fourth, Nancy her third, Barry his second, and Bill his first. Their incomes reflect their years of working experience.

In year 2, Sheila leaves the scene. Juan now earns what Sheila used to earn, Nancy earns what Juan used to earn, Barry earns what Nancy used to earn, and Bill earns what Barry used to earn. Jill has just achieved adulthood and enters the labor market earning what Bill used to earn.

Table 14.1

Incomes Over a Five-Year Period

	Year 1 ($)	Year 2 ($)	Year 3 ($)	Year 4 ($)	Year 5 ($)	Total ($)
Sheila	168,170	11,352	28,777	49,223	76,329	333,851
Juan	76,329	168,170	11,352	28,777	49,223	333,851
Nancy	49,223	76,329	168,170	11,352	28,777	333,851
Barry	28,777	49,223	76,329	168,170	11,352	333,851
Bill	11,352	28,777	49,223	76,329	168,170	333,851

Table 14.2

Income Over a Five-Year Period Allowing for Entry and Exit

	Year 1 ($)	Year 2 ($)	Year 3 ($)	Year 4 ($)	Year 5 ($)
Sheila	168,170				
Juan	76,329	168,170			
Nancy	49,223	76,329	168,170		
Barry	28,777	49,223	76,329	168,170	
Bill	11,352	28,777	49,223	76,329	168,170
Jill		11,352	28,777	49,223	76,329
Li			11,352	28,777	49,223
Sammy				11,352	28,777
Anna					11,352

In each subsequent year, the oldest adult leaves the scene and is replaced by a new, younger adult.

Similar to the first example, this society is one in which there is a high degree of inequality in annual incomes, but the process of intragenerational mobility will equalize annual incomes.

A third situation is shown in Table 14.3. Assume Sheila and Bill populate the economy in the first generation and Sheila is rich while Bill is poor.[3] Each has one child. Sheila has Sheila Jr. and Bill has Bill Jr. After Sheila and Bill retire or die, Sheila Jr. and Bill Jr. replace them in the workforce, but Bill Jr. is rich and Sheila Jr. is poor. Then they each have a child. Sheila III is the child of Sheila Jr. and Bill III is the child of Bill Jr. When the two Juniors retire or die, the IIIs take their place, but each earns the same moderate income. What we have here is a case of almost complete intergenerational mobility. Humble beginnings are no bar to achieving fabulous success in life, and being born with a silver spoon in your mouth does not guarantee the "good life" later on.

The point of the preceding three examples is this: It does not make sense to evaluate the inequality of any variable without at the same time looking at the degree of mobility in that variable. For example, with respect to income, annual data on the distribution of income by household, family, and individual is readily available and is frequently the source of information for critical commentaries. Yet this data is potentially misleading. Gathered at a particular point in time, it lumps together units (households, families, or

Table 14.3

Changes in Income by Generation

	Generation 1		Generation 2		Generation 3
Person	Income ($)	Person	Income ($)	Person	Income ($)
Sheila	168,170	Sheila Jr.	11,352	Sheila III	49,223
Bill	11,352	Bill Jr.	168,170	Bill III	49,223

individuals) that differ greatly from each other along numerous dimensions, such as age, education, job market experience, region of the country, and many more. That some inequality exists is inevitable, and some of it would be considered completely legitimate by nearly everyone. The fact of the matter is that things change, people change, and incomes fluctuate over time. A more complete picture of inequality has to take into account income mobility—how incomes fluctuate over the life cycle (intragenerational mobility) and between generations (intergenerational mobility).

This chapter focuses on intragenerational earnings mobility. It will look at models explaining why people's earnings change over their lifetime. Chapter 15 examines intergenerational earnings mobility. To complete our look at mobility, Chapter 16 throws the accumulation and transfer of wealth into the mix.

How Earnings Change Over the Life Cycle

My Earnings History

Figure 14.1 shows my yearly earnings from when I was sixteen years old to the present.[4] The vertical axis has been masked to save me from embarrassment because the actual dollar values have been exceedingly modest. The earnings recorded in the graph were not my only income most of those years. I did receive interest and occasional consulting fees and made nontaxable contributions to a pension fund, but these other sources of income were always unexceptional. The bulk of my income from the sweat of my brow is displayed in the figure.[5]

One thing to note is the fluctuation in my earnings from year to year. Note the big drop in 2003, primarily the result of not teaching summer school for the first time ever, and not having a summer research grant. It is not the least bit unusual for people's incomes to fluctuate dramatically from year to year. The economy tanks, people get sick, their union goes on strike, they get a chance to work overtime, and so on.

Another thing to notice is the long-term upward trend for my earnings. I have apparently gotten more productive over time despite the fact that my last year of formal schooling was 1975.

My pattern is not unusual. Figures 14.2 and 14.3 show age-earnings profiles for full-time, year-round workers by gender and level of education for the nation as a whole. The shapes of these profiles, although a little bit messy, look suspiciously like mine.[6]

Although my pattern is not unusual, there is probably no one else in the entire world who has had the exact same pattern. Undoubtedly some people, contrary to my

Figure 14.1 **My Age-Earnings Profile**

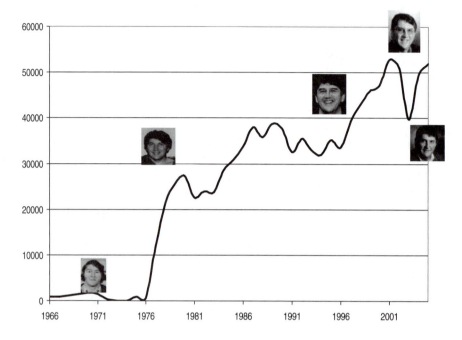

Figure 14.2 **Mean Earnings for Men by Age and Education, 2006, Full-time, Year-Round Workers**

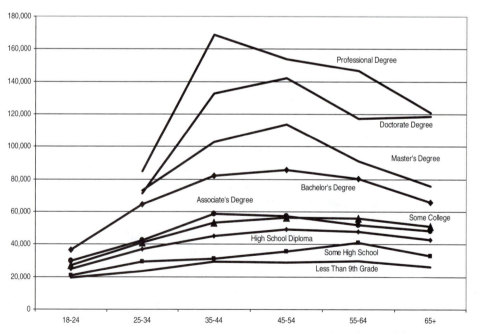

Source: U.S. Census Bureau, Historic Income Tables, P-32, http://www.census.gov/hhes/www/income/ histinc/p32.html, accessed 25 June 2008.

Figure 14.3   **Mean Earnings for Women by Age and Education, 2006, Full-time, Year-Round Workers**

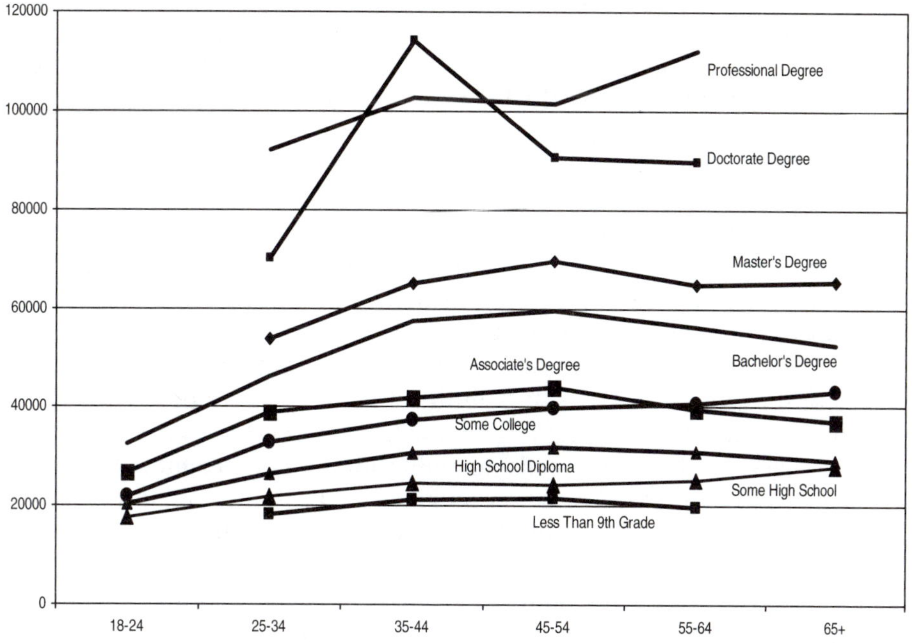

Source: U.S. Census Bureau, Historic Income Tables, P-32, http://www.census.gov/hhes/www/income/histinc/p32.html, accessed 25 June 2008.

pattern, have had their earnings shoot up spectacularly over relatively short periods of time. Think of any winner of *American Idol* or *Survivor.* Others have seen their earnings rise much more steadily than mine. Still others have had to suffer through severe reverses that lasted for varying lengths of time, perhaps the result of a failure of a business, a lay-off, or illness. Some have had their careers end prematurely and been forced to retire early. All this churning of earnings is a major contributor to intragenerational mobility.[7]

This chapter will investigate models that attempt to provide a systematic explanation of why people's earnings change over their working careers and why they tend to follow the pattern of Figures 14.1, 14.2, and 14.3. The models in this chapter do not provide the entire story of intragenerational mobility, of course. As the discussion above pointed out, frequently earnings change due to random events. Also, earnings are only one of the elements that determine well-being. The discussion in Chapter 16 on wealth accumulation and transfer over the life cycle extends the picture.

THEORIES OF EARNINGS GROWTH

Individual earnings are likely to grow over time simply as an outcome of the process of economic growth. Chapter 2 provided a demand-and-supply analysis of the impact of growth on wages. The story is not a simple one, and long-run wage growth is not to be taken for granted. If, however, technological change and increases in the supply of other factors of production raise labor productivity to more than offset the effect of increased labor supply on wages, then wages will grow over time. This theory does not adequately explain the distinctive age-earnings profiles of individuals as represented by Figures 14.1–14.3.

Human Capital Theory

One of the more durable theories of the labor market is human capital theory. Economists use it to explain both short-run and long-run earnings differentials as well as the pattern of wage growth over time. The theory can also be used to suggest very specific policy interventions. It is an extraordinarily versatile theory.[8]

Your human capital is the personal attributes that determine your productivity and, consequently, your earning ability. Examples of human capital include education, skills, information, health, and location. While the impact that education and skills have on productivity needs no elaboration, the other three are probably not as obvious. Job market information includes such things as knowledge of what jobs have vacancies, what wages are being offered, and what the working conditions are like. Everything else held constant, workers with more job market information should have an easier time finding satisfactory jobs and, consequently, their earnings will be higher. Your health helps determine how hard and long you can work and what job stresses you can handle. Healthier individuals will earn more. Location also influences your earning ability. Workers in declining regions will have fewer opportunities than workers in expanding areas.

Human capital is similar to physical capital in a very important respect. Physical capital consists of machinery, factories, and equipment, all of which can make human labor more productive, just like skills, information, health, and location make human labor more productive. But the analogy cannot be carried too far. Unlike physical capital, human capital cannot be sold because the human capital cannot be separated from the actual human. Of course, human capital can be rented. You can rent your skills to an employer for a wage. Also the individual renting human capital cares about such things as working conditions and personal interaction on the job. Physical capital could care less.

Human capital theory makes two claims. First, a person's earning capacity depends on the amount of human capital possessed. *Ceteris paribus,* those with greater human capital will have higher earnings. Poverty then can be attributed to lack of human capital. Income inequality is associated with inequality in the distribution of human capital. Wage growth reflects human capital accumulation over the career.

Second, the amount of human capital you have depends on actions that you (or your parents) take. Skills can be acquired by attending school or a job training program, or through experience. Information can be obtained through reading, asking around, or experience. You can improve your health by dieting, exercise, and cutting out various vices. Your location can be changed by migration.

Acquiring human capital is called investing in human capital for a very good reason. The defining characteristic of an investment is that a cost is incurred today in exchange for a payoff in the future. This is true for each of the five types of human capital mentioned. There are tuition, books and equipment fees, and foregone earnings associated with going to school or a training program, but the skills acquired will allow the holder to earn more in the future. Reading want ads or perusing Monster. com are time-consuming activities, but will pay off later in job opportunities. Dieting all the time and exercising some of the time are a source of disutility. The benefit comes in the longer and healthier life to be lived later. Migration requires that tickets be purchased and ties to old friendships and familiar surroundings be cut. Better jobs will appear only once you get to where you are going.

Present Value. (If you read and understood this material in Chapter 4, you may skip to the next section.) What would you rather choose—for me to give you $100 now or for me to give you $100 one year in the future? If you are rational, you would take the $100 now. Even disregarding the risk (I might be nowhere to be found in a year), the money in your hands right now can be put to work now and start earning now. It could be invested and earn interest. The money you need to wait for cannot do anything for you now. This example shows that money in the future is not worth the same as money today. Rather, money in the future in worth less than money today. In other words, the present value of money in the future is less than the present value of money today. The present value of $100 one year in the future is less than the present value of $100 today.

What is $100 one year in the future worth today? Your internal rate of time preference is a measure of the reward you require to postpone consumption. If you would postpone $100 in consumption today only if you were given $110 in consumption next year, your internal rate of time preference is 10 percent [= (110–100)/100]. People are likely to differ in their internal rate of time preference. People with high internal rates of time preference are frequently called impatient, present-oriented or, more pejoratively, unable to defer gratification. These are people who are so eager to consume now that they demand a large reward for abstaining. People with low rates of time preference are patient or future-oriented or able to defer gratification.

Your internal rate of time preference helps determine the present value of future money. If your internal rate of time preference is p, then $X today is equivalent to $X*(1 + p) one year in the future: $X today = $X(1 + p) in one year. To get what $X in one year is worth today, divide both sides of that expression by (1 + p). Therefore: $X/(1 + p) today = $X in one year.

Using numbers, if your internal rate of time preference is 8 percent, then $100 in one year is worth $100/(1.08) = $92.59 today. The process of converting a future value into a present value is sometimes called discounting and the internal rate of time preference is sometimes called the discount rate.

What is the present value of $100 two years in the future? With an internal rate of time preference of p, you expect a p reward for waiting one year and will expect an additional p for the second year. So $X today is equivalent to $X(1 + p)(1 + p) in two years: $X today = $X(1 + p)(1 + p) in two years. Therefore: $X/(1 + p)^2$ today = $X in two years.

At an 8 percent rate of time preference, $100 in two years in worth $85.73 today.

What is the present value of $100 three years in the future? With an internal rate of time preference of p, you expect a p reward for waiting one year, an additional p for waiting the second year, and p more for the third year. So $X today is equivalent to $X(1 + p)(1 + p)(1 + p) in three years: $X today = $X(1 + p)(1 + p)(1 + p) in three years. Therefore: $X/(1 + p)^3$ today = $X in three years.

At an 8 percent rate of time preference, $100 in three years in worth $79.38 today.

Are you starting to see a pattern? The present value of $X in n years is equal to $X/(1 + p)^n$.

The present value of a stream of money can easily be calculated following this model. Assume you are fortunate enough to win a $1 million lottery that pays its prizes in $50,000 increments over a twenty-year period. You really do not win $1 million because the present value of your winnings (assuming an 8 percent rate of time preference) is:

$$PV = \$50,000 + \$50,000/(1 + .08) + \$50,000/(1 + .08)^2 + \ldots + \$50,000/(1 + 0.08)^{19} = \$530,180.$$

Since you receive your first payment right away (when you rush on down to the lottery office to claim your prize), it is not discounted. The remaining payments are then paid out over nineteen years.[9]

An important complication arises from the fact that people's rate of time preference is not a constant, but rather changes with their level of consumption. The more you consume today, the less valuable an additional dollar of consumption becomes. This is simply the law of diminishing utility in action. From the standpoint of time preference, this means the more you consume now, the less impatient you become. Your rate of time preference declines as you consume more today.

There is an important implication of this. People's saving and consumption is influenced by their rate of time preference and the market rate of interest. If the interest rate on savings is less than your rate of time preference, you will consume now rather than save, simply because the market reward for saving is insufficient. Conversely, people whose rate of time preference is less than the market rate of interest, will save now because they receive a larger reward than they require. But the rate of time preference of the consumers will fall and the rate of time preference of the savers will rise. In equilibrium everyone's rate of time preference will equal the market rate of interest. Consequently, in calculations of present value, an appropriate rate of interest can be used instead of a separate rate of time preference for each person.[10]

Investments in Schooling. In this section we will use a way-too-simple example to show how decisions are made in a human capital model. Assume everyone graduates from high school at age eighteen having learned the exact same thing. At that point a choice must be made whether to enter the workforce directly or attend college for four years. If the individual enters the workforce, he or she will find a job paying W^H a year and work until retirement at age sixty-seven. If he/she chooses the col-

Figure 14.4 **The Schooling Model**

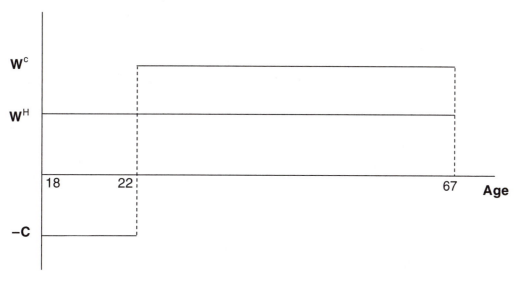

lege route, then there will be four years of full-time studying at C per year.[11] At age twenty-two, the person will graduate and find a job paying W^C per year (where $W^C >$ W^H) and work until retirement at age sixty-seven. Figure 14.4 shows the yearly monetary outgo and income from the two choices.

Assume nonmonetary characteristics of the two jobs are equivalent. The choice simply becomes which job pays more. But which job pays more is not such a simple concept. The college graduate's job pays more each year, but you cannot start earning that money right off the bat and there are significant upfront costs that must be paid. To make an intelligent decision requires that the present value of the two choices be computed.

The present value of taking a job immediately upon graduation from high school is given by the following equation:

$$PV^H = W^H + W^H/(1 + p) + W^H/(1 + p)^2 + \ldots + W^H/(1 + p)^{49} = \Sigma W^H/(1 + p)^{t-18}.$$

The present value of going to college first and then taking a job is given by a slightly more complicated equation.

$$PV^C = -C - C/(1 + p) - C/(1 + p)^2 - C/(1 + p)^3 + W^C/(1 + p)^4 + W^C/(1 + p)^5 + \ldots + W^C/(1 + p)^{49} = \Sigma (W^C - C)/(1 + p)^{t-18}$$

The job that pays more is the one with the higher present value.

There is an alternative way to analyze this choice. It requires the computation of the internal rate of return from going to college. The internal rate of return (r) is the value that causes $\Sigma 9W^H/(1 + r)^{t-18}$) to be equal to $\Sigma((W^C - C)/(1 + r)^{t-18})$. The math necessary to solve this problem is not pretty, but the problem can be solved by most electronic spreadsheet programs. An individual would attend college if r > p.

In most cases the decision of the present value approach will be the same as the decision of the internal rate of return approach. In a few cases they might conflict, but these cases are unlikely to be significant in actual practice. Computing the internal rate of return is the preferred approach, but, to repeat, the math is not pretty.

A Numerical Example. To demonstrate some of the complexities, consider the following numerical example. Assume everyone can work for three periods after graduation from high school. The wage a high school graduate can command is $25,000 per year. Going to college takes one period and costs $25,000. The wage a college graduate can command is $55,000, but college graduates can only work two periods. If the interest rate is 5 percent, the problem can be set up this way: $PV^H = \$25,000 + \$25,000/(1+.05) + \$25,000/(1+.05)^2 = \$71,485.26$ for going to work directly after high school and $PV^C = \$-25,000 + \$55,000/(1+.05) + \$55,000/(1+.05)^2 = \$77,267.57$ for going to college and then work. The choice is a clear. Go to college.

But now assume the rate of time preference is 15 percent. The problem then becomes: $PV^H = \$25,000 + \$25,000/(1+.15) + \$25,000/(1+.15)^2 = \$65,642.72$ for going to work directly after high school and $PV^C = \$-25,000 + \$55,000/(1+.15) + \$55,000/(1+.15)^2 = \$64,413.99$ for going to college and then work. Here the decision is do *not* go to college.

The difference between the two cases is the interest rate. While the college wage is over twice the high school wage, it can only be earned in the future. The higher the interest rate, the more those future earnings are discounted.

Do People Think This Way? The foregoing might seem a bit fantastic to you. In your senior year of high school did you sit down and calculate present values of going to college versus not going or for different occupations? Of course not. And neither did I. Of what relevance then is the foregoing analysis?

The question of "do people think this way" is a great way to begin thinking about the role of models in economics. Human capital theory is a model. It is an abstract replica of reality. It is a simplification of reality where the simplification takes place so that the human mind can comprehend what is taking place. Reality is too complex. It must be simplified before understanding can occur.

The human capital model does not say that people think this way. Rather it says people act *as if* they think this way. There is a big difference between these two sentences. The first sentence focuses on what happens inside the brain. It says that people think a certain way and that is why they act a certain way. The second sentence only focuses only on how people act. To provide some logical basis for why people act that way we make up a story about what is happening inside their brain. The story might not be accurate, but never mind. What is really important is how they act.

How do we validate the human capital model? Given the current state of brain science, we cannot look inside peoples' brains and discover what is happening. However, we can test the predictions of the model against people's actions. If the predictions are accurate, then the model might be useful, even if it is not very realistic.

Consider some predictions of the human capital model. What does the model say would happen to college attendance if the earnings of college graduates rose? The model clearly implies that college attendance would increase. Is that the case? Apparently, yes.[12] According to the model, college attendance rises because people recognize that the present value of going to college and taking those types of careers has increased. Whether people actually think that way is unknown, but not essential. The fact that people do increase their college attendance when the earnings of college graduates increase means they act *as if* they thought this way

There are a number of other predictions from the model. What happens to college attendance if the cost of going to college falls or if people's internal rate of time preference rises? We could test this against the data. If our predictions are borne out, then we have a useful model, even if it is not very realistic.

Who is more likely to attend college—the young or the old? According to the model, it makes more sense for the young to attend. It is a reasonable assumption that since the young have a longer career ahead of them, they stand to benefit more.[13] Is the prediction of the model borne out? If you are reading this as a college student, just take a look around. If not, use your imagination.

So back to the initial question: Do people think this way? Probably not. But they act as if they do and that makes the human capital model a useful tool for analyzing what happens in the labor market.[14]

How Does Schooling Raise Earning Power? The exact mechanism by which schooling raises earning power is an area of significant controversy. Many, almost without thinking, naturally assume that the essential skills nurtured by human capital investment are cognitive skills. Cognitive skills are technical skills. Think of them as the "3 Rs": readin', ritin', and 'rithmetic. After all, we need to read, write and be able to do arithmetic to perform in high-level jobs and what do schools do if not teach us the 3 Rs?

The recent rise in inequality is often attributed to technological change that influences the demand for labor. The development of computers and information technology has created a demand for people who have the technical skills to work with this technology. These individuals have a high level of cognitive skill.

However, empirical analysis has not been kind to that position (Bowles and Gintis 1976; Bowles, Gintis, and Osbourne 2001). The issue is not whether cognitive skills are important or not. Clearly they are essential. Rather the issue is whether they are scarce or not, and the evidence seems to be that they are not especially scarce. They are not so scarce that they make the crucial difference in explaining earnings differences. More concretely, very few people hold jobs where they are required to solve problems using advanced calculus. Most people hold jobs where algebra will do, and algebra skills are not all that scarce.

The alternative view states that the crucial factor in determining earnings is motivational and behavioral traits. Employers are not just looking for people who can solve complex mathematical equations, program computers, design rocket engines, and do all those things that require cognitive skills. They also seek people with ambition, stamina, trustworthiness, dependability, perseverance, and consistency for a couple of reasons. One has to do with the principal-agent problem. Employers cannot oversee all their employees all the time. They have to rely on their employees to be self-motivated and this requires people with certain personalities. Also, since markets are not always in equilibrium, employers need employees who are adept at taking advantage of the unforeseen opportunities that arise. People who are fatalistic or impatient cannot do this. Ambitious, self-confident people can. Schools are not simply where people learn to do math. They are where people develop these vital behavioral traits.[15] Consequently, the return to human capital investment does not reflect its impact on cognitive skills. Rather, the motivational and behavioral traits fostered by schools are really crucial.

Another point of view is the screening hypothesis. Simply stated, it says that schooling does not necessarily make people more productive, but rather that more productive people necessarily get more schooling. The problem is one of information. How does a really productive individual make him- or herself stand out to an employer? One way is to acquire a credential, such as a diploma (Spence 1973). Since the most productive people are likely to be most adept at succeeding at schooling, these folks will get the most schooling and will get the best jobs on that basis. Employers will only see that their most productive employees in fact have the most schooling and put two and two together and arrive at what they think is four.

The weight of the evidence has not been strongly supportive of this hypothesis.[16] For example, one implication of the theory is that self-employed individuals do not need as much education as others because the only person they have to impress is themselves. One study found that self-employed workers received nearly as much education as salaried workers (Wolpin 1977). However a subsequent study muddied the waters a bit. This study looked at wages received by takers of the GED exam.[17] While there is a uniform GED exam administered everywhere in the country, different states have different passing standards. Two individuals could get the exact same score on the test, but one would pass and one would fail because of the state they took the exam in. If educational credentials act merely as a screen, then the person who passed should receive a higher wage than the person who failed. The finding was that among those with the same GED score, passers received a higher wage than those who failed (Tyler, Murnane, and Willett 2000). Consequently, educational credentials act at least partly as a screening device, and so this interesting hypothesis cannot be completely rejected.

On-the-Job Training. The age-earnings profiles in Figures 14.1–14.3 do not look like that of Figure 14.4. The former show earnings continuing to rise even after the completion of schooling until they reach a peak a few years before retirement. How come?

There are a couple of reasons for the difference. One is that Figure 14.4 does not allow for subsequent schooling or training. It is not at all unusual for some workers to go back to school or to enter a training program mid-career. Sometimes these programs are used to upgrade skills. Other times they are used to obtain replacement skills after a layoff. These sorts of programs are likely to create discreet jumps in the age-earnings profile, not produce the curvature shown.

The second reason is more fundamental. Subsequent to the end of schooling most workers accumulate what is known as on-the-job training (OJT). This training is just what its name says. It is training acquired while you are working for a particular employer. OJT is often simply the result of experience. It is practice makes perfect (sometimes called learning by doing) or learning by observing. It is often acquired informally.

A couple of summers during my high school years I worked as a laborer in a warehouse.[18] I mainly loaded and unloaded boxcars full of tires. In the morning we would open a boxcar filled with tires and unload it. We would place the tires in four stacks of eight on a pallet and crown it with one tire. Then a lift truck would carry the pallet away and place an empty pallet in its place. Unloading a fifty-foot boxcar would take all morning.[19] After lunch we would go to the same boxcar and load it up again. The lift truck driver would bring pallets of tires and we would break them down and fit them in the boxcar. Believe it or not, there are special ways to do this that allows for the work to proceed smoothly and permits all the tires to fit in the volume of the boxcar.

My coworker one summer was a young man who had just graduated from high school. He was undecided about a career, but did know one thing. He did not want to load and unload boxcars the rest of this life. During breaks or lunchtime, instead of relaxing with the rest of us, he persuaded the foreman to let him drive the lift truck around. Driving a lift truck is no easy task. The truck is heavy, warehouses have many obstacles in them, and the wheels of a lift truck turn in the opposite way from those of a car.[20] Since the lift trucks need to be driven quite rapidly in order for all the work to be done, it requires some training but practice is essential.

What my coworker was doing was OJT. He was given minimal training but was primarily developing his skills by practice. Should an opportunity have arisen, he was increasing his chances of being selected for what would have been a promotion. Lift truck drivers spend most of their day seated, at least.

Like any human capital, OJT raises the productivity of the person receiving it. As people acquire training, their productivity will rise and we would expect their earnings to rise even after they have completed formal schooling.

There are two types of OJT. General training is defined as training that raises the recipient's productivity equally in all firms (Becker 1993b, 33–40). Specific training is training that raises the recipient's productivity only in the firm providing the training (Becker 1993b, 40–51). An example of general training might be a very basic skill such as learning how to use a specific word processing program. Since many firms might use that word processing program, learning how to use it at one firm would also be beneficial at other firms. In fact, most schooling is general training.

A definite example of specific training is harder to come by. Assume a firm using a very idiosyncratic technology in production. In other words, it produces the product differently than any other firm. For example, one beer company advertises that its beer is cold-brewed as opposed to the warm-brewing technology of other beer firms. Learning how to use that technology is specific training because knowing how to use it will raise your productivity at that firm, but would not help you at all at any other firm.

The type of training received has important implications for who pays for the training and for turnover. Consider general training. What if the employer were to pay for general training? Before going forward, let us talk about what is meant by paying for the training. An employer can pay for training in two ways. One way is by paying the tuition to a training program. Another way is by continuing to pay you your normal wage while letting you learn the skill the hard way, namely by making mistakes, such as breaking tools, damaging goods, and disrupting the other workers.

Regardless, what will happen if the employer pays? You will earn a skill that will make you more productive to your employer and to everyone else. The only way the employer can reap any advantage by incurring the cost to train you is if the employer can keep the extra productivity that you are responsible for by paying you a wage less than your now higher productivity. But will that happen? Why would you stay with that employer if you could take your now higher productivity self to some other employer and command a wage equal to your productivity? In short, no employer would be willing to pay for general training because there is no guarantee that the worker will stay with the firm.[21]

As a result, the worker will be forced to pay for the training. The worker might pay the tuition out of pocket or else the worker might accept a starting (or training) wage less than the value of his or her marginal productivity during the training period.[22] At the end of the period, the worker's productivity is now higher and the worker will be able to reap a return from any firm willing to pay a wage equal to the new, higher productivity.

Specific training works a bit differently. Here workers do not have an incentive to pay for the training because since their productivity is only raised in one firm they cannot use their new skills as a bargaining chip to gain a higher wage. Employers would have to pay, but then employers find themselves in a dilemma. What happens if the employer pays for the training but the worker subsequently decides to leave the firm? The employer's investment is lost. Therefore the employer will pay the worker a slightly higher wage at the end of the training period simply to retain the worker's services. But if that happens, then that job becomes particularly attractive, thereby creating a surplus of applicants for the job, which would allow the employer to shift a portion of the training costs onto the worker. The bottom line is that the worker and employer will share both the costs and the benefits of the training. A clear prediction of the theory is that workers with specific training will have lower turnover rates than other workers.

How does all this fit into a theory of lifetime earnings? First, consider when it makes the most sense to invest. Investing in yourself makes more sense earlier rather than later. There are two reasons. First, the earlier you invest in yourself, the more years you have to recoup your investment. Second, the opportunity cost of investment is lower. A major component of the cost of investment is foregone earnings. The younger you are the lower your earnings.

Therefore individuals should begin investing early. This is true for both schooling and OJT. Therefore wages are likely to be low during the early years both because productivity is low and because the worker is paying the cost of investment. As the worker ages, wages will rise as the investments start paying off. Of course, as the worker ages, it makes less sense to invest in oneself. Also, earlier human capital investments may depreciate or become obsolete so wages may flatten out or actually decline near the end of the career.

What we have just done here is provide a theory that helps explain intragenerational mobility.

Incentives[22]

What are some other reasons why wages might change over the life cycle? The wage structure can be used as an incentive to get people to work hard.

How do you motivate workers to give a full day's work for a full day's a pay? In some instances adequate supervision is all that is required. In others, a piece rate compensation scheme might do the trick. But what do firms do when intense supervision is expensive or impractical or when output is difficult to observe?

Refer to Figure 14.5. Let MP be the worker's productivity over his or her career. Note that it rises during the early years of the worker's career, presumably as a result of human capital investment. At some point a peak will be hit after which productivity declines. The decline in productivity might be the result of depreciation or obsolescence of human capital, a decision to reduce hours of work, or the simple effects of aging. Let W be a wage profile constructed in such a way that the present value of wages was exactly equal to the present value of MP.

How should labor be compensated? At first glance, it might appear that both employers and workers would not be concerned about whether the wage was W or MP, but the fact is that employers would prefer to pay W, and workers would prefer to receive W, rather than MP. The argument goes like this: From the standpoint of the employer, W is preferable to MP because it reduces the incentive for workers to shirk. Early in their careers, since workers receive a wage less than their productivity is worth, they want to work hard and retain their job or else they will never see their extra productivity reflected in their paycheck. Later in their careers, workers will continue to work hard because they are earning a wage that exceeds their productivity and they do not want to blow that opportunity.

Workers also prefer the compensation scheme of W. Workers will work harder over their entire careers if they receive W than if they were paid MP each year. If all workers work harder, the firm's productivity increases, so every worker will receive a higher wage than otherwise.

> This is like the apocryphal story of the Chinese merchant boat with a cruel taskmaster. In earlier times, boats were powered by men with oars. The faster they rowed, the faster the boat traveled and the more money they made. The story goes that an observer was remarking to an oarsman about the cruelty of the taskmaster, who whipped the rowers when they slacked off. The observer says, "It must be terrible to have to work for such a cruel master." The oarsman replied, "He works for us. We do not work for him. The oarsmen own the boat and hire him to make sure that we do not shirk on the job" (Lazear 1998, 285–86).

Figure 14.5 **Incentives**

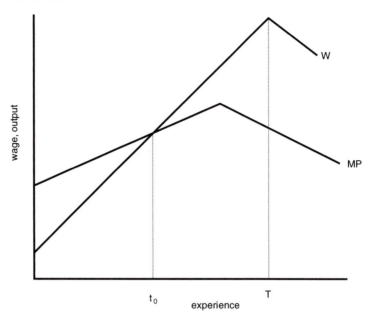

So workers have an incentive to keep their "nose to the grindstone" throughout their career under this pay scheme. The downside is that at point T the present value of wages paid to the worker will just be equal to the present value of the worker's productivity. If the worker keeps working, the worker's wage will be greater than productivity and the present value of the wages received will then exceed the present value of the productivity provided. The worker would not want to quit, but the employer no longer benefits from employing that worker. Thus we have an explanation for why many firms once had mandatory retirement ages. Of course, in the United States today mandatory retirement ages are viewed as age discrimination and are illegal. That legislation has complicated the problem facing the employer. The employer needs to devise some other way to get workers to retire "on time." Buy-outs are a common device.

The Tournament Model

Another way for a firm to use lifetime earnings as a motivating device is to employ a hierarchy of job levels with opportunities for promotion from within the firm from lower to higher levels. To analyze this we can make use of the so-called tournament model (Lazear and Rosen 1981). In the tournament model, the firm establishes a job pyramid and promotes from within after a competition among workers for jobs at the lowest level. In Figure 14.6 the job pyramid really looks like a pyramid. There are six job levels. The job gets "better" as you move up the pyramid from level 6 to level 1. The number of jobs decreases as you move up the pyramid from level 6 to level 1. Workers are hired at level 6, known as a

Figure 14.6 **The Tournament Model**

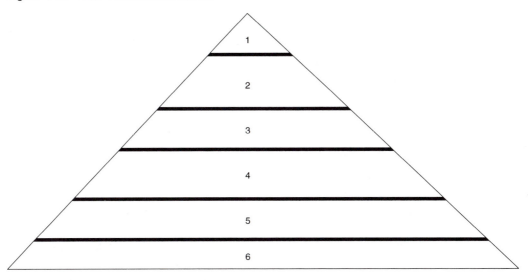

port of entry. As they acquire skill and experience and if they perform well they can get promoted up the pyramid.

Given what we have said earlier, it is not surprising that people's earnings increase over their lifetime as they acquire skill and experience and are promoted up the job pyramid. What the tournament model adds to the mix is an explanation of earnings differentials as one moves up the pyramid. In many corporations, the earnings differentials between one level and another increase as you move up the pyramid. For example, in one study of corporate compensation schemes (base plus bonuses) for the top four executive levels (where level 1 was the CEO) using a sample of over 200 publicly held corporations, a promotion from level 4 to level 3 increased compensation by 44 percent, from level 3 to level 2 increased compensation by 75 percent, and from level 2 to level 1 increased compensation by 141 percent (Main, O'Reilly, and Wade 1993, 610–611). Or consider the compensation scheme on the television show *Survivor.* The ultimate survivor gets $1 million. The second place person gets $100,000. Everyone else just gets expenses reimbursed.

The explanation for why compensation schemes are structured this way is as follows: Pay differentials motivate people to make the effort toward promotion to higher levels. But as people move up the job pyramid, they achieve "comfortable" levels of compensation. Moving up higher will raise compensation, but why put forth the extra effort if the gain in compensation will only be modest? Consequently, compensation increases must be greater and greater in order in get people to continue to strive for "the brass ring."

A clear prediction of the theory is that the structure of compensation in tournament models is economically efficient. This is not a particularly easy proposition to test. Knoeber and Thurman found that growers of broiler chickens raised larger birds when their compensation depended on relative performance (Knoeber 1989). In an interesting experiment, Bull, Schotter, and Weigelt found weak evidence that players put forth more effort in tournament situations (Bull, Schotter, and Weigelt 1987). Sports provide a particularly interesting venue in which to test tournament model predictions. Ehrenberg and Bognanno looked at scores on the European Professional Golfers Association tour. They found that the same golfer achieved better average scores on the same course when the difference between prizes by finish position is greater. Also, players near the top played harder at the end of the tournament (Ehrenberg and Bognanno 1990). There is evidence that participants in foot races run faster in races with a bigger payoff (Maloney and McCormick 2000).

CEO Compensation

With the tournament model in mind, consider a currently hot topic. The relative compensation of CEOs has skyrocketed in recent decades. In 1980, CEOs of large U.S. corporations received as compensation about forty times what the average American worker received (Anderson et al. 2007, 7). In 2006, they received about 364 times what the average American worker received (Anderson et al. 2007, 2). To put this number in perspective, if the average worker makes $29,670 a year, then the average CEO makes $29,670*364 = $10,800,000. Most of you reading this book are unlikely to become average workers. Rather you are likely to be salaried, white-collar employees making well above the average. Assume your salary is $100,000. That would mean the CEO would make 108 times what you make.

CEO compensation is a hot topic for a number of reasons. One reason is simply because it is a big pile of money. Anybody could live quite comfortably on half that! Another reason is there appears to be no close connection between CEO compensation and corporate performance. Since 2001, *Forbes Magazine* has ranked CEOs by compensation and efficiency, where efficiency is a measure of corporate performance (DeCarlo 2008). The best-compensated CEOs typically do not lead the league in efficiency. A third reason for concern is that workers have not kept up with CEO compensation, or, for that matter, overall productivity growth. Figure 14.7 shows cumulative nonfarm productivity and wages since 1959. By 2006 productivity had increased 68.74% over what it was in 1959. Wages had only increased 48.24 percent. The gap in growth rates began to show itself in the early 1960s, and became especially pronounced starting in the mid-1970s. A fourth reason is because CEOs in the United States make far more than CEOs in the rest of the world. The most instructive comparison is with European CEOs. CEOs at the top twenty European corporations make about a third of what CEOs at the top twenty U.S. corporations make.

A fifth reason that CEO compensation is being scrutinized is the general public's awareness of several highly publicized instances of corporate executive bad behavior. For example, in 2002 Kmart declared bankruptcy and eliminated 22,000 jobs, but CEO Charles Conway walked away with a $9.5 million severance package; but at least he lost his job. Rich McGinn, CEO of Lucent Technologies received a $5.5 million severance package while the company's workforce was cut in half and the workers' 401(k) plan was frozen. Douglas Daft of Coca-Cola cut 5,200 jobs, lost do-

Figure 14.7 **Productivity and Worker Pay**

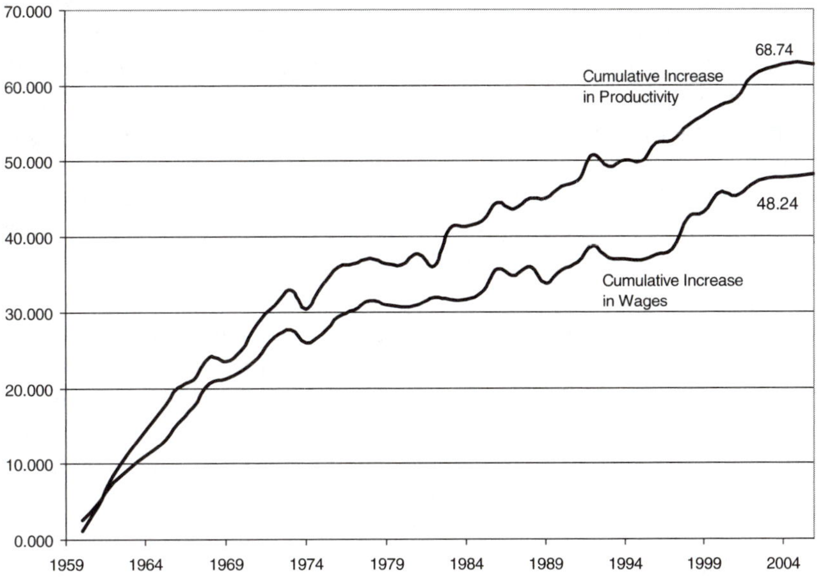

Source: Economic Report of the President

mestic market share, and failed to meet earnings goals, but he received $105 million in compensation. Enron Corporation went bankrupt, 6,100 employees lost their jobs, and many employees lost their pensions. The late CEO Kenneth Lay is alleged to have deceived employees about the direction the company was taking and pocketed $123 million. And don't forget Martha Stewart!

How are CEOs compensated? Generally speaking, there are four components to CEO compensation: salaries and fringes, bonuses, perks, and stock options. Salaries and fringes are what you would expect them to be. While CEOs receive handsome salaries and fringes, they are not extraordinarily disproportionate to what others receive. Bonuses are frequently given for meeting certain goals laid down by a company's board of directors. Often the bonuses can be quite generous. Examples of perks are paid country club membership, use of a corporate jet, and tickets to the Super Bowl. The real money for CEOs comes about as the result of stock options.

A stock option is a financial device that allows the holder to buy a particular stock at a particular price.[24] For example, let us say that a CEO is given an option to buy 100 shares of a stock at $75 a share (the strike price). If the stock price is currently $70 a share, then the CEO will not exercise the option. If the stock rises to $85 a share, the CEO can do two things. One is to continue to hold onto the option and hope the stock rises even further (there is usually an expiration date for an option). The second is to exercise the option. In that case the CEO can buy the stock at $75, realizing a capital gain of $10 a share. In this instance the CEO might hold the stock or turn around and sell it. For some options, the corporation simply gives the CEO the difference between the option price of the stock and the current selling price.

There is a good reason why options might be used to compensate CEOs. The owners of a corporation are its stockholders, and what stockholders want most of all is for the value of their shares to appreciate. If the CEO owns neither stock nor options, then the CEO is likely to be indifferent toward that goal (by deeds if not by words). By issuing options, the goals of the CEO are aligned with the goals of the stockholders, and, in theory, that should motivate the CEO to act in the manner most consistent with what the owners of the corporation want.

The really huge paydays that CEOs have enjoyed, such as the more than $570 million Michael Eisner of The Walt Disney Company received in 1997, were the result of options being exercised. One point that needs to be made is that options are granted only intermittently so big paydays are sporadic. Also, the discussion of stock options begs the question of how many options will be issued to the CEO and what the strike price of the stock will be. The really big paydays were not only the result of the CEO being able to raise the corporation's stock price. They were also the result of the CEO receiving a large number of options at a very favorable strike price.

Nevertheless, many CEOs have done quite well in recent years, and the justice of this is a matter of national concern.

Internal Labor Markets

Many firms have established what are called internal labor markets (Doeringer and Piore 1971). An internal labor market can be thought of as a job ladder (see Figure 14.8). Workers are hired from the external labor market at ports of entry, typically a relatively low-skilled job, and jobs higher on the ladder are filled by promoting from within.

Blue- and white-collar examples abound. In traditional steel and auto plants, kids straight out of high school would be placed in hot, sweaty, menial jobs. If they stuck out the probationary period, they were promoted to slightly better jobs, and if they continued to show their worth, they would keep getting promoted. As they moved their way up the ladder they would receive training, the jobs would require more skills, and their wages and fringe benefits would improve. About forty years later they would be at the top rung and ready to retire.

The federal government structures many of the white-collar jobs at its agencies this way. College graduates are hired to work at jobs that if not hot, sweaty, and menial, do not require much in the way of creativity—research assistant, database manager, and so on. But with good performance and some training these workers will move up the ranks.

Colleges and universities have what amounts to an internal labor market. People get hired as assistant professors. After a probationary period of six years, tenure is granted with a promotion to associate professor. Then after a period of time you get promoted to professor.

A leading interpretation of internal labor markets is that they represent an efficient solution to a labor supply problem. These arrangements developed where the skills necessary to produce the work that needed to be done were largely specific rather than general. (The jobs required for many of the production processes were not the type of thing you would necessarily learn about in shop class.) By creating an inter-

Figure 14.8 **Internal Labor Markets**

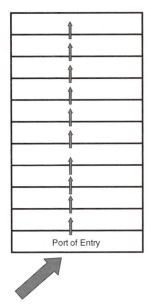

Port of Entry

nal labor market, firms could provide the necessary training, often in a very informal environment. The skills needed for the next job on the rung could be developed by working at the preceding job and/or watching the guy at the next step.[25] To minimize investment losses from turnover, firms would backload wages and benefits.[26] Wages and benefits would increase as the worker moved up the ladder, creating an incentive for the worker to stay with the firm even though the first several years of employment might involve some fairly undesirable jobs. Workers, even those with fairly modest levels of education, would be assured stable, long-term employment and a constantly rising living standard.

The perception by workers that they were being treated fairly was necessary for the strategy to succeed. What developed was a complex set of rules and norms that governed many aspects of worker-management interaction, from the procedures governing promotions, lay-offs, and recalls, to how supervisors spoke to workers. These rules could be explicit, such as those defined by a company handbook or the written contract between a union and the employer,[27] or implicit, such as those defined by the development of a specific workplace culture and that employers and employees violated only at their peril.

A major issue today is whether internal labor markets have become less important in the highly competitive markets created by globalization, where downsizing, outsourcing, flexible production methods, total quality management, and worker empowerment, among other things, have become buzzwords. Surprisingly enough, despite all the hoopla, the average length of job tenure has not declined significantly (Schultze 2000). There has, however, been a rise in the contingent or part-time labor force, so the picture is mixed.

The view that internal labor markets represent an efficient and equitable solution to a labor market problem is not held by everyone. The opposite point of view is that the development of these structures is more a reflection of the roles of nonmarket forces such as custom, reciprocity, and so on, or they are just the way the capitalists squeeze more labor out of the workers while preventing the development of working class solidarity (Stone 1973).

Labor Supply Over the Life Cycle

How does labor supply change over the life cycle? Chapter 3 discussed the mainstream approach to labor supply. Review it now if this is not clear in your mind. In this section we will extend that analysis to an explanation of how labor supply changes over the life cycle. This discussion will take place at a much more intuitive level than what was presented in Chapter 3.[28]

Continue with the assumption that there are only two uses for time—work and leisure—but recognize that the category leisure includes a much wider variety of activities than simply sunning yourself at the beach. Leisure can include housework, yard work, home repair, and child care, among many other things. Granted these activities do not involve much of what is normally thought to be leisure, but at least they are not paid employment, which is the key distinction.

At each moment over the life cycle, individuals have a level of productivity in both activities. In the case of market work, that productivity is probably best measured by the wage that could be earned. In the case of leisure, productivity can be measured by the work accomplished or the money saved by doing things yourself. At every moment in time, a rational individual will allocate his or her time to activities that are more productive. In periods of time when market productivity is relatively high, the individual will choose to work. When leisure productivity is relatively high, the individual will opt for leisure. If we assume that leisure productivity is relatively constant over the life cycle, then the discussion of life-cycle wage growth would imply that individuals would devote relatively more time to work activities as they age, at least up until the point where potential wage peaks. Figure 14.9 shows this point rather impressionistically. The top graph shows a common pattern of wage growth over time. The bottom graph shows labor supply under the assumption that leisure time productivity remains relatively constant over time. As individuals become more productive in work activities, they respond by devoting a larger proportion of their time to work. This reaction of labor supply to wage growth acts to strengthen the tendency toward upward earnings mobility over the life cycle. If leisure productivity declines over time, as it well might as children grow up and become more independent and as aging reduces the zest with which one performs housework, yard work, and home repair, this would only reinforce the tendency to greater labor supply and upward earnings mobility.

One question you might have at this point is what happened to the income effect? The analysis in the preceding paragraph argues that people respond to a higher wage as they age by supplying more labor. Might the higher wage have an income effect leading to less labor supply? The explanation depends on the distinction between

Figure 14.9 **Wage and Labor Supply Over the Life Cycle**

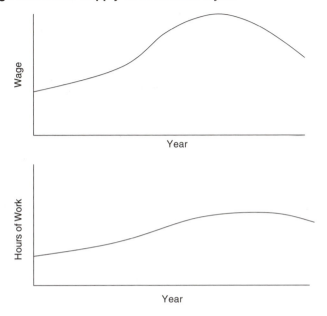

expected and unexpected increases in wages. If the wage increase is unexpected, then it has an income effect along with the substitution effect because the wage increase is like a windfall. If the wage increase is not unexpected, and wage growth over the life cycle is something that most people expect, then the wage increase does not have a windfall aspect and, consequently, no income effect.

Of course, in a family context, things get a bit more complicated. There the partners have to decide how to jointly allocate their time so that money is earned and the household tasks are accomplished. A purely economic analysis of the situation would rely on the law of comparative advantage. Even if both partners are more productive in market work than in leisure activities, it may be more advantageous for the partner who is relatively more productive in the market to work while the other stays home. However, even in this case, the partners respond to economic incentives. If the rewards to market work become large enough, the stay-at-home partner can be drawn into the labor market and a cleaning service hired to maintain the house. Whether a purely economic explanation to the household division of labor is reasonable remains a highly contentious point.

The data would appear to provide some support to this theory. Figure 14.10 shows hours of work for males over the life cycle by birth cohort. Figure 14.11 shows the same for females. In each case, the shape is similar to that of the typical age-earnings profile. Both males and females supply more hours to the marketplace during the periods of their careers when their potential wage is likely to be highest. The case of females is particularly interesting. The earliest birth cohorts seem to have decreased their work hours between the ages of twenty and thirty. This makes sense when you remember that job opportunities were none too good for women of those eras and those were the

Figure 14.10 **Male Labor Supply Over the Life-Cycle**

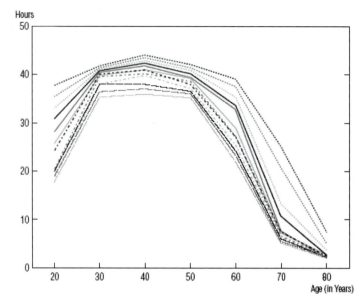

Source: McGrattan and Rogerson (2004): 26. (Any views expressed are those of the authors and not necessarily those of the Federal Reserve Bank of Minneapolis or the Federal Reserve System.)

Figure 14.11 **Female Labor Supply Over the Life-Cycle**

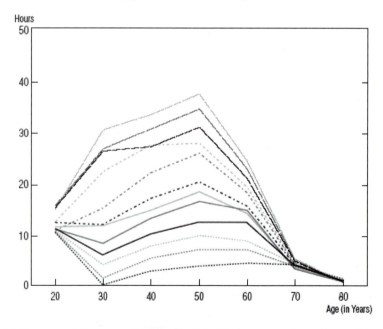

Source: McGrattan and Rogerson (2004): 27. (Any views expressed are those of the authors and not necessarily those of the Federal Reserve Bank of Minneapolis or the Federal Reserve System.)

ages when women were most likely to give birth and have small children. For most of these women, their leisure time productivity would have been much greater than their work productivity. Later, as the children entered school, women began returning to the workforce. While women still have to grapple with career and home conflicts today, more recent female birth cohorts have increased their labor supply during their twenties, in a manner similar to the way men have always done. Another interesting finding is that while more recent male birth cohorts have worked fewer hours, more recent female birth cohorts have worked more hours.

ANNUAL VERSUS LIFETIME INEQUALITY

What the analysis makes clear is that an important distinction must be made between annual inequality and lifetime inequality. Because of expected income growth during a career and the significant fluctuations in income that can take place from year to year for all sorts of random reasons, lifetime income may be distributed significantly more equally than income in any particular year. For example, in Table 14.1, even though the Gini coefficient in any particular year was 0.70, the lifetime Gini coefficient was 0; in other words, perfect equality.[29]

Adjusting the measurement of inequality to take into account lifetime income is no mean feat, primarily because we do not have data with individual lifetime incomes. We have to estimate lifetime incomes using data from much shorter time periods and incorporating what we know about typical age-earnings profiles. Morton Paglin found that adjusting the Gini coefficient formula to take into account lifetime income resulted in a decrease in the measured level of inequality of approximately 33 percent (Paglin 1975). Friesen and Miller modified Paglin's approach and found an approximately 40 percent decrease in measured inequality (Friesen and Miller 1983). Regardless of the exact number, we have every reason to expect that incomes are distributed much more equally on a lifetime basis.

RELATIVE VERSUS ABSOLUTE MOBILITY

What about the degree of mobility in the United States? Unlike the case of poverty and inequality, there is no "official," readily available data. There are, however, longitudinal data surveys, such as the Panel Study of Income Dynamics (PSID) (University of Michigan. Institute for Social Research 2007) and National Longitudinal Surveys (NLS) (United States Department of Labor. Bureau of Labor Statistics 2007b), which can be used for that purpose.

Table 14.4 shows a mobility table (sometimes called a transition matrix) for families in the United States for the period 1968–1970 to 1989–1991 (Gottschalk and Danziger 1998). The table is constructed in the following manner. A sample of families was selected in 1968–1970 and ranked on the basis of family income-to-needs ratio. The family income-to-needs ratio takes into account family size and composition so that, for example, a two-person family with income of $40,000 is ranked higher than a five-person family with the same income. The families are then divided into five quintiles, from poorest to richest. In 1989–1991 the same

Table 14.4

Intragenerational Mobility in the United States from 1968–70 to 1989–91

1968–70 Quintile	Quintile in 1989–91				
	Lowest (%)	Second (%)	Third (%)	Fourth (%)	Highest (%)
Lowest	53.8	21.8	18.8	4.8	0.9
Second	22.7	25.4	18.5	25.8	7.7
Third	11.1	21.4	24.4	27.8	15.4
Fourth	5.3	22.6	23.0	19.3	29.8
Highest	7.0	8.6	16.2	22.2	46.1

Source: Gottschalk and Danziger (1998).

Table 14.5

A Caste Society

t Quintile	Quintile at t + n				
	Lowest	Second	Third	Fourth	Highest
Lowest	100	0	0	0	0
Second	0	100	0	0	0
Third	0	0	100	0	0
Fourth	0	0	0	100	0
Highest	0	0	0	0	100

families were located and again divided into quintiles on the basis of family income-to-needs ratio.

The table is interpreted in the following way: The number 53.8 in the upper left-hand cell shows that 53.8 percent of the families that started in the poorest quintile in 1968–1970 were in the poorest quintile in 1989–1991. Moving across to the upper right-hand cell, the number 0.9 says 0.9 percent of the families that were in the poorest quintile in 1968–1970 were in the richest quintile in 1989–1991. Similarly, 46.1 percent of the families that were in the richest quintile in 1968–1970 were in the richest quintile in 1989–1991, while 7.0 percent of the families in the richest quintile in 1968–1970 fell to the poorest quintile in 1989–1991.

What story is told by a transition matrix? Table 14.5 is a hypothetical transition matrix. It shows a society where everyone stays put. One hundred percent of the people who start in the lowest quintile in period t are there in period t + n. Likewise with starters in every other quintile. No one is able to rise (or fall) beyond their starting point. This represents a caste society, one with no mobility.

The polar opposite society is shown in Table 14.6. Here starters in each quintile in period t end up being distributed equally to all the quintiles in period t + n. Everyone has an equal chance of landing in any quintile, n years later. This might be thought of as a perfectly mobile society.

What about American society between 1968–1970 and 1989–1991? It was not a caste society by any means, but it was not perfectly mobile either. Families that

Table 14.6

Perfect Mobility

t	Quintile at t + n				
Quintile	Lowest (%)	Second (%)	Third (%)	Fourth (%)	Highest (%)
Lowest	20	20	20	20	20
Second	20	20	20	20	20
Third	20	20	20	20	20
Fourth	20	20	20	20	20
Highest	20	20	20	20	20

Table 14.7

Intragenerational Mobility in the United States, 1988 to 1998

1988	Quintile in 1998				
Quintile	Lowest (%)	Second (%)	Third (%)	Fourth (%)	Highest (%)
Lowest	53.3	23.6	12.4	6.4	4.3
Second	25.7	36.3	22.6	11.0	4.3
Third	10.9	20.7	28.3	27.5	12.6
Fourth	6.5	12.9	23.7	31.1	25.8
Highest	3.0	5.7	14.9	23.2	53.2

Source: Bradbury and Katz (2002) Appendix Table A.

started poor ended up rich and vice versa all within the course of a decade, but poor families were much more likely to stay poor and rich families were much more likely to stay rich.

What has happened to mobility in the United States over time? Table 14.7 shows family income-to-needs mobility for the period 1988–1998 (Bradbury and Katz 2002). A comparison of Table 14.5 and Table 14.8 shows that mobility over 1988–1998 was only slightly higher than in the earlier period.[30] What is the significance of this? We know the inequality increased significantly during that time. It would have been one thing if the higher inequality had been accompanied by significantly higher mobility, but since mobility was only slightly higher, it suggests a deteriorating situation for many Americans (McMurrer and Sawhill 1998, 35).

In addition, mobility rates in the United States are no higher than in the few countries for which we have comparative data (Aaberge et al. 1996; Burkhauser, Holtz-Eakin, and Rhody 1997; Duncan et al. 1993).

CONTROVERSY: HOW MUCH INTRAGENERATIONAL MOBILITY?

Table 14.8 shows the transition matrix from Table 14.4 on top and another matrix from the same authors for the very same time period using the same data on the bottom.

Table 14.8

Relative versus Absolute Mobility

Relative Mobility

1968–70 Quintile	Quintile in 1989–91				
	Lowest (%)	Second (%)	Third (%)	Fourth (%)	Highest (%)
Lowest	53.8	21.8	18.8	4.8	0.9
Second	22.7	25.4	18.5	25.8	7.7
Third	11.1	21.4	24.4	27.8	15.4
Fourth	5.3	22.6	23.0	19.3	29.8
Highest	7.0	8.6	16.2	22.2	46.1

Absolute Mobility

1968–70 Quintile	Quintile in 1989–91				
	Lowest (%)	Second (%)	Third (%)	Fourth (%)	Highest (%)
Lowest	31.0	25.4	11.1	21.1	11.4
Second	9.5	14.6	17.0	16.3	42.5
Third	4.5	8.2	12.7	17.4	57.1
Fourth	1.6	4.9	13.2	16.6	63.7
Highest	3.6	5.2	4.4	6.8	80.1

Source: Gottschalk and Danziger (1998).

This bottom matrix appears to tell a very different story with a much higher degree of mobility. According to this matrix only 31.0 percent of the lowest quintile stayed there and 11.4 percent made it to the top. While 80.1 percent of the top quintile in 1968–1970 were still there in 1989–1991, only 3.6 percent fell to the lowest quintile.

What distinguishes the two matrices in Table 14.8 is that the top matrix measures *relative mobility* while the bottom matrix measures *absolute mobility*. The difference between the two is quite significant. To construct the top matrix, the quintile level of each member of the sample was determined by comparing that member's income to the income of every other member of the sample *in both years*. To be in the lowest quintile in 1968–1970 meant that the member's income was among the lowest 20 percent in the sample. To be in the lowest quintile in 1989–1991 meant the member's income was among the lowest 20 percent of that same sample of persons. However every member of the sample was twenty-one years older in 1989–1991 than they had been in 1968–1970 and, presumably, most were earning more money. Even if you were in the lowest quintile in 1989–1991, your standard of living was probably much improved over what it had been in 1968–1970. To be mobile, then, required more than simply an increase in the member's income. Rather, the member's income had to increase relative to everyone else in the sample.

The bottom matrix was constructed a bit differently. In 1968–1970 quintile membership was determined by seeing where each sample member's income stood relative to every other sample member's income. In 1989–1991, quintile membership was determined not by comparing each sample member's income to other members of the sample (who were twenty-one years older than when the research began), but by comparing their income to that of society as a whole. Society as a whole includes individuals of all ages. The members of the sample were a decidedly older group than society as a whole. Mobility would occur if a sample member's absolute level of income rose, even if they did not pass anyone else in the sample.

How mobility is measured is not just a technical issue. It is an issue with real economic significance. Focusing on relative mobility, and the fact that relative mobility has not increased much in recent decades while inequality has risen, suggests a worsening situation with respect to opportunity in the United States. Focusing on absolute mobility suggests that opportunity is still alive and well. People still move up, and with greater inequality, which means that their income gains are greater as they move up the pyramid. "A steeper lifetime earnings profile reflects greater opportunity" (Cox and Alm 1999, 83).

Which focus is the right one? The whole issue would appear to depend on whether you think a person's standard of living is best determined by how much stuff they have or by how much stuff they have relative to the stuff everybody else has.[31] This is the second time we have encountered this issue. The first time was in Chapter 12's discussion of relative poverty measures.

CONCLUSION

Snapshots show us something. Movies show us more. Often all we have to go on is a snapshot, but, as the introduction to this chapter demonstrates, we should be wary of the reality it purports to show. People's earnings and incomes tend to grow over their careers. The human capital model, incentive-based models, and the theory of labor supply can all be usefully employed to explain his. Earnings and incomes also fluctuate a great deal over shorter periods of time. These fluctuations reflect choices people make to invest in themselves or to supply labor, but also the vicissitudes of luck, both good and bad. Today's poor may be tomorrow's rich, and vice versa. In short, mobility can offset inequality.

Has mobility offset inequality in the United States? Only partly. The empirical evidence we have shows lifetime income inequality 33 to 40 percent less than annual income inequality (Paglin 1975; Friesen and Miller 1983). Whether this decrease is large or small is your call. The recent sharp increase in annual income inequality in the United States could only be offset by an increased degree of intragenerational mobility. There is no persuasive evidence that this has occurred (McMurrer and Sawhill 1998). Rising inequality within a generation is not an issue that can be easily swept under the rug.

In the next chapter we will extend the analysis to successive generations, and see if rising inequality can be swept under the rug by intergenerational mobility.

QUESTIONS FOR REVIEW AND PRACTICE

1. Explain how your actions influence your lifetime earnings. What factors influencing lifetime earnings are outside your control? Why might two people born at the same time end up with different lifetime earnings? Did the person with the higher lifetime earnings have a "better life?"

2. What would you rather live in—a society with a high degree of absolute mobility but a low degree of relative mobility, or a society with a high degree of relative mobility and a low degree of absolute mobility? You cannot answer that you prefer a high degree of both kinds of mobility.

3. Peter has just graduated from high school. He will live for three more periods, and he is considering three alternative education-work options. He can start working right away, earning $100,000 in period 1, $110,000 in period 2 (as his work experience leads to higher productivity), and $90,000 in period 3 (as his skills become obsolete and physical abilities deteriorate). He can also go to college in period 1, spending $10,000 in that period, and then earn $150,000 in periods 2 and 3. Finally, he can get a doctorate degree after completing his college education. Going to graduate school in period 2 will cost $15,000. After getting his doctorate, he will become a professor in a business school and earn $350,000 in period 3. What should Peter do if his rate of discount is 20 percent? What should Peter do if his rate of discount is 5 percent? What explains the difference in the results?

4. Three human capital puzzles:
   a. A proposal calls for the expansion of college tuition tax credits for middle-class families. A tuition tax credit would allow the family to reduce its taxes, making college more affordable. Using the human capital model, what effect should this policy have on the distribution of earnings?
   b. Why are wages "indeterminate" under specific training?
   c. What effect does on-the-job training have on earnings inequality?

5. Women receive lower wages, on average, than men of equal age, and the disparity between the earnings of men and women grows with age. *Use human capital theory* to explain why. (To help you develop your answer, it may be useful to know that women have a lower labor force participation rate at every age, are more likely to work part-time, and are more likely to move in and out of the labor force than men. Consider certain realities of men's and women's lives.)

6. Assume a job requires no on-the-job training and worker skills do not increase with the simple passage of time. If the present value of the wage payments were the same, why might the worker prefer being paid less than the value of his or her marginal product at the beginning of the career and less than the value of the marginal product at the end of the career, as opposed to being paid his or her value of the marginal product very year?

7. Differentiate between intragenerational mobility and intergenerational mobility.

8. What types of human capital are you investing in right now? What are the costs and benefits of each?

9. Junior must decide whether to accept $125 today or $150 one year from today.
   a. If Junior's internal rate of time preference is 14 percent, what will be do?
   b. If Junior's internal rate of time preference is 22 percent, what will be do?
   c. What does Junior's internal rate of time preference say about him?

Notes

1. The incomes were not randomly chosen. Rather the values were exactly the same as the mean household income by quintile for the United States in 2006. This means the inequality of incomes in the example is roughly comparable to inequality in household incomes in the United States, although probably not exactly the same due to how income is distributed within each quintile. Also note that the lowest income was below the poverty line for a three-person family.

2. There are complications associated with just when someone earned income. For example, earning a low income today with a higher income in the future may not be viewed as equivalent to earning a high income today and a lower income in the future. These can safely be ignored at the present time.

3. Read no significance into Sheila being a typical woman's name and Bill being a typical man's name. They are just names to allow us to trace the family line.

4. For yearly earnings I am using the sum of all Medicare earnings from all W-2 statements received. Medicare earnings are subject to Medicare tax. Since 1994 there has been no upper limit on earnings subject to the tax (not that it would have made a difference for me prior to 1994 or for several years after for that matter).

5. Many of my early jobs involved literal, not just figurative, sweat.

6. There are not values for every age category for every educational level. This reflects a tiny sample for some of these categories. For example, there are not many eighteen- to twenty-year-olds who hold doctorates.

7. Remember people earn income from labor, but also from their ownership of the other factors of production. This discussion abstracts from these other sources.

8. It has been used to explain marriage and divorce (Becker 1993a), fertility (Becker 1993a), child rearing practices (Becker 1993a), and also why teenagers do not clean their rooms (Fender and Fletcher undated).

9. Today many lotteries offer the winner a lump sum in lieu of payments stretched out over a long time. The lump sum is not $1 million. Rather it is the present value of the stream of payments discounted at some interest rate.

10. Which market rate of interest to use is a matter of considerable debate, but beyond the scope of this book. It is an issue likely to be studied in courses in public finance.

11. The costs represent tuition, books, fees, and any other monetary outlay required to receive an education.

12. Goldin, Katz, and Kuziemko attribute part of the reversal of the gender gap in college attendance and graduation rates (females have recently overtaken males in both regards) to the fact that the college wage premium is now relatively higher for females than males (Goldin, Katz, and Kuziemko 2006).

13. Another reason is that the cost of schooling is lower for the young than the old since the wages of the young tend to be less than those for the old. Variation of wages by age is not in this stripped-down model so this comment is confined to a footnote.

14. The human capital model has been subjected to a number of other criticisms. There is no implication here that the model is flawless, or we would have no need to search for even better models.

15. The other locations are the family and the community.

16. It is nice to know something worthwhile happens in the classroom.

17. The GED is an exam used to establish high school equivalent learning for high school dropouts. A GED certificate serves as a substitute for a high school diploma. Whether the level of learning required to get a GED is the same as for a high school diploma is a matter of debate (Carneiro and Heckman 2003).

18. To be completely up front, it was my father's warehouse, but I had a pretty dirty job.

19. And was very boring.

20. To better facilitate driving in reverse.

21. Sometimes worker and employer might be able to work out some agreement obligating the employee to stay with the firm for a certain amount of time after the training ends or else reimburse the employer for the training.

22. Other arrangements are possible. Employers might pay the tuition but the worker's wage might be low enough to offset the tuition payment.

23. The material in the section is based primarily on Edward P. Lazear (1979).

24. To be precise here, there are actually two types of options. A *call* gives the holder the right to buy a stock at a specified price. A *put* gives the holder the right to sell a stock at a specified price. Most CEO options are calls.

25. Think back to the lift truck example discussed previously.

26. Since wage levels reflected a long-term strategy on the part of the firm, they did not respond much to the business cycle. As the economy slows, firms are more likely to use lay-offs and demotions instead of wage decreases. Wages were more flexible at the port of entry.

27. The first contracts between the United Autoworkers Union and the auto manufacturers were one to two pages in length. By the mid-1970s contracts exceeded 800 pages, with most of the pages being devoted to the delineation of workplace rules. Of course, this might be a bit misleading. The contracts were printed in booklets narrow enough to be carried in the back pocket by employees.

28. For a more rigorous (translation: math and graphs) analysis, see Solomon W. Polachek and W. Stanley Siebert (1993).

29. This conclusion ignores the impact of discounting on lifetime incomes.

30. These tables used the same accounting unit (families) and same measure of income (income to needs ratio), but were prepared by different researchers. Consequently they are probably not done in exactly the same way so we need to be careful not to attribute too much precision to the results. Nevertheless the conclusion ventured above that mobility did not change very much seems reasonable.

31. *Stuff* refers to the goods and services that money can buy.

15 How the Size of a Slice Changes From Generation to Generation

> . . . that even operating under the most stringent meritocratic guidelines, success is cumulative and self-reinforcing, and gets passed on to children as "privilege," or unearned advantage (Metcalf 2005).

INTRODUCTION

Does everybody have an equal opportunity to achieve success in life, or, as the opening quote implies, is success "rigged"? This chapter looks at how your parents[1] influence your accumulation of human capital and subsequent economic success. The role of parents cannot be overemphasized. Your parents give you your genes and are also the major factor determining the "quality" of the environment you grow up in. Your parents' money and choices are decisive in determining the quantity and quality of schooling you receive, what neighborhood you live in, who your peers are, who your role models are, and how healthy you are. Your parents determine how much nurturing you receive, give you "connections,"[2] and teach you social graces. Your parents determine your race, ethnicity, and skin tone, and help determine your health, beauty, sexual orientation, and religion. (Your gender is a more random event.) Children do not "inherit" only human capital from their parents; some inherit significant amounts of financial wealth. In short, you can thank or blame your parents for much of your economic success. *Ceteris paribus,* a child with "good" parents will have greater opportunities than a child with "bad" parents.

MEASURING INTERGENERATIONAL MOBILITY

As in the case of intragenerational mobility, transition matrices for intergenerational mobility can be examined. Table 15.1 shows a transition matrix based on the research of economist Thomas Hertz (Hertz 2005). It compares the decile standing of a sample of children with the decile standing of their parents. Therefore, it shows relative mobility.

According to the matrix, while movement all the way from bottom to top is possible, it is highly unlikely. Only 0.5 percent of the offspring of parents at the bottom made it to the top. More than 50 percent of the offspring of parents at the bottom remained mired in the bottom two deciles. Nearly 27 percent of the offspring of parents on the

Table 15.1

Intergenerational Transition Matrix

Parents	Children									
	Bottom	2	3	4	5	6	7	8	9	Top
Bottom	36.6	20.5	13.4	9.6	6.6	4.7	4.3	2.1	1.8	0.5
2	20.7	18.1	11.0	13.0	8.9	11.1	6.6	5.3	3.0	2.2
3	13.7	13.1	14.4	13.1	11.0	8.5	8.4	8.9	5.1	3.9
4	8.3	11.7	11.7	10.8	12.0	10.0	9.6	10.1	7.4	8.4
5	5.6	8.2	12.3	11.4	13.8	13.0	13.1	8.1	7.0	7.6
6	4.5	9.1	9.4	5.9	14.4	12.7	10.4	11.5	13.7	8.3
7	3.1	6.1	11.2	14.4	11.0	9.1	9.4	14.9	11.9	8.9
8	3.7	6.0	7.2	9.3	8.5	10.8	10.7	12.5	16.8	14.7
9	2.6	3.8	5.2	7.3	5.7	8.1	15.6	16.1	16.8	18.8
Top	1.4	3.6	4.2	5.0	8.1	12.4	11.5	10.6	16.5	26.7

Source: Thomas Hertz, "Rags, Riches, and Race: The Intergenerational Economic Mobility of Black and White Families in the United States," In Samuel Bowles, Herbert Gintis, and Melissa Osborne Groves, *Unequal Chances: Family Background and Economic Success,* Princeton: Russell Sage Foundation and Princeton University Press, 2005, p. 186. Reprinted by permission of Princeton University Press.

top landed on the top themselves. Over 50 percent of them remained in the top three deciles. Only 1.4 percent fell all the way to the bottom.

Another commonly used approach to measure intergenerational mobility is to compute what is called the intergenerational elasticity. The equation represents the relationship between parent income and offspring income: $\ln y_{oi}^{t+1} = \alpha + \beta^* \ln y_{pi}^{t} + \varepsilon_i^{t+1}$.

Let y equal income. The subscripts identify the generation (o for offspring and p for parent) and the individual (i). The variable y_{pi} refers to parent i. The variable y_{oi} is the offspring of parent i. The superscript refers to the generation. Superscript t means the parents' generation while t+1 means the offspring's generation. The symbol ln means natural logarithm and ε is a stochastic (or random) error term. The error term represents the random factors influencing y_{oi} in addition to y_{pi}. β is the intergenerational elasticity. The equation says that income achieved by the offspring depends on the income of the parent plus random factors.

A brief digression on natural logarithms is in order. The natural logarithm (or natural log) of a number is an exponent. If x is the number, then if $\ln(x) = a$, $e^a = x$. The number e is a weird thing that appears in many mathematical formulas. It equals 2.71828182845904 . . . (it goes on forever). The natural log of a number is the power to which e can be raised in order to get the number x. If $x = 100$, then $\ln(100) = 4.60517$. Therefore $e^{4.60517} = 100$.

One important property of natural logs is the following. For small changes in x, $\Delta \ln(x) \approx \% \Delta x$; the change in the natural log of x is approximately equal to the percentage change in x. For example, the difference between 100 and 101 is 1 percent. $\text{Ln}(100) = 4.60517$ and $\ln(101) = 4.61520$. The difference between $\ln(100)$ and $\ln(101)$ is 0.01003, which is approximately 1 percent.

Let the following equations represent the relationship between offspring and parent income for two families. Pat Sr. has a child named Pat Jr. Kim Sr. has a child named Kim Jr.

$$\ln y_{\text{Pat Jr}}^{t+1} = \alpha + \beta * \ln y_{\text{Pat Sr}}^{t} + \varepsilon_{\text{Pat Jr}}^{t+1} \qquad 15.2$$

$$\ln y_{\text{Kim Jr}}^{t+1} = \alpha + \beta * \ln y_{\text{Kim Sr}}^{t} + \varepsilon_{\text{Kim Jr}}^{t+1} \qquad 15.3$$

Now subtract (15.3) from (15.2). This gives:

$$(\ln y_{\text{Pat Jr}}^{t+1} - \ln y_{\text{Kim Jr}}^{t+1}) =$$

$$\beta * (\ln y_{\text{Pat Sr}}^{t} - \ln y_{\text{Kim Sr}}^{t}) + (\varepsilon_{\text{Pat Jr}}^{t+1} - \varepsilon_{\text{Kim Jr}}^{t+1}) \qquad 15.4$$

Since the random terms are unpredictable, we can ignore the last term in (15.4). That leaves:

$$(\ln y_{\text{Pat Jr}}^{t+1} - \ln y_{\text{Kim Jr}}^{t+1}) = \beta * (\ln y_{\text{Pat Sr}}^{t} - \ln y_{\text{Kim Sr}}^{t}) \qquad 15.5$$

The term in parentheses on the left-hand side is (approximately) the percentage difference between the incomes of Pat Jr. and Kim Jr. The term in parentheses on the right-hand side is the percentage difference between the incomes of Pat Sr. and Kim Sr. For example, if $\beta = 0.5$, then if the incomes of Pat Sr. and Kim Sr. differed by 10 percent, the income of Pat Jr. and Kim Jr. would differ by 5 percent [5% = 0.5*(10%)].

The value that β takes on has economic meaning. If $\beta = 0$, there is perfect intergenerational mobility,[3] meaning regardless of the percentage difference in the parent generation's income, there would be no difference in the offspring generation's income. In other words, the income of the offspring is completely unaffected by parent income. This does not mean the offspring incomes will all be equal. In fact, they likely will be different, but the cause of the difference is the values of ε for each offspring. The value of ε reflects the skills each have that are not derived directly from their parents, as well as market luck. If B=1, there is no mobility. The differences between the offspring are the same as the differences between the parents. If $0 < \beta < 1$, then there is regression to the mean.

How do we determine the value of β? In principle, if we had data on the income of parents and their offspring, we could estimate a regression equation.[4] A number of practical problems arise. For one thing, there are not many reliable sources of data on both offspring and parent income. Second, even when data exists, it may be inadequate to the task. If we regressed a single year's observation of offspring income on a single year's observation of parent income, we would run into the difficulty that neither year's value would be representative of either person's lifetime income. The values could be influenced by temporary fluctuations, such as might result from a layoff or sickness or an unexpectedly good year. The econometric evidence suggests that using income data from a short-term period tends to bias estimates of β downward (Solon 1992; Zimmerman 1992).

There have been many attempts to estimate β using different data sets and a variety of estimating techniques. Most economists today simply use 0.4 as the intergenerational elasticity for the United States.[5] [Intergenerational elasticities for other economic characteristics have also been estimated (Mulligan 1997, 186–213).]

What does this mean? If $\beta = 0.4$, then the following should be true: If two sets of parents differ in income by 10 percent, their offspring should differ by approximately 4 percent. The offspring of the offspring (the grandchildren of the parents) should differ by only 1.6 percent. In other words, a fairly significant difference in one generation can decline to insignificance by the third generation.

In the late nineteenth century a famous American tycoon named Andrew Carnegie is said to have uttered, "Shirtsleeves to shirtsleeves in three generations."[6] Carnegie emigrated to the United States from Scotland and began his career with modest means and eventually became a very successful steel man. He created the Carnegie Steel Company, which later became one of the building blocks of U.S. Steel. In achieving success, Carnegie was not reluctant to use forceful tactics (Standiford 2005). This led some of his critics to call him a robber baron.[7] Nonetheless, upon retirement, instead of bequeathing his entire massive estate to his heirs (he had no children), he became a world-class philanthropist. Among the monuments to his generosity today are several Carnegie libraries in the United States and the United Kingdom, Carnegie Mellon University, the Carnegie Hero Fund, the Carnegie Endowment for International Peace, and Carnegie Hall in New York City. Carnegie's philosophy was at least partly influenced by the observation that when many of his fellow tycoons passed their wealth on to their heirs, the heirs promptly squandered it on "riotous living" and by making bad investment decisions.

A MODEL OF INTERGENERATIONAL MOBILITY

Human capital investment decisions, while made on behalf of an individual, are not always made by that individual. The investment process begins early, literally in the womb,[8] and for much of your life—your formative years—most of the decisions are made by parents or guardians on your behalf, and you do not have much input into the process.

Modeling the impact of parents on human capital investment and subsequent economic success is no mean feat. Economists have had only limited success with it.[9] This section develops a simplistic version of a model that is already very simple. But the model is useful because it forces us to recognize some of the fundamental considerations regarding this issue (Mulligan 1997, 72–136).

The most fundamental consideration is this: Children are brought into this world and then must be supported. In most human societies, the parents or guardians (hereafter just parents) shoulder most of this responsibility.[10] By and large, the provision to children limits what is available for the parents.[11]

Assume that every family consists of two parents and one child and that the productive life of the child begins after the productive life of the parents ends. The parents' lifetime wealth will put an upper limit on their lifetime consumption. Figure 15.1 measures the lifetime consumption of the parents (C_p) on the x axis. Point A shows lifetime parental consumption if the parents spend every penny on themselves.

Of course, a child complicates things. Assume every penny parents divert from their own consumption provides human capital to the children. For example, the money

Figure 15.1 **Parental Investment in Children**

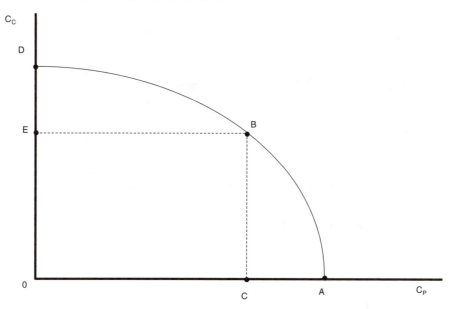

the parents could have spent on their second honeymoon is used to pay college tuition or for music or tennis lessons. Or, parents could cut back on the time they devote to work and spend it reading to the child and taking the child on museum trips or to the symphony.[12] The curve AD is a production function. It shows how parents' consumption contributes to the child's human capital and consequently the child's lifetime consumption. For example, at point B the parents choose to spend C on themselves. This frees up A–C for their child. The spending on the child will allow the child to consume E during his or her lifetime.

The negative of the slope of AD is equal to $1 + r_h$, where r_h is the rate of return on the next increment of human capital investment. As we move from A to D, r_h gets smaller, which reflects diminishing returns to investments in children's human capital (Lord 2002, 193–95). The model could be extended to allow parents to make financial bequests to their child, which will be discussed in Chapter 16.

The curve can shift due to differences in wealth and child's ability. The left panel in Figure 15.2. shows the impact of a change in wealth. AD is the initial production function. If parent wealth increases, then the curve will shift to FG. The greater wealth will allow the parents to consume more themselves and to provide greater support for their child. The right panel shows the impact of greater child ability. AD is the initial production function for a child of moderate ability. AG would be the production function for a child of greater ability. Regardless of ability, if the parents spend nothing on their child, they will be able to consume at point A while the child will be unable to consume anything under both scenarios. A child of greater ability will be able to turn every dollar of parental spending into his or her own greater consumption.

What provides the motivation for parental spending? We will assume that altruism is the leading motive.[13] Altruism is said to exist when parents get utility from the well-being

Figure 15.2 **Differences in Income and Ability**

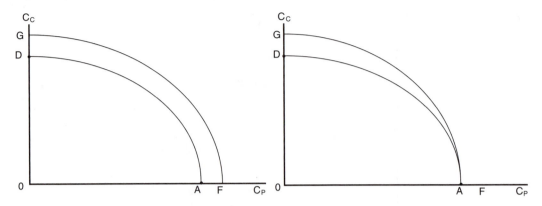

Figure 15.3 **Equilibrium**

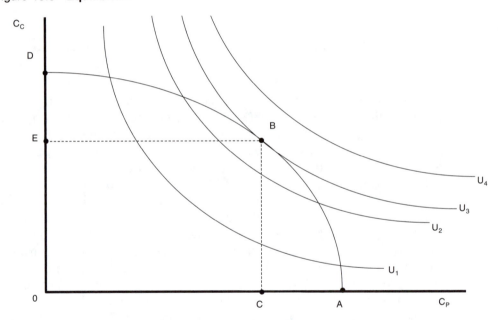

of the child. Altruism allows us to draw indifference curves as in Figure 15.3. The curve U_1 shows all combinations of parental and child consumption that yield the same level of utility for the parents. U_2, U_3, and U_4 show increasing levels of parental utility.

The parental equilibrium point is where the production function is just tangent to the highest indifference curve. In Figure 15.3, that would be point B. There, parents will consume C themselves, using A–C to finance human capital development for their child, which will allow the child to consume E.

Figure 15.4 shows the impact of income on parental investment in children. Assume a poor family and a rich family. The poor family has the production function AD while the rich family has production function FG. Assume both families have the

Figure 15.4 **Equilibrium with Differences in Income**

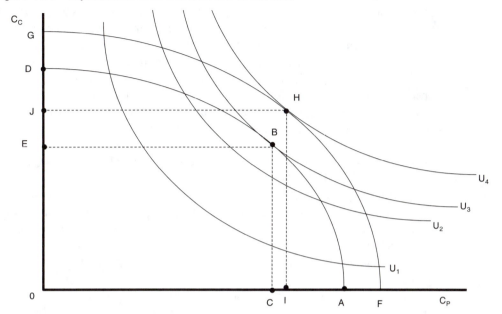

exact same tastes so the indifference curves U_1 to U_4 apply to both. From inspection of the graph, we can see that the poor family would choose point B while the rich family would choose point H. The rich family ends up consuming more, but it also invests more in its child, which allows the child to consume more.

As a set of exercises, try drawing the cases where the child of the rich parents is more able and less able then the child of the poor parents.

WHY DOES IT PAY TO BE BORN RICH?

Regardless of whether you think an intergenerational elasticity of 0.4 is a big or small number, it is not 0. Why do the children of rich parents end up relatively advantaged while the children of poor parents end up relatively disadvantaged? Why is the extent of mobility so limited? This section will argue that the children of rich parents can more easily accumulate human capital than the children of poor parents. Further, to the extent that children inherit the discriminatory "markers" of their parents (for example, skin color, hair texture, accent, beauty, etc.) and discrimination persists from generation to generation, the roadblocks placed in front of parents will be roadblocks for the children as well.

Much of this section will emphasize what parents are able to do for their children. The acquisition of human capital is a lifelong process. For nearly the first two decades of anyone's life parents are the initiators and directors of the process. But emphasizing parental decision making is not the same as blaming parents for everything that goes wrong or crediting parents for everything that goes right, because parents are not free agents in this process. What parents are able to do for their children partially reflects constraints imposed by society and the push-back from their children. Even the best-intentioned parent can be thwarted by an unsupportive society. For example, poor parents who seek the best education for their children may be unable to avoid sending their children to drug-infested, crime-ridden, underperforming public schools; and the children are not simply putty in the hands of parents and society. Even the "best" families can produce rebellious children who make bad, irreversible decisions. Parents, society, and the children themselves can all share some of the blame.

When it comes to human capital accumulation, the children of rich parents[14] have several advantages over the children of poor parents:

- *Education.* Rich parents can afford to give their children more and higher quality education than poor parents can. For example, in the United States, family income is a predictor of college attendance for children. Currently, about 80 percent of the children from the highest-income families and about two-thirds of the children from middle-income families attend college, but only about half of the children from low-income families do (Lederman 2007). The children of the rich are more likely to attend expensive, top-notch private schools.[15] Rich parents can also afford all sorts of support services to help their children succeed in school. Examples are private tutors and SAT prep courses.
- *Home Environment.* Rich parents may be able to provide their children with a home environment that is more supportive to the development of human capital. There is some evidence that rich parents are more likely to have books in the home and to read to their children. Rich parents may be more likely to attend school functions, such as back-to-school night, and be more adept at acting as advocates for their children in negotiations with teachers and school administrators. Rich parents can also afford to involve their children in numerous enriching activities, such as foreign travel or cultural events like the symphony, opera, or ballet.
- *Neighborhood Effects.* Rich parents can buy homes in the better neighborhoods. This allows their children access to the best public schools. It also puts them in touch with positive role models and peer groups. The discussion in Chapter 12 of William Julius Wilson's thesis in *The Truly Disadvantaged* is relevant here (Wilson 1987).
- *Social Capital.* This encompasses a wide variety of skills that are acquired from an individual's cultural environment. It includes behaviors that allow some people to move into and in certain social spheres. Rich parents enable beneficial social connections. "Knowing someone" is a tremendous advantage in obtaining jobs and awareness of other opportunities (Granovetter 1974). Rich parents can teach their children the social graces necessary for acceptance in the desirable niches of society, such as the knowledge of which fork to use; how to dress, groom, and speak properly; and simple self-confidence.

    A special type of social capital is ethnic capital, defined as "the whole set of ethnic characteristics—including culture, attitudes and economic opportunities—that children in particular ethnic groups are exposed to" (Borjas 1999, 148). Some evidence on the role that ethnic capital plays comes from George Borjas's research on immigrants (Borjas 1999, 146–60). He essentially found that with everything else held constant, intergenerational elasticity is influenced by ethnic group membership. Intergenerational elasticity is higher or lower for some people than for others simply because they are members of certain ethnic groups.

> Skill differentials across ethnic groups tend to persist across generations, and much of this persistence arises because ethnicity matters, and it matters above and beyond parental inputs. In an important sense, ethnicity is like glue: it has spillover effects that stick for a long time. These ethnic spillover effects help "prop up" the skills of persons who belong to advantaged groups, slowing down the natural process of regression toward the mean. The same spillover effects help "keep down" the skills of persons belonging to disadvantaged groups, again arresting the natural process of regression toward the mean. In effect, ethnic capital simultaneously creates both a glass ceiling and a glass floor, preventing workers from deviating too much from the norms of their ethnic group. In an important sense, ethnic capital makes it harder to escape the economic destiny implied by one's ethnic background (Borjas 1999, 152–154).

Some ethnic cultures might be more conducive to success in the modern American economy than others. Consider the following hypothetical situation involving two families that are identical in all respects except the parents in the first family were born in Mexico and live in a barrio in eastern Los Angeles, while the second family's parents were born in Korea and live in a Korean enclave in Orange County just south of Los Angeles. "Even though the parents in these two families are high school graduates, the child in the Mexican household will likely grow up in an ethnic enclave where many of the neighbors are high school dropouts and where few of the child's friends go on to college. In contrast, the child in the Korean household will likely grow up in an area where many neighbors have some college education and where many of the child's friends will go on to college" (Borjas 1999, 148).

- *Health Capital.* Wealthier people tend to be healthier than poor people (Schiller 2004, 120). They use their knowledge and wealth to lead healthier lifestyles, to live in better environments that protect health (Schiller 2004, 199–21), and to have access to better health care either because they are more likely to be insured or because they can afford expensive medical procedures out of personal funds. From an intergenerational standpoint, their lifestyle example is instructive, their environment is conducive, and their access to high-quality health care is beneficial to their offspring

  The relationship between health and income is one of two-way causation. Bad health causes low income while at the same time low income causes bad health. This makes it difficult to analyze many health-related economic issues. Generally, is it more effective to devote resources to improving health outcomes or economic outcomes? Specifically, should we augment children's diets or parents' incomes?

- *Discrimination.* It will not be a newsflash to anyone that discrimination has played an important role in the past and probably continues to play a role in determining economic outcomes in our society. Such factors as race, skin color, ethnicity, gender, social class, physical attractiveness, age, sexual orientation, and religion, among many others create advantages for some and disadvantages for others. Rich parents are rich, at least partly, because they have enough of those factors that create advantages and few of those factors that create disadvantages. To the extent that privileged parents are able to pass advantage-creating factors on to their offspring—and many of these factors, such as race, skin color, ethnicity, social class, physical attractiveness, sexual orientation, and religion, can either be bequeathed genetically or learned as a result of the environment created by the parents—their children will have a leg up on the children of less privileged parents.

WHY IS B < 1?

Given the tremendous advantages noted above associated with rich parents, it is a wonder that there is any social mobility at all. What factors contribute to mobility?

REGRESSION TO THE MEAN IN ABILITY

A phenomenon that has been remarked upon for more than a century is *regression to the mean*. The first clear demonstration of the phenomenon is usually attributed to Sir Francis Galton.[16] For a whole host of anatomical characteristics of humans he showed that if parents exhibit extreme values of the characteristic, the children will be less likely to exhibit extreme values. For example, the children of exceptionally tall parents tend to be shorter on average than their parents, and the children of exceptionally short parents tend to be taller than their parents on average. In other words, the heights of children tend to regress toward the mean (or regress toward mediocrity as he put it). Galton also showed regression to the mean for various measures of "success" or "eminence" for relatives (Galton 1969).

The relevance of this concept is that the achievements of the children of exceptionally high-achieving parents are likely to be less impressive. The achievements of the children of exceptionally low-achieving parents are likely to be more impressive.

The preceding discussion of regression to the mean in no way "explains" why regression to the mean takes place. It just suggests that it is a "natural" phenomenon.

ENDOGENOUS ALTRUISM

A more systematic explanation looks at the degree of altruism among parents. Figure 15.5 shows two sets of indifference curves. The indifference curves U_1, U_2, U_3, and U_4 are steeper than the set U_5, U_6, and U_7. The slope of the indifference curve has an important economic interpretation. It shows how parents trade off their child's consumption for their own. The former set of indifference curves represents parents who are not very concerned about their child's consumption. They are not willing to sacrifice much of their own consumption so that their child can consume more. The relative steepness of indifference curves U_1, U_2, U_3, U_4 can be interpreted this way: In order to get one more unit of consumption for themselves, they are willing to give up many units of their child's consumption. The latter set represents parents who are very concerned about their child's consumption. They would willingly sacrifice a large quantity of their own consumption so that their child could consume more. The relatively flat indifference curves U_5, U_6, and U_7 mean to get one more unit of

Figure 15.5   **Equilibrium with Differences in Altruism**

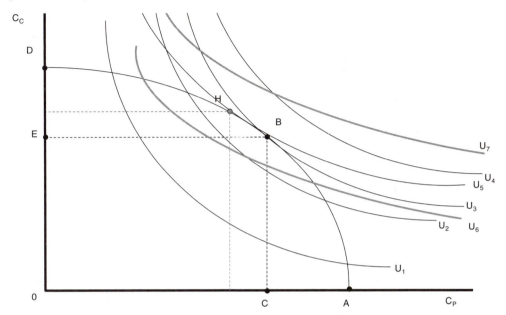

consumption for themselves, they would sacrifice only a small amount of their child's consumption. It is logical to say that parents with the latter set of indifference curves are more altruistic than parents with the former set.

Assume two parents with the same level of income. The production function of both is represented by AD. The graph shows that the equilibrium point for the less altruistic parents is point B, while H is the equilibrium point for the more altruistic parents. The more altruistic parents invest more in their child allowing that child to consume more.

What determines the parent's level of altruism? Traditionally, economic theory has taken tastes as a given, and not attempted an explanation. Newer research has begun to study taste formation (Becker 1996). Mulligan uses endogenous taste formation as a key element in his model of intergenerational mobility (Mulligan 1997, 72–136). In the Mulligan model, parents are assumed to be born selfish, but are capable of developing concern for the well-being of their children. As parents get to know their children, they learn what makes them happy and sad, and getting to know their children is a product of devoting time and effort to caring for the children. Parents who devote more time and effort to their children will be, everything else held constant, more altruistic.

The degree of altruism that parents display is not merely a matter of individual tastes randomly distributed among the population. Rather the degree of altruism responds to economic incentives. Everything else held constant, families with greater total income will tend to be more altruistic because altruism is likely to be a normal good. But, to the extent that the higher income is the result of higher wages and if time is a crucial input in caring for children, then higher wages will lead to less time devoted to caring for children and less altruism.[17]

In Figure 15.6, AD is the production function for a low-income family. FG is the

Figure 15.6 **Equilibrium with Differences in Income and Altruism**

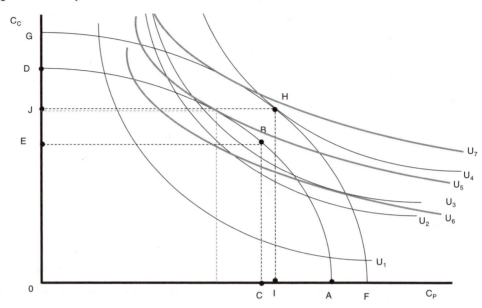

production function of a high-income family. If the high-income family has high income primarily because of a higher wage, then it is likely that the high-income family is less altruistic because the high wage will lead them to devote less time to caring for their child. Their indifference curves will be steeper than those of the poor family. This suggests that the consumption level of the children of these two families are likely to be quite similar despite the differences in the incomes of the families. This then is consistent with an intergenerational elasticity less than 1. This is one possible outcome (see Mulligan for a thorough analysis of the rich menu of alternative outcomes).

Essentially we have shown that, despite all the advantages the children of rich parents have, regression to the mean in economic status is a likely outcome when we take into account parental altruism.

Redistributive Policy

As the discussion in Chapter 7 pointed out, the net effect of government tax and transfer policy is to redistribute income from the rich to the poor. Any policy that boosts the income of the poor has the potential to allow them to purchase more human capital for their children. In addition to general redistribution, there are many specific government policies that aid lower-income children in their acquisition of human capital. An illustrative but not complete list would include the following:

- All states offer "free" (and compulsory up to the age of 16) public education.
- Title I of the Federal Education Act provides federal subsidies for particularly poor school districts.

- Through the Stafford, Ford, Perkins, and PLUS programs, the federal government provides a system of subsidized loans directly for students and for parents.
- Federal Pell Grants provide college tuition aid to students from low-income families. The federal Supplemental Educational Opportunity Grant provides additional funding to the poorest Pell Grant recipients.
- Veterans of military service are eligible to benefit from the GI College Fund, a program that subsidizes college expenses.
- The federal government supports work-study programs at colleges.
- The AmeriCorps program allows college graduates to work at public service jobs for a period of time to acquire money for graduate training.
- The HOPE Scholarship and Lifetime Learning Credit are tax expenditures for lower-income parents who qualify.
- Some states have begun to offer college savings programs. Sometimes called 529 plans, the programs allow parents to invest money while the child is growing up. Although the contributions are not tax deductible, the investment grows tax-free and will not be taxed when it is eventually withdrawn to be used to cover college expenses. The Federal Coverdell Education Savings Account program works in a similar manner.
- Some states allow parents to lock in tuition at the existing level when their child is born by beginning to make tuition payments at that time.
- The state of Georgia has a scholarship program called Helping Outstanding Pupils Educationally (HOPE). HOPE allows any student in the state who maintains a B average or better to attend state schools at a reduced tuition.

Government policy does not uniformly lead to redistribution from rich to poor, even in the area of human capital investment. An example of that is the method most states still use to fund their public education system, discussed in Chapter 7.

Reduction in Discrimination

There seems to be general agreement that some of the more overt forms of discrimination have been on the decline in the United States. Assuming that this is true, the children of parents who have been discriminated against should have an easier time rising in the world. Of course, these children will still be disadvantaged as a result of their humble origins. As the discussions of regression to the mean in ability, endogenous altruism, and redistributive policy have shown, their disadvantage will slow their rise, not prevent it.

Issues in Intergenerational Mobility

To What Extent Should We Facilitate Greater College Attendance?

It is well known there are substantial differences in college attendance rates across family income classes. These differences are not a recent development, and the differences do not seem to have changed over time (Carneiro and Heckman 2003). There are three, not necessarily mutually exclusive, interpretations for these differences:

1. Children of the poor have higher internal rates of time preference. In other words, they are less able to defer gratification, which acts to limit the amount of schooling they receive.
2. Short-term credit constraints: This explanation argues that low-income parents simply cannot afford to send their child to college when the time comes. The parents have been unable to accumulate enough savings of their own, and the child is unable to earn enough by working to finance college. Also, neither the parents nor the child can borrow the funds needed. The parents are not considered a good enough credit risk. The child cannot borrow on the basis of expected future earnings because he or she cannot offer acceptable collateral nor provide assurance that he or she will select a career providing adequate earnings to pay back the loan.
3. Long-term credit constraints: This explanation argues that children who grow up in low-income families lack access to the "whole package." Their parents are unable to provide them with the resources needed to develop the cognitive and noncognitive abilities required for success in school.[18]

Children's tastes for education and their expectations about their life chances are shaped by those of their parents. Educated parents are better able to develop scholastic aptitude in their children by assisting and directing their studies. It is known that cognitive ability is formed relatively early in life and becomes less malleable as children age. By age 8, intelligence as measured by intelligence quotient (IQ) tests seems to be fairly well set (see the evidence summarized in Heckman 1995). Noncognitive skills are more malleable until the late adolescent years (Heckman 2000). The influences of family factors present from birth through adolescence accumulate to produce ability and college readiness. By the time individuals finish high school and their scholastic ability is determined, the scope of tuition policy for promoting college attendance through boosting cognitive and noncognitive skills is greatly diminished (Carneiro and Heckman 2003, 100–01).

The evidence on this issue is not conclusive, but is not unfavorable to the long-term credit constraints view (Carneiro and Heckman 2003, 96–128). For example, in equations explaining both college attendance and completion, the impact of family income is sharply reduced when measures of scholastic ability are included. If scholastic ability is largely determined by long-term family and environmental factors, then this result suggests that long-term factors are more important than short-term factors. This result does not mean that short-term credit constraints are unimportant. Rather it suggests that the policies already in place to make college affordable (for example, Pell Grants and subsidized student loans) work fairly well.

Differences in ability across family types appear at early ages and persist. In tests of cognitive ability, the children of the poor start out behind as early as age 6 and the gap only increases (Carneiro and Heckman 2003, 130). Controlling for school quality does not account for the increase in the gap. The same pattern holds for noncognitive abilities. On the Anti-Social test, a measure of the frequency of dishonest, cruel, non-cooperative, violent or disobedient behaviors, as was the case with the cognitive test above, the children of the poor start out with lower scores as early as age 6 and the gap increases over time (Carneiro and Heckman 2003, 134). Adjusting for measures of family background reduces, but does not eliminate, the gaps.

"Good" families promote cognitive, social, and behavioral skills. "Bad" families do not. The major implication of this from a policy standpoint is that improving equality of opportunity requires that interventions begin early. We cannot wait until late in the game and simply send everyone to college.

THE ROLE OF GENES

Children receive their genetic make-up from their parents. There the agreement ends. What this means for the intergenerational mobility process is highly controversial, and over the years the controversy has generated more heat than light. What follows in this brief section is a hopefully balanced discussion of what is of the greatest interest to an economist about this topic.

Undoubtedly the concept that first leaps to mind when the role of genes is mentioned is IQ. For our purposes, the term IQ will be used in the most general fashion, to refer to how "smart" someone is. A "smart" person can be said to have a high IQ; a "not-so-smart" person has a low IQ. To be a bit more precise, think of IQ as a measure of cognitive ability. People who are good writers and have high mathematical abilities are what are referred to as having a high IQ.

The common perception is that IQ is inherited and that a high IQ is essential for economic success. The former perception seems fundamentally correct. Estimates of the correlation between parent and offspring IQs range from 0.42 to 0.72 (Bouchard Jr. and McGue 1981). The perception that IQ impacts an individual's level of success is the key, and is much more controversial.

Richard J. Herrnstein and Charles Murray used statistical techniques to argue for an important place for IQ in this discussion (Herrnstein and Murray 1994). Their studies of siblings[19] raised together (hence a common environment) have concluded that the sibling with the higher IQ does considerably better than the one with the lower IQ. The validity of their statistical analysis has been widely criticized. As has always been the case in IQ research, much of the criticism has been of the emotional, knee-jerk variety that has not addressed the issues, but there have been many thoughtful and telling critiques (Heckman 1995; Devlin et al. 1997).

The consensus of the scientific community today would appear to be that IQ, while unquestionably a causal factor in determining earnings, does not play a significant role in the intergenerational elasticity (Bowles, Gintis, and Groves 2003, 9–12). Assuming that IQ affects earnings both directly and indirectly via educational attainment, a rough estimate of the impact of IQ on earnings is that a standard deviation difference in IQ leads to a 0.226 standard deviation difference in log earnings (Bowles and Gintis 2002, 10). The correlation between parent and offspring income resulting from genetic inheritance of IQ depends on the impact of IQ on earnings for the parents (use 0.226), the impact of IQ on earnings for the offspring (again use 0.226), and the correlation between parental and offspring IQ that can be attributed to the genetic inheritance of IQ. For arcane mathematical reasons that need not detain us,[20] these three factors can be multiplied together to get the correlation of interest. Since multiplying the parents (0.226) and the offspring (0.226) yields 0.051, the highest the correlation between parent and offspring incomes as a result of genetic inheritance can be is 0.051, and this is if parental and offspring IQ are perfectly correlated. The number 0.051 is less than 10 percent of the estimated intergenerational income correlation.[21] The actual value is likely to be much less than 10 percent, which supports the conclusion in the first sentence of this paragraph. The economic explanation of this result is that while cognitive skills are essential, they are not scarce enough to be valuable. Other types of skills, the so-called noncognitive skills, are often the crucial determinant of economic success.

Genetics does play an obvious role that is frequently overlooked. One of the preconditions for discrimination to take place is that there must be an easy way to differentiate between the "in-group" and the "out-group." Among the most commonly used markers are physical traits such as skin color and hair texture, and these traits are strongly influenced by the genetic bequest of parents. Chapter 10 reviewed research that concluded, *ceteris paribus*, more beautiful people are more successful in the labor market than those who are less beautiful. How beautiful you are is obviously the product of several factors, including diet, exercise, and grooming skill, but it also reflects the symmetry of the face, bone structure, the quality of your skin, and many other things that you are likely to inherit from your parents. In short, Brad Pitt and Angelina Jolie are likely to have better looking kids than Fat Albert and Ugly Betty, regardless of anything else.

CONCLUSION

The issue of intergenerational mobility speaks directly to the equity of the economic system. How close have we come to equal opportunity? The consensus estimate of the intergenerational elasticity of income is problematic. What do you make of the number 0.4? One interpretation is that children surrender over half the advantage that their parents had in one generation. Given all the obvious advantages that growing up in a comfortable environment provides, this is a remarkable degree of mobility. The polar opposite interpretation is that an intergenerational elasticity of 0.4 means the advantages provided by a family line take more than three generations to disappear. If your grandparents made it big, you are still benefiting, but your children might not do as well.

The most important thing is to avoid is overconfidence with respect to the extent of our knowledge in this area. The analysis of intergenerational mobility is still in its infancy. More fully specified models are needed.

QUESTIONS FOR REVIEW AND PRACTICE

1. What does the intergenerational elasticity measure? What is the current consensus on the value of the intergenerational elasticity for income? Explain

why the intergenerational elasticity is not equal to 0. Explain why the intergenerational elasticity is not equal to 1.

2. Assume all parents have one child, parents can be either rich or poor, parents can be either highly altruistic or not very altruistic toward their child, and the child can be either dumb or smart. For each case, draw a graph that shows your result and provide an intuitive explanation for the result.

   a. Assuming their children are equally intelligent, show how the child of poor parents might have greater lifetime consumption than a child of rich parents.

   b. Assuming the parents are equally rich, show how a dumb child might have greater lifetime consumption than a smart child.

3. Explain how **your** actions influence your children's lifetime earnings. How confident should you be that your children will live better than you?

4. Is there a healthy degree of intergenerational mobility in the United States or is the degree of intergenerational mobility distressingly low?

NOTES

1. The term *parents* is being used very broadly here. It essentially refers to the environment you grew up in and any elements of biological inheritance that are relevant to your success—in short, the nurture and nature in your upbringing.

2. The social networks you are plugged into are sometimes called your social capital.

3. It would be similar to the perfect mobility society defined earlier.

4. See the discussion on regression equations in Chapter 10.

5 Mazumder argues that better estimating techniques actually place β nearer to 0.6 (see Mazumder 2005, 81).

6. This quote is frequently traced back to a Lancashire proverb "Theres nobbut three generations atween clog and clog."

7. *Robber baron* is a pejorative term that refers to a businessperson who uses hardball tactics.

8. Your mother's diet, whether she smokes or drinks, whether she perms her hair, and, some say, the type of music she listens to, all are thought to influence fetal development.

9. For a review of the literature and view of the current state of the art in this area see Casey B. Mulligan (1997). Another useful source is William A. Lord (2002, 188–218).

10. An African saying of unknown origin is that "it takes a village to raise a child." This means that parents are not enough. Children are also guided by relatives, neighbors, schools, the media, and community norms, among many others. But it is hard to deny that parents are the single most important influence.

11. This is not to deny that accompanying children on such activities as visiting a museum is not enjoyable for the parents.

12. Of course, some of the money parents spend on children probably does not make much of a contribution to their human capital, such as money for candy, an iPod, or violent video games. The model abstracts from these complications.

13. Altruism is not the only possible motive. Another is a sense of obligation toward that helpless creature the parents brought into the world. Still another is reciprocity. The parents may feel that if they take care of the child while the child is dependent, then the child will take care of them when they are old and gray. Predictions from models using other motives will not be discussed.

14. In this context, I am simply dividing families into two categories: rich and poor. Rich does not mean fabulously wealthy. It just means the people with incomes higher than the people classified as poor. Think of the rich as the middle class and up.

15. Stories abound of the competition among rich parents to place their children in the "best" preschools. To many parents the right preschool is the crucial first step toward Harvard.

16. The Englishman Galton (1822–1911) developed the concepts of regression and correlation. But he also did much more in an impressively accomplished career. Galton was a polymath, geographer, meteorologist, anthropologist, eugenicist, inventor, and explorer.

17. A more complete analysis of the determinants of altruism can be found in Mulligan (2004, 72–136).

18. The reason this is called long-term credit constraints probably reflects the idea that the child does not have enough money to buy a good enough parental environment and genes.

19. Y is a sibling of X if X and Y share at least one parent.

20. See the discussion of the mathematics behind this in Samuel Bowles and Herbert Gintis (2002, 10–13).

21. The intergenerational income correlation is the correlation of parent and offspring incomes. It is closely related to the intergenerational income elasticity. Thomas Hertz reports intergenerational income elasticities of between 0.47 and 0.53 (Hertz 2005, 188).

16

The Accumulation, Distribution, and Transfer of Wealth

INTRODUCTION

Flow variables such as wages, income, and consumption have played the key roles in the analyses of the preceding chapters. In this chapter, a stock variable—wealth—takes center stage. Wealth (its level and distribution) is an important factor influencing economic well-being. Income from wealth—interest, dividends, and capital gains—makes up a significant chunk of the national income, approximately 23 percent,[1] and the mere possession of wealth is a source of security and a creator of opportunity. This chapter reviews models of the accumulation of wealth with special emphasis placed on the always interesting topic of inheritance.

PRELIMINARIES

Chapter 1 defined the following terms: wealth, assets, liabilities, net worth, income, stock, flow, and money. If you have forgotten the definitions, please review immediately. We will wait until you return.

Where does wealth come from? Ultimately all wealth comes from saving. Out of our flow of income, we divert the larger proportion to finance the things we consume in order to survive and enjoy life. The portion that we do not consume becomes our savings, which is what we use to accumulate wealth in the form of real, financial, and human capital.

However, while you cannot accumulate wealth without having an income, you cannot have an income without having wealth. It is a bit of a chicken and the egg problem that we will not try to solve here. It is safe to say that once society is a "going concern" all new wealth can only come from saving.

What is true for society as a whole is not necessarily true for individuals. Certainly individuals can accumulate wealth by saving, but individuals can also obtain wealth from transfers in the form of gifts, bequests, and theft. These transfers, however, are redistribution of already existing wealth.

IS WEALTH DIFFERENT?

Families who have assets have significant advantages over families who do not, even at the same level of income.

Assets act as a safety net. In difficult times, a family with assets can maintain their standard of living for a time until their fortunes change. Families without assets may have to rely on welfare or face homelessness.

Families with assets can take advantage of opportunities, such as starting businesses and buying homes in good neighborhoods with good schools. Often modest amounts make the difference when it comes to a business start-up or home down payment.

Here, a personal story may be relevant. Right after we were married, my wife and I rented an apartment in Hyattsville, Maryland. A few years later we rented a townhouse in Alexandria, Virginia. Then, in quick succession, I took a job with the University of Mary Washington (then Mary Washington College) in Fredericksburg, Virginia, and we had a child. Living in Alexandria necessitated more than two hours of commuting each workday. The next year, to decrease my commuting time, we decided to buy a house in Fredericksburg. At the time, my salary was miniscule, my wife was not working, and our savings were virtually nonexistent. If we had to rely on our own resources, we would not have been able to buy a house. We would have either stayed in Alexandria or rented some modest and uninspiring apartment or townhouse in the Fredericksburg vicinity. What allowed us to move was the generosity of my in-laws, Al and Mary, who gave us $10,000 toward the down payment. To put this in perspective, at the time, the $10,000 was 23 percent of the cost of the house. The result is that we were able to move into a nice home (one we still live in and which has probably appreciated more than ten times) in a nice neighborhood with nice neighbors, and I was close enough to my job so that I was able to walk to work each day. If we had not been able to do that, our lives would have been very different and probably not as good. Having ready access to assets (in this case, my in-laws' assets) allowed us to take advantage of a great opportunity.

Was it fair for us the get this money? Probably not. There are certainly many families who do not have such an advantage. But consider this question: Would it have been fair to prohibit Al and Mary from giving us the money? Both of them came from large working class families, and neither of them had had it easy. Mary was a high school graduate who became a nurse. She worked at that job most of her life except when she took some time off to raise her children. Al had an even tougher life. His father died when he was young and he had to quit school after the sixth grade. He joined the army during World War II and was a POW. Afterward he worked in factories. Neither of them ever inherited a penny, but they worked hard, played by the rules and put three daughters through college and one through graduate school. They owned a home, but it was very unassuming.[2] The only vacations they ever took were to visit family, they owned modest cars, and hardly ever ate out. Should Al and Mary have been prohibited from using their wealth as they saw fit?

The point of this little trip down memory lane is that wealth is not simply a sum of money. The possession of wealth can potentially create, as it did in our case, life-changing opportunities.

WEALTH ACCUMULATION OVER THE LIFE CYCLE

Let's consider a representative single individual named Pat who begins life with nothing and will not receive any bequests or gifts over his or her lifetime. In Figure

Figure 16.1 **Wealth Accumulation Over the Life Cycle**

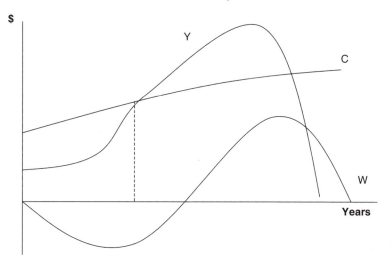

16.1 Y is Pat's earnings, year by year. The pattern of earnings is consistent with both theory and empirical evidence as shown in Chapter 14.

There are well-accepted economic theories that say individuals try to smooth out their consumption over their lifetime (Modigliani and Brumberg 1954; Friedman 1957). Instead of consuming Y each year, Pat would choose to consume along path C. The simple reason for this has to do with the law of diminishing marginal utility. If Pat consumed along Y, then in years when Y was high, the utility of the marginal units of consumption would be quite low. In years when Y was low, the utility of marginal units of consumption would be high. By consuming relatively more when Y is low and relatively less when Y is high, Pat would maximize lifetime utility.

Less abstractly, Pat will consume more than Y while young and old. The young years may correspond with Pat starting a household and family. Spending requirements may be relatively high as Pat buys a car, buys a house, and decorates the nursery, among other things. During the old years, Pat may be retired either voluntarily or because of physical disabilities. In order to maintain a recognizable lifestyle, Pat may very well have to spend beyond his or her current income.

To achieve this desired path of consumption, Pat will either have to be able to borrow or draw down on assets during the young and old years. Between those time periods, Pat will want to save in order to pay back earlier borrowing and to build up a cushion of assets for the retirement years.

The line W in Figure 16.1 represents the pattern of wealth-holding that would result from the plan described in the previous paragraph. Initially Pat would go into debt (represented by negative wealth), but then assets would rise as Pat entered peak earning years. Toward the end of Pat's life, his/her assets would decline.

It is the period near the end of life that is a source of some controversy in economics. Presumably if Pat knew exactly when he/she was going to die and had no children, friends, or causes, then Pat would end life with no wealth remaining. Pat would spend his/her last dollar just as he/she takes his/her last breath. Of course, we know that is not the case. Most people end their life with some assets—their house, car, a few antiques, some money in the bank and so on—and a few pass with enormous sums of wealth. Why is this?

Reasons are not hard to come by. For one thing, no one knows the exact moment of their death so people hold on to their wealth as insurance against destitution. There are likely some parents who use their wealth strategically to cement the allegiance of their children. And there are many who have deep concern for succeeding generations, either their own children or for society as a whole. They build and hold their wealth so they can bequeath it to their heirs or favorite causes. Undoubtedly, this is not a case where one explanation holds true and the rest are irrelevant. There is probably a little bit of all three in every parent's behavior.

How much of our wealth is the result of life-cycle savings and how much is the result of gifts and bequests? Economists have looked at this issue and concluded that life-cycle savings account for between 20 and 80 percent of total national wealth.[3] This fairly wide range is indicative of how imprecise our knowledge is in this area.

THE FORM OF BEQUEST

Among those with deep concern for succeeding generations, there exist options with respect to how wealth can be transferred. One set of options has to do with the form of the transfer. Parents who want to provide for their children can give them cash or heirlooms, or invest in their human capital. Philanthropists can give cash, financial assets, or real assets to charities or other nonprofit organizations. Another set of options has to do with the timing of these bequests. Should donors begin making transfers during their lifetimes or wait until death?

A MODEL OF INHERITANCE INCLUDING FINANCIAL BEQUESTS

A variety of things can be inherited at variety of times. Wealth that is inherited consists of goods and services, financial wealth, and human capital, and can be inherited at any time between conception of the recipient and the benefactor's death. Children inherit genes (a part of their human capital) from their parents at the moment of conception. Parental investment in their children's schooling can begin in preschool and continue through graduate or professional school. Children can receive items of wealth, such as cars, a down payment on a home, and vacations, from their parents and others throughout their lifetime. Wealth received while the benefactor is alive is called an *inter-vivos* transfer. Wealth received upon the death of the benefactor is called a bequest.

This discussion of the form of bequest uses the human capital inheritance model from Chapter 15. To briefly review, each family consists of two parents and one child. Parents know what the value their own lifetime wealth and what the value of the lifetime wealth of their child will be under a variety of circumstances.

The horizontal axis in Figure 16.2 measures lifetime parental consumption (C_p),

Figure 16.2 **A Model of Inheritance**

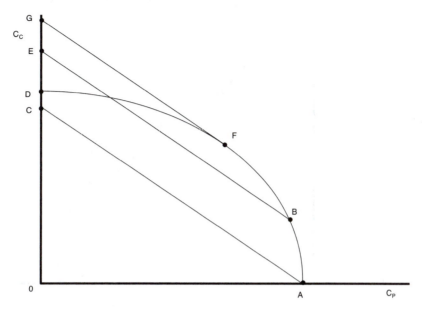

and the y axis measures lifetime consumption of the child (C_c). The curved line AD shows the trade-off between parent's and child's consumption. If parents sacrifice their own consumption, they can provide human capital to the child, which will finance a certain level of consumption. Let r_h be the rate of return on human capital investment. At any point along AD, the slope is $-(1 + r_h)$. As we move from A to D along AD, r_h gets smaller. This is simply a reflection of the law of diminishing returns applied to investments in human capital. Because human beings have a limited capacity to absorb new knowledge and because human capital investment takes time, additional increments of investment are likely to be less productive than the initial increments. In Chapter 15 we added parental indifference curves to show what choice the parents would make.

Parents have another choice to make. In addition to transfers of human capital, parents can simply save money at interest and later transfer the entire lump sum to their children. Let r be the rate of return on saving. The choice parents make is likely to depend on the relative rate of return. If $r_h > r$, then the parent will invest in the child's human capital. If the opposite is the case, then the parent will simply give the child money.

Start at point A and assume at that point $r_h > r$. The line AC represents parental and child consumption possibilities when the parents save. It shows the impact that one dollar transferred from parent's wealth will have on the consumption of the child. It is a straight line with the slope $-(1 + r)$. The reason it is straight in contrast to AD is because there will not be diminishing returns to family saving. Since each family's saving is just a small percentage of the total pool of savings (even in the case of someone like Bill Gates), the amount they save has no influence over the market interest rate.

Figure 16.3 **Equilibrium with Altruistic and Non-altruistic Parents**

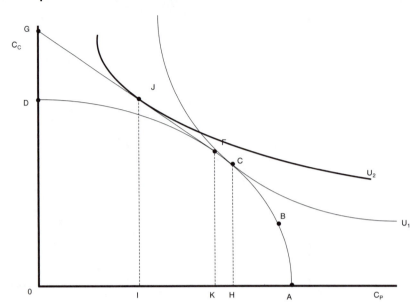

Here things get a bit complicated. At point A the family will obviously invest in the child's human capital. Now consider point B. At this point the family can continue to invest in human capital and continue following the path along AD or it could invest in financial wealth and follow the path represented by line BE (where BE is parallel to AC). Given the relative rate of return, human capital investment remains the better choice. At point F, however, saving has the same rate of return as human capital investment, and to the left of point F the parent would prefer financial investment. Therefore the consumption possibilities frontier becomes AFG.

What the parents ultimately do depends on their indifference curves. Figure 16.3 shows two indifference curves. U_1 is the indifference curve of relatively nonaltruistic parents. U_2 is the indifference curve of relatively altruistic parents. The nonaltruistic parents will invest AH in their child, all in the form of human capital investments. The altruistic parents will invest AI. AK will be human capital investment and the rest will be a financial bequest. The model is not detailed enough to allow us to ascertain when the transfer takes place.

An interesting complication is what happens if the straight line FG is extended to the horizontal axis. With appropriately shaped indifference curves, the parents could end at a point along that line segment. Practically speaking, that would mean they borrowed against their children's future income to finance their own consumption. Since this does not seem to be very common in the real world, we can safely ignore that outcome.

COMPARATIVE STATICS

Many of the same comparative statics exercises covered in the previous chapter apply here. We can show the effects of different levels of parental wealth, child's ability,

Figure 16.4 **A Change in the Interest Rate**

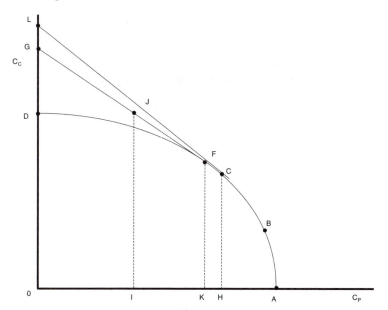

and different degrees of parental altruism. If you understood them in Chapter 15, you will understand them here. If not, please review Chapter 15.

A new exercise demonstrates the effect of a change in the rate of interest. In Figure 16.4 line CL shows a higher interest rate. It is tangent to the production function further to the right. The impact of a higher interest rate on the size of a bequest is theoretically ambiguous (income versus substitution effect). The higher interest rate makes it easier to transfer a larger sum of money, but it also means the parent can achieve a certain target transfer amount by saving less money. Regardless of the sum, the transfer will consist of less human capital and more financial wealth.

THE ACCUMULATION OF HUGE FORTUNES

In this section we will ask and answer two questions: How do people accumulate huge fortunes, and why do people accumulate huge fortunes?

HOW DO PEOPLE ACCUMULATE HUGE FORTUNES?

Every year, *Forbes Magazine* publishes "The Forbes 400," a list of the 400 wealthiest Americans.[4] Studying the list shows two things that are quite interesting. One, typically at least half the people listed are "self-made" billionaires. Their enormous wealth was not simply the result of inheritance. Rather they created it during their careers.[5] Two, their wealth was not the result of several decades of patient saving and investment; their fortunes were essentially accumulated over a relatively short period of time—ten to fifteen years in many cases (Thurow 1972).

How does anyone end up with tens of billions of dollars of wealth? Pat's accumulation process described in the previous section is not how it's done. Consider the math. To accumulate Bill Gates' $48 billion would only require saving $25 a year assuming two conditions: the savings would have to earn 10 percent annually (plausible) and you would have to have started saving 200 years ago! Of course, you could start the process and bequeath what you accumulated to your heir, hoping your heir and your heir's heir and also subsequent generations would continue to save and bequest just as you had. If so, then eight generations later your successor as head of the dynasty would be worth $48 billion. Of course, this assumes all your ancestors bequeathed to one heir, and there were no messy divorces and financial disasters over the entire 200-year period. There are some members of the Forbes 400 list who inherited their wealth. The wealth of the Walton and Mars families was inherited, and there are also Rockefellers and Hearsts further on down the list. But these dynasties cannot be traced back 200 years.

If you want to accumulate $48 billion during your lifetime, the task is a bit harder. At a 10 percent rate of return for investments, you could accumulate the $48 billion in 50 years by saving $40 million a year! Many of the fortunes on the *Forbes* list did arise during the career of the creator. Prominent examples are the fortunes of the computer moguls Bill Gates, Paul Allen, Michael Dell, Lawrence Ellison, and Steve Ballmer.[6] However none of their fortunes took fifty years to create. Many arose within only a couple of decades. For example, Bill Gates and Paul Allen founded Microsoft Corporation in 1975. It only took Gates until 1986 to enter the Forbes 400. By 1996 he had taken first place and he has been at or near that position ever since.

A $48 billion "overnight" fortune requires entrepreneurial success combined with imperfect real capital markets and perfect (or nearly perfect) financial capital markets. Consider this simple model:[7] Assume the economy has two capital markets. The real capital market is the market for factories, machinery, and tools. The financial capital market is the market for stocks, bonds, and other similar financial instruments.

The two markets are related. Assume that $100,000 in real capital is needed to start a business and that this amount can be raised by selling stock. Now operate the business for a year and assume a $20,000 profit was earned and that this profit would continue to be earned until the end of time. We can say that the rate of return to the investment in real capital was $20,000/$100,000 = 20 percent.[8] Since the profits earned accrue to the stockholders, we can also say that the rate of return to the financial investment of $100,000 was also $20,000/$100,000 = 20 percent.

Now assume that two firms, A and B, are initially capitalized at $100,000 each. For some reason, A's product proves highly popular and earns a $30,000 annual profit and this profit is expected to continue until the end of time. Firm B's product is not as successful, earning only $10,000, again expected to continue until the end of time. The rate of return to both real and financial investment in A is 30 percent; the rate of return for B is 10 percent.

If the economy was competitive with perfect capital mobility, capital would flow into the industry represented by Firm A. New firms would be established that would produce either an identical or similar product to that produced by Firm A. This would reduce the profitability and rate of return to Firm A. Capital would probably also be leaving the industry represented by Firm B with the ultimate effect of raising the prof-itability and rate of return to Firm B. In equilibrium, the rate of return to both firms would be equal. Firm A's good year would simply provide a temporary windfall, but is unlikely to cause an appreciation in the stock price. Investors look to the future, and the future they see for Firm A is simply normal profits. In the same vein, Firm B's stock is unlikely to depreciate in price.

In the real world, though, capital is not always that mobile. For example, Firm A may have established a brand name, which insulates it against new competition. Another consideration is that the managerial expertise needed to be successful in Firm A's industry may be in short supply. If Firm A produces computers while Firm B produces textiles, there may not be many textile executives who would have any idea what to do in the computer industry. Another possibility is that there are artifi-cial barriers to capital mobility. For example, the government may have established regulatory barriers to entry into Firm A's industry. Another barrier may be the result of Firm A's hardball business practices. Firm A may have established relationships with suppliers or retailers that would make it very difficult for new firms to enter the industry.

Regardless of the source of the barriers, their very existence means that Firm A's supranormal profit can continue to be earned for many years. The rate of return to Firm A's real capital investment may be continuously high. But the barriers that limit real capital mobility do not exist for financial capital. If Firm A earns supranormal profits, its stock becomes especially attractive. Investors will start bidding up the price of the stock. The stock price will rise until the rate of return to financial investment in Firm A is at the equilibrium level. If the equilibrium rate of return is 20 percent, with $30,000 a year in profits, Firm A's stock price will be bid up to $150,000 ($30,000/$150,000 = 20 percent). Early birds, the founders of Firm A and the early investors, will enjoy a dramatic increase in their wealth (50 percent) that will take place almost overnight (the stock market will quickly capitalize the return). Latecomers, those who purchase Firm A's stock after the market movement, will only get the normal rate of return.

To summarize, when capital is highly mobile, investors can only expect the normal rate of return. Investors may enjoy windfall profits, but not permanent increases in the value of their wealth. To become really wealthy one must first have a good idea and have been an early bird. Significant wealth accumulation will only take place if there are barriers to real capital mobility that cause profits to be capitalized into the price of the stock

Many try, but only some get rich. What differentiates the successful tycoons from all the wannabes? To help explain, we will make use of an interesting theory from finance known as the efficient markets hypothesis.[9]

This hypothesis is based on a number of propositions:

1. Within any risk class, the expected return to any financial investment is the same. The reason is this: If the expected return on one instrument was higher than on others, then everyone would try to buy that instrument raising its price and lowering its return until it was just equal to the others.
2. Any useful information about an investment is quickly incorporated into

Figure 16.5 **Distribution of Investment Returns**

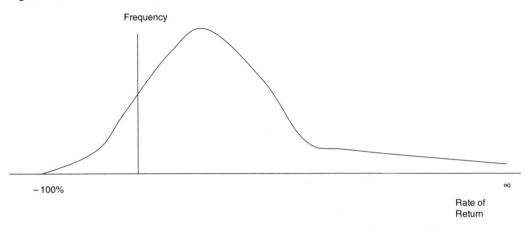

the price of the asset. Assume a firm develops a new product or process that promises great success, or the CFO absconds with the company treasury to Rio. Once the information is announced or is leaked, it will take approximately one nanosecond for it to be incorporated into the price of the stock. This is because there are so many intently interested people a quick reaction is a virtual certainty. This implies that information is essentially worthless. The colorful explanation of this point is that you could do as well in the stock market by throwing darts at the stock pages and buying those investments as you could by consulting with (and paying for) an investment guru. Be careful here. The analysis does not mean that information is useless. Information is obviously very valuable. What it does mean is that the only way to get rich is to consistently know more than everyone else. With all the millions of smart people monitoring the stock market, how could you ever hope to be first most of the time?

3. Even though the expected return is the same on all investments, the actual return over any period of time will differ. Figure 16.5 shows a hypothetical skewed distribution of actual investment returns. The distribution is skewed because on the negative side there is a definite limitation. You cannot lose more than 100 percent of your investment. On the positive side of things, investment returns cannot literally be infinite, but they can be quite high. Comparing Google, a major player in the internet sector, with Pets.com, a venture that attempted to sell pet food over the internet and failed miserably (but did leave us with the legacy of some of the cleverest TV commercials of all time), illustrates that point. Because of this, even if people start from a position of equal wealth or their investment abilities are highly similar, the end result will be great disparities in wealth.

What can we say about those who do manage get rich? In this model, luck would appear to be the operative word. Of course, good luck can be followed by bad luck, but here the principle of diversification comes to the rescue. After hitting it big, an investor can then diversify his or her portfolio. This will reduce the level of risk markedly while allowing the investor to earn the market rate of return.

This theory applies directly to financial investments, but what we are talking about here is entrepreneurial ability. Might the same theory hold? There are certainly plenty of people trying to make it big as entrepreneurs, and it is hard to believe that a small number of them are just that much more capable than the others. More importantly, how many have done it more than once? If one individual is demonstrably better at acquiring wealth than the others, then that individual should be able to achieve exceptional success multiple times. That is hardly ever the case.

WHY DO PEOPLE ACCUMULATE HUGE FORTUNES?

Bill Gates has accumulated a fortune of approximately $48 billion. If he stopped accumulating today and began to spend on himself and if he had twenty years left to live, he would have to spend approximately $6.5 million a day to go through his entire fortune![10] Not only does this seem extravagant, it is very likely impossible, not to mention irrational. Consumption is more than just spending money. It also requires time. For example, you cannot buy an around-the-world vacation unless you take the time to go around the world sightseeing. It is unlikely that there are enough hours in the day for you to spend $6.5 million on yourself, not to mention day after day after day for twenty years.

In addition, the value of future consumption is bound to fall precipitously, simply because the older you are the less likely you are to be around to enjoy future consumption. Consequently, a rational individual is unlikely to accumulate an amount that he or she could not consume.

Of course, the person may not just be worried about his or her consumption. He or she may be concerned about the consumption of future generations. But even there, things are more complicated then they might seem. In an intergenerational context, a person must not only weigh the value of current consumption against future consumption, but also against current and future consumption of offspring. If the person consumes more now, that means less future consumption for the person and less current and future consumption for the offspring. Consuming less now could benefit the individual's future or the present or future of the offspring. The outcome of all this weighing is not obvious. Regardless, there is a limit to how far the person will look forward. The value of the offspring's future consumption will be quite low at any reasonable discount rate. For example, the value of an additional $100 in consumption for the offspring forty years in the future is only $14.20 today at a discount rate of 5 percent.

It is therefore unlikely that consumption could ever be a motivation for the accumulation of enormous wealth. So what else might provide motivation? Something that is valuable to everyone, but is not subject to diminishing marginal utility, is economic power. Large accumulations of wealth give people influence within the family, the community, and society as a whole. Power is closely associated with the possession of wealth, which would explain why people tend to distribute their wealth only upon

Table 16.1

Gini Coefficients for Net Worth and Income, 1989–2004, Selected Years

Year	Net Worth	Income
1989	0.7863	0.5399
1992	0.7808	0.5005
1995	0.7841	0.5146
1998	0.7935	0.5302
2001	0.8034	0.5643
2004	0.8047	0.5406

Source: Kennickell (2006), Table 4.

their death. Carroll provides convincing evidence that the rich are different from you and me in their drive to accumulate wealth (Thurow 1972, 141–42; Carroll 1998).

THE DISTRIBUTION OF WEALTH

Table 16.1 shows the Gini coefficients for net worth and income in the United States for selected years between 1989 and 2004 inclusive.[11] There are two things that are particularly notable about this table. First, the distribution of net worth is more unequal than the distribution of income, which should not be too surprising. People with higher income should be able to save disproportionately more. Their internal rate of time preference is probably lower because consumption for mere survival is no longer a concern.[12] Second, the distribution of net worth became more unequal over time. The increased inequality was not simply random variation over a relatively short period. A trend toward increased inequality in the distribution of wealth over a half century is evident (Mishel, Bernstein, and Allegretto 2007, 251). Despite the half-century trend, wealth inequality now may be less than it was in the third decade of the twentieth century (Wolff 2003, 353).

Table 16.2 shows mean and median values of net worth over the same time period. Note the dramatic difference between the median and mean value of both measures of net worth each year. As discussed in Chapter 1, a distribution with this characteristic is the log-normal distribution. The reason it is skewed is that in the United States there are a few people with disproportionately enormous amounts of wealth (Bill Gates and the others mentioned earlier), and their wealth pulls the mean well above the median.

Table 16.3 is another way to view the distribution of net worth. It shows the percentage of net worth held by different groupings of people. It shows, for example, that in 2004 the wealthiest 1 percent of the population held 33.4 percent of the net worth while the 50 percent least wealthy held only 2.5 percent of the net worth.

For another take on the distribution of wealth, *Forbes Magazine* annually ranks the richest people in the world (Kroll 2008). In 2008, American investor Warren Buffett headed the list with wealth totaling $62 billion. Bill Gates was third with $48 billion. Only two other Americans were in the top 25, Sheldon Adelson in twelfth place with

Table 16.2

Mean and Median Values of Net Worth, 1989–2004, Selected Years

Year	Mean	Median
1989	277.9	68.8
1992	246.1	65.3
1995	260.7	70.8
1998	328.5	83.2
2001	428.9	91.7
2004	448.0	93.1

Note: Amounts given in thousands of dollars.
Source: Kennickell (2006), Table 3.

Table 16.3

Proportions of Total Net Worth Held by Various Percentile Groups, 1989–2004, Selected Years

Year	Net Worth Percentile Group 0–50%	50–90%	90–95%	95–99%	99–100%
1989	3.0	29.9	13.0	24.1	30.1
1992	3.3	29.6	12.5	24.4	30.2
1995	3.6	28.6	11.9	21.3	34.6
1998	3.0	28.4	11.4	23.3	33.9
2001	2.8	27.4	12.1	25.0	32.7
2004	2.5	27.9	12.0	24.1	33.4

Source: Kennickell (2006), Table 5.

$26 million and Lawrence Ellison in fourteenth place with $25 billion. How do you measure up relative to them? The accuracy of the lists is unclear. *Forbes* does not claim to have precisely measured the wealth of the individuals mentioned. Its estimates are "highly educated guesses" based on a variety of sources. Many items that would be important components of the wealth of "normal" people, such as the value of automobiles and checking accounts, are not included. Of course, their omission would probably not significantly impact the standing of Warren Buffett et al. The *Forbes* list is more for entertainment value than anything else.

There is an apparent tendency for the rich to get richer. Over the period 1989–2004, the combined wealth of the people listed in the Forbes 400 increased nearly 2.5 times over this relatively short interval (Kennickell 2006, 6).

Table 16.4 shows average wealth (net worth) by various demographic characteristics. The results are not all that surprising. Wealth increases with age, up to age sixty-five; the self-employed are wealthier than employees, the retired, and nonworkers; and having a college education, being married, and being a male correlate with wealth.

Important differences in net worth exist between individuals of various ethnicities

Table 16.4

Wealth by Demographic Characteristics, 1998

Characteristic	Average Wealth
Age	
25 and under	17,593
26–30	46,453
31–35	127,456
36–40	162,264
41–45	257,981
46–50	347,994
51–55	470,694
56–60	514,013
61–65	609,059
Over 65	381,643
Employment Status	
Worker	170,347
Self-employed	958,484
Retired	361,005
Nonworker	107,986
Education	
No High School	78,548
High School	189,983
College	541,128
Marital Status	
Married	386,900
Single	
With dependents	105,251
Without dependents	164,886

Source: Rodriquez, Diaz-Gimenez, Quadrini, and Rios-Rull (2002); 1998 Survey of Consumer Finances. Any views expressed herein are those of the authors and not necessarily those of the Federal Reserve Bank of Minneapolis or the Federal Reserve System.

and races. Mean net worth for African-American and Hispanic families in 2004 was $111,200 and $152,700, respectively, well below the $448,000 of all families (Kennickell 2006, 34). Wealth is distributed a bit less equally among African-Americans (Gini = 0.7955) than among all families, but the Hispanic distribution (Gini = 0.8334) is a bit more equal. The differences in Gini coefficients are not statistically significant.

Differences in wealth-holding depend on a variety of factors, some peculiar to the individual and others representing social factors. People differ in lifetime income because of the choices they make and the obstacles placed in their way. People differ in risk aversion and thriftiness. People differ in the interest rates they face and the returns they manage to achieve on their investments. People differ in the wealth of the family they were reared in. People differ in their access to borrowing and investment opportunities.

THE ROLE OF BEQUESTS IN WEALTH INEQUALITY

To what extent do bequests contribute to wealth inequality? At first glance, this might seem like a fairly straightforward question. People born with silver spoons in their mouths generally inherit large sums of wealth, which perpetuates their privileged position and the inequality associated with it. At second glance, the problem is a bit more complicated. There are a number of intervening factors that can lessen the impact of bequests on the degree of inequality. These factors include:

A. *Regression to the mean in skills*: High-wealth parents are likely to be above average with respect to skills. The regression to the mean principle implies that their offspring are unlikely to be as talented. The offspring's lower earning ability may offset the impact of the inheritance on inequality. In that sense, the bequest might be thought of as insurance for less capable offspring.

B. *Labor-supply behavior*: Accumulating a large sum of wealth in order to bequeath it to the offspring may have motivated a high level of parental labor supply. However, some heirs might be attracted to the jet-setting lifestyle and live off of their inheritance. In economic terms, the receipt of a bequest is likely to have an income effect that may lead the offspring to reduce their labor supply. Empirically, however, inheritances do not lead to large reductions in labor supply of both men and married women (Joulfarian and Wilhelm 1994).

C. *Consumption and saving behavior*: While the parental generation obviously had a high propensity to save, this trait is not necessarily passed on to the offspring. The offspring may simply look at the inheritance as a windfall leading to wild, irresponsible consumption. The evidence we have is that family consumption does increase after an inheritance, but the effect is rather small (Joulfarian and Wilhelm 1994).

D. *Mating patterns*: The impact of inheritance on the distribution of wealth reflects the mating patterns of the society. If the children of rich parents tend to marry the children of other rich parents (positive assortive mating), then large accumulations of wealth can be maintained or even grow. If the pattern of mating based on the wealth of parents is more random, then a different distribution will result.

E. *Number of children*: Large estates can be dissipated over time if the parents have many children. If richer families tend to have more children than poorer families, this will act as a mitigating factor on inequality in the distribution of wealth.

F. *Inheritance customs*: It is the current custom in the United States for estates to be more or less evenly divided among offspring. Obviously, the division is seldom precise. Black sheep can be disinherited, and the child who provides the parents with the most care during their senior years may sometimes be rewarded. Nevertheless, the evidence implies that wealth is typically evenly distributed among offspring. In foreign countries wealth must be evenly distributed for tax reasons. This custom was not always the case (DeLong 2003; Pestieau 2003). In Europe and colonial America the custom known as primogeniture was common. Under this custom, an estate was passed intact to the eldest son, with the proviso that the eldest son had certain responsibilities toward his siblings. This system made it easier to maintain large accumulations of wealth.

What is the net impact of all these complicating factors? While wealth is highly correlated across generations, most people inherit very little. This suggests that bequests play only a small role in the intergenerational transmission of inequality, although it plays a large role for very wealthy families (Bowles, Gintis, and Groves 2005).

THE "DEATH TAX"

For many years, politicians in the United States have argued over the so-called death tax. There is not now nor has there ever been in the United States a tax officially known as a death tax. There is, however, a tax known as the Unified Estate and Gift Tax, which is what the politicians are referring to, whether they know it or not.

The tax works like this: Within nine months of death, the executor of an estate is required to file a tax return, but only if there is a taxable estate. See Figure 16.6. The executor begins by totaling the decedent's gross estate. The gross estate consists of all decedent's assets, the decedent's share of jointly held assets, all proceeds from life insurance, and all gifts made during life in excess of the gift exemption. Typically assets are valued at market value at date of death, but there are some complicated rules that can be followed if the value of the estate declines after the decedent's death. These need not detain us. An important exception is the case of closely held businesses and farms where the value of assets is set at "use value," which is typically less than market value. This rule can drastically reduce an estate's value.

From that value several subtractions can be made. All bequests to a surviving spouse, all charitable contributions, all payments of debts, administrative and legal fees, funeral expenses, and all payments for state inheritance and estate taxes can be subtracted.

Then the Unified Estate and Gift Tax Credit can be applied. In 2008 the credit was $1.5 million dollars, but rose to $3 million dollars in 2009. Essentially this means that only estates that far exceed $3 million dollars will be subject to any tax.

Once the tax base is determined, a tax rate can be applied. The tax rates currently run from 18 to 55 percent depending on the value of the estate. The 18 percent rate applies to an estate of $10,000 while the high rate would apply to estates whose tax base exceeds $3 million.

The writers of the legislation were well aware that people would attempt to find loopholes in the law. One potential loophole comes about as a result of people who attempt to give their estate away before they die. People are allowed to give away $11,500 tax free each year to as many individuals as they choose. After that, the gifts must be included in the value of the estate. What this suggests is that if you expect to die very rich, you need to start keeping good financial records early on.

Another potential loophole results from people who make bequests to people two or more generations removed. For example, what if grandparents leave part of their estate to their grandchildren, skipping their children? The loophole is that the estate avoids one round of taxation—the taxation that would take place when the estate was transferred to the parents. To avoid this and to preserve the principle that

Figure 16.6 **Computation of the Estate Tax**

> Gross Estate
> –Bequests to Spouse
> –Charitable Contributions
> –Debts, Administrative and Legal Fees, Funeral
> Expenses
> –Credit for State Inheritance and Estate Taxes
> –Unified Estate and Gift Tax Credit
> Taxable Estate
> * tax rate
> Tax

estates should be taxed once per generation, Congress has created what is called the generation-skipping tax. The purpose of this complicated tax is to capture the revenue that would be lost. As currently instituted, the tax does not completely capture the lost revenue, but it is the thought that counts.

What impact does the inheritance tax have on incentives, specifically the incentive to save and accumulate wealth? The typical critic of the inheritance tax will argue that if people are not allowed to distribute their wealth as they see fit, they will not bother to accumulate it in the first place. This implies both less work and less saving on their part. This not only reduces what the decedent accumulates and what the heirs receive, but also potentially has a negative impact on the rest of society. The work the inheritance tax–beleaguered individuals did not do in their lifetime may have allowed them to build a better mousetrap or find a cure for cancer; and the saving not done could have created jobs or led to higher wages.

It turns out that at the theoretical level, things are not that simple. The impact of an inheritance tax ultimately depends on why people choose to accumulate wealth in the first place (Gale and Slemrod 2001).

- One possible reason for bequests is that people simply die before they "plan" to and the bequest is the wealth they did not have a chance to consume. In that instance, since the donor never had any intention of making a bequest in the first place, the inheritance tax is not taken into account in the making of work, saving, and investment decisions.

- Another approach is to look at the promise of bequests as a way for the donor to induce certain types of behavior on the part of potential recipients. A very cold example is that it is a way for Mom and Dad to get their children to visit them in the nursing home. In other words, a bequest is a payment for services rendered. In that case, the inheritance tax is much like an excise tax on the donor. If the demand for services on the part of donors is highly elastic, an inheritance tax will greatly reduce the quantity demanded of services and that will negatively impact the donors' willingness to work, save, and invest. Unfortunately, the problem can get much more complicated. We also need to consider elasticity of supply and strategies employed by both donor and recipient to manipulate the size of the bequest (Bernheim, Shleifer, and Summers 1985). These more complicated situations are not yet well understood (Gale and Slemrod 2001, 35).

- When altruism is the motive, there is a potential positive externality situation. The donor is considered altruistic because he or she gets utility from the recipient's utility. The donor must trade off the reduced utility from his or her own reductions in consumption against the utility received from the recipient's happiness. However, what is important from the standpoint of society is not just the net effect on the donor's utility, but also the utility the recipient gets. In other words, since donors do not take into account the recipient's utility (they only take into account the utility they get from the recipient's utility—a crucial distinction), they are likely to provide too small a bequest. A clear implication is that bequests should be subsidized, not taxed. But this conclusion is further complicated by the so-called Samaritan's dilemma. If the recipient knows that the donor will behave altruistically toward him or her, the recipient has an incentive to act in a way to increase the likely bequest (Bruce and Waldman 1990). For example, the recipient may not work, save, or invest in order to nudge the donor to provide an even more generous bequest.
- Still another possible bequest motive is "the joy of giving" on the part of the donor. The donor gets utility simply as a result of providing a transfer. Here the donor trades off the loss of his or her utility from a reduction of consumption against the utility received from giving. But, as in the altruism model, the donor ignores the recipient's utility and hence is likely to transfer too little wealth.[13]

To most people, the equity issue trumps the efficiency issue. Call it the Paris Hilton effect (even though this issue predated Paris by several centuries). Why should some people be given a leg up in life just because they happened to be born lucky? No one doubts that the mere existence of a Paris Hilton strongly strengthens the case for near confiscatory estate taxation, but there are other considerations. One that has already been alluded to is that empirically inheritance does not play a very large role in maintaining wealth inequality. Presumably the factors listed in the section on the role of bequests in wealth inequality play a role here. Since the wealth tax is relatively expensive to collect, a major expansion might actually serve to shrink the pie. The second consideration has already been introduced with the story of Al and Mary from the beginning of this chapter. Why shouldn't hard-working, thrifty people be allowed to dispose of their wealth as they see fit?

CONCLUSION

The distribution of wealth is a remarkable and complicated issue in its own right. Interestingly enough, despite the fact that stories of family dynasties have been a colorful part of our society for a long time, bequests may be overrated as an element contributing to the intergenerational transmission of inequality. The reason is that there are simply too few people receiving sizable inheritances. Over the period 1960–95 only between 2 and 4 percent of estates were large enough to be subject to the inheritance tax (Mulligan 1997). "Even though this figure leaves out quite substantial inheritances as well as transfers that occur during life, it seems unlikely that for most of the population a substantial degree of economic status is transmitted directly by the intergenerational transfer of property or financial wealth" (Bowles, Gintis, and Groves 2005, 18–19).

QUESTIONS FOR REVIEW AND PRACTICE

1. How does the degree of parental altruism affect the composition of the bequest given to their children?
2. What is the relationship between imperfect capital mobility and the accumulation of large personal fortunes?
3. What conditions would be required for bequests to add to wealth inequality? What is the likelihood those conditions will occur simultaneously?
4. Should the United States tax inheritances?

NOTES

1. These forms of income were approximately 23 percent of adjusted gross income in 2004 in the United States (Internal Revenue Service 2007).

2. It made Archie Bunker's or Roseanne's homes look palatial.

3. For the lower estimate see Franco Modigliani (1988). For the higher estimate see Laurence J. Kotlikoff (1988).

4. From time to time *Forbes Magazine* also publishes other breakdowns of wealthy individuals, for example, the wealthiest individuals in the world.

5. We need to be careful here. Few of them were dirt-poor as children. Most grew up in very comfortable circumstances. But the wealth they ended up with far exceeded the wealth of their parents. A good example of this is Warren Buffett. While his parents were quite well-to-do, Warren had himself removed from the will because he was doing so well on his own. The family wealth was eventually inherited by his sister Doris, who is an active philanthropist in her own right.

6. None of these is a true "rags-to-riches" story. Bill Gates, for example, came from a fairly affluent family who could afford to send him to Harvard University (from which he dropped out after a year), but his family was not worth $48 billion, $1 billion, or even $50 million. Besides, as of this writing, his parents are still alive. Bill created well over $47.9 billion on his own.

7. The following discussion is based on Lester Thurow (1972: 129–54).

8. The assumption that constant profits would be earned until the end of time is just for the purpose of simplifying the math.

9. This discussion is also based on Lester Thurow (1972: 142–54). Thurow, however, uses the wrong name for the theory. He calls the theory the random walk. While the random walk and efficient markets hypothesis are often discussed in tandem, there is an important distinction between the two (Landsburg 1993, 188–196).

10. Remember we are talking here about consumption. Many of the expenditures that might first come to mind, like mansions and great art and Ivy League educations, are more properly classified as investment.

11. The source of the net worth data is the Federal Reserve System's triennial Survey of Consumer Finances (SCF). The SCF's collection of asset data is actually quite extensive. It includes the respondent's primary residence and other real estate holdings; net equity position in closely held businesses; value of all types of vehicles; miscellaneous nonfinancial assets such as antiques and artwork; and all types of financial assets, including bank accounts, stocks, bonds, mutual funds, retirement accounts like

IRAs and 401(k)s, cash value of life insurance, annuities, trusts, and managed investment accounts; and the value of miscellaneous financial assets such as futures contracts, oil leases, and royalties. There is also data on a rich menu of liabilities, including mortgages, installment loans, credit card debt, pension loans, and other debts.

12. That people with higher incomes are more likely to save is suggested by the following thought experiment. Who is likely to have a higher rate of time preference, a person with a low income or someone with a high income? Recall that the rate of time preference measures the reward people require for abstaining from consuming today. Presumably if today's level of consumption is high, additional consumption is unlikely to be very valuable, which suggests a low rate of time preference. This leads to more saving and less consumption on the part of the already rich.

13. We will not discuss the distinction between altruism and joy of giving models. If you must know, the latter model allows for equilibria with lower total consumption. The utility the donor receives from simply giving could offset lowered consumption for both the donor and recipient. The former type of model never allows for lower consumption because utility in such a model is only a function of the donor's and recipient's consumption (Gale and Slemrod 2001, 36).

PART V

FINAL THOUGHTS

17 Equalizing and Enlarging the Slices

INTRODUCTION

In a provocative article, Gary Becker, the 1992 recipient of the Nobel Prize in Economics, and Kevin Murphy, the 1997 recipient of the John Bates Clark Medal,[1] discuss the "upside" of the recent increase in income inequality (Becker and Murphy 2007). They argue that the rise in inequality largely reflects increased demand for educated and highly skilled labor resulting from technological advances and globalization. In short, there has been an increase in the rate of return to human capital investment. Nothing new here. Further, they go on to say that the increase in inequality will ultimately be good for us. Why? An increase in the rate of return to human capital, like an increase in the rate of return to physical capital, represents greater productivity in the economy. In short, the pie will get larger.

Nevertheless, the rise in inequality is problematic. The "normal" working of the market should lead to greater investment in human capital, a reduction in the returns to education and, eventually, a decrease in inequality. This "normal" response does not, however, appear to be taking place. The expected increase in educational attainment appears to be stalled. There has not been a significant decrease in the proportion of students who drop out of high school, nor has there been a significant increase in the proportion of high school graduates who go on the college or college students who complete their degrees (Becker and Murphy 2007, 5). What is standing in the way of the "normal" working of the market? According to Becker and Murphy, "The answers to these and related questions lie partly in the breakdown of the American family, and the resulting low skill levels acquired by many children in elementary and secondary school—particularly individuals from broken households" (Becker and Murphy 2007, 5).

As we have seen, the causes of inequality and poverty are many and varied. What the preceding analysis suggests, however, is that policies to equalize and enlarge the slices likely to have the greatest payoff are those that focus on how we nurture our children. Saying that, however, hardly simplifies the problem. Bringing up children right is a complicated and vexing problem. It also takes a village. There are many things to keep our eye on and they interact with each other in unpredictable ways.

What To Do

Will all those opposed to strengthening education please raise their hands? Everybody is in favor of stronger education, and, of course, everyone is right. We cannot have too much high-quality education. The sticking point lies in the question of which specific policies should be used to improve education.

What we apparently know is this:

- The United States spends more per pupil than almost every other country that might be considered similar to us in level of development, yet the test scores of American students only put them in the middle of the pack internationally (Rosen and Gayer 2008, 140).
- No clear evidence of a positive relationship between educational spending and student test scores has arisen from the voluminous studies of the issue (Hanushek 2002).
- Noncognitive skills play a surprisingly large role and cognitive skills play a surprisingly small role in explaining both educational and subsequent economic success (Carneiro and Heckman 2003).
- "Cognitive and noncognitive deficits emerge early, before schooling, and if uncorrected, create low-skilled adults" (Carneiro and Heckman 2003, 205).

What this suggests is that simply throwing money at the problem is not likely to be very effective. Rather, policy should be targeted at the very young (including preschoolers), and should emphasize the development of noncognitive skills. What it also suggests is that the policies should not so much target the schools as the families that are sending their kids to school.

Are there any templates we can follow? There are a couple of examples of early intervention programs that are suggestive of positive results from this approach:

1. Perry Preschool Program: The Perry preschool program took disadvantaged children with below-normal IQs in Ypsilanti, Michigan, and divided them into control and treatment groups. The treatment group received weekly home visits and intensive, high-quality preschool services (including the teaching of parenting skills) for 1–2 years. By their late twenties, the children of the treatment group had higher earnings and less criminal behavior than the control group children (Carneiro and Heckman 2003, 164–169, 171).
2. Syracuse Preschool Program: This program provided family development support for disadvantaged children from prenatal care through age five, weekly home visits for the family, and year-round day care. The result was that girls in the treatment group had better school achievement and were less likely to get involved in criminal activities. Boys, unfortunately, did not fare so well (Carneiro and Heckman 2003, 164–169).
3. Head Start: It is widely believed that the Head Start program has been quite successful in serving its clients. The evidence, however, is not crystal-clear on Head Start's effectiveness (Carneiro and Heckman 2003, 169–170).

There are a number of programs that are designed to provide intervention during the adolescent years. One example is the ubiquitous Big Brothers/Big Sisters program in which an adult is paired with an adolescent from a broken family. The adult is supposed to provide mentoring and serve as an appropriate role model for the child. A second example is Philadelphia's Futures' Sponsor-a-Scholar program, which provides mentoring and some financial support to help students make it to college. Both these program have demonstrated some success (Carneiro and Heckman 2003, 175–78). Children in Big Brothers/Big Sisters have obtained better grades, have had a better relationship with their parents, and have exhibited less antisocial behavior. The Sponsor-a-Scholar children had better grades and increased college attendance. However, these beneficial effects were only shown for students who were still in school. High school dropouts were hardly affected.

The policies that receive the most attention include raising school quality (by reducing class sizes and improving teacher quality), school choice, and more adequate provision of public and private job training. What is often passed over is the fact that these policies are far from smashing successes. Reducing class size does have a positive impact on test scores, but the impact is small and test scores have a small impact on earnings (Carneiro and Heckman 2003, 156–159). Policies to reduce class size are unlikely to pass a cost-benefit test. While we have substantial evidence that the quality of teachers matters, we have no reliable way of predicting who will be a good teacher. Conservatives are big supporters of school choice programs, and, while there is some evidence of better school outcomes from increased competition, it is far from definitive (Carneiro and Heckman 2003, 159–163). The underwhelming record of job training programs was discussed in Chapter 13.

Here we run into an enormous roadblock. So much of the success of students in school is predicated on what happens at home, and, unless society wants to put tight curbs on who can have children and who cannot and regulate child-rearing practices, there is only so much we can do about it. The philosophical approach known as "luck egalitarianism" may be relevant here. Luck egalitarianism takes the view "that inequalities resulting from responsible choices are just, while those due to factors beyond people's control are not"(Swift 2005).

From the standpoint of parents and kids, the essential issues are these: Parents can benefit their children in two ways. Parents can share their resources with their children, for example by paying their tuition to a top college or providing a trust fund. Parents also share with their children their genes, personalities, identity, and preferences. The former "gifts" are more along the lines of luck, and, in principle, society could employ policies that neutralize their impact. The latter represent responsible choices. Not only would it be impractical to prevent their sharing, but it is likely farther than we want to go.

THE DOWNSIDE OF INEQUALITY AND THE TAX ANGLE

Although educational bottlenecks are problematic, Becker and Murphy still see an upside to rising inequality to the extent that it encourages greater human capital investment and, ultimately, faster economic growth. Because of this, they would counsel strongly against "soak the rich" tax schemes because higher taxes would reduce the incentive to acquire human capital.

Others are not so reluctant to use taxes as a club against the rich. In some cases, the rationale would appear to be little more than envy or the sneaking suspicion that the rich obtained their advantages illegitimately. Regarding the latter point, we have Balzac's injunction, "Behind every great fortune, there is a crime."[2] An argument of more recent vintage is that rising inequality is ultimately unsatisfying to the rich and harmful to the middle class, and increasing taxes may be the simplest way to extract ourselves from a damaging "positional arms race" (Frank 2007b).

It has been an axiom of economics that "more is better." The more goods and services we consume, the happier we are likely to be. However, a substantial amount of psychological research, a limited amount of economic research, and simple introspection suggests there are some goods where the happiness derived depends less on the absolute amount consumed and more on the amount consumed relative to everyone else. These are called positional (or context-sensitive) goods (Frank 2007b, 2). Consider the hypothetical case of housing (Robert H. Frank 2007b, 2). Would you rather live in a 3,000-square-foot house or a 4,000-square-foot house? Most people would answer 4,000 square feet, contemplating what they could do with all the extra space. Now let us add some context. The 4,000-square-feet answer makes perfect sense based on the world we live in where most houses are much smaller than 4,000 square feet (and probably smaller than 3,000 square feet). What if the choices you faced were as follows: One choice is that you could live in a 3,000-square-foot house in a world where the typical house was 2,000 square feet. The second choice is you could live in a 4,000-square-foot house in a world of 6,000 square feet houses. Opting for the second world over the first would consign you to a world in which your house no longer "kept up with the Joneses." Regardless of what you would choose, this example demonstrates that context is influential in determining the utility obtained from a particular purchase. It is probably easy to think of other instances, for example, with respect to clothing, cars, yachts, and vacations.

The problem with positional goods is that positional arms races are almost inevitable. If utility depends on relative position, and if everyone is trying to improve their relative position, then a likely end result is that no one will. In fact, the end result is that everyone will end up worse off. Not only have they not improved their relative position, but the effort required to participate in the "arms race" might be substantial. In the case of houses, buying and maintaining a bigger house may require longer hours on the job, commuting, doing more housework, and greater indebtedness.

In the case of the United States, the lion's share of recent economic growth has gone to the super-rich. This has set off an orgy of extravagant spending among that group (Frank 2007).[3] While the middle class tends not to compare themselves directly with the super-rich, the middle class has been caught in the rip tide. Extravagance by the super-rich is noted by families one notch down on the income scale, and they have to increase their spending to "maintain appearances." As these one-notch-down families spend more, families at the second notch down follow suit. Soon enough, the ripple sucks in the middle class. The consequence is families increasingly stressed by work, commuting, debt, and lack of sleep, along with deteriorating public services, and no one is much happier even though they own an abundance of "stuff" (Frank 2007b, 78–86).

In this instance, more progressive income taxes or instituting a consumption tax may serve to ameliorate the situation. Reducing the ability and desire on the part of the super-rich for a really extravagant lifestyle should lower stress levels throughout the income distribution. The tax revenue raised could be used to improve the schools, extend health insurance to all, and restore our crumbling infrastructure, among other things. And we could all be happy in our 2,500-square-foot houses.

WHAT NOT TO DO

Some commentators argue that a high degree of inequality is inevitable under free market capitalism, not because it is necessary to provide needed incentives, but rather because it serves the purpose of dividing the "working class" (Gordon 1982). Workers who are on different rungs of the job hierarchy are less likely to perceive their common interests and more likely to support a system that promises some prospect of modest upward mobility. This makes them less likely to band together to rise up and overthrow their capitalist oppressors. Consequently, policies that work on labor supply are only going to have modest ameliorative effects.

The judgment of history, as of this writing at least, seems to be that free-market capitalistic systems grow richer faster, and that economic growth tends to facilitate democracy, tolerance, and equality (Friedman 2005).

Even among those who do not subscribe to such radical views, there appears to be widespread belief that the economic system will always need low-wage workers to perform various and sundry low-skill and menial tasks. As a description of the way the economic system works, that is not quite accurate. What is more accurate is that employers need low-cost employees. The cost of an employee depends not only on the wage received, but also the productivity of that employee. Employee A with a wage of $20 per hour and a productivity of 100 widgets an hour costs just as much as employee B with a wage of $10 per hour and a productivity of 50 widgets per hour. Both produce a widget for 20 cents.[4]

Individual workers and the economy as a whole will benefit from any policy that raises their human capital and productivity. Employers will simply redesign jobs to take advantage of the skills being offered in the market.

Using government power to fix wages and restructure jobs is generally not the thing to do. Economic growth requires a relatively unfettered marketplace. Interventions should be primarily on the supply side.

"FAR-OUT" POLICIES

If you do not like the ideas presented thus far in this chapter, consider the following from all over the ideological spectrum. Hopefully these will make the previous ideas more palatable.

ENTREATIES

One of my colleagues at the University of Mary Washington maintains a blog (Web-liminalblog; http://cherrycoated.com/wordpress/index.php). A posting on January 4, 2005, raised an interesting issue.

> The *New York Review of Books: Inside the Leviathan* is a good article detailing many of the costs we all incur through the existence of Wal-Mart and their practices.
> Here are two quotes:

> "One of the most telling of all criticisms of Wal-Mart is to be found in a February 2004 report by the Democratic Staff of the House Education and Workforce Committee. In analyzing Wal-Mart's success in holding employee compensation at low levels, the report assesses the costs to US taxpayers of employees who are so badly paid that they qualify for government assistance even under the less generous rules of the federal welfare system. For a two-hundred-employee Wal-Mart store, the government is spending $108,000 a year for children's health care; $125,000 a year in tax credits and deductions for low-income families; and $42,000 a year in housing assistance. The report estimates that a two-hundred-employee Wal-Mart store costs federal taxpayers $420,000 a year, or about $2,103 per Wal-Mart employee. That translates into a total annual welfare bill of $2.5 billion for Wal-Mart's 1.2 million US employees."

> "The exploitation of the working poor is now central to the business strategy favored by America's most powerful and, by some criteria, most successful corporation. With the re-election of a president as enamored of corporate power as George W. Bush, there is every prospect that this strategy and its harsh practices will continue to spread throughout the economy."

> Another reminder that we shouldn't shop at Wal-mart (I did once about 2 years ago, but haven't since) and why we should discourage our friends from shopping at Wal-Mart.

> *Posted by ernie at 07:09 PM* (Ackermann 2005)

As of this writing, Wal-Mart is the largest American corporation. It offers one-stop shopping. Wal-Mart sells virtually everything you would ever want to buy from food to clothing to computers to music to books to toys to furniture, and so on. Everyone reading this has been there. You know what Wal-Mart is all about. Wal-Mart advertises its low prices, and, on the basis of casual empiricism,[5] its advertising seems fundamentally accurate in that regard.

To produce its product, Wal-Mart employs a huge workforce, most of whom work at jobs such as salesperson, cashier, stocker, and warehouse operative that require only modest amounts of skill.[6] In the United States, Wal-Mart's employees are not unionized. By any standard, many Wal-Mart employees receive only modest wages and benefits.

Like any large corporation, Wal-Mart has become a lightning rod for criticism. One criticism, already mentioned, is Wal-Mart's wage and benefits policies. Some people believe Wal-Mart's wages and benefits are just too low. Wal-Mart has vigorously defended itself in a series of national television ads that stress employee satisfaction with the way they are treated. And Wal-Mart always seems to be able to hire an adequate workforce. But this is an issue that will never go away. The government report cited in Ernie's blog claims that many Wal-Mart employees are eligible for and draw a variety of government welfare benefits. A related criticism is that since Wal-Mart is such a large employer, its wage and benefit policies become the de facto standard in the local labor market. In other words, everyone ends up paying Wal-Mart's inadequate compensation. There have been communities that have rejected Wal-Mart for that reason. Why firms hiring similarly skilled labor to the type Wal-Mart hires would provide better compensation in the absence of Wal-Mart is not entirely clear.

What Ernie thinks is that people should not patronize Wal-Mart. Presumably under the pressure of falling sales, Wal-Mart will respond by raising wages and benefits as a public relations gesture, if not as an act of contrition.

Ernie is concerned about what Wal-Mart's compensation policies cost society in terms of government expenditures. What is not discussed is what the cost to society would be if Wal-Mart were to raise compensation. If Wal-Mart increased compensation, presumably its costs of production would rise and that would inevitably lead to higher prices, to the detriment of many people of modest income who shop at Wal-Mart precisely because prices are so low. Quite possibly Ernie has the following notion in mind: Perhaps Wal-Mart could raise compensation but would not have to raise prices because the rich people who own Wal-Mart would just accept lower profits. Maybe, but Wal-Mart is not a closely held corporation. Its stock is held by millions of people either directly or as part of 401(k) or other pension systems. Many of these stockholders are of modest means. A lowering of stock values would negatively affect them. The point is that there is no free lunch. Worker compensation cannot be raised without affecting many, many people, most of whom are individuals of fairly modest means.

Of course, if Ernie really wanted to do something for the poor folks at Wal-Mart he could go to the store and pass out cash to any employee he met. But of course that would mean he would have less to spend elsewhere. Alleviating poverty is an important social goal, but one that will not be achieved by such simplistic means as boycotting one of the nation's largest employers.

TRY ECONOMIC FREEDOM

A relentless blogger and chair of the George Mason University Department of Economics, Don Boudreaux, posted the following on January 28, 2005.

> Former Senator John Edwards "is planning to set up a center to study ways to alleviate poverty"—so reports the Washington Post's E.J. Dionne.
>
> My first reaction is: Don't need it. We already know how to alleviate poverty: achieve economic freedom.
>
> My second reaction is: At least in the United States, we have not only alleviated poverty— Would even Edwards insist that America's poor are today no better off than they were 100 or even 50 years ago?—we have *eliminated* poverty.
>
> I stand by both of my reactions. But I know that the second one is especially controver-

sial. We have indeed eliminated poverty in the United States. By historical standards, no one—not a single person in our civilization—lives in poverty. (I suspect there are a handful of people who voluntarily live like hermits in the wilderness of places such as Montana or North Carolina's mountains. These people might well live in deep material poverty, but they live this way by choice—by choosing to remove themselves from our commercial civilization.)

The typical reaction I get when I insist that poverty is eliminated in the U.S. is this: "How can you say that?! Many Americans are homeless, having to bed-down in shelters. Many Americans have no health insurance. Many Americans go to bed hungry? Many Americans are without jobs."

I respond by pointing out that, unlike people living in absolute poverty, no American starves to death; almost all Americans without homes of their own have ready access to homeless shelters and to soup kitchens; lack of health insurance is not the same thing as lack of health care—and much health care is readily affordable even with a shred of insurance; and losing a job in America doesn't mean starvation and death.

"Of course," comes the retort, "but surely you, Boudreaux, don't mean to say that people who eat in soup kitchens and sleep in homeless shelters aren't living in poverty?!"

I reply that, yes, such people do live in poverty *by the standards of our astonishingly wealthy society.* And I agree that these standards are appropriate. What was middle-class comfort in 1905 might well be poverty by the standards of 2005.

But (I continue) it's important to recognize that in the U.S., Canada, Western Europe, and many other countries that are well-integrated into the global market economy, absolute poverty *is* eliminated. And more to the point, if we agree that the relevant standard for poverty is a *relative* one, then barring complete equality of material standards of living, some people living below the median will be classifiable as living in poverty. This classification will arise no matter how materially affluent these 'poor' people are in any absolute sense.

So any center for the study of ways to alleviate poverty in the United States, if it does its job seriously, will either push for as much income equality as possible, or attempt that which is impossible by definition—the elimination of relative poverty.

Again, if poverty is defined as a relative concept—as it must be defined in America today by those who wish to do battle against domestic poverty—then there is no solution, no alleviation or elimination of poverty, short of bringing about total income equality.

Put differently, if we define the poor as those who live, say, in the bottom quintile of the income distribution, then the poor will indeed always be with us—and centers such as the one planned by John Edwards will always have a 'problem' to 'solve' even as the real curse that such institutions *appear* to address—material deprivation—shrinks into an ever-more-distant memory (Boudreaux 2005).

So how about the "try economic freedom" idea? What Boudreaux and others of his ilk have in mind is a drastic retrenchment of government. Government should spend, tax, borrow, and regulate less. Let the market allocate and reward labor and capital. Such a system would grow more rapidly. The poverty problem would disappear as the pie got larger (in fact, we have already eliminated poverty so this is a nonissue). Might such a system generate a significant degree of inequality? Maybe yes, maybe no, but the central point is that the degree of inequality is also a nonissue. We probably need inequality to generate appropriate incentives for productive activity. As long as everyone has a big enough slice of the pie, the relative sizes do not matter.

What is problematic about this approach is the implicit assumption that all members of every generation are able to begin the race at the same starting line—that the intergenerational elasticity is 0. But it is not 0, and inequalities arising during one generation will work to the detriment/advantage of the offspring of the poor/rich. Admittedly this would not go on forever, but with an intergenerational elasticity of 0.4, it could take as long as four generations for inequalities to be corrected. Why should any member of the newest generation have to suffer any disadvantage at the starting line? Fighting relative poverty would seem an appropriate task in any society, regardless of the material standard of living the society has been able to achieve.

UNIVERSAL BASIC INCOME (UBI)

While our government has never used a program exactly like the "straight transfers" (review Chapter 7), there have been no shortage of proposals for the enactment of such a program. The most recent is Philippe Van Parijs's Universal Basic Income (UBI) program.[7] "By universal basic income, I mean an income paid by a government, at a uniform level and at regular intervals, to each adult member of society. The grant is paid, and its level is fixed, irrespective of whether the person is rich or poor, lives alone or with others, is willing to work or not" (Van Parijs 2001, 5).

Everybody from Bill Gates on down would receive a monthly check. In Van Parijs's formulation, the UBI would be set at a relatively generous level enabling everyone to at least live at a subsistence level without doing a lick of work.

Van Parijs justifies UBI by arguing that it is just and will help generate jobs and growth.[8] While everyone receives a UBI monthly check (most people would continue to earn the bulk of their income from work; the UBI check would only cover a basic standard of living), the money to fund the program would come from progressive taxes. The rich would pay more in taxes than they receive in benefits while the opposite would be true for the poor. The end result is that under UBI, money ends up being taken from the rich and given to the poor. What makes this just? Van Parijs believes the high incomes of the rich are essentially unjustified because they are, for the most part, a matter of luck. "Our race, gender, and citizenship, how educated and wealthy we are, how gifted in math and how fluent in English, how handsome and even how ambitious, are overwhelmingly a function of who our parents happened to be and of other equally arbitrary contingencies. Not even the most narcissistic self-made man could think that he fixed the parental dice in advance of entering this world" (Van Parijs 2001, 25). Consequently, taking from the rich is morally acceptable. Likewise, the low incomes of the poor are essentially the result of their lack of luck. so giving to the poor is also morally acceptable. Redistribution to the poor would allow them to enjoy what everyone else already has, namely, *real freedom*, which basically means not only having the right to do what you want, but the resources to make it happen. Since real freedom is a good thing, this method of achieving it is also good (Van Parijs 2001, 14).

Van Parijs also argues that UBI would contribute to jobs and growth. Employers could offer lower wages to recruit labor, while labor would not have to demand as high a wage to take a job. Workers would not be forced to take dirty, demeaning jobs, so the overall quality of jobs offered would improve, making work more attractive. Without the pressure to find work fast, unemployed workers could use their idle time to develop new skills that would make them more productive when they returned to the workforce (Van Parijs 2001, 15–19).

The indifference curve analysis of straight transfers in Chapter 7 predicted that such a program could lead to reductions in labor supply. Van Parijs's response is "So what?" (Van Parijs 2001, 23). Working is overrated. "Boosting the labor supply is no aim in itself. No one can reasonably want an overworked, hyperactive society" (Van Parijs 2001, 23). Besides, he doubts that there will be major reductions in labor supply. For one thing, UBI only allows a subsistence standard of living. To rise above that level, people would have to work, and would not forfeit any UBI by doing so. Another thing that Van Parijs believes is that people have a natural need to work. "Everything we know suggests that nearly all people seek to make some contribution" (Van Parijs 2001, 25).

Would UBI be affordable? Assume $9,500 is the annual subsistence level of income for an individual.[9] With a population of approximately 300 million,[10] that works out to approximately $2.8 trillion dollars per year! By way of comparison, total federal government outlays were $2.3 trillion in 2004. Of course, if we used UBI this way, many existing federal outlays could be eliminated or reduced. For example, transfers such as Social Security, welfare, and unemployment benefits would likely be reduced. We might also have less expenditure for prisons and hospitals. Any way you cut it, UBI would not be cheap.

CONCLUSION

So ends this survey of policies to deal with inequality and so ends this book. As promised in Chapter 1, there is a great deal of controversy in this field because there is a great deal of uncertainty and much is at stake. The issue is nothing less than how we are able to look ourselves in the mirror and how we rate the society we inhabit and the one we will bequeath to our children. Have we done all that could be done about the biggest problem of this age and any age?

QUESTIONS FOR REVIEW AND PRACTICE

1. Compare Becker and Murphy to Frank. Where do you stand on the issue of increased taxes on the rich?
2. Is it morally objectionable for corporations to pay the market wage for employees if the market wage does not provide a "decent" standard of living?
3. In the 1960s President Lyndon Johnson declared a War on Poverty. Has the war been won?
4. How convincing is Van Parijs on the UBI?
5. Is it appropriate for a highly affluent society to create policies to fight relative poverty?

NOTES

1. The John Bates Clark Medal is presented every two years by the American Economic Association to the most outstanding economist under the age of forty. It is very prestigious.

2. Actually the English version of the quotation has been modified a bit. The exact quote from French reads, "*Le secret des grandes fortunes sans cause apparente est un crime oubilie, parce qu'il a ete proprement fait*" (Balzac 1991). A literal translation is "The secret of great fortunes without apparent cause is a forgotten crime because it has been neatly done." The translation is from Professor Scott Powers of the University of Mary Washington.

3. To be fair, it has also made possible some innovative philanthropy (Frank 2007, 157–179).

4. The math is cost per widget = hourly wage/hourly productivity.

5. I have shopped there plenty of times, although I am not a regular.

6. For a jaundiced-eye view of what working at Wal-Mart is like, see Barbara Ehrenreich (2001).

7. Van Parijs traces the UBI idea back a century and a half to Charles Fourier, an early eighteenth-century French utopian socialist (Van Parijs 2001, 6). The most recent heyday for UBI-like proposals was the 1960s. The most noted proposals were the similar "negative income tax" programs put forth by the very liberal economist James Tobin and the very conservative economist Milton Friedman (Friedman 1962; Tobin 1968). Also of interest was the guaranteed annual income plan of Robert Theobald (1965).

8. A third argument advanced in support of his program is that UBI appropriately addresses "feminist" and "green" concerns, but this is of lesser interest and will not be discussed here (Van Parijs 2001, 19–21).

9. This number is not simply drawn from thin air. It is the "official" United States poverty threshold for a single individual. See Chapter 12 for a more complete discussion of the poverty threshold.

10. See www.census.gov for an up-to-date estimate of the U.S. population.

Bibliography

Aaberge, Rolf, Anders Björklund, Markus Jäntti, Mårten Palme, Peder J. Pedersen, and Nina Smith. 1996. "Income Inequality and Income Mobility in the Scandinavian Countries Compared to the United States." Discussion Papers 168, Research Department of Statistics, Norway.

Acemoglu, Daron. 2002. "Technological Change, Inequality and the Labor Market." *Journal of Economic Literature* 40(1):7–72.

Ackermann, Ernest C. 2005. "What Wal-Mart Costs Us." WebliminalBlog. http://cherrycoated.com/wordpress/2005/01/04/what-wal-mart-costs-us/ (accessed 28 June 2008).

Adams, Scott and David Neumark. 2005. "A Decade of Living Wages: What Have We Learned?" *California Economic Policy* 1(3):1–23.

American Medical Association. 2007. AMA Homepage. http://www.ama-assn.org/ (accessed 1 August 2007).

Anderson, Donna M. and Michael J. Haupert. 1999. "Employment and Statistical Discrimination: A Hands-On Experiment." *The Journal of Economics* 25(1):85–102.

Anderson, Sarah, John Cavanagh, Chuck Collins, Sam Pizzigati, and Mike Lapham. 2007. *Executive Excess 2007: The Staggering Social Cost of U.S. Business Leadership.* Institute for Policy Studies and United for a Fair Economy. http://www.faireconomy.org/files/ExecutiveExcess2007.pdf (accessed 25 June 2008).

Andreoni, James. 1995. "Warm-Glow Versus Cold-Pickle: The Effects of Positive and Negative Framing on Cooperation in Experiments." *Quarterly Journal of Economics* 110(1):1–21.

Andrews, Margaret, Linda Scott Kantor, Mark Lin, and David Ripplinger. 2001. "Using USDA's Thrifty Food Plan to Assess Food Availability and Affordability." *Food Access* 24(2):45–53.

Anheier, Helmut K. 2005. *Nonprofit Organizations: Theory, Management, Policy.* New York: Routledge.

Arrow, Kenneth J. 1972. "Models of Job Discrimination." In *Racial Discrimination in Economic Life*, ed. A. H. Pascal, 83–102. Lexington, MA: D.C. Heath.

Arrow, Kenneth J. and Gerald Debreu. 1954. "The Existence of an Equilibrium for a Competitive Economy." *Econometrica* 22:265–90.

Autor, David H., Lawrence F. Katz, and Alan B. Krueger. 1998. "Computing Inequality: Have Computers Changed the Labor Market?" *Quarterly Journal of Economics* 113(4):1169–1213.

Averett, Susan L. and Sanders Korenman. 1996. "The Economic Reality of the Beauty Myth." *Journal of Human Resources* 31(2):37–49.

Badgett, M. V. Lee. 1995. "The Wage Effects of Sexual Orientation Discrimination." *Industrial and Labor Relations Review* 48(4):726–739.

Ball, Sheryl B. and Catherine C. Eckel. 1996. "Buying Status: Experimental Evidence on Status in Negotiation." *Psychology and Marketing* 13(4):381–405.

Ball, Sheryl B. and Catherine C. Eckel. 1998. "Stars Upon Thars: Status and Discrimination in Ultimatum Games." Working paper.

Balzac, Honore de. 1991. *Pere Goriot.* New York: Knopf.

Banfield, Edward C. 1974. *The Unheavenly City Revisited.* Boston: Little, Brown and Company.

Bardham, Pranab, Samuel Bowles, and Herbert Gintis. 2000. "Wealth Inequality, Credit Constraints, and Economic Performance." In *Handbook of Income Distribution*, ed. Anthony Atkinson and Francois Bourguignon, 541–604. Dortrecht: North Holland.

Becker, Gary S. 1971. *The Economics of Discrimination.* 2nd ed. Chicago: University of Chicago Press.

———. 1993a. *A Treatise on the Family.* Enlarged edition. Cambridge, MA: Harvard University Press.

———. 1993b. *Human Capital: A Theoretical and Empirical Analysis with Special Reference to Education*, 3rd edition. Chicago: The University of Chicago Press.

———. 1996. *Accounting for Tastes.* Cambridge, MA: Harvard University Press.

Becker, Gary S. and Kevin M. Murphy. 2007. "The Upside of Income Inequality." *The American. com: A Magazine of Ideas.* http://www.american.com/archive/2007/may-june-magazine-contents/the-upside-of-income-inequality.html (accessed May 10, 2007).

Belman, Dale. 1992. "Unions, the Quality of Labor Relations, and Firm Performance." In *Unions and Economic Performance*, ed. Lawrence Mishel and Paula B. Voos, 41–108. Armonk, NY: M.E. Sharpe, Inc.

Bergmann, Barbara. 1971. "The Effects on White Income of Discrimination in Employment." *Journal of Political Economy* 79(2):294–313.

———. 1986. *The Economic Emergence of Women.* New York: Basic Books.

———. 1997. *In Defense of Affirmative Action.* New York: Basic Books.

Bernard, Didem. 2007. "Out-of-Pocket Expenditures on Health Care Among the Nonelderly Population, 2004." *Medical Expenditure Panel Survey, Statistical Brief #159.* Rockville, Md.: Agency for Healthcare Research and Quality.

Bernheim, B. Douglas. 2002. "Taxation and Saving." In *Handbook of Public Economics 3*, ed. Alan J. Auerbach and Martin Feldstein, 1173–1249. Amsterdam: Elsevier.

Bernheim, B. Douglas, Andrei Shleifer, and Lawrence H. Summers. 1985. "The Strategic Bequest Motive." *Journal of Political Economy* 93(December):1045–76.

Bertrand, Marianne and Sendhil Mullainathan. 2004. "Are Emily and Greg More Employable than Lakisha and Jamal? A Field Experiment on Labor Market Discrimination." *American Economic Review* 94(4):991–1013.

Billig, M. and H. Tajfel. 1973. "Social Categorization and Similarity in Intergroup Behaviour." *European Journal of Social Psychology* 3:27–52.

Blank, Rebecca M. 2000. "Distinguished Lecture on Economics in Government: Fighting Poverty: Lessons Learned from Recent U.S. History." *Journal of Economic Perspectives* 14(2):3–19.

———. 2002. "Evaluating Welfare Reform in the United States." *Journal of Economic Literature* 40(4):1105–1166.

Blau, Francine D. and Lawrence M. Kahn. 2007. "Changes in the Labor Supply Behavior of Married Women: 1980–2000." *Journal of Labor Economics* 25(3):393–438.

Blinder, Alan S. 1973. "Wage Discrimination: Reduced Form and Structural Estimates." *The Journal of Human Resources,* 8(4):436–455.

Bluestone, Barry and Stephen Rose. 1997. "Overworked and Underemployed: Unraveling an Economic Enigma." *The American Prospect* (March-April): 58–69.

Borjas, George J. 1999. *Heaven's Door: Immigration Policy and the American Economy.* Princeton: Princeton University Press.

Bouchard, T.J. Jr. and M. McGue. 1981. "Familial Studies in Intelligence." *Science* 212:1055–9.

Boudreaux, Donald. 2005. "Eliminating Poverty." Café Hayek Blog. http://cafehayek.typepad.com/hayek/2005/01/eliminating_pov.html (accessed 3 March 2005).

Bowles, Samuel and Herbert Gintis. 1976. *Schooling in Capitalist America: Educational Reform and the Contradictions of Economic Life.* New York: Basic Books.

———. 2002. "The Inheritance of Inequality." *Journal of Economic Perspectives* 16(3):3–30.

Bowles, Samuel, Herbert Gintis and Melissa Osborne. 2001. "The Determinants of Earnings: A Behavioral Approach." *Journal of Economic Literature* 39(4):1137–1176.

Bowles, Samuel, Herbert Gintis and Melissa Osborne Groves, eds. 2003. "Introduction." In *Unequal Chances: Family Background and Economic Success*, 1–22. Princeton, NJ: Princeton University Press.

Bradbury, Katharine and Jane Katz. 2002. "Women's Labor Market Involvement and Family Income Mobility When Marriages End." *New England Economic Review* (Q4):41–74.

Brenner, Lynn. 2005. "What Did You Do?" *Parade Magazine* (13 March): 4–10.

———. 2008. "How Does Your Salary Stack Up?" *Parade Magazine* (13 April): 6–17.

Brown, Charles, Curtis Gilroy and Andrew Kohen. 1982. "The Effect of the Minimum Wage on Employment and Unemployment." *Journal of Economic Literature* 20(2):487–528.

Bruce, Neil. 2001. *Public Finance and the American Economy.* 2nd ed. New York: Addison Wesley.

Bruce, Neil and Michael Waldman. 1990. "The Rotten Kid Theorem Meets the Samaritan's Dilemma." *Quarterly Journal of Economics* 105(1):155–65.

Bryant, Carleton R. 1992. "GOP Staff Study Finds Liability in Luxury Tax." *The Washington Times*, 24 February 1993, A3.

Bull, Clive, Andrew Schotter, and Keith Weigelt. 1987. "Tournaments and Piece-Rates: An Experimental Study." *Journal of Political Economy* 95(1):1–33.

Burkhauser, Richard V., Douglas Holtz-Eakin, and Stephen Rhody. 1997. "Labor Earnings Mobility and Inequality in the United States and Germany During the 1980s." *International Economic Review* 38(4):775–794.

California Supreme Court. 1971. *Serrano v. Priest,* 5 Cal.3d 584 (Serrano I).

———. 1976. *Serrano v. Priest,* 18 Cal.3d 728 (Serrano II).

———. 1977. *Serrano v. Priest,* 20 Cal.3d 25 (Serrano III).

Caplan, Bryan. 2007. *The Myth of the Rational Voter.* Princeton, NJ: Princeton University Press.

Card, David E. and Alan B. Krueger. 1994. "Minimum Wages and Employment: A Case Study of the Fast-Food Industry in New Jersey and Pennsylvania." *American Economic Review* 84(4):772–93.

———. 1995. *Myth and Measurement: The New Economics of the Minimum Wage.* Princeton, NJ: Princeton University Press.

Carliner, Geoffrey. 1976. "Returns to Education for Blacks, Anglos, and Five Spanish Groups." *Journal of Human Resources* 11(2):172–89.

Carneiro, Pedro and James J. Heckman. 2003. "Human Capital Policy." In *Inequality in America: What Role for Human Capital Policies?* ed. James J. Heckman and Alan B. Krueger, 77–239. Cambridge, MA: The MIT Press.

Carroll, Christopher D. 1998. "Why Do the Rich Save So Much?" Unpublished paper (April 17).

Chang, Roberto. 1994. "Income Inequality and Economic Growth: Evidence and Recent Theories." *Federal Reserve Bank of Atlanta Economic Review* 79(1):1–10 .

Chiswick, Barry R. 1983. "The Earnings and Human Capital of American Jews." *Journal of Human Resources* 18(3):313–336.

Cipriani, Giam Pietro and Angelo Zago. 2007. "Productivity or Discrimination? Beauty and the Exams." Unpublished paper.

Citro, Constance F. and Robert T. Michael. 1995. *Measuring Poverty: A New Approach.* Washington, DC: National Academy Press.

Cleveland, Gordon, Morley Gunderson, and Douglas Hyatt. 2003. "Union Effects in Low-Wage Services: Evidence from Canadian Childcare." *Industrial and Labor Relations Review* 50(2):295–305.

Coate Stephen and Glenn C. Loury. 1993a. "Will Affirmative-Action Policies Eliminate Negative Sterotypes?" *American Economic Review* 83(5):1220–40.

———. 1993b. "Antidiscrimination Enforcement and the Problem of Patronization." *American Economic Review* 83(2):92–98.

Cofer, Eloise, Evelyn Grossman, and Faith Clark. 1962. *Family Food Plans and Food Costs.* USDA Home

Economics Research Report No. 20. Alexandria, VA: Center for Nutrition Policy and Promotion.

Cox, Stan. 2008. "A Wal-Mart Wage Doesn't Go Very Far—Even at Wal-Mart." http://members.cox.net/t.s/walmart.html (accessed 15 May 2008).

Cox, W. Michael and Richard Alm. 1999. *Myths of Rich and Poor: Why We're Better Off Than We Think.* New York: Basic Books.

Dahl, Molly, Tom DeLeire, Ed Harris, and Ralph Smith. 2007. "Response to a Request by Senator Grassley About the Effects of Increasing the Federal Minimum Wage versus Expanding the Earned Income Tax Credit." Unites States Congressional Budget Office Report. 9 January.

Danziger, Sheldon, Robert Haveman, and Robert Plotnick. 1981. "How Income Transfer Programs Affect Work, Savings, and the Income Distribution: A Critical Review." *Journal of Economic Literature* 19(3):975–1028.

Darity, Jr., William, Jason Dietrich, and David Guilkey. 1997. "Racial and Ethnic Inequality in the United States: A Secular Perspective." *American Economic Review* 87(2):301–305.

DeCarlo, Scott. 2008. *CEO Compensation.* Forbes.com. http://www.forbes.com/2008/04/30/ceo-pay-compensation-lead-bestbosses08-cx-sd_0430ceo_land.html (accessed 25 June 2008).

DeLong, J. Bradford. 2003. "A History of Bequests in the United States. In *Death and Dollars: The Role of Gifts and Bequests in America.,* ed. Alicia H. Munnell and Annika Sunden, 33–53. Washington, DC: The Brookings Press.

DeNavas-Walt, Carmen, Bernadette D. Parker, and Cheryl Lee Hill. 2006. "Income, Poverty and Health Insurance Coverage in the United States: 2005." U.S. Census Bureau, *Current Population Reports, P60–231.* Washington, DC: U.S. Government Printing Office.

Devlin, Bernie, Stephen E. Fienberg, Daniel P. Resnick, and Kathryn Roeder. 1997. *Intelligence, Genes, and Success: Scientists Respond to The Bell Curve.* New York: Springer.

Doeringer, Peter B. and Michael J. Piore. 1971. *Internal Labor Markets and Manpower Analysis.* Lexington, MA: D.C. Heath and Company.

Duncan, Greg J., Bjorn Gustafsson, Richard Hauser, Gunther Schmauss, Hans Messinger, Ruud Muffels, Brian Nolan, and Jean-Claude Ray. 1993. "Poverty Dynamics in Eight Countries." *Journal of Population Economics* 6(3):215–234.

Easterlin, Richard. 1973. "Does Money Buy Happiness?" *The Public Interest* 30 (Winter): 3–10.

Ehrenberg, Ronald G. and Michael L. Bognanno. 1990. "Do Tournaments Have Incentive Effects?" *Journal of Political Economy* 98(6):1307–24.

Ehrenreich, Barbara. 2001. *Nickel and Dimed: On (Not) Getting By in America.* New York: Henry Holt and Company.

F.I.S.T. 1978. Produced and directed by Norman Jewison. Chateau Productions.

Fehr, Ernst, Georg Kirchsteiger, and Arno Riedl. 1993. "Does Fairness Prevent Market Clearing? An Experimental Investigation." *The Quarterly Journal of Economics* 108(2):437–459.

Fender, Ann Harper and Jean Fletcher. 2001. "Technological Change, Opportunity Costs and Enforcement Costs in Home Production." Unpublished paper.

Fershtman, Chiam and Uri Gneezy. 2001. "Discrimination in a Segmented Society: An Experimental Approach." *Quarterly Journal of Economics,* 116(1):351–77.

Firestone, David. 1999. "Agriculture Department to Settle Lawsuit by Black Farmers." *The New York Times*, January 5, 1999: A1.

Fix, Michael and Raymond J. Struyk. 1993. "Clear and Convincing Evidence: A Measurement of Discrimination in America." Washington, DC: Urban Institute.

Frank, Robert H. 2007a. *The Economic Naturalist: In Search of Answers to Everyday Enigmas.* New York: Basic Books.

———. 2007b. *Falling Behind: How Rising Inequality Harms the Middle Class.* Los Angeles: University of California Press.

———. 2008. *Microeconomics and Behavior.* 7th ed. New York: McGraw-Hill Irwin.

Frank, Robert H. and Ben S. Bernanke. 2007. *Principles of Economics.* 3rd ed. New York: McGraw-Hill Irwin.

Frank, Robert H. and Philip J. Cook. 1995. *The Winner-Take-All Society: Why the Few at the Top Get So Much More Than the Rest of Us.* New York: Penguin Books.

Frank, Robert L. 2007. *Richistan: A Journey Through the American Wealth Boom and the Lives of the New Rich.* New York: Crown Publishers.

Freeman, Richard B. 1975a. "Supply and Salary Adjustments to the Changing Science Manpower Markets: Physics 1948–1973." *American Economic Review* 65(1):27–39.

———. 1975b. "Legal Cobwebs: A Recursive Model of the Market for New Lawyers." *Review of Economics and Statistics* 57(2):171–80.

———. 1976. "A Cobweb Model of the Starting Salary of New Engineers." *Industrial and Labor Relations Review* 29(2):236–48.

Freeman, Richard B. and James Medoff. 1984. *What Do Unions Do?* New York: Basic Books.

Friedman, Benjamin. 2005. *The Moral Consequences of Economic Growth.* New York: Knopf.

Friedman, Milton. 1957. *A Theory of the Consumption Function.* Princeton, NJ: Princeton University Press.

———. 1962. *Capitalism and Freedom.* Chicago: University of Chicago Press.

Friedman, Milton and Rose Friedman. 1979. "Who Protects the Worker?" In *Free to Choose: A Personal Statement*, ed. Milton and Rose Friedman. New York: Harcourt Brace Jovanovich.

Friesen, Peter H. and Danny Miller. 1983. "Annual Inequality and Lifetime Inequality." *The Quarterly Journal of Economics* 98(1):139–156.

Fryer, Roland G. and Steven D. Levitt. 2004. "The Causes and Consequences of Distinctively Black Names." *Quarterly Journal of Economics* 119(3):767–805.

Fryer, Roland G., Jacob K. Goeree, and Charles A. Holt. 2005. "Experience-Based Discrimination: Classroom Games." *Journal of Economic Education* 36(2):160–70.

Fuchs, Victor. 1969. "Comment on Measuring the Low-Income Population." In *Six Papers on the Size Distribution of Wealth and Income*, ed. Lee Soltow, 198–202. New York: National Bureau of Economic Research.

Furchtgott-Roth, Dianna and Christine Stolba. 1999. *Women's Figures: An Illustrated Guide to the Economic Progress of Women in America.* Washington, DC: The AEI Press.

Gale, William D. and Joel Slemrod. 2001. "Overview." In *Rethinking Estate and Gift Taxation,* ed. William G. Gale, James R. Hines Jr., and Joel Slemrod. Washington, DC: Brookings Institution Press.

Galton, Francis. 1969. *Hereditary Genius: An Inquiry into Its Laws and Consequences.* London: Macmillan.

Gilens, Martin. 2004. "The American News Media and Public Misperceptions of Race and Poverty." In *Race, Poverty and Domestic Policy*, ed. C. Michael Henry. New Haven, CT: Yale University Press.

Gini, Corrado. 1912. "Variabilità e mutabilità." In *Libreria Eredi Virgilio Veschi*, ed. Pizetti E, Salvemini and T. Rome. Reprinted in *Memorie di metodologica statistica.* 1955.

Glanz, James. 2004. "Truckers of Iraq's Pony Express Are Risking It All for a Paycheck." http://query. nytimes.com/gst/fullpage.html?res=9C00E3DB1638F934A1575AC0A9629C8B63.

Gold, Michael Even. 1983. *A Dialogue on Comparable Worth.* Ithaca, NY: ILR Press.

Goldin, Claudia and Cecilia Rouse. 2000. "Orchestrating Impartiality: The Impact of 'Blind' Auditions on Female Musicians." *American Economic Review* 90(4):715–41.

Goldin, Claudia, Lawrence F. Katz, and Ilyana Kuziemko. 2006. "The Homecoming of American College Women: The Reversal of the College Gender Gap." *Journal of Economic Perspectives* 20(4):133–56.

Gordon, David M., ed. 1977. *Problems in Political Economy: An Urban Perspective.* 2nd ed., Lexington, MA: D.C. Heath and Company.

———. 1982. *Segmented Work, Divided Workers: The Historical Transformation of Work in America.* New York: Cambridge University Press.

Gottschalk, Peter and Sheldon Danziger. 1998. "Family Income Inequality, How Much Is There and

Has It Changed?" In *The Inequality Paradox: Growth of Income Disparity*, ed. James A. Auerbach and Richard S. Belous. Washington DC: National Policy Association.

Granovetter, Mark. 1974. *Getting a Job: A Study of Contacts and Careers*. Chicago: University of Chicago Press.

Green, Carole A. and Marianne A. Ferber. 1984. "Employment Discrimination: An Empirical Test of Forward versus Reverse Discrimination." *Journal of Human Resources* 19(4):557–569.

Gruber, Jonathan and James Poterba. 1996. "Tax Subsidies to Employer-Provided Health Insurance." In *Empirical Foundations of Household Taxation*, ed. Martin Feldstein and James Poterba, 135–164. Chicago: University of Chicago Press.

Hamermesh, Daniel and Jeff Biddle. 1994. "Beauty and the Labor Market." *American Economic Review* 84(5):1174–1194.

Hanushek, Eric A. 2002. "Publicly Provided Education." In *Handbook of Public Economics*, ed. Alan J. Auerbach and Martin Feldstein, 2045–2141. Amsterdam: Elsevier.

Harford, Tim. 2008. *The Logic of Life: The Rational Economics of an Irrational World*. New York: Random House.

Haveman, Robert H. 1988. *Starting Even: An Equal Opportunity Program to Combat the Nation's New Poverty*. New York: Simon and Schuster.

Hays, Sharon. 2003. *Flat Broke with Children: Women in the Age of Welfare Reform*. New York: Oxford University Press.

Heckman, James J. 1995. "Lessons from *The Bell Curve*." *Journal of Political Economy* 103(5):1091–1120.

———. 1998. "Detecting Discrimination." *Journal of Economic Perspectives* 12(1):101–16.

———. 2000. "Policies to Foster Human Capital." *Research in Economics* 54(1):3–56.

Heckman, James J. and Alan Krueger. 2003. *Inequality in America: What Role for Human Capital Policies?* Cambridge, MA: The MIT Press.

Henrekson, Magnus and Anna Dreber. 2007. "Female Career Success: Institutions, Path Dependence and Psychology." Paper presented at the annual meeting of the Eastern Economics Association, New York.

Herrnstein, Richard and Charles Murray. 1994. *The Bell Curve: Intelligence and Class Structure in American Life*. New York: The Free Press.

Hertz, Thomas. 2005. "Rags, Riches, and Race: The Intergenerational Economic Mobility of Black and White Families in the United States." In *Unequal Chances: Family Background and Economic Success* ed. Samuel Bowles, Herbert Gintis, and Melissa Osborne Groves, 165–91. Princeton, NJ: Princeton University Press.

Hoffa. 1992. Produced by Caldecut Chubb and Danny DeVito. Directed by Danny DeVito. Twentieth Century Fox Film Corporation.

Hotz, V. Joseph, Charles Mullin, and John Karl Scholz. 2000. "The Earned Income Tax Credit and Labor Market Participation of Families on Welfare." In *The Incentives of Government Programs and the Well-Being of Families*, ed. Bruce Meyer and Greg Duncan. http://www.jcpr.org/book (accessed 6 August 2007).

Hytrek, Gary and Kristine M. Zentgraf. 2008. *America Transformed: Globalization, Inequality, and Power*. New York: Oxford University Press.

Internal Revenue Service. 2007. *SOI Tax Stats–Individual Income Tax Returns*. http://www.irs.gov/taxstats/indtaxstats/article/0,,id=133414,00.html (accessed 13 August 2007).

International United Brotherhood of Teamsters. 2007. http://www.teamster.org/ (accessed 1 August 2007).

Jarrell, Stephen B. and T. D. Stanley. 2004. "Declining Bias and Gender Wage Discrimination: A Meta-Regression Analysis." *Journal of Human Resources* 39(3):828–838.

Jones, Jeffrey M. 2006. "Gallup: Heavy Support for Raising Minimum Wage." Gallup News Service. http://henwood.blogspace.com/?p=1274 (accessed 26 July 2007).

Joulfaian, David and Mark O. Wilhelm. 1994. "Inheritance and Labor Supply." *The Journal of Human Resources*. 29(4), Special Issue: *The Family and Intergenerational Relations*: 1205–1234.

Karelis, Charles. 2007. *Persistent Poverty: Why the Economics of the Well-Off Can't Help the Poor.* New Haven, CT: Yale University Press.

Keefe, Jeffrey H. Dale. 1992. "Do Unions Hinder Technological Change?" In *Unions and Economic Performance*, ed. Lawrence Mishel and Paula B. Voos, 109–41. Armonk, New York: M.E. Sharpe, Inc.

Keith, Verna M. and Cedric Herring. 1991. "Skin Tone and Stratification in the Black Community." *American Journal of Sociology* 97(3):760–78.

Kennickell, Arthur B. 2006. "Currents and Undercurrents: Changes in the Distribution of Wealth, 1989–2004." SCF Working Paper. http://www.federalreserve.gov/pubs/oss/oss2/method.html (accessed 10 June 2008).

Kerbo, Harold R. 2006. *Social Stratification and Inequality: Class Conflict in Historical, Comparative, and Global Perspective.* Boston: McGraw Hill.

Klein, Daniel B. and Charlotta Stern. 2007. "Is There a Free-Market Economist in the House? The Policy Views of American Economic Association Members." *American Journal of Economics and Sociology* 66(2):309–334.

Knoeber, Charles R. 1989. "A Real Game of Chicken: Contracts, Tournaments, and the Production of Broilers." *Journal of Law, Economics and Organization* 5(3):271–92.

Kondratas, S. Anna. 1984. "The Problems of Measuring Poverty." *Backgrounder.* The Heritage Foundation (1 November): 1–14.

Kotlikoff, Laurence J. 1988. "Intergenerational Transfers and Savings." *Journal of Economic Perspectives* 2(2):41–58.

Kroll, Luisa. 2008. *The World's Billionaires.* Forbes.com. http://www.forbes.com/2008/03/05/richest-people-billionaires-billionaires08-cx_lk_0305billie_land.html (accessed 25 June 2008).

Kroll, Luisa and Lea Goldman, eds. 2005. "The Richest People on Earth." *Forbes Magazine* 175(6):166–67.

Krueger, Alan B. 1993. "How Computers Have Changed the Wage Structure: Evidence from Microdata 1984–89." *Quarterly Journal of Economics* 108(1):33–60.

Landsburg, Steven. 1993. *The Armchair Economist: Economics and Everyday Life.* New York: The Free Press.

Lane, Robert E. 1993. "Does Money Buy Happiness?" *The Public Interest.* 113(Fall): 56–66.

Lang, Kevin. 2007. *Poverty and Discrimination.* Princeton, NJ: Princeton University Press.

Lang, Kevin and Jay Zagorsky. 2000. "Does Growing Up with an Absent Parent Really Hurt?" *Journal of Human Resources* 36(2):253–73.

Lazear, Edward P. 1979. "Why is There Mandatory Retirement?" *Journal of Political Economy* 87(6):1261–64.

———. 1998. *Personnel Economics for Managers.* New York: John Wiley & Sons, Inc.

Lazear, Edward P. and Sherwin Rosen. 1981. "Rank-Order Tournaments as Optimum Labor Contracts." *Journal of Political Economy* 89(5):841–64.

Lederman, Doug. 2007. "Closing the College Achievement Gap." *Inside Higher Education* (31 October). http://www.insidehighered.com/news/2007/10/31/system (accessed 31 October 2007).

Levitt, Steven D. and Stephen J. Dubner. 2005. *Freakonomics: A Rogue Economist Explores the Hidden Side of Everything.* New York: William Morrow.

Lewis, H. Gregg. 1963. *Unionism and Relative Wages in the United States: An Empirical Inquiry.* Chicago: University of Chicago Press.

Long, James E. and Albert N. Link. 1983. "The Impact of Market Structure on Wages, Fringes, and Turnover." *Industrial and Labor Relations Review* 36(2):239–250.

Lord, William A. 2002. *Household Dynamics: Economic Growth and Policy.* New York: Oxford University Press.

Lorenz, M.O. 1905. "Methods of Measuring the Concentration of Wealth. *Publications of the American Statistical Association* 9:209–219.

Loury, Glenn C. 1992. "Incentive Effects of Affirmative Action." *The Annals of the American Academy* 523(September): 19–29.

Lundberg, Mattias and Lyn Squire. 2003. "The Simultaneous Evolution of Growth and Inequality." *The Economic Journal* 113 (April): 326–44.

Lundberg, Shelly J. and Richard Startz. 2000. "Inequality and Race: Models and Policy." In *Meritocracy and Economic Inequality*, ed. Kenneth Arrow, Samuel Bowles, and Steven Durlauf, 269–95. Princeton, NJ: Princeton University Press.

Luxembourg Income Study. 2008. http://www.lisproject.org/ (accessed 8 July 2008).

Main, Brian G.M., Charles A. O'Reilly III, and James Wade. 1993. "Top Executive Pay: Tournament or Teamwork?" *Journal of Labor Economics* 11(4):606–628.

Maloney, M. and R. McCormick. 2000. "The Response of Workers to Wages in Tournaments: Evidence from Foot Races." *Journal of Sports Economics* 1(2):99–123.

Malthus, Thomas R. 1989. *An Essay on the Principle of Population.* New York: Cambridge University Press.

Mangum, Garth L., Stephen L. Mangum, and Andrew M. Sum. 2003. *The Persistence of Poverty in the United States.* Baltimore, MD: The Johns Hopkins University Press.

Mankiw, N. Gregory. 2007. *Principles of Economics.* 4th ed. Mason, OH: Thomson South-Western.

Manning, Alan. 2003. *Monopsony in Motion: Imperfect Competition in Labor Markets.* Princeton, NJ: Princeton University Press.

Marx, Karl. 1957. *Capital.* New York: Dutton.

Mason, Patrick L. 2001. "Annual Income and Identity Formation Among Persons of Mexican Descent." *American Economic Review* 91(2):178–183.

Mazumder, Bhashkar. 2005. "The Apple Falls Even Closer to the Tree Than We Thought." In *Unequal Chances: Family Background and Economic Success*, ed. Samuel Bowles, Herbert Gintis, and Melissa Osborne Groves, 80–99. Princeton, NJ: Princeton University Press.

McConnell, Campbell R., Stanley L. Brue, and David A. MacPherson. 2006. *Contemporary Labor Economics.* 7th ed. New York: McGraw-Hill Irwin.

McGratton, Ellen R. and Richard Rogerson. 2004. "Changes in Hours Worked, 1950–2000." *Federal Reserve Bank of Minneapolis Quarterly Review* 28(1):14–33.

McIntosh, Peggy. 1988. "White Privilege and Male Privilege: A Personal Account of Coming to See Correspondences through Work in Women's Studies." Working Paper #189, Wellesley College Center for Research on Women, Wellesley, MA 02181

McKenzie, Richard B. 1999. "The Minimum Wage Debate: Always Off Course." *The Southwest Economy* 4(July/August): 8–13.

McMurrer, Daniel P. and Isabel V. Sawhill. 1998. *Getting Ahead: Economic and Social Mobility in America.* Washington, DC:The Urban Institute Press.

Mean Girls. 2004. Produced by Lorne Michaels. Directed by Mark Waters. Paramount Pictures.

Metcalf, Stephen. 2005. "Unfair Harvard: The Real Story Behind One Graduate's Gripes. *Slate Magazine* (March 10, 2005). http://slate.msn.com/id/2114657 (accessed 13 March 2005).

Miller, G.A. 1956. "The Magical Number Seven, Plus or Minus Two: Some Limits on Our Capacity for Processing Information." *Psychological Review* 63:81–97.

Miller, Preston J. 1994. "The High Cost of Being Fair." *Federal Reserve Bank of Minneapolis 1993 Annual Report.* http://www.minneapolisfed.org/pubs/ar/ar1993.cfm?js=0 (accessed 11 July 2008).

Mishel, Lawrence, Jared Bernstein, and Sylvia Allegretto. 2007. *The State of Working America 2006/2007.* An Economic Policy Institute Book. Ithaca, NY: ILR Press, an imprint of Cornell University Press.

Mishkin, Frederic S. 2004. *The Economics of Money, Banking and Financial Markets.* 7th ed. New York: Addison-Wesley.

Modigliani, Franco. 1988. "The Role of Intergenerational Transfers and Life Cycle Saving in the Accumulation of Wealth." *Journal of Economic Perspectives* 2(2):15–40.

Modigliani, Franco and Richard E. Brumberg. 1954. "Utility Analysis and the Consumption Function: An Interpretation of Cross-section Data." In *Post-Keynesian Economics*, ed. K.K. Kurihara. Rutgers, NJ: Rutgers University Press.

Mulligan, Casey B. 1997. *Parental Priorities and Economic Inequality.* Chicago: The University of Chicago Press.

——. 1999. "Galton versus the Human Capital Approach to Inheritance." *Journal of Political Economy* 107(6):S184–224.

Munnell, Alicia H. and Annika Sunden. *Death and Dollars: The Role of Gifts and Bequests in America.* Washington, DC: The Brookings Press.

Murray, Charles. 1997. "IQ Will Put You in Your Place." *Sunday Times* 25 May 1997. http://www.eugenics.net/papers/murray.html (accessed 22 June 2005).

National Bureau of Economic Research. 2008. "Business Cycle Expansions and Contractions." http://www.nber.org/cycles/cyclesmain.html (accessed 8 July 2008).

National Coalition for the Homeless. 2007. *How Many People Experience Homelessness.* NCH Fact Sheet #2 (August).

Neumark, David and William Wascher. 2000. "Minimum Wages and Employment: A Case Study of the Fast-Food Industry in New Jersey and Pennsylvania: Comment." *The American Economic Review* 90(5):1362–1396.

——. 2007. "Minimum Wages and Employment." *Foundations and Trends in Microeconomics* 31(1–2):1–182.

Nordheimer, Jon. 1993. "Laid-Off Boatyard Workers Rehired." *The New York Times*, August 16, 1993, B 4.

Nozick, Robert. 1974. *Anarchy, State and Utopia.* New York: Basic Books.

Oaxacca, Ronald. 1973. "Sex Discrimination in Wages." In *Discrimination in Labor Markets*, ed. Orley Ashenfelter and Albert Rees. Princeton, NJ: Princeton University Press.

OECD. 2007. *Health Costs Per Day.* OECD Health Data. http://www.globalhealthnet.com/Hospital-CostsperDay.html (accessed 13 July 2007).

Office of Policy Development and Research. 1996. "Expanding Housing Choices for HUD-Assisted Families: First Biennial Report to Congress: Moving to Opportunity Fair Housing Demonstration." Washington DC: U.S. Department of Housing and Urban Development.

Okun, Arthur M. 1975. *Equality and Efficiency: The Big Tradeoff.* Washington, DC: The Brookings Institution Press.

Orshansky, Mollie. 1965. "Measuring Poverty." In *The Social Welfare Forum 1965.* New York: Columbia University Press.

——. 1969. "How Poverty is Measured." *Monthly Labor Review* 92(2).

Osberg, Lars and Kuan Xu. 2000. "International Comparisons of Poverty Intensity: Index Decomposition and Bootstrap Inference." *The Journal of Human Resources* 35(1):51–81.

Padavic, Irene and Barbara Reskin. 2002. *Women and Men at Work.* 2nd Edition. Thousand Oaks, CA: Pine Forge Press.

Page, Benjamin I. and James R. Simmons. 2000. *What Government Can Do: Dealing with Poverty and Inequality.* Chicago: The University of Chicago Press.

Paglin, Morton. 1975. "The Measurement and Trend of Inequality: A Basic Revision." *The American Economic Review* 65(4):598–609.

Pendakur, Krishna and Ravi Pendakur. 1998. "The Colour of Money: Earnings Differentials among Ethnic Groups in Canada." *The Canadian Journal of Economics* 31(3):518–548.

Persson, Torsten and Guido Tabellini. 1994. "Is Inequality Harmful for Growth?" *American Economic Review* 84(3):600–21.

Pestieau, Pierre. 2003. "The Role of Gift and Estate Transfers in the United States and in Europe." In *Death and Dollars: The Role of Gifts and Bequests in America*, ed. Alicia H. Munnell and Annika Sunden, 64–85. Washington, DC: The Brookings Press.

Polachek, Solomon W. and W. Stanley Siebert. 1993. "Labour Supply." *The Economics of Earnings.* New York: Cambridge University Press.

Queen, Edward L. 2004. "Charitable Choice." In *Philanthropy in America: A Comprehensive Historical Encyclopedia*, ed. Dwight F. Burlingame. Vol. I. Santa Barbara, CA: ABC-Clio, Inc.

Raff, Daniel M.G. Lawrence H. Summers. 1987. "Did Henry Ford Pay Efficiency Wages?" *Journal of Labor Economics* 5(October, Part II): S57–S86.

Rainwater, Lee. 1977. "Perceptions of Poverty and Economic Inequality." In *Problems in Political Economy: An Urban Perspective*, ed. David M. Gordon, 285–93. Lexington, MA: D.C. Heath and Company.

Rawls, John. 1999. *A Theory of Justice.* Cambridge, MA: Belknap Press of Harvard University Press.

Ray, Margaret A. and Paul W. Grimes. 1993. "Jockeying for Position: Winnings and Gender Discrimination on the Thoroughbred Racetrack." *Social Science Quarterly* 74(1):52–61.

Rector, Robert, Kirk A. Johnson, and Sarah E. Youssef. 1999. "The Extent of Material Hardship and Poverty in the United States." *Review of Social Economy* 57(3):351–387.

Rees, Albert. 1963. "The Effects of Unions on Resource Allocation." *The Journal of Law and Economics* 6 (October): 69–78.

Reich, Michael, David M. Gordon, and Richard C. Edwards. 1973. "A Theory of Labor Market Segmentation." *American Economic Review* 63(2):65–71.

Reich, Robert B. 1989. "As the World Turns." *The New Republic.* 23(1 May): 26–28.

Ricardo, David. 1969. *The Principles of Political Economy and Taxation.* New York: Dutton.

Robinson, Joan. 1971. "Euler's Theorem and the Problem of Distribution." In *Readings in Microeconomics,* ed. William Breit and Harold M. Hochman, 2nd ed, 399–410. New York: Holt, Rinehart and Winston, Inc.

Robinson, John P. and Geoffrey Godbey. 1997. *Time for Life: The Surprising Ways Americans Use Their Time.* University Park, PA: The Pennsylvania State University Press.

Rodriguez, Santiago Budria, Javier Diaz-Gimenez, Vincenzo Quadrini, and Jose-Victor Rios-Rull. 2002. "Updated Facts on the U.S. Distributions of Earnings, Income and Wealth." *Federal Reserve Bank of Minneapolis Quarterly Review* 26(3):2–35.

Roemer, John E. 1995. Equality and Responsibility. *Boston Review: A Political and Literary Forum* (April/May). http://bostonreview.net/br20.2/roemer.html (accessed 13 January 2005).

Rogers, Annette L. and Camille L. Ryan. 2007. *Extended Measures of Well-Being: Living Conditions in the United States, 2003.* United States Bureau of the Census, Household Economic Studies, P70–110. http://www.census.gov/prod/2007pubs/p70–110.pdf (accessed 25 July 2007).

Rones, Philip L., Randy E. Ilg, and Jennifer M. Gardner. 1997. "Trends in Hours of Work Since the Mid-1970s." *Monthly Labor Review* 120(4):3–14.

Roosevelt, Franklin Delano. 1937. *The Second Inaugural Address.* http://www.feri.org/archives/speeches/jan2037.cfm (accessed 3 August 2007).

Rosen, Harvey S. and Ted Gayer. 2008. *Public Finance.* 8th ed. New York: McGraw-Hill Irwin.

Rosenbaum, James E. 1995. "Changing the Geography of Opportunity by Expanding Residential Choice: Lessons from the Gautreaux Program." *Housing Policy Debate* 6:231–69.

Roth, Alvin E. 1995. "Bargaining Experiments." In *The Handbook of Experimental Economics*, ed. John H. Kagel and Alvin E. Roth. Princeton, NJ: Princeton University Press.

Russell, Thaddeus. 2001. *Out of the Jungle: Jimmy Hoffa and the Remaking of the American Working Class.* New York: Alfred A. Knopf.

Rycroft, Robert S. undated. *The Lorenz Curve and the Gini Coefficient.* http://people.umw.edu/~rrycroft/JEE/LG.htm (accessed 27 May 2008).

———. 2004. "Estimating a Plane: Economics in the Third Dimension." *Computers in Higher Education Review* 16 (April). http://www.economicsnetwork.ac.uk/cheer/ch16/rycroft.htm (accessed 11 July 2008).

Schiller, Bradley R. 2004. *The Economics of Poverty and Discrimination.* 9th ed. Upper Saddle River, NJ: Pearson Prentice Hall.

Schor, Juliet. 1991. *The Overworked American: The Unexpected Decline in Leisure.* New York: Basic Books.

Schotter, Andrew and Keith Weigelt. 1992. "Asymmetric Tournaments, Equal Opportunity Laws, and Affirmative Action: Some Experimental Results." *Quarterly Journal of Economics* 107(2):511–539.

Schultze, Charles L. 2000. "Has Job Security Eroded for American Workers?" In *The New Relationship: Human Capital in the American Corporation*, ed. Margaret M. Blair and Thomas A. Kochan, 28–65. Washington, DC: The Brookings Institution.

Schwartz, Barry. 2004. *The Paradox of Choice: Why More is Less.* New York: Harper Perennial.

Shackett, Joyce and John Trapani. 1987. "Earnings Differentials and Market Structure." *The Journal of Human Resources* 27(4): 518–531.

Shipler, David K. 2004. *The Working Poor: Invisible in America.* New York: Alfred A. Knopf.

Slesnick, Daniel T. 2001. *Consumption and Social Welfare: Living Standards and Their Distribution in the United States.* New York: Cambridge University Press.

Sloane, Arthur A. 1991. *Hoffa.* Cambridge, MA: The MIT Press.

Smith, Adam. 1991. *The Wealth of Nations.* New York: Alfred A. Knopf.

Smith, Sharon P. 1976. "Pay Differentials between Federal Government and Private Sector Workers." *Industrial and Labor Relations Review* 29(2):179–197.

Solon, Gary. 1992. "Intergenerational Income Mobility in the United States." *American Economic Review* 82(3):393–408.

Sowell, Thomas. 1981. *Ethnic America: A History.* New York: Basic Books.

———. 1983. *The Economics and Politics of Race.* New York: William Morrow and Company, Inc.

———. 1994. *Race and Culture: A World View.* New York: Basic Books.

———. 1998a. *Race, Culture and Equality.* Stanford, CA: Hoover Institution on War, Revolution and Peace.

———. 1998b. "Race Dialogue: Same Old Stuff." *Jewish World Review* (14 July). http://jewishworldreview.com/cols/Sowe11071498.html (accessed 24 July 2007).

Spence, A. Michael. 1973. "Job Market Signaling." *Quarterly Journal of Economics* 87(3):355–74.

Standiford, Les. 2005. *Meet You in Hell: Andrew Carnegie, Henry Clay Frick, and the Bitter Partnership That Transformed America.* New York: Three Rivers Press.

Stone, Katherine. 1973. "The Origins of Job Structures in the Steel Industry." In *Labor Market Segmentation,* ed. Richard C. Edwards, Michael Reich, and David M. Gordon, 27–84. Lexington, MA: D.C. Heath and Company.

Swift, Adam. 2005. "Justice, Luck and the Family: The Intergenerational Transmission of Economic Advantage From a Normative Perspective." In *Unequal Chances: Family Background and Economic Success,* ed. Samuel Bowles, Herbert Gintis, and Melissa Osborne Groves. Princeton, NJ: Princeton University Press.

Tajfel, Henri. 1970. "Experiments in Inter-Group Discrimination." *Scientific American* (November): 96–102.

The Economist. 2007. "The Frayed Knot." *The Economist* (24 May). http://www.economist.com/world/na/displaystory.cfm?story_id=9218127 (accessed 5 June 2007).

The University of Maryland Medical Center. 1999. "The 'Breakeven' Cost of Kidney Transplants is Shrinking." News Release (May). http://www.umm.edu/news/releases/Kidcost.htm (accessed 13 July 2007).

The Urban Institute. 2006. "Maximum Monthly Benefit for a Family of Three with No Income (Table L5)." ANF Data Resources. Welfare Rules Database. http://anfdata.urban.org/WRD/WRDWelcome.cfm (accessed 24 June 2008).

Theobald, Robert. 1965. *Free Men and Free Markets.* Garden City, NY: Anchor Books.

Thurow, Lester. 1972. *Generating Inequality: Mechanisms of Inequality in the Economy.* New York: Basic Books.

Tobin, James.1968. Raising the Incomes of the Poor. In *Agenda for the Nation: Papers on Domestic and Foreign Policy*, ed. Kermit Gordon. Washington, DC: The Brookings Institution Press.

Tyler, John H., Richard J. Murnane, and John B. Willett. 2000. "Estimating the Labor Market Signaling Value of the GED." *Quarterly Journal of Economics* 115(2):431–468.

United Autoworkers. 2007. *Welcome to the UAW.* http://www.uaw.org/index.cfm (accessed 1 August 2007).

United Brotherhood of Carpenters and Joiners of America. 2007. *The UBC*. http://www.carpenters. org/ (accessed 1 August 2007).

United States Bureau of the Census (USBC). 2003. "Poverty in the United States: 2002." Current Population Reports. Washington, DC United States Government Printing Office.

———. 2006. "Income, Poverty and Health Insurance Coverage in the United States, 2005." Current Population Reports. Washington, DC: U.S. Government Printing Office.

———. 2007a. "Survey of Income and Program Participation, 2007." http://www.sipp.census.gov/ sipp/ (accessed 24 July 2007).

———. 2007b. "The Effect of Taxes and Transfers on Income and Poverty in the United States, 2005." http://www.census.gov/prod/2007pubs/p60-232.pdf.

———. 2007c. "Income, Poverty and Health Insurance Coverage in the United States, 2006." Current Population Reports. Consumer Income. Washington, DC: U.S. Government Printing Office.

——— 2007c. "Longitudinal Employer—Household Dynamics." http://lehd.dsd.census.gov/led (accessed 24 July 2007).

———. 2008. "The Effect of Taxes and Transfers on Income and Poverty in the United States, 2006." http://pubdb3.census.gov/macro/032007/alttoc/toc.htm (accessed 7 July 2008).

United States Code. 1963. The Equal Pay Act of 1963. 29, 206(d). http://www.eeoc.gov/policy/epa. html (accessed 11 July 2008).

———. 1964. Title VII of the Civil Rights Act of 1964. 42, 2000e. http://www.eeoc.gov/policy/vii. html (accessed 11 July 2008).

———. 1967. Age Discrimination in Employment Act of 1967. 29, 621. http://www.eeoc.gov/policy/ adea.html (accessed 11 July 2008).

———. 1990. The Americans with Disabilities Act of 1990. 42, 12101. http://www.eeoc.gov/policy/ ada.html (accessed 11 July 2008).

United States Congress. 2004. Committee on Ways and Means. *Green Book*. prepared by Members of the Staff. 108th Cong., 2nd sess. Committee Print (March 2004).

United States Congress. 2007. "Prescription Drug Pricing in the Private Sector." Washington D.C.: Congressional Budget Office.

United States Court of Appeals. 1970. *Shultz v. Wheaton Glass Co.* 421 F. 2d 259 (3rd Cir.).

United States Department of Agriculture. 1956. "Food Consumption in Households in the United States." *Household Food Consumption Survey, 1955*, Report 1. Washington, DC: U.S. Department of Agriculture.

United States Department of Commerce. Bureau of Economic Analysis. 2007. "Interactive Access to National Income and Product Accounts Tables." http://www.bea.gov/national/nipaweb/Index.asp (accessed 30 April 2007).

United States Department of Housing and Urban Development. 2007. "HUD Reports Drop in Number of Chronically Homeless Persons Living on Nation's Streets." HUD No. 07–167 (7 November 2007). Washington, DC: US Department of Housing and Urban Development.

United States Department of Labor. 2007. "Minimum Wage Laws in the States." http://www.dol.gov/ esa/minwage/america.htm (accessed 26 July 2007).

United States Department of Labor. Bureau of Labor Statistics. 2006. *Women in the Labor Force: A Databook* (2006 Edition). http://www.bls.gov/cps/wlf-table18–2006.pdf (accessed 24 June 2008).

———. 2007a. "National Census of Fatal Occupational Injuries in 2006." http://www.bls.gov/news. release/pdf/cfoi.pdf (accessed 14 August 2007)

———. 2007b. "National Longitudinal Surveys." http://www.bls.gov/nls (accessed 24 July 2007).

———. 2007c. "Union Members in 2006." http://www.bls.gov/news_release/union2.nr0.htm (accessed 16 July 2007).

———. 2008. "Overview of BLS Statistics on Wages, Earnings, and Benefits." http://www.bls.gov/ bls/wages.htm (accessed 10 July 2008).

United States Equal Employment Opportunity Commission. 1968. Senator Clifford Case (R, NJ) and Senator Joseph Clark (D, PA), "Interpretive Memorandum on Title VII." *Legislative History of*

Titles VII and XI of Civil Rights Act of 1964. Washington, D.C.: United States Government Printing Office.

United States Supreme Court. 1937. *NLRB v. Jones & Laughlin Steel Corp.*, 301 U.S. 1.

———. 1954. *Brown v Board of Education* 347 U.S. 483.

———. 1971. *Griggs et al. v. Duke Power Company* 401 U.S. 424.

———. 1973. *San Antonio Independent School District v Rodriguez* 411 U.S. 1.

———. 1977. *Dothard, Director, Department of Public Safety of Alabama, et al. v. Rawlinson et al.* 433 U.S. 321.

———. 1979. *United Steelworkers of America, AFL-CIO-CLC v. Weber et al.* 443 U.S. 193.

———. 1987a. *Paul E. Johnson, Petitioner v Transportation Agency, Santa Clara County, California, et. al.* 480 U.S. 616.

———. 1987b. *United States v Paradise et al.* 480 U.S. 149.

———. 1989a. *Ward's Cove Packing Co., Inc., et al. v. Atonio et al.* 490 U.S. 642.

———. 1989b. *Wygant et al. v. Jackson Board of Education et al.* 476 U.S. 267.

———. 1999a. *Albertson's Inc. v. Kirkingburg.* 527 U.S. 555.

———. 1999b. *Murphy v. United Parcel Service, Inc.* 527 U.S. 516.

———. 1999c. *Sutton v. United Airlines, Inc.* 527 U.S. 471.

———. 2002. *Toyota Motor Manufacturing, Kentucky, Inc. v. Williams.* 534 U.S. 184.

University of Michigan. Institute for Social Research. 2007. "Panel Study of Income Dynamics." http://psidonline.isr.umich.edu (accessed 24 July 2007).

Van Parijs, Philippe. 2001. *What's Wrong With a Free Lunch?* Boston: Beacon Press.

Vaughan, Graham M., Henri Tajfel, and Jennifer Williams. 1981. "Bias in Reward Allocation in an Intergroup and an Interpersonal Context." *Social Psychology Quarterly* 44(1):37–42.

Vickery, Claire. 1977. "The Time-Poor: A New Look At Poverty." *Journal of Human Resources* 12(1):27–48.

Waldfogel, Jane. 1998. "Understanding the 'Family Gap' in Pay for Women with Children." *Journal of Economic Perspectives* 12(1):137–56.

Waltman, Jerold L. 2008. *Minimum Wage Policy in Great Britain and the United States.* New York: Algora Publishing.

Wellington, Harry H. and Ralph K. Winter. 1971. *The Unions and the Cities.* Washington, DC: Brookings Institution.

Whalen, Charles and Barbara Whalen. 1985. *The Longest Debate: A Legislative History of the 1964 Civil Rights Act.* Cabin John, MD: Seven Locks Press.

Wikipedia. 2008. "Cabrini-Green." http://en.wikipedia.org/w/index.php?title=Cabrini-Green&oldid=224066684 (accessed 7 July 2008).

Wilson, William Julius. 1987. *The Truly Disadvantaged: The Inner City, the Underclass, and Public Policy.* Chicago: University of Chicago Press.

Wolff, Edward N. 2003. The Impact of Gifts and Bequests on the Distribution of Wealth. In *Death and Dollars: The Role of Gifts and Bequests in America*, ed. Alicia H. Munnell and Annika Sunden, 345–88. Washington, DC: The Brookings Press.

Wolpin, Kenneth I. 1977. "Education and Screening." *American Economic Review* 67(4):949–58.

Yinger, John. 1998. "Evidence on Discrimination in Consumer Markets." *Journal of Economic Perspectives* 12(2):23–40.

Yitzhaki, Shlomo. 1987. "The Relation Between Return and Income." *Quarterly Journal of Economics* 102(1):77–95.

Zimmerman, David J. 1992. "Regression Toward Mediocrity in Economic Stature." *American Economic Review* 82(3):409–29.

Index

About the Author

Robert S. Rycroft, Professor of Economics, University of Mary Washington, earned a Ph.D. (1978) and M.A. (1974) from the University of Maryland, after having received a B.A. (1972) in economics from the College of William and Mary. A member of Phi Beta Kappa and the American Economic Association, Dr. Ryroft is the author of *Essentials of Macroeconomics I and II* and a contributor to *The Economics Problem Solver* and *GRE Economics Test*. His current research interests include the economics of inequality, poverty, mobility and discrimination, philanthropy and service learning, and personal response pads. He is president of Omicron Delta Epsilon. Dr. Rycroft is married and the father of two children.